THE BRAZILIAN LEGAL PROFESSION IN THE AGE OF GLOBALIZATION

This book provides the first comprehensive analysis of globalization's impact on the Brazilian legal profession. Employing original data from nine empirical studies, the book details how Brazil's need to restructure its economy and manage its global relationships contributed to the emergence of a new "corporate legal sector" – a sector marked by increasingly large and sophisticated law firms and in-house legal departments. This corporate legal sector in turn helped to reshape other parts of the Brazilian legal profession, including legal education, pro bono practices, the regulation of legal services, and the state's legal capacity in international economic law. The book, the second in a series on Globalization, Lawyers, and Emerging Economies, will be of interest to academics, lawyers, and policymakers concerned with the role that a rapidly globalizing legal profession is playing in the development of key emerging economies and how these countries are integrating into the global market for legal services.

Luciana Gross Cunha is Professor and Associate Dean of the Center for Applied Legal Research at Fundação Getulio Vargas Law School in São Paulo, Brazil.

Daniela Monteiro Gabbay is Professor of Civil Procedure, Strategies and Mediation at Fundação Getulio Vargas Law School in São Paulo, Brazil.

José Garcez Ghirardi is Professor at Fundação Getulio Vargas Law School in São Paulo, Brazil, where he acted as the methodology coordinator from 2009 to 2010. He is an accredited member of the Brazilian Bar Association.

David M. Trubek is Voss-Bascom Professor of Law and Dean of International Studies Emeritus at the University of Wisconsin–Madison and Senior Research Fellow at the Center on the Legal Profession, Harvard Law School.

David B. Wilkins is Lester Kissel Professor of Law, Vice Dean for Global Initiatives on the Legal Profession, and Faculty Director of the Center on the Legal Profession at Harvard Law School. He is also Senior Research Fellow of the American Bar Foundation and Fellow of the Harvard University Edmond J. Safra Foundation Center for Ethics.

The Brazilian Legal Profession in the Age of Globalization

THE RISE OF THE CORPORATE LEGAL SECTOR AND ITS IMPACT ON LAWYERS AND SOCIETY

Edited by

LUCIANA GROSS CUNHA

Fundação Getúlio Vargas Law School, São Paulo

DANIELA MONTEIRO GABBAY

Fundação Getúlio Vargas Law School, São Paulo

JOSÉ GARCEZ GHIRARDI

Fundação Getúlio Vargas Law School, São Paulo

DAVID M. TRUBEK

University of Wisconsin–Madison

DAVID B. WILKINS

Harvard Law School

CAMBRIDGE
UNIVERSITY PRESS

CAMBRIDGE
UNIVERSITY PRESS

University Printing House, Cambridge CB2 8BS, United Kingdom

One Liberty Plaza, 20th Floor, New York, NY 10006, USA

477 Williamstown Road, Port Melbourne, VIC 3207, Australia

314–321, 3rd Floor, Plot 3, Splendor Forum, Jasola District Centre,
New Delhi - 110025, India

79 Anson Road, #06-04/06, Singapore 079906

Cambridge University Press is part of the University of Cambridge.

It furthers the University's mission by disseminating knowledge in the pursuit of education, learning and research at the highest international levels of excellence.

www.cambridge.org
Information on this title: www.cambridge.org/9781107183544
DOI: 10.1017/9781316871959

First published 2018

Printed in the United States of America by Sheridan Books, Inc.

A catalogue record for this publication is available from the British Library

ISBN 978-1-107-18354-4 Hardback

Contents

Figures

Tables

Contributors

Frederico de Almeida is Assistant Professor of Political Science at University of Campinas.

Camila de Pieri Benedito is a PhD candidate in sociology at Universidade Federal de São Carlos.

Maria da Gloria Bonelli is Professor of Sociology at Universidade Federal de São Carlos.

Adriane Sanctis de Brito is a PhD candidate in legal theory and philosophy at University of São Paulo.

Luciana Gross Cunha is Professor of Political Science at Escola de Direito de São Paulo da Fundação Getúlio Vargas, São Paulo.

Vitor M. Dias is a PhD candidate in sociology at Indiana University–Bloomington.

Ary Oswaldo Mattos Filho is professor of law at Escola de Direito de São Paulo da Fundação Getulio Vargas (FGV DIREITO SP), former dean of FGV DIREITO SP, and founding partner of Mattos Filho, Veiga Filho, Marrey Jr. e Quiroga Advogados.

Daniela Monteiro Gabbay is Professor of Law at Escola de Direito de São Paulo da Fundação Getúlio Vargas, São Paulo.

José Garcez Ghirardi is Professor of Law at Escola de Direito de São Paulo da Fundação Getúlio Vargas, São Paulo.

Rubens Glezer is Professor of Law at Escola de Direito de São Paulo da Fundação Getúlio Vargas, São Paulo.

Vikramaditya S. Khanna is William W. Cook Professor of Law and faculty director of the Directors' College for Global Business and Law University of Michigan School of Law.

Paulo André Nassar is a PhD candidate and Professor of Law at Universidade Federal do Pará.

Fabiana Luci de Oliveira is Assistant Professor of Sociology at Universidade Federal de São Carlos.

Luciana Ramos is Professor of Law and Coordinator for Applied Legal Research at Escola de Direito de São Paulo da Fundação Getúlio Vargas, São Paulo.

Ligia Pinto Sica is Professor of Law at Escola de Direito de São Paulo da Fundação Getúlio Vargas, São Paulo.

Fabio de Sa e Silva is Assistant Professor of International Studies and Wick Cary Professor of Brazilian Studies at the University of Oklahoma.

David M. Trubek is Voss-Bascom Professor of Law and Dean of International Studies Emeritus at the University of Wisconsin–Madison and Senior Research Fellow at the Harvard Law School Center on the Legal Profession.

David B. Wilkins is Lester Kissel Professor of Law, Faculty Director of the Center on the Legal Profession, and Vice Dean for Global Initiatives on the Legal Profession at Harvard Law School.

Rafael A. F. Zanatta is a MS candidate at University of São Paulo Faculty of Law.

Acknowledgments

The editors would like to thank all the contributors to this volume, without whom none of this work would have been possible. They would also like to thank the support provided by the Harvard Law School Center on the Legal Profession, which serves as the institutional home of the Globalization, Lawyers, and Emerging Economies (GLEE) project and has provided essential support of every kind. The editors would also like to thank the Escola de Direito de São Paulo da Fundação Getulio Vargas (FGV DIREITO SP), which served as the in-country hub for the GLEE Brazil work. This book would not have been possible without the generous support – in time, advice, and funding – of the Center's world-class Advisory Board. Indeed, the initial impetus for the GLEE project came at the 2010 spring annual meeting of the Advisory Board in New York City, where Cyril Shroff suggested that we begin a project on the impact globalization was having on the legal profession in the world's most important emerging economies. We would also like to thank the other sources of support the GLEE Brazil Project has received, including from Pinheiro Neto Advogados and the David Rockefeller Center for Latin American Studies at Harvard University. Finally, the editors thank the hundreds of Brazilian lawyers who generously devoted their time, insights, and talents through countless interviews and surveys. Without their contributions, this book would never have been possible. We are eternally grateful.

Foreword

Ary Oswaldo Mattos Filho

This book is an important and pioneering analysis of transformations in the world of legal practice being undertaken today by lawyers in Brazil. Through a detailed survey of the major changes the legal world in Brazil has gone through over the last decades, this book illuminates the most recent phase in the evolution of the profession.

From the creation of law courses in Brazil in the early nineteenth century to today, Brazil's legal profession has gone through several major phases. This has occurred, as is natural, because of the different political and economic phases that the country has gone through since independence. In order to facilitate the understanding of those not familiar with the reality of Brazil, I trust it will assist the reader's understanding to divide this history into three major phases the legal profession and lawyers have gone through. For this analysis to make sense, we should bear in mind that, as in any country, political and economic developments tend to shape the actions of Brazil's citizens and, as such, the creation of laws and their application. Therefore, in this analysis, it will be important to illustrate the historical facts that resulted in the current practice of the legal profession, richly researched in this book.

I PHASE 1: FROM COLONY TO AN AGRICULTURAL EXPORTING REPUBLIC

The first phase commences timidly in the then colony of Portugal with the arrival of the Portuguese court in 1808. Up until that time, Brazil was one of Portugal's lethargic colonies like the innumerable ones existing on the African continent. The application of the law, if it even existed, was erratic. The center of political, economic, and cultural power was Lisbon, where an absolutist monarchy prohibited any economic activity not in the interests of the king and the exports of the colony had to be sent first to Lisbon before they could be traded with other countries. Until 1808, the colony was prohibited from having any equipment for the reproduction of newspapers, books, or pamphlets of any type. In addition, there could be no factories, financial institutions, universities, or any other facilities that would allow the inhabitants of the colony to develop an idea of technical, cultural, or industrial progress.

We should be grateful to Napoleon Bonaparte for the introduction of the minimum elements for the process of modern civilization among us, because, with the beginning of the invasion of Portugal by French troops in 1808, the Portuguese king, when fleeing from Lisbon, transferred to Brazil the seat of the Portuguese kingdom. This change forced the creation of the first bank (Banco do Brasil), the first printing presses for printing books and newspapers, most importantly, the official gazette of the Crown, the creation of the first rudimentary local industries, and the establishment of the first Brazilian university, the university of medicine in Bahia.

We should also be grateful to the English for the independence of Brazil to the extent that, with the defeat of Napoleon Bonaparte, there was the beginning of the movement toward the return of the king and the kingdom to Portugal, leaving the king's son as regent. At this time, an incipient Brazilian legal elite who had graduated from Coimbra started to develop separatist ideas that culminated in 1821 in the independence of the country and the severing of relations with Portugal.

Owing to this break, the country lost the possibility of having its nascent legal elite graduate in Portugal, and this led to the creation of our law courses in 1827. The creation of law schools in Brazil was due to the fact that the youth of the former colony were perceived as enemies of the Portuguese kingdom and were not allowed to continue attending the schools in Coimbra. This forced the creation of the first two universities, one in São Paulo and the other in Olinda. In this first phase, which lasted until the beginning of the twentieth century, preparation in law courses was more focused on forming a ruling elite to conduct the affairs of the young and independent country than on preparing students for the exercise of the legal profession itself.

It was these two law schools that came to supply Brazil with almost all of its political/administrative elite. Almost all of the deputies, senators, ministers of state, judges, and other professionals who were engaged in making and applying the law emerged from their ranks. But what was this youth supposed to learn? In the absence of a better paradigm, the new schools copied the curriculum of the law school in Coimbra, which was already outdated in dealing with the economic progress occurring at the time in Europe and the United States. If we analyze the parliamentary discussions in Brazil as to the composition of the subjects that would necessarily be taught, we will see that a good part of the discussions – if not the hottest parliamentary debate – was about the usefulness of making it compulsory to teach Roman law and canon law. Even if Roman law did not appear as one of the mandatory subjects in 1827, canon law did.[1] However, Roman law has survived to this day in the curriculum of some good law schools.

This first phase, in practice, ultimately formed personnel for the exercise of activities relating to the administration of the emerging Brazilian state. In the early years, the most important area of legal practice involved application of the rules of family law, succession, and matters relating to property. This occurred due to the low level of business development at that time, with the country focusing on the production and export of agricultural goods, mainly coffee. This phase, in my view, lasted until the beginning of the twentieth century, when the second phase, with more specialized legislative production and a growing number of judges and public prosecutors, started.

II PHASE 2: LAWYERS AND INDUSTRIALIZATION

The demand for the exercise of the legal profession in several areas of commercial law commenced in the 1930s with the beginning of the process of industrialization. This process was kicked off by the growing capitalization of coffee producers who invested in industry and by the efforts of entrepreneurs, many of whom were descendants of immigrants from Europe and the Middle East. The process of industrialization accelerated considerably with the Second World War, which led to increased demand from European countries and the United States. As a consequence, demand for the provision of legal services grew in the areas of corporate law, bankruptcy, and insolvency, as well as in export and import law, and contract law became an important area of work in legal practice.

At the same time, as a result of the growth of the role of the state in the life of the country, the dictatorship of Getulio Vargas demanded expanded legal services in the area of administrative law. Yet, while more and more lawyers were engaged in professional work, members of the profession also continued to play important roles in politics. If we research the professional background of the senators, deputies, governors, and even presidents of the republic established after World War II, we will note that they mostly came from

[1] The curriculum of the two law schools, created by law, provided that the following subjects be taught during the five years of the course: natural law, public law, analysis of the constitution, *ius gentium*, diplomacy, ecclesiastic public law, civil law, criminal law, criminal procedure, mercantile and maritime law, political economics, and theory and practical procedure.

law schools, although occasionally, a medical doctor, engineer, or another professional pursued a political career.

The second phase is characterized by a greater insertion of lawyers in professional work, with an increase in tax laws, a new corporate law, and the enactment of the criminal code. But in this second phase, while the demand for legal services increased, Brazilian lawyers and lawmakers of the Republic established after World War II continued to look to Europe for inspiration, and the influence of French, Italian, and Iberian European law was strongly maintained. The profession was exercised by sole practitioners, and usually with the death of the founding partner, the law firm died also. The profession was exercised by individuals, never by firms of lawyers.

The greatest changes occurred after 1964, upon the removal of the president and assumption of power by the military. With the establishment of a dictatorial regime, the world of law went into decline, power being taken over by a group of economists who sought a great change of direction, moving much closer to the US model as to the management of the economy, without, however, decreasing the leading role of the state.

For such purpose, there were created, among other state bodies, the central bank, the national monetary council, the national housing bank, and a national tax code. Also, there was an attempt to create a securities market, and several laws on securities were passed. In 1976, still under the military regime, the Brazilian securities commission was created, as well as new corporation law. In other words, ironically, the repressive regime created new fields of law for lawyers, even though it had erased human rights from the rule of law.

At this time, the US government, through the US Agency for International Development (USAID), along with the Ford Foundation, supported scholarships to the United States for lawyers as well as other professionals.[2] This phase caused an increasing number of Brazilians to go to the United States to undertake master's or doctoral degrees in the most varied professions. As such, lawyers, economists, engineers, company administrators, and so on, radically changed their preferences to US education, to the detriment of the universities of Europe, until then absolute in the preference of graduate students.

These professionals returned to Brazil impregnated with values different from those with which they departed. This preference of lawyers and economists to do their graduate courses in US universities had a profound impact on the life of the country after the decade of 1970–1980. The economists brought new paradigms for the activities of the financial market

[2] This writer was one of the persons selected, obtaining a scholarship to study at the Harvard Law School in 1967.

and, consequently, for Brazilian companies. The merger of ideas of the economic world with the legal world brought for lawyers a growing area of work in what is today called business law. This included new ways of financing the private sector, which generated an enormous increase in practice in the area of contracts.

III PHASE 3: LAWYERS AND GLOBALIZATION

In the early 1990s, two other factors created an enormous and different line of work for Brazilian lawyers. On one hand, foreigners were permitted to invest directly in the Brazilian capital markets, and Brazilian companies were permitted to issue securities in foreign markets. Both overseas and here, there was the beginning of the participation of large investment funds sponsoring capitalization mechanisms for the large Brazilian private companies, as well as some Brazilian companies going overseas by means of branches. With all of this, there was the beginning of a process of conglomeration of Brazilian financial institutions, creating large-sized banks capable of generating extensive funding for the business sector.

On the other hand, the process of privatization of state-owned companies began, which continue in the form of concessions of activities previously exercised by the state. These two new activities – the contact with the capital markets overseas and the arrival of foreign capital to participate in privatizations or concessions of state assets – necessarily require cooperation between Brazilian and US or UK lawyers, since, normally, the laws of both countries are applied. This contact between lawyers of both countries – fed by the growing number of Brazilians returning with master's degrees from the United States – facilitated and came to influence national practices. These professional connections reached another level when many of those who finished their LLMs started to get training in US law firms. Economists, who at an increasing number started to work in financial institutions and even with governmental entities, also contributed with the adoption of new financing models that became part of the national legal world, with alien names such as leasing, factoring, merger, spin-off, board, swaps, and derivatives.

It was only from the convergence of the aforementioned factors that the services of the corporate legal profession began to be demanded on a large scale, thus creating the need for the emergence of a much larger number of full-service law firms in addition to the very few that had existed up to then (which were dedicated almost exclusively to servicing foreign capital companies). As such, it is possible to mark in time the emergence of the large law firms at the beginning of the 1990s. At the same time, there were other transformations.

One was the rise in the prestige of the general counsels, many of them now with an overseas LLM degree and ready to follow the changes brought by the internationalization of law. They started to dialogue with financial directors and discuss agreements overseas, and a completely new range of legal services appeared, demanding a different type of professional.

But this brave new world includes only a portion of the lawyers. As also occurs in other countries, lawyers, for the most part, continue to provide everyday legal services. This majority has the voting power in the Bar, causing the entity that represents lawyers to act partly in defense of the greatest interests of the country and partly in defense of the interests of its members. In this latter case, sometimes it is confronted with the dilemma between serving the interests of the majority of its members – preserving exclusive fields of work – and more generous interests, such as what occurred in the case of pro bono, which was initially outlawed by the Bar. In this area, despite initial hostility, the large law firms finally won the right to provide free legal services to non-governmental organizations. It is to be praised that generosity won.

Major transformations occurred in the world of business law, with enormous effects on the law of obligations, which had remained static. Even criminal law started to absorb new possibilities of financial crimes, in the defense of nature, against pollution, in the defense of the capital markets investor, and so on. This world that globalizes increasingly quickly has also elevated the importance of women in the legal profession, also due to the influence of international feminist movements. Today the number of female students at law schools is greater than the number of male students.

However, if the world of the legal profession has been transforming rapidly, the same cannot be said of the willingness or capacity of the law schools to adapt to the not-so-new role that the lawyer has come to play in Brazilian society. This gap between the demands made on lawyers by Brazilian society and the training offered in most law schools exists in the choice of subjects taught and in other areas. Most of the law faculties continue to ignore transformations occurring all around them and fail to prepare lawyers for the demands now made on the providers of legal services.

This book illuminates the transformations and the challenges they create. It is the first time the new reality of the Brazilian legal profession has been surveyed through extensive empirical research. As such, it is one of the most important contributions ever made for legal educators, lawyers, and representatives of professional associations in Brazil, all of whom should take ownership of the results so that we can work to meet the demands that are emerging from the worlds of entrepreneurs and society. Not only is this book important to understanding what is happening in Brazil: being part of surveys of the corporate legal profession in China and India, it will also help people understand general trends for legal professions in all emerging economies in the age of globalization.

Good reading and good ideas are necessary for the practice of law in this globalized world.

1

Globalization, Lawyers, and Emerging Economies

The Case of Brazil

Luciana Gross Cunha, Daniela Monteiro Gabbay, José Garcez Ghirardi, David M. Trubek, and David B. Wilkins

I GLOBALIZATION, LAWYERS, AND EMERGING ECONOMIES

In the 1990s, Brazil and other emerging economies went through a major transformation. Closed economies were opened, foreign investment was encouraged, and many state-owned enterprises were privatized. This "global transformation" had a major impact on the Brazilian legal system.

While many parts of the legal system were affected, the corporate law profession changed the most. This sector includes all the institutions and actors that provide legal advice to corporations whether domestic or foreign, public or private. Global transformation brought about major changes in the national political economy, led to a flood of new laws governing corporate activity, and created a demand for new kinds of legal services to help companies manage the new legal environment. This led to rapid growth of the complex of institutions that provide corporate legal services and affected the way lawyering was practiced and organized. Many forces came together to give new shape to the professional identity of lawyers, the structures they work in, and the roles they play. The result was the creation of a new and powerful segment of the legal profession whose activities had profound impacts on the rest of the profession, the legal system, the operation of enterprises (both public and private), state policy, and global governance.

In this book, we describe the growth of the corporate legal sector in Brazil and the impact of this development on lawmaking, legal education, regulation of the legal profession, public interest law, trade policy, and gender roles. The book is part of a larger study of global transformation and its impact on the legal profession carried out by GLEE, the project on Globalization, Lawyers, and Emerging Economies.[1] Based at the Harvard Law School's Center for the Legal Profession, GLEE is currently studying these developments in Brazil, India, and China, with plans to expand the project into Africa and the states of the former Soviet Union. In Brazil, GLEE's research has been based at the law school of the Fundação Getulio Vargas (FGV) in São Paulo.[2]

II THE LITERATURE

For more than half a century, a growing body of scholarship has documented the complex relationship between legal institutions and economic, social, and political development in the Global South. GLEE builds on this rich tradition and seeks to relate it to the Brazilian scene by exploring the impact of globalization on the legal profession, and vice versa.

The literature on the Brazilian legal profession as such is limited. To be sure, there have been numerous studies of the role of *law* in recent Brazilian development. Studies include the impact of new laws on the development of the capital market (Trubek 2011a), the legal architecture that allowed Brazil's successful conditional cash-transfer program to operate (Coutinho et al. 2013), the impact of international trade law, and other topics. But these studies paid little attention to the role of lawyers.

A lot has also been written about the role of Brazilian lawyers as statesmen and the effects of lawyers' presence in governance. Studies showed that from the beginning of the Brazilian state, lawyers played roles other than that of professionals serving clients. The first lawyers trained after independence were supposed to serve as statesmen. People with law training dominated the state at least until the 1930s and maintained some influence until the 1960s (Adorno 1998; Venâncio Filho 1978). Furthermore, while the military regime that took over in 1964 displaced lawyers from the peaks of state power,

[1] The first volume from this project, *The Indian Legal Profession in the Age of Globalization: The Rise of the Corporate Legal Sector and its Impact on Lawyers and Society*, edited by Wilkins, Khanna, and Trubek, was published by Cambridge University Press in 2017.

[2] Around twenty researchers and scholars in law, sociology, and political science were involved in the GLEE project's study of the corporate legal sector in Brazil and its impact. The research was conducted in 2013–2014. It focused on the states of São Paulo and Rio de Janeiro, which make up 44 percent of the Brazilian GDP and are home to almost half the lawyers in the country, the headquarters of the main Brazilian corporate law firms, and the legal departments of the largest domestic and foreign companies. To create a profile of the corporate sector, the team conducted more than fifty in-depth interviews with partners in major law firms and legal directors of large national and international companies. We also created a database that included information about the top 367 business law firms in the country. Other studies were done of the corporate sector in lawmaking, legal education, gender roles, provision of pro bono services, and trade relations.

a mass of lawyers were trained to serve the lower-level bureaucracy (Venâncio Filho 1978; Adorno 1988; Faoro 2001). During this period, and despite some efforts at reform, the formalist and generalist tradition that was imported from Portuguese universities in the nineteenth century was deepened (Venâncio Filho 1978; Lyra Filho 1980; Faria 1987; Warat 2002; Falcão Lacerda e Rangel 2012; Trubek 2012). As a result, when the military regime ended and democracy was reestablished, lawyers within and beyond the state were not up to the needs of a society growing in complexity and diversity of interests (Lyra Filho 1980; Falcão 1984; Faria 1987; Arruda 1989; Sousa and Geraldo 1997; Warat 2002).

While there is a rich literature on law in Brazilian development and on lawyers in the Brazilian state, there has been less written on the legal profession as such. However, this has begun to change. Starting in the 1990s, scholars began to look directly at practicing lawyers and address structural tensions between the legal profession and the changes stemming from the country's development process. Topics were varied, such as gender roles in law firms (see Chapter 5), the role of lawyers in judicial reform (Almeida 2006) and access to justice (Almeida 2010; Santos and Carlet 2010; Sa e Silva 2011), and legal education (Junqueira 1999; Sa e Silva 2007). But new and even more complex challenges were to come, some of the most pressing resulting from globalization. Changes in the global economy would not only lead to a push for liberalization of the local markets and changes in balance between the state and the market but would also unleash a boom in new legislation and set in motion processes that would blur the lines between indigenous and foreign forms of law practice.

Very little has been done to capture and account for the role of lawyers in globalization and liberalization in Brazil. There is one study of efforts to train Brazilian lawyers to deal with the World Trade Organization (WTO). The most influential study to date is the pioneering work of Yves Dezalay and Bryant Garth in *The Internationalization of Palace Wars: Lawyers, Economists and the Contest to Transform Latin American States* (Dezalay and Garth 2002). This book really launched the worldwide study of lawyers and globalization and provided the first analysis of this relationship in Brazil. In addition to Dezalay and Garth, Professors Shafer, Sanchez, and Rosenberg conducted a detailed study of Brazil's efforts to train lawyers to represent the country's interests in the WTO (Shafer et al. 2012). As we indicate below, GLEE builds on both of these seminal works to construct a new account of how globalization is reshaping the market for corporate legal services in Brazil and other emerging economies, and the broader implications of this restructuring.

Our theory begins with Dezalay and Garth's trenchant observation that the massive legal changes that occurred during the 1990s were making US laws and legal institutions especially influential in the global economy. To explain this, they built accounts that rested to one degree or another on four pillars: the logic of capital accumulation in open economies, diffusion, core-periphery relations, and the sociology of the legal profession.[3]

The first pillar was a theory of capital accumulation in an open world economy. The grand transformation in the 1990s, which the GLEE project refers to as the "global shift," can be seen as an effort to create a single world market open to global capital. The project included efforts to integrate emerging economies into this universal system.[4] This in turn impacted domestic law in "peripheral countries." The process included diffusion of legal rules from the core to the periphery. Dezalay and Garth noted that US legal ideas and institutions tended to be favored during the global shift even in countries with very different legal traditions and historical ties. They suggested that asymmetrical power and US hegemony are among the factors that explain why the US approach to regulation of the economy was so influential, US laws were transplanted, US styles of lawyering diffused, and US legal education was sought out by aspiring lawyers.

[3] The original Dezalay-Garth theory is based on a model of institutional diffusion under conditions of core-periphery hierarchy, with economic and legal developments determined by the interaction of intraelite struggles within the legal profession and policy conflicts at the state level – which the authors refer to as "palace wars." This in turn takes place in a global context in which strong interests in the core work to engage actors in the periphery in policy changes that will benefit global capital. At the same time, local elites are able to resist some pressures from the core, leading to hybrid solutions. The overall picture that emerges from this analysis is one in which "double agents" in the North and South work together in ways that preserve and enhance international hegemony. By constructing a market for new legal forms and economic ideas while adapting them to local conditions and the interests of local elites, these double agents shore up both international hegemony and domestic systems of dominance.

[4] Since the postwar period, many developing countries had tried to insulate themselves from the world economy. They focused on building domestic industries, protected them by high tariff walls, and placed limits on foreign investment. The state played a central role in the economy, and many sectors were dominated by state-owned enterprises (SOE). But by the 1990s, this model had become exhausted, and other possibilities had become available. Inspired in part by the model of the Asian Tigers, emerging economies began to shift to export-led growth. That, in turn, increased the need to make domestic industries competitive and attract the kinds of foreign investment that would strengthen export capacity. It also pointed to the benefits from privatizing at least some SOEs. The turn to the market and the outside world was encouraged by core countries that saw in these liberalizing and rapidly growing emerging economies prospects for new markets, opportunities for high-yielding investment, and sources of labor. Through the WTO, BITs, and the use of conditional development assistance that required market-oriented reforms, core countries helped shape global norms in ways that facilitated their entry into these emerging markets.

This Americanization process was driven in part by the dynamics of the legal profession. Legal and corporate elites are key players in transplanting and/or implementing new legislation or professional models from developed countries (Dezalay and Trubek 1998). The impact produced by globalization in corporate law and practice depends on how it is translated by the elites involved. While traditional legal elites in many emerging economies looked to Europe for cultural inspiration and legal models, a new "modernizing" faction in countries like Brazil built closer ties to the United States. By deploying this US-oriented expertise during debates over the grand transformation, these rising elites helped steer reform in one direction while simultaneously advancing their own position within the Bar and the state.[5]

Focusing on Brazil, Dezalay and Garth described a "classic pattern" in which a legally trained elite dominated the field of state power in the nineteenth and first half of the twentieth centuries. Generalist lawyers, often trained in Europe, occupied key positions in both the legal field and the state. This socially and politically conservative elite served as a brake on efforts to modernize the economy. By the 1960s, however, this elite was losing influence. And when the military took power in 1964, the legal elite was sidelined and legal institutions, never too strong, were weakened.

Dezalay and Garth note that during the 1980s, as the military regime waned, elements in the legal elite sought to turn this situation around by exploiting US links, building on US legal ideas, and getting support from US institutions. One example they give was the development of the Pinheiro Neto law firm, which broke with the Brazilian pattern of small, family-dominated business law firms to create a US-style, full-service, corporate law firm with close ties to Wall Street firms. Another is the role played by the graduates of the Centro de Estudos e Pesquisas no Ensino do Direito (CEPED) legal education experiment. This project, which was supported by USAID and the Ford Foundation, trained several hundred Brazilian lawyers. Dezalay and Garth note that this project, run by Brazilian lawyers with close connections to international companies and contact with US-style law firms, and including visiting professors from the United States, introduced students to US legal ideas and global lawyering models. It also offered some of them access to US legal education. Once they completed the course (and some returned from LLMs in the United States), this group of CEPED alumni was able to parlay these credentials into important positions in business law, academia, and government. When Brazil began to restructure its economy

5 For subsequent applications of Dezalay and Garth's framework to analyze the legitimation of business law in Brazil, see Engelmann (2012).

in the 1990s, privatize state-owned firms, and attract foreign investment, there was a cadre ready, willing, and able to use its US-oriented expertise to help shape the new legal environment and build the public and private institutions it demanded.[6] This included efforts to make the legal order more autonomous.[7]

While GLEE builds on the insights of scholars like Dezalay and Garth, the project also seeks to address critical new issues. Among them is the role of the new corporate law sector once it grew to be a major element of the profession. Dezalay and Garth and other pioneering students of law and globalization studied the early years of legal response to the global shift; GLEE has looked at this development after two decades of rapid growth of the new corporate legal sector. The GLEE project is the first effort to provide detailed data on the growth of the sector, including both in-house offices and outside law firms; to trace the interaction between Brazilian law firms and foreign ones; and to study the impact of a robust corporate law sector on other parts of the legal system.

In addition to taking account of over two decades of rapid growth of the sector, GLEE deals with changes in global and Brazilian governance and policy that have occurred since the 1990s, when the study of law and globalization began. GLEE operates in a world in which traditional ideas about the "core" and the "periphery" and the dominance of the neoliberal Washington Consensus that animated the reforms of the 1990s are far less clear than they were even a decade ago. With the rise of a "new developmental state" in the twenty-first century, Brazil saw the reemergence of industrial policy and a more robust social policy, which have created new conditions for the operation of the corporate law sector (Trubek et al. 2013).

III THE TRANSFORMATION OF BRAZIL IN THE 1990S: LIBERALIZATION, PRIVATIZATION, INTERNATIONALIZATION, DEMOCRATIZATION

Brazil was late to industrialize.[8] As the country broke free from Portuguese colonial power (1822) and abolished slavery (1888), coffee production became the driver of the first transformation in its economic structure. Capital accumulation funded by coffee exportation led to an incipient urban bourgeoisie,

6 For detailed information on the CEPED experience, see Falcão et al. (2012).

7 Ironically, according the Dezalay and Garth, the dominance of lawyers in the state in the earlier period had discouraged efforts to make law autonomous from power.

8 This section draws on Trubek (2012) and Trubek et al. (2013).

while government incumbents at the federal level emphasized investments in heavy infrastructure, particularly in railroads (Furtado 2007).

From the 1930s to the 1950s, stronger and more conscious industrialization efforts were put in place. In the wake of the crash of 1929, Brazil took a route that would be later known as *import substitution* (Furtado 2007; Tavares 2011). This included both protectionist trade policy and stronger state activism in the economy. Imports tariffs were raised, local currency devalued, and commodity surpluses purchased by the state, thus creating resources that could be used for further industrial investments by domestic capitalists. Also, the state itself became an economic agent, whether by getting directly involved in basic industry – such as in metalwork via SOE *Volta Redonda* and oil production and processing via SOE *Petrobras* – or by funding investment projects in heavy infrastructure via the national investment bank *BNDES*. From 1930 until the end of the 1980s, economic policies basically consisted of state-led initiatives to promote import substitution, industrialization and growth using "economic law" tools, such as state-owned enterprises, economic planning, price control, sectorial regulatory and administrative authorities, and the use of tax and financial incentives.

However, between 1988 and 2004, Brazil partially dismantled these structures and policies and shifted to more market-oriented approaches. In 1988, after twenty-four years of military dictatorship and in a context of a threat of hyperinflation,[9] Brazil passed a new constitution that has influenced and shaped policy ever since. The 1988 Constitution is a social-democratic document that includes both civil, political, and social rights and several policy goals like building a free, just, and solidarity society, fostering national development, acquiring technological autonomy, eradicating poverty and marginalization, and reducing inequalities. Many of its provisions have direct effect on government policy and budgetary allocations.

In 1989, immediately after the new constitution came into force, President Collor de Mello was elected. Adopting a rhetoric based on the need for "modernization," Collor de Mello abruptly started a liberalization period that included drastic tariff reduction, privatization, as well as flawed attempts to control inflation.[10] Under Itamar Franco, the vice president who replaced

[9] In January 1990 inflation in Brazil reached 56 percent per month, raising to 73 percent in February and peaking at 84 percent per month in March. During the same period, inequality reached its worse level ever since it started to be measured (the Gini coefficient peaked at 0.647, according to IBGE, the Brazilian Office of Statistics).

[10] Paradoxically enough, Collor harshly confiscated savings and deposits owned by Brazilian citizens. This controversial measure has raised several discussions in the Brazilian judiciary.

Collor de Mello after he was impeached, a stabilization plan (Plano Real) was successfully adopted and inflation controlled.[11] Also, new legislation on social assistance and welfare for the poor was passed. Franco's Minister of Finance, Fernando Henrique Cardoso, known popularly as FHC, became the next president in 1994. During Cardoso's eight years in office, Brazil continued to move away from the *dirigiste* policies of the "developmentalist" period, embracing many of the neoliberal prescriptions favored by the Washington Consensus.[12]

In the Cardoso period, state-owned enterprises were privatized, direct subsidies for certain industries scaled back, areas of the economy deregulated, import barriers reduced, competition fostered and enforced, intellectual property rights tightened, efforts to attract foreign capital undertaken,[13] and fiscal responsibility enhanced. Also, the currency (real) was constantly kept overvalued, and monetary stability was pursued and attained.[14] Foreign investment increased and Brazilian firms could raise money in the international capital market. In place of direct state control of sectors like telecommunications and state ownership of major enterprises in steel, mining, and aircraft production, many SOEs were sold to private groups.

This process was accompanied by a veritable flood of new legislation, much of it new to the Brazilian scene. US-style independent regulatory agencies were created to monitor and regulate the newly privatized sectors. Antitrust law was updated and enforcement strengthened. New laws governing capital markets were passed and a vibrant capital market began.

These changes created whole new areas of law and generated new demands from corporate clients. Companies and governmental entities found themselves operating in a new, complex, transnationalized regulatory matrix. This created a huge demand for corporate legal services. Many of the new laws were both complex and unfamiliar to most Brazilian practitioners: for example, the independent regulatory agencies were based on foreign models that were shoe-horned into Brazilian legal categories. Lawyers had to deal with new clients and unfamiliar transactions. More and more Brazilian companies

11 As Castro notes, "Despite that, a period of strong deterioration of the Balance of Payments began, which led the current-account deficit to achieve 4.0 percent of the GDP in 1998 (Castro 2008).

12 FHC has always rejected the neoliberal label and claimed that his goal simply was to modernize the economy.

13 Among the measures were a series of bilateral investment treaties protecting foreign investors that were signed but never ratified.

14 Ban notes, "The goal of price stability has remained sacrosanct and the instruments for achieving this goal have been in line with the latest international fashions: central bank independence and inflation targeting" (Ban 2013, 6).

found themselves working with foreign corporations. Transactions rarely seen in Brazil like transnational mergers and acquisitions and overseas bond and stock issues were introduced. Moreover, some of the new legal rules were derived from international sources like the WTO requiring Brazilian lawyers to master international texts and understand international institutions.

Such measures marked the beginning of a process which would ultimately led to a substantial reform of the Brazilian State. It aimed at fostering development within the new global reality by modernizing Brazilian society and economy to strengthen Brazil's position in global market. The bulk of this process, which took place between 1990 and 2000, was carried out by means of amendments to the Constitution, substantial changes in legislation and institutions, and the creation of new regulatory agencies.

While from a legislative standpoint, this new regulatory framework emerged as a result of intense political negotiation involving different social actors, its effectiveness required the existence in the country of practicing lawyers able to deal with the new reality. Regulation could only work if Brazil could count on legal professionals who, working both in the public and the private sectors, had the skills to respond to the needs of a global market whose dynamics were often at odds with the country's legal tradition and practices. Such a demand ended up by profoundly reshaping the legal profession in Brazil as it inevitably led, notably from the 1990s onward, to transformation of Brazilian law firms and to competition among them.

IV BRAZIL'S REDEMOCRATIZATION REVIVES THE RULE OF LAW AND GIVES THE LEGAL PROFESSION A CENTRAL ROLE

While primarily economic forces were influencing change in the laws affecting business and creating new demands for legal services, political developments affected the nature and status of the Brazilian legal profession and strengthened its role in the country. During the military regime (1964–1985) the profession was somewhat marginalized as technocrats took over lawmaking and political repression limited lawyer's role in civil affairs. But by the end of the 1970s social movements, in which lawyers played a prominent role, had started the transition from a military regime toward democracy. A group of legal professionals, organized around a commitment to liberal values and the rule of law, emerged and gave the country's legal elite a prominent role in the new Brazilian political and social scene. With the rule of law enshrined as a fundamental principle, this elite played a role in the development of the new environment, including the laws affecting business and the creation of the new corporate law sector.

The reemergence of the Brazilian legal elite during redemocratization was the result of actions by individual lawyers and the Ordem dos Advogados do Brasil – the Brazilian Bar Association or OAB. They fought for human rights and defended political prisoners during the military regime. With democratization, they pushed for reforms to guarantee civil rights, protect social and economic rights, and improve access to justice. These efforts culminated in the Federal Constitution of 1988.

The 1988 Constitution ushered in other changes that strengthened the rule of law and thus increased the importance of legal professionals in the Brazilian economy, polity, and society. These included strengthening the Public Prosecutor's Office and the Judiciary which ensured greater scrutiny of executive and legislative adherence to the law and the Constitution. These measures enhanced the role of legal professionals as guardians of the new rule of law order. This capacity was used to defend clients of all types, from victims of civil rights violations to corporations, and ensured that lawyers would be in high demand as the economy grew.

V THE TRANSFORMATION OF THE CORPORATE LEGAL HEMISPHERE, 1990–2014

The global shift deeply affected the Brazilian legal market. Apart from a boom of new practice areas (e.g., capital markets, ADR, mergers and acquisitions, antitrust), there have been changes in the profile of clients, who became significantly more demanding in an increasingly competitive legal market.

Prior to the global shift, the typical Brazilian law firm in the corporate sector was relatively small. A handful of lawyers joined together to form a firm. In many cases, they were led by a "notable," a lawyer who had gained a reputation as one learned in the law. These legal notables combined intellectual and social capital built on family connections, academic positions, and publications of doctrinal texts. The firms were managed informally and developed clients through social contacts and the reputation of the leading partner. The practice would be focused on the area of the lead lawyer's expertise. There were some exceptions, particularly in that part of the sector that catered primarily to foreign clients. There you could find larger firms offering a fuller range of services, more professional management, and emphasis on the firm's brand, not just that of an individual notable. In some cases, these firms were founded by expatriates with experience in large law firms in the United States who settled in Brazil or Brazilians with overseas experience.[15]

[15] See Krishnan et al. (2016).

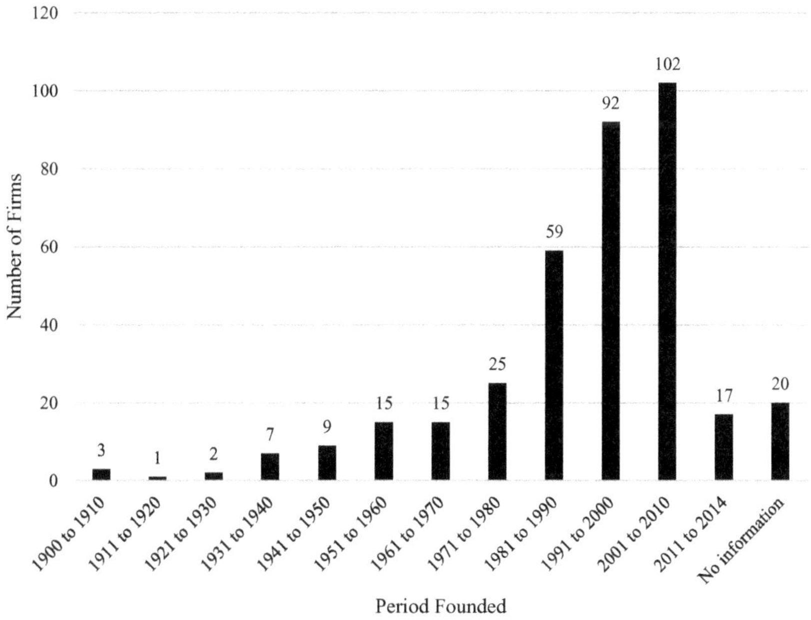

FIGURE 1.1 Number of law firms by decade.
Source: Gabbay, Ramos, and Sica, chapter 2, this volume.

But even the largest of these firms in the pre-1990s period was small by global norms or today's Brazilian standards.

All that changed after 1990. Figure 1.1 shows the rapid rise of the corporate sector in the 1990s after the economy was opened and privatization began. As Chapter 2 of this volume develops, in the two decades starting in 1991 more corporate law firms were added (194) than had been created in the entire period since 1900 (136). Not only did the number of firms grow rapidly after 1991; there was an increase in the size of law firms driven in part by the emergence of new practice areas so that by 2014 there were 10 firms with more than 300 lawyers and many with more than 100.

The privatization drive and other changes created whole new areas of law affecting business. Take, as an example, telecommunications. This sector had previously been a state monopoly but in the 1990s it was privatized, opened to foreign firms, and subjected to new forms of regulation including the creation of a US-style regulatory agency called ANATEL.[16] All of a sudden, corporations were faced with a legal regime that had no precedent in the country. This

[16] For a detailed discussion of the transformation of telecoms market and regulation, see Sa e Silva and Trubek in Chapter 10 of this volume.

created a big demand for lawyers who had both knowledge of the new telecoms laws and international expertise. Similar things happened in other legal fields. As demand increased and the economy grew, mergers, spin-offs, and associations between law firms occurred and new firms were created. The old "gentleman's agreement" against poaching lawyers from other firms eroded as the market became more competitive.

While many firms grew substantially and began to resemble global full-service firms to one degree or another, these two decades also saw the rise of "boutique" firms claiming a high level of specialized expertise. Many firms refer to themselves as boutique firms to achieve greater prestige and to differentiate themselves from generalist law firms, which are sometimes associated with somewhat impersonal services.

In addition to the growth of corporate law firms, in-house offices also grew in size, sophistication, and importance within the corporation (see Chapters 3 and 4). Since the expansion of legal departments in Brazil, which gained strength in the 1990s with privatizing of companies and further opening of the Brazilian market to foreign capital, the profiles and the careers of legal directors have undergone several transformations, culminating in more value and more prestige being given to those professionals inside companies. These transformations have a series of implications for the corporate legal sector, ranging from changing the criteria for hiring professionals, to creating new demands for more sophisticated legal services.

VI THE RISE OF THE NEW DEVELOPMENTAL STATE AND ITS IMPACT ON LAWYERING

In the heyday of neoliberalism, it might have seemed that the era of the developmental state was over and industrial policy a thing of the past. But Brazil never fully accepted neoliberal reforms and the role of the state continued robust even under Cardoso. With the election of Lula, ideas of developmentalism returned and more attention was paid to industrial policy. This trend accelerated in Lula's second administration and was further deepened under Dilma with the enactment of the Brasil Maior (Greater Brazil) plan. While the Lula-Dilma developmental state maintained elements of past forays into industrial policy, there was no effort to reprivatize major industries like minerals giant Vale or the recently privatized telecoms sector. Rather, this new developmentalism operated more like a public-private partnership with various incentives provided to firms that contributed to industrial policy goals. The new political economy of development affected lawyering in various ways, including creating a need for new skills and negotiating tactics as corporate lawyers found themselves dealing with state agencies of various types that sought to shape investment and output. These policies seemed to work well for a while, but with the end of the commodity boom the Brazilian economy went into decline. Efforts to deepen state engagement to keep growth going may have aggravated the situation and the country fell into a steep recession. In 2016, Dilma was impeached, and Michael Temer assumed the presidency, resulting in the formation of a conservative government. While this government has pledged to reduce the role of the state in the economy, as of the date of writing, relatively little had been changed and many of the forces affecting lawyering were still in place.

VII THE SCOPE OF THE STUDY

The GLEE Brazil Project aimed at identifying the globalization process and its impact by asking a set of questions specifically focusing on the corporate law environment in Brazil, including its structures, organizations, and actors. Key research questions were as follows:

1. What impact has globalization had on law firms serving corporate clients in Brazil? Has a new model of law firm arisen and what does it look like?
2. How have in-house legal departments responded to the new business needs, including the new international dimensions of Brazilian companies? What major changes have in-house legal departments undergone as a result of such changes?
3. What role has the corporate legal sector played in creation of new legal regimes designed to manage Brazil's role following the global shift?
4. What skills do lawyers working in new-model law firms and new in-house offices require? Where do they secure the needed skills and knowledge? How has the rise of the corporate sector affected Brazil's many law schools?
5. To what extent are the changes in law, lawyering, and law office organization influenced by foreign, especially US, models? What tensions has that created?
6. How did the regulation of the legal profession, including that of law offices, respond to globalization, in general, and to the internationalization of legal services, in particular?
7. How has the corporate law sector responded to calls for corporate social responsibility and pro bono services, and how has the rest of the profession reacted?

8. What is the structure of the new mass-litigation law offices and how do they work and how do they affect access to justice?
9. How have new kinds of law offices in the corporate and mass-litigation areas impacted gender issues?
10. How has Brazil responded to the need to prepare lawyers to handle trade-related litigation including WTO cases as well as antidumping and other trade remedies?
11. How has the reemergence of industrial policy under Lula and Dilma affected corporate legal practice?

VIII MAJOR FINDINGS

Taken together, the chapters offer a detailed overview of the Brazilian corporate legal sector and the transformations it has undergone since the 1990s. Although the papers cover a wide range of topics, a complex overall picture emerges. As Maria da Gloria Bonelli and Camila de Pieri Benedito point out in Chapter 5 of this volume, discourses on globalization and professions should always use both terms in the plural, not the singular. Professional globalization is not a one-way street, in which the North exports expertise to professionals in the South, who, in turn, merely absorb and implement the technological advances generated abroad. And legal professions are not monoliths. The GLEE research suggests a multidirectional movement and a complex interplay between foreign models and Brazilian institutions and practice. The ten most important findings follow.

A *The Rise of the Corporate Legal Sector Has Transformed an Important Sector of the Brazilian Legal Profession*

Since the 1990s, the landscape encountered by the legal profession has changed substantially especially in the Southeast region where most of the corporate headquarters and most of the corporate lawyers are located. Changes can be found in all dimensions including the laws themselves, legal institutions, lawyering practices, the profession's hierarchical structures and the political dynamics of actors in the legal field. They are the result of the interaction of various actors in the profession, including traditional elites and newcomers, domestic and foreign lawyers, in-house legal directors and outside law firm management, local bar officials and national OAB leadership, as well as government agencies such as the Ministerio Publico (Public Prosecutors).

B *These Changes Have Been Driven by a Boom in New Laws That Were in Part Created by Corporate Lawyers*

With the opening of the economy, privatization of state own enterprises, and increasing flow of foreign investment, new laws had to be produced to structure changes and govern new forms of economic activity. Corporate lawyers played a role in the making of this boom which then created new demands for their services.

C *Many Developments Have Been Influenced by Diffusion of Global Models and Styles, but There Has Been Resistance*

Global processes of diffusion have had an influence but the impact has varied from area to area. In some, Brazil has followed global trends. The role of in-house counsel is an example: Brazilian corporations, following global models, have raised the stature of the general counsel within the company, increased the sophistication of the company's legal staff, expanded the size of in-house offices, and changed the relationship between the in-house offices and outside firms. Even with respect to in-house counsel, however, there continue to be important differences between Brazilian practices and the in-house counsel movement in the United States. In other areas, global actors, models, and processes have encountered resistance. Imported laws and legal institutions have not always worked as expected, and hybrids have emerged. While the global law firm model, based largely on the US approach, has influenced the growth of the corporate law firm sector, it has also met resistance from the rest of the profession and there is tension between the US-influenced corporate firm's operation and the regulatory structure governing law offices.

D *The Organized Bar Has Been a Source of Resistance*

In some cases, diffusion has led to direct conflict. A lot of resistance has come from the organized Bar – the OAB. The Bar has adopted a conservative stance, seeking to protect existing markets against innovations like pro bono; limit the role of foreign firms in the country; and police alliances between Brazilian and foreign law firms. Thus, the effort by elite corporate firms to follow global models for pro bono was initially blocked by the OAB forcing the firms to seek creative ways to maintain such programs which are important for their relationship with major clients, and to their image as "world-class" firms. The OAB has also placed strict limits on the role of foreign law firms established in Brazil, although the firms have found ways to circumvent the restrictions.

Finally, efforts by some Brazilian firms to create formal, visible, and permanent alliances with foreign firms met with stiff resistance by the Bar which essentially outlawed such relationships.

E *The New Legal Services Market Has Demanded a New Type of Lawyer*

The growth of the corporate sector and the internationalization of corporate law practice created a demand for a new kind of lawyer. To succeed in this new environment, lawyers must not only have basic legal skills and knowledge of the Brazilian system; they must also have knowledge of advanced and specialized disciplines like international economic law; understand business practice, and be familiar with global lawyering styles.

F *Women Have Found Employment Opportunities in the Globalizing Sectors but Still Face Gender Inequality*

In two sectors affected by globalization – large corporate firms and mass-litigation outsourcing firms – women have found new job opportunities. More than half the associates in large corporate firms in São Paulo are female as are 65 percent of the lawyers in JPM Advogados, the leading mass-litigation firm. But women lag behind men in the senior ranks of the large corporate firms and most jobs in mass litigation are low-paying, routine, and low quality. A similar story can be told with respect to in-house legal departments. While women constitute a significant percentage of the lawyers employed by these departments, there are far fewer women general counsels – although, as in the United States, their percentage in these positions is increasing and is still greater than it is in equivalent positions in leading law firms.

G *Diffusion and Resistance Have Led to Hybridization*

The overall process of diffusion and resistance has led to the creation of hybrids in many areas as global models interact with Brazilian tradition, custom, practice, and law. Such hybrids can be found in law firms, in-house legal departments, legal education, pro bono, and gender relations. For example, the clash between corporate lawyers wishing to develop US-style pro bono efforts and resistance by the organized Bar led to a hybrid pro bono practice unique to Brazil. Other examples include the Bar's restriction on the foreign law firms, which have led to new strategies and relations between local and foreign law firms that ensure they are effectively inserted in global networks and international operations. However, small even such small changes are still largely absent in the educational area, where for the most part law schools have resisted change and kept traditional curricula and methodologies untouched.

H *Brazilian Law Schools Have Failed to Prepare Lawyers for Global Practice*

GLEE studies the ways that Brazilian lawyers developed the capacities needed for global lawyering. We found that law schools have been very slow to respond to the need for such training. To secure the needed skills and experiences, Brazilian lawyers have relied more on continuing legal education, study abroad, and training in law firms and GC offices than on formal legal education.

I *The Rise of the New Developmental State Has Created New Challenges for Corporate Lawyers*

Finally, the reemergence of the developmental state had an effect on the corporate law sector. GLEE observed these effects in two areas. In the field of telecommunications, corporate lawyers are seeking to cope with a series of demands from the state inspired by new developmental state industrial and social policy. This has changed the nature of advocacy in this sphere. Another major impact of the new developmental state on the profession can be seen in the area of international trade law. In the early 2000s, the Brazilian government and the private sector worked together to create a cadre of lawyers who could handle WTO cases. However, as WTO litigation declined, demand for this kind of work declined and there was an oversupply of trade law experts. The return of industrial policy changed the situation. Concerned with the impact of imports on domestic manufacturers, the government strengthened domestic antidumping laws thus creating a new market for lawyers with trade expertise.

IX CHAPTER SUMMARIES

A *Rapid Growth of Corporate Law Firms since 1990*

Gabby, Ramos, and Sica argue in Chapter 2 of this volume that in the twenty-five years since 1990, the corporate law firm sector in Brazil has grown substantially. The number of firms has more than doubled and average firm size increased dramatically. At the same time, firms have changed their methods of operation, recruitment, and management. Until 1990, the sector was small and largely focused on serving local clients; today it includes many large firms as well as numerous specialized "boutiques" serving both domestic and foreign corporations. Many of these firms have instituted management systems, hired professional managers, and employed technology to control operations and maintain communication. The firms have paid attention to branding, marketing themselves as collective entities with stress on the firm's capabilities, not those of an individual notable. They have established career ladders and regular performance reviews. Brazilian firms have sought foreign as well as domestic clients and have looked for ways to work with foreign law firms in the growing number of transactions with transnational elements.

Starting in the late 1990s, foreign law firms began establishing themselves in Brazil. In 2013, there were twenty-three such law firms operating in Brazil. Under OAB rules, these firms can only serve as consultants on foreign law and cannot advise on Brazilian law or appear in court. But they have found ways to get around some of these restrictions and to build alliances with Brazilian law firms.

The changing nature of the Brazilian corporate law firms is the product of rising overall demand for business law services as well as new client requirements. The arrival of more foreign corporations, and the increased importance and sophistication, of the in-house offices in both foreign and domestic companies, has led to demands for great sophistication in the services performed by outside firms as well as new lawyering styles and skills.

The rise of the corporate sector has created tension between an emerging model of professional organization and practice and traditions of the Brazilian legal profession including some OAB regulations. This has sometimes been manifested in a certain distance between what people say about how lawyers can and should operate and what is actually going on. Thus, while the Bar imposes minimum fee schedules and prohibits advertising, the new-model corporate firms compete actively for business and have engaged in various methods to market their brands. Similarly, while the Bar has sought to impose restrictions on alliances between domestic and foreign law firms and limit the activities of foreign firms established in Brazil, the largest Brazilian law firms are inserted in global networks of international operations and foreign firms operating in Brazil find ways to get around the restrictions on their practice. Finally, while corporate law firms are not "companies" under Brazilian law and thus are not supposed to be "entrepreneurial," and the Bar prohibits law firms with "mercantile forms or characteristics," the new-model corporate law firms operate like business entities as they respond to market demand and adopt corporate management technologies. The result is that there is often a gap between rhetoric and reality in the corporate law sector, as well as the development of hybrid organizational forms as the new-model law firms seek to adopt global forms and practices to Brazilian culture and regulation.

B *The "In-House Counsel Movement" Begins to Take Hold in Brazil, but with Important Differences from Both US Models and Similar Developments in Other Emerging Economies*

By almost any measure, one of the most significant developments in the corporate legal services market in the United States over the past thirty years has been the growth in the size, stature, and influence of internal legal counsel (Wilkins 2012; Heineman 2016). This "in-house counsel movement," as the American legal scholar Robert Eli Rosen aptly labeled this transformation (Rosen 1989), has been based on three interrelated arguments: *economic value* (i.e., that handling legal work internally is more efficient than hiring outside law firms), *substantive expertise* (i.e., that because of their proximity to the business, in-house lawyers can give better advice than outside counsel), and *professional independence* (i.e., that because general counsel are better able to understand and protect the company's long-term interests and reputation than law firm partners that they are more likely to uphold the legal profession's traditional ideal of the "Lawyer Statesman" who counsels clients to conform their conduct to the public purposes of the legal system) (Kronman 1993; Heineman 2016). Two chapters in this volume examine the degree to which this movement has come to Brazil, and how developments in that country compare with the evolution of internal lawyering in India, where the GLEE project is also conducting research.

Oliveira and Ramos begin this analysis in Chapter 3. Using quantitative data on a large cross section of Brazilian companies, as well as qualitative interviews of legal directors from prominent Brazilian firms, the authors investigate whether Brazil's legal departments exhibit six characteristics that have come to define the growth in status and influence of general counsels in the United States and other jurisdictions in the Global North: (1) the overall size of the legal department; (2) the demographic and educational profile of in-house lawyers (particularly of the GC); (3) the degree the GC exerts control over external law firms and other legal providers; (4) the prestige and authority of the GC within the company; (5) the status of in-house counsel within the legal profession as a whole; and (6) the participation and influence of GCs within wider debates over legislation and public policy (Wilkins 2012). Based on this data, Oliveira and Ramos conclude that since the expansion of legal departments in Brazil, which began during the 1990s coinciding with the increased privatizing of companies and the opening of the Brazilian market to foreign capital, the profiles and careers of legal directors have undergone several transformations, culminating in more value and prestige being given to these professionals within their companies. Prior to this period, few domestic Brazilian companies had in-house legal departments. By the end of the 1990s, however, with growing globalization and the arrival of more foreign capital in Brazil, it became increasingly necessary for legal professionals working in the corporate world to have a more complete background, including knowledge of corporate law disciplines, as well as of business, accounting, and international law. Legal departments therefore increased in size, and the legal directors operating these departments became increasingly sophisticated and influential. These transformations, in turn, generated a series of implications for the country's corporate legal market, changing the criteria for hiring in-house lawyers – including foreign law firms, which GCs now view as an important part of the Brazilian legal market.

Although the authors therefore conclude that important aspects of the in-house counsel movement have indeed come to Brazil, they also document how the structure and functioning of internal legal departments in Brazilian companies continues to differ from the US model. Thus, while many legal directors are moving from solely occupying the role of "cop," perceived as a necessary evil involved in managing the business's legal risks, to the role of "counselor," balancing legal risk management, compliance, and business recommendation, few have made the transition to an "entrepreneur" role where they play a key role in the company's strategic decision making. The stature and prestige of legal directors promised by the in-house counsel movement in the United States and other countries is therefore still a work in progress in Brazil. Nevertheless, the trajectory toward greater importance for the role is strong, and there are likely to be further changes in this direction in the coming years.

In Chapter 4, Wilkins and Khanna extend this analysis by examining how Brazil's internal legal departments compare to those in India. Given the similarities between these two rising powers, it is not surprising that some version of the in-house counsel movement has come to both jurisdictions. Like Brazil, India also underwent a global shift in the 1990s when the country moved from a closed socialist economy to one that is now more or less open, creating the kind of foreign direct investment and privatization that fuels the demand for sophisticated internal counsel. Notwithstanding these broad similarities, however, there are important differences in the economic structure, proximity to the West (particularly the United States), and the state of the legal profession in Brazil and India that plausibly impact how the in-house counsel movement develops in each country.

To explore these potential similarities and differences Wilkins and Khanna present the results of a comprehensive survey of general counsels in Brazil and India. The samples in each jurisdictions are broadly representative of large companies, including foreign multinationals (FMNCs) as well as domestic companies, and capture a significant percentage of Brazil and India's market capitalization, and an even greater percentage of the respective economic activity. As a result, Wilkins and Khanna are able not only to chart the growth in the size, sophistication, and impact of general counsel offices in each jurisdiction, but can also examine differences between FMNCs and domestic companies within each country's corporate counsel sector.

As predicted, the survey demonstrates that important aspects of the in-house counsel movement have come to each country. Legal departments in both jurisdictions have grown larger, and general counsels more sophisticated, across all company types. Consistent with the core tenets of the in-house counsel movement, GCs in both countries exercise primary control over the company's legal function, including putting together the list of "preferred providers" who do the company's outside legal work. Notwithstanding these changes, however, legal departments in both jurisdictions continue to spend more than half of their budgets on outside counsel and other legal service providers, with half of their overall budgets going to routine legal work. And while Brazilian and Indian GCs spend more time on public policy matters than they have in the past – and expect to spend even more time on these matters in the future – in neither country are these issues as important a part of the GC's job as they are in the United States and other more developed legal markets.

In addition to these core similarities, however, the survey results also underscore important differences, both between Brazil and India, and between domestic and FMNCs. The legal budgets of companies in Brazil are far larger than those in India, particularly with respect to FMNCs operating in the two jurisdictions. GCs in Brazil also appear to be more integrated into the company's senior management and business decision making than their Indian counterparts, with the former being more likely to advising the board, participate in senior leadership discussions, and counsel the CEO than GCs in India. Brazilian legal departments also tended to keep a greater percentage of the company's "high value" work in-house than similarly situated departments in India, while sending more "routine" work to outside providers. These differences, which are similar across both domestic and foreign companies in both jurisdictions, are consistent with the hypothesis that Brazil's more open economy and proximity to the United States has led to greater diffusion of the American model of internal lawyering where law is integral to business, and where GCs are considered both important members of the senior leadership team and capable of handling more sophisticated legal work. And while GCs in both countries report that they terminate important law firm relationships infrequently – significantly less frequently than GCs in the United States – Brazilian legal directors are more likely to do so than GCs in India. Once again, this difference underscores that the shift in power between inside and outside lawyers that has been at the core of the in-house counsel movement in the United States is currently more firmly established in Brazil than it is in India.

Taken together, these two studies provide ample support for the hypothesis that the US model of internal lawyering is diffusing through the Global South, led by FMNCs who are looking for the same levels of support and function from their legal departments in countries like Brazil and India that they receive in their home jurisdiction. But while this aspect of the American Mode of the Production of Law (Trubek et al. 1994) appears to be more firmly entrenched in Brazil than in India, neither country has yet to achieve the level of transformation on the six indicators identified by Wilkins as characterizing general counsel offices in the United States. Moreover, given the potential for "disruptive innovation" to transform the way that companies produce and consume legal services, it is far from clear that the evolution of internal lawyering will follow the established tenets of the in-house counsel movement in these and other rapidly changing emerging economies – particularly as law is increasingly absorbed into broader "business solutions" that may not need to be handled by specialized legal departments.

C *Women Find New Employment Opportunities in Globalized Practices but Encounter Barriers to Promotion in Large Firms and Low-Quality Jobs in Mass-Litigation Firms*

Bonelli and Benedito argue in Chapter 5 that globalization has had an important impact on gender relations in the Brazilian legal profession. The traditional Brazilian law firm tended to be male dominated; if women were hired they rarely made partner. Globalization has changed this situation not only in the elite corporate law firm sector, but also in mass-litigation law firms that emerged in the 1990s to handle a litigation explosion.

As indicated in Chapter 2, the large-scale corporate law firm is the best-known product of globalization in Brazil. But mass-litigation firms are the product of globalization as well. Starting in the 1990s, corporations in Brazil began to outsource mass litigation to specialized firms set up for this purpose. Like the elite corporate firms, they represented a major break with the traditional law firm pattern as they employ business methods, handle thousands of small-scale, relatively routine cases and employ assembly-line methods.

A study of gender roles in a sample of corporate law firms in São Paulo and in JBM Advogados, the largest mass-litigation firm, shows that both of these "globalized" practices are more likely to hire and promote women than is the case in the traditional law firm sector. In the corporate law firm sector, half the associates and up to a quarter of the partners are women. While women lag behind men in gaining partnership in this sector, they do better than in traditional firms. Women also have found employment opportunities in JBM Advogados which hires hundreds of low-paid lawyers to handle routine tasks in what some describe as "factory-like" conditions. At the time the study was done, 65 percent of JPM's lawyers were women, and women equaled or outnumbered men in managerial positions.

Globalization has therefore created more opportunities for women at both the top (corporate) and bottom (mass litigation) end of the profession. But gender hierarchies still remain: men are more likely to make partner in the corporate sector, and most of the jobs in the mass-litigation sector are low quality, paying little and involving routine work under close supervision in assembly-line conditions.

D *The Rise of New-Model, Large-Scale Corporate Law Firms and the Arrival of Foreign Law Firms Create Regulatory Challenges for the Brazilian Bar Association (OAB)*

The rise of the corporate law sector has presented regulatory challenges for the Brazilian Bar Association (Ordem dos Advogados do Brasil or OAB) which has had to deal with new forms of organization, employment, and lawyering styles, new kinds of practice, as well the presence of foreign firms. OAB regulations played an important role in the growth of the corporate law firm sector. Almedia and Nassar argued in Chapter 6 that as Brazilian lawyers began to adopt corporate law firm models from the United States and other developed countries, the OAB was faced with a new entity that operated differently than the traditional Brazilian law firm. These "new-model" firms were relatively large, highly specialized, organized in a hierarchical fashion, and profit seeking. Although there were concerns that this "commercialized" approach to law practice was at odds with principles of professionalism, the OAB created a regulatory framework that accommodated the new model, allowing the corporate sector to grow substantially in the 1990s and early 2000s.

The rise of the corporate sector created a new actor in OAB politics. The Association had been dominated by two groups: the traditional elite of prestigious lawyers who had dominated the profession since the beginning, and the OAB's organizational elite of elected Bar leaders who occupied important posts within the Association and were responsive to the great mass of members. With the rise of the corporate law firms, a third elite made up of business lawyers from large law firms entered the picture.

These three elites struggled as the OAB dealt with two issues that arose as a result of globalization and the rise of the corporate sector: (1) the rules governing pro bono practice and (2) the regulation of foreign law firms and their relationship with Brazilian firms. The struggles took place within the complex federal structure of the OAB with various actors seeking to secure rulings at levels most favorable to their claims. This meant that some issues remained at state level while others ended up in the OAB's Federal Council.

The first case arose because the large law firms, influenced by global trends, wanted to create pro bono units but ran into opposition from the São Paulo State Bar Association who voted to ban the practice to protect the solo practitioners and small law firms that constitute the bulk of the Bar's membership business lawyers, joined by prestigious representatives of the traditional legal elite, challenged the ruling. Bar leaders, however, fought to maintain the ban on pro bono, which their constituency feared threatened a lucrative legal and market for lawyers under São Paulo's judiciary system. After considerable debate, the alliance of traditional and business lawyers could strike a compromise with the São Paulo Bar Association under which pro bono was allowed but only for NGOs without resources to hire lawyers. This compromise lasted for more than a decade until the Federal Prosecutor's Office challenged the ban on pro bono for individuals. Faced with a possible constitutional proceeding, the Federal Council of the OAB weighed in, suspended the São Paulo ban on individual pro bono, and announced that it would allow this practice in the future.

In the second regulatory debate, some among the new corporate elite wanted the OAB to outlaw alliances between foreign law firms and local firms. The controversy arose after a few Brazilian corporate law firms had created formal alliances with foreign firms, including some that were licensed to practice foreign law in Brazil and others operating outside the country. Once again the issue erupted in São Paulo, home of most of the large law firms. Many of the large firms favored strict restrictions on such alliances and supported actions of the São Paulo Bar that punished several firms for establishing alliances.

However, large firms benefiting from this practice disagreed and sought a ruling from the Federal Council. This generated a debate on the issue of foreign firm alliances with some large–law firm leaders pushing for draconian restrictions and others proposing more limited ones. Some members of the traditional elite weighed in, supporting some but not all the proposed restrictions. With the São Paulo business law elite split and the traditional elite not in favor of all the proposed restrictions, the issue could not be contained at the state level and gravitated to the Federal Council. In the face of strong opinions on all sides of the issue, the Federal Council issued a very general opinion stating that permanent and visible alliances with foreign firms licensed to operate in Brazil were not allowed but leaving room for other kinds of relations both with such firms and those outside the country.

E *Competing Interests, Local Institutions, and Diverse Interactions across Borders Affect the Diffusion of US Practices and Ideologies: The Case of Pro Bono*

In Chapter 7, Sa e Silva extends the regulatory debate concerning the rise of pro bono in Brazil referenced in the proceeding section to provide a more comprehensive examination of how globalization has influenced the development of this increasingly important practice. By the time the global shift was taking place and impacting the legal profession in emerging economies, pro bono – traditionally defined as free legal services for the poor – was becoming a core institutional feature of US corporate law firms and access to justice practices. But whereas this trend quickly saw correspondence among local entrepreneurs in Brazil, pro bono found less chance to grow and prosper among Brazilian corporate lawyers and law firms showing the limits to diffusion of US practices and ideologies. Competing interests and institutions at the local level, along with diverse interactions across the North/South border have produced a unique meaning for pro bono in São Paulo.

Initially, pressures from clients seeking to advance corporate social responsibility projects and support from traditional elite lawyers allowed pro bono to grow. But struggles for shares of the legal market at both the top and the bottom of the bar's structure constrained its institutionalization among corporate lawyers and law firms.

As indicated above, to mediate these conflicts, the bar enacted regulations allowing pro bono services to be offered only to NGOs and in transactional matters, not litigation. And while law firms initially resisted these restrictions, over time some of them compromised with the bar leadership as part of a wider bargain that also restricted the entry of foreign law firms into the Brazilian legal market. Faced with this strong opposition by the bar and some corporate elites, pro bono promoters responded by not only reinforcing the "traditional" roots of pro bono, but also by developing strong alliances with public defenders, litigation-oriented NGOs, and human rights advocacy groups. The result is a very different profile for pro bono in Brazil than what tends to exist in the United States and other jurisdictions, where this practice focuses primarily on individual representation.

As indicated in the prior section, the deal struck in São Paulo limiting pro bono to work for NGOs lasted for over a decade. But recently the Federal Prosecutor's Office's threat to challenge the ban on individual representation has led the OAB to void the restrictions. This leaves pro bono in Brazil at a crossroads, which can lead to many different forms of engagement among both pro bono activists and corporate lawyers and law firms. These can be more traditional or more innovative; more technical or more politicized; more systematic or more ad hoc.

F *Brazilian Law Schools Fail to Meet the Challenge of Globalization, and Aspiring Lawyers Seek Alternative Paths to Acquiring Needed Skills and Experience*

In Chapter 8, Cunha and Ghirardi shine a light on changes in legal education in Brazil. The transformation of the corporate law sector created demand for new skills. Corporate law firms and GC offices sought lawyers with basic legal skills, knowledge of advanced areas of corporate and international economic law, familiarity with global lawyering styles, and a grasp of business fundamentals. Brazilian law schools failed to respond to this demand. With minor exceptions, the established law schools resisted changes. While a wave of new law schools was created, often by profit-seeking institutions, these new entrants concentrated on low-level, mass legal education, replicating traditional curricula and focusing on preparation for the bar exam. While a few law schools in Rio and São Paulo have introduced innovative undergraduate law programs and addressed global issues, the mass of law schools failed to respond to the new needs.

As a result, aspiring corporate lawyers had to seek alternative paths to gain the capacities required by the new market. These paths included continuing legal education programs which have proliferated, study abroad principally in the United States, internships in foreign law firms, and in-house training. Some of the institutions that created new, internationally oriented law undergraduate courses have also started offering MA programs and high-level continuing education courses. They thus meet a substantial portion of the local market demand for lawyers with new skills and knowledge. Although continuing education has helped provide knowledge of advanced legal subjects it rarely if ever offers training in business fundamentals or global lawyering styles. These capabilities are best found through foreign degrees and internships as well as training programs directly offered (in-house) or financed by law firms, including a growing number of executive education programs in the United States and United Kingdom that cater to a global clientele. Many students, having finished the undergraduate course in Brazil and often doing some work in corporate firms, have gone abroad for LLMs and internships and many law firms now offer substantial in-house training.

G *Lawyers Trained in WTO Law Find New Outlets for Their Skills in the Surge of Trade Remedies Generated by New Industrial Policies*

Glezer, Dias, Brito, and Zanatta in Chapter 9 describe how Brazil's entry into the WTO created a demand for lawyers who could understand the WTO's rules and defend Brazil's interests in the organizations' dispute resolution system. Lawyers were needed who could use WTO law to support Brazilian exporters seeking access to foreign markets and protect domestic policy against complaints in the WTO. To meet this need, the Brazilian Ministry of Foreign Affairs, working with the private sector, created a program in Geneva to train lawyers from the public and private sector in WTO law. This project created a cadre of lawyers familiar with the mechanics of foreign trade and WTO law and procedure. An elite group, trained in the Geneva Program and/or through study and work abroad, emerged. Most found work in large full-service law firms.

While the initial idea behind capacity building was to create a cadre of lawyers who could work in the WTO itself, the decline of WTO cases involving Brazil, and the need for legal expertise in other areas of trade law including antidumping and customs law, has changed the profile of the trade law bar and the work its members do.

The initial capacity-building efforts actually created an oversupply of trade law experts. With WTO litigation work declining, these lawyers needed to find other outlets for their skills. When New Developmental State industrial policies led to a tougher antidumping law, legal capacity that had been developed for WTO litigation was adapted and deployed in trade remedy litigation and foreign trade consulting. Demands by Brazilian and foreign clients for representation in antidumping actions grew. WTO-trained lawyers became active in the Brazilian trade remedy system and set themselves up as consultants offering economic and business as well as legal analysis. Stimulated by this new demand, work increased and new organizational models for legal practice emerged. The trade law bar has increased participation in global consulting networks, created "foreign desks" in large-scale law firms, gone to work for firms specializing in government relations, and lobbied government agencies. These moves have ensured employment for the trade law elite, helping to absorb the oversupply. A few lawyers are added to the field from time to time, largely through in-house training. But most trade lawyers do not predict major growth in the future.

H *Corporate Lawyers Help Create the New Regime*

Much of the GLEE study explores how changes in economic policy led to legal changes which in turn generated demand for new kinds of lawyering. But there is another side to the story. As Sa e Silva and Trubek argue in Chapter 10 of this volume, corporate lawyers did not sit back passively waiting for technocrats and legislators to create the postglobal transformation legal regime: they actively participated in the creation of the new laws, procedures, and institutions. To explore this issue, GLEE studied one important area – telecommunications. Until 1990, telecommunications was a state monopoly and the sector was run by Telebras, a major state-owned enterprise. In the 1990s a decision was made to privatize the sector and seek foreign investment. To make the sector attractive to foreign investors, it was subjected to new forms of regulation including the creation of a US-style regulatory agency called ANATEL.

GLEE looked at four incidents in the history of this process. The first two stories focus on the transition between state monopoly and a regulated market (late 1980s–1997). They reveal two ways in which corporate lawyers contributed to that process. Initially, corporate lawyers sought to provide legal legitimacy and the necessary legal tools for ongoing attempts to open the telecom sector: they engaged in creative interpretation of existing laws and produced suggestive drafts of administrative norms that could enable private participation in the telecom sector. None of these efforts were sufficient to produce an atmosphere favorable to private investment. When the government made a more decisive move to open the sector and seek foreign investment, it was convinced of the need to make a major change in Brazilian laws in order to make the sector more attractive to foreign investors. This reform, which involved creating a regulatory structure based on foreign approaches to industry regulation and administrative law institutions not recognized in Brazilian law, required a distinct kind of legal assistance. Corporate lawyers helped the government identify specialized professionals who could get the job done.

The third story focuses on the initial operation of the sector as an aspiring regulated market operating under an imported legal structure (1998–2007).

This time, corporate lawyers ensured that the previous legal reforms were administered the way they were intended. Initially, the new legal forms conflicted with an enduring technocratic ethos held among ANATEL directors, who had been socialized in the context of the Telebras system. By undertaking opaque and idiosyncratic regulatory practices, which translated into demands that companies saw as exceeding legitimate regulatory concerns, these old-style technocrats tried to pour the old wine of developmentalism into the new bottles of the regulatory state. But by imposing legal constraints on regulatory discretion through the use of Courts and administrative proceedings, corporate lawyers curbed the powers of these technocrats. At the end of this period, with regulation operating under stricter legal constraints and ANATEL placing more value on the law and legal reasoning, corporate lawyers had acquired considerable professional power, which they could use to place substantive constraints on the workings of the agency and drive the sector toward the original aspiration of a regulated market in which private companies exercised substantial discretion.

The fourth story focuses on the changing scene in the sector with the emergence of a new developmental state in the late 2000s. Now, reinvigorated state activism informed by concerns for social inclusion and industrial development led to new demands on the companies and new challenges to the legal infrastructure inherited from the 1990s. Corporate lawyers have resisted these moves by continuous legal mobilization and production of market-friendly legal ideologies. But they confront a more effective state apparatus and increased social and public participation in the sector, potentially limiting their ability to resist the new policies. There is a tension between two approaches: resistance and challenge to the legitimacy of the procedures used and new demands being made, and pragmatic advocacy which accepts the legitimacy of government action and seeks the best deal possible in that context. The outcome of this struggle is unclear. Yet it shows that the rise of a new developmental state is changing the context in which corporate lawyers act and may influence their orientations in ways that challenge the some of the theories concerning lawyers and globalization.

This final chapter, therefore, provides a fitting conclusion to this volume. As indicated at the outset, the GLEE project's primary goal is to open a new field of study in Brazil and other emerging economies, as opposed to resolving the complex questions raised by our research regarding the evolving relationship between the emergence of a new and increasingly defined corporate legal hemisphere and broader issues of economic, political, and social development. We hope that Brazilian and international scholars will be inspired by the work we have done here to pursue these questions.

REFERENCES

Adorno, Sérgio. 1998. *Os Aprendizes do Poder: O Bacharelismo Liberal na Política Brasileira*. São Paulo: Paz e Terra.

Almeida, Frederico. 2006. "A Advocacia e o Acesso à Justiça no Estado de São Paulo (1980–2005)." Master's Thesis in Political Science. São Paulo: FFLCH/USP.

2010. "A Nobreza Togada: Elites Jurídicas e a Política da Justiça no Brasil." PhD in Thesis in Political Science. São Paulo: FFLCH/USP.

Arruda, Edmundo Lima de, Jr. 1989. *Ensino Jurídico e Sociedade: Formação, Trabalho e Ação Social*. São Paulo: Acadêmica.

Ban, Cornel. 2013. "Brazil's Liberal Neo-developmentalism: New Paradigm or Edited Orthodoxy?" *Review of International Political Economy* 20 (2): 298–331.

Bonelli, Maria da Gloria, et al. 2008. "Profissionalização por Gênero em Escritórios Paulistas de Advocacia." *Revista de Sociologia da USP* 20 (1): 265–290.

Bresser Pereira, Luis Carlos, and Yoshiaki Nakano. 1991. "Hiperinflação e estabilização no Brasil: O primeiro Plano. Collor." *Revista de Economia Política* 11 (4): 89–114.

Castro, Antonio B. 2008. "From Semi-stagnation to Growth in a Sino-centric Market." *Review of Economics and Politics* 28 (1): 3–27.

Coutinho, Diogo R. 2012. "Decentralization and Coordination in Social Law and Policy: The Bolsa Familia Program." In *Law and the New Developmental State: The Brazilian Experience in Latin American Context*. Edited by David M. Trubek, Helena Alviar Garcia, and Diogo R. Coutinho. New York: Cambridge University Press.

Coutinho, Diogo R., David M. Trubek, and Mario Gomes Schapiro. 2012. "Toward a New Law and Development: New State Activism in Brazil and the Challenge for Legal Institutions." *The World Bank Review* 4: 281–314.

Coutinho, Diogo R., Mario G. Schapiro, and David M. Trubek. 2013. "New State Activism in Brazil and the Challenge for Law." In *Law and the New Developmental State: The Brazilian Experience in Latin American Context*. Edited by David M. Trubek, Helena Alviar Garcia, and Diogo R. Coutinho. New York: Cambridge University Press.

Dezalay, Yves, and Brian Garth. 2002. *The Internationalization of Palace Wars: Lawyers, Economists and the Contest to Transform Latin American States*. Chicago: University of Chicago Press.

Dezalay, Yves, and David M. Trubek. 1998. "A reestruturação global e o direito: A internacionalização dos campos jurídicos." In *Direito e Globalização Econômica*. Edited by José Eduardo Faria. São Paulo: Malheiros.

Engelmann, Fabiano. 2012. "Globalization and State Power: International Circulation of Elites and Hierarchies in the Brazilian Legal Field." *Dados* 55 (2): 487–516.

Falcão, Joaquim de Arruda. 1984. *Os Advogados: Ensino Jurídico e Mercado de Trabalho*. Recife: Fund. J. Nabuco, Massangana.

Falcão, Joaquim A., Gabriel Lacerda, and Tânia Ragel. 2012. *Aventura e Legado no Ensino do Direito*. Rio de Janeiro: FGV Direito Rio.

Faoro, Raymundo. 2001. *Os Donos Do Poder – Formação do Patronato Político Brasileiro*. 3rd ed. São Paulo: Editora Globo.

Faria, Jose Eduardo. 1987. *A Reforma do Ensino Jurídico*. Porto Alegre: SAFE.

Furtado, C. 2007. *Formação Econômica do Brasil*. São Paulo: Companhia das Letras.

Heineman, Ben. 2016. *The Inside Counsel Revolution: Resolving the Partner-Guardian Tension*. New York: Ankerwycke.

Junqueira, Eliane Botelho. 1999. *Faculdades de Direito ou Fábricas de Ilusões?* Rio de Janeiro: LetraCapital/IDES.

Krishnan, Jayanth K., Vitor M. Dias, and John Pence. 2016. "Legal Elites and the Shaping of Corporate Law Practice in Brazil: A Historical Study." *Law and Social Inquiry* 41 (2): 346–370.

Kronman, Anthony. 1993. *The Lost Lawyer*. Cambridge, MA: Harvard University Press.

Lyra Filho, Roberto. 1980. *O Direito que se Ensina Errado*. Brasília: Centro Acadêmico de Direito da UnB.

Rosen, Robert Eli. 1989. "The Inside Counsel Movement, Professional Judgment and Organizational Representation." *Indiana Law Journal* 64 (3): 479–553.

Sa e Silva, Fabio. 2007. *Ensino Jurídico. A Descoberta de Novos Saberes para a Democratização do Direito e da Sociedade*. Porto Alegre: Sergio Antonio Fabris Editor.

2011. "É Possível Mas Agora Não: A Democratização da Justiça no Cotidiano dos Advogados Populares." *Texto para Discussão* – IPEA. Brasília 1567 (1).

Sanchez Badin, Michelle. 2013. "Developmental Responses in the International Trade Legal Game: Cases of Intellectual Property and Export Credit Law Reforms in Brazil." In *Law and the New Developmental State: The Brazilian Experience in Latin American Context*. Edited by David M. Trubek, Helena Alviar Garcia, and Diogo R. Coutinho. New York: Cambridge University Press.

Santos, Boaventura de Sousa, and Flávia Carlet. 2010. "The Movement of Landless Rural Workers in Brazil and Their Struggles for Access to Law and Justice." In *Marginalized Communities and Access to Justice*. Edited by Yash Ghai and Jill Cottrell. Abingdon, UK: Routledge.

Shafer, Gregory, Michelle Sanchez Badin, and Barbara Rosenberg. 2012. "The Transnational Meets the National: The Construction of Trade Policy Networks in Brazil." In *Lawyers and the Construction of Transnational Justice*. Edited by Yves Dezalay and Bryant Garth. New York: Routledge.

Sousa, J. R., and Jose Geraldo. 1997. "Movimentos Sociais e Práticas Instituintes de Direito: perspectivas para a pesquisa sócio-jurídica no Brasil." *OAB Ensino Jurídico: 170 Anos de Cursos Jurídicos no Brasil*. Brasília: OAB.

Tavares, Maria da Conceicao. 2011. "O Processo de substituição de importações como modelo de desenvolvimento na América Latina: o caso do Brasil." In *Desenvolvimento e Igualdade: Homenagem aos 80 Anos de Maria da Conceição Tavares*. Edited by V. P. Corrêa and M. Simioni. Rio de Janeiro: IPEA.

Trubek, David M. 2011a. *Direito, Planejamento, e Desenvolvimento do Mercado de Capitais Brasileiro*. São Paulo: Saraiva.

2011b. "Reforming Legal Education in Brazil: From the CEPED Experiment to the Law Schools at the Getulio Vargas Foundation" (Univ. of Wisconsin Legal Studies research paper no. 1180). http://ssrn.com/abstract=1970244.

2012. "Reopening the CEPED File: What Can We Learn From a 'Cold Case'"? In *Aventura e Legado no Ensino do Direito*. Edited by Joaquim Falcão, Gabriel Lacerda, and Tânia Rangerl. Rio de Janeiro: FGV Direito Rio.

Trubek, David M., Yves Dezalay, Ruth Buchanan, and John R. Davis. 1994. "Global Restructuring and the Law: Studies of the Internationalization of Legal Fields and the Creation of Transnational Arena." *Case Western Law Review* 44 (2): 407–498.

Trubek, David, Helena Alviar Garcia, and Diogo R. Coutinho. 2013. *Law and the New Developmental State: The Brazilian Experience in Latin American Context*. New York: Cambridge University Press.

Venâncio Filho, Alberto. 1978. "Análise Histórica do Ensino Jurídico no Brasil." In *Encontros da UnB: Ensino Jurídico*. Brasília: Editora Universidade de Brasília.

Warat, Luis Alberto. 2002. "Confissões Pedagógicas diante da Crise do Ensino Jurídico." In *OAB Ensino Jurídico: diagnósticos, perspectivas e propostas*. Brasília: OAB.

Wilkins, David B. 2012. "Is the In-House Counsel Movement Going Global? A Preliminary Assessment of the Role of Internal Counsel in Emerging Economies." *Wisconsin Law Review* 4 (2): 251–304.

Wilkins, David B., and Vikramaditya S. Khanna. 2017. "Globalization and the Rise of the In-House Counsel Movement in India." In *The Indian Legal Profession in the Age of Globalization: The Rise of the Corporate Legal Sector and Its Influence on Lawyers and Society*. Edited by David B. Wilkins, Vikramaditya S. Khanna, and David M. Trubek. Cambridge: Cambridge University Press.

Wilkins, David B., Vikramaditya S. Khanna, and David M. Trubek (eds.). 2017. *The Indian Legal Profession in the Age of Globalization: The Rise of the Corporate Legal Sector and Its Influence on Lawyers and Society*. Cambridge: Cambridge University Press.

2

Corporate Law Firms

The Brazilian Case

Daniela Monteiro Gabbay, Luciana Ramos, and Ligia Pinto Sica

I INTRODUCTION

In the nearly three decades since 1990, the corporate law sector in Brazil has been dramatically transformed. The number of firms has more than doubled, firms have grown substantially in size, and the methods of management and operation and have all been revolutionized. Prior to the early 1990s, the corporate legal sector in Brazil mostly consisted of small firms focused on serving local clients. Today, the sector includes a combination of full-service corporate firms as well as specialized boutiques, each serving large domestic and foreign companies.[1]

As Chapter 1 addresses, many of these developments resulted from a "global shift" in the Brazilian economy that occurred in the early 1990s and resulting in a set of major legal changes. For instance, at that time, Brazil began moving away from the centralized, state-dominated, and closed economy model that had prevailed since the 1930s. Facing a financial crisis and a sluggish economy, the country sought to revive growth by opening to the world economy, attracting foreign investment, and privatizing many state-owned enterprises. These developments were accompanied by a legislative "boom" that created new areas of law designed to govern these newly privatized sectors, to attract additional foreign direct investment, and to stimulate domestic investment. New regulations were passed, creating the need for professionals capable of operating in areas such as capital markets, infrastructure, telecommunications, energy, arbitration, competition, and mergers and acquisitions (M&A).

These changes, along with the increasing presence of national and multinational corporations and foreign investors in the market, altered the demand for

[1] For an analysis of the growth of foreign lawyers in Brazil and their partnerships with local Brazilian firms, see Krishnan et al. (2014).

corporate legal services in Brazil. Domestic, and increasingly foreign clients, began looking for legal expertise in the new areas of law, such as cross-border transitions and M&A, the effect of which made well-trained, corporate lawyers in high demand. Clients, especially foreign companies, were looking not only for a high-level technical expertise, but increasingly also global lawyering skills. As such, individuals with international expertise and global know how became highly valued (Englemann 2011).

As this the demand for these new types of lawyers grew, a new model of the modern Brazilian corporate law firm began to take shape. In stark contrast to the typical Brazilian firm of the pre-1990s, these new firms tended to be larger, more internationalized, and have greater levels of professional management. Moreover, as the corporate sector became increasingly competitive, both by the growth of new firms as well as increased clients demand, firms were forced to pay greater attention to things like marketing and branding, training programs (including sending lawyers abroad), upgrades in management and technology, and building foreign alliances.

A *The Research*

This chapter examines these changes, paying particular attention to the core characteristics of the modern, Brazilian corporate law firm. We sought to understand the impact of globalization on the Brazilian corporate legal market using two major data sources: (1) a law firm database built from publically available sources, including law firm rankings and other similar publications, and (2) interviews with managing partners and founders of major law firms.[2] Put together, the database includes 367 law firms that provide corporate legal services. With respect to the publically available data sources, the database was created based on the information available at four national and international rankings: *Análise Advocacia* 500 (2010, 2013), *Chambers Latin America* (2011, 2013), *Latin Lawyer* (2013), and *The Legal* 500 (2013).[3] These rankings are based on data provided by the companies who are clients of the law firms. The database of 367 corporate law firms is structured and based on objective information from these publications, including: (1) number of lawyers, (2) number of partners, (3) year of establishment, and (4) headquarters. To

[2] For the purposes of this chapter, globalization is understood as a multifaceted phenomenon not restricted to economic integration. Adopting the view of Wilkins and Papa, three globalization processes play a significant role in the globalization of legal services: economic, knowledge, and governance (Wilkins and Papa 2012).

[3] As this book was going to press, the 2016 edition of *Análise Advocacia* 500 was released. Where and when appropriate, it is incorporated into the analysis.

build the database, we followed the classification of legal areas used by the magazine *Análise Advocacia 500* and excluded the law firms dedicated exclusively to criminal, labor, consumer rights, and insurance.

The interviews supplement this data and provide insights on how key players see the transformation of the Brazilian corporate legal market that has resulted from the opening of the economy and globalization. We conducted interviews with founding partners and/or managing partners of thirteen corporate law firms that operate in São Paulo and Rio de Janeiro, including those with different founding dates and sizes. The interviews were conducted from a semistructured script of questions involving: (1) the respondents' professional career, (2) how they view globalization's impact on law firms and the Brazilian legal market, (3) hiring models and career structures within firms, and (4) firm management and operation models. Interviews were conducted between November 2013 and February 2014.

Finally, as this book was going to press we supplemented these data sources with pertinent information from the 2016 edition of *Análise Advocacia*. It is important to note that our analysis of this data is not comprehensive. Instead, we use this most recent publicly available data about the Brazilian corporate law firm market to highlight important trends that appear to have taken place since the conclusion of our primary data collection in 2013 as an invitation to further research. As indicated in the Chapter 1, Brazil has been in a period of tremendous political, economic, and social upheaval since 2014. We hope that our study will encourage future research about how these large-scale forces will affect Brazil's corporate legal market.

B *Tensions in a Fast-Changing Sector*

The rise of the corporate sector in Brazil created tension between an emerging model of professional organization and the traditional practices of the Brazilian legal profession, including some regulations by the organized bar (Ordem dos Advogados do Brasil or OAB). This created a disconnect between the official rules under which firms operate, and what is taking place on the ground. For example, while the Bar still imposes minimum fee schedules and prohibits advertisement, the new corporate law firm model entailed active competition for business, including robust brand development. Similarly, while the Bar has sought to impose restrictions on alliances between domestic and foreign law firms, the largest Brazilian law firms participate in global networks of international operations.[4] Finally, while corporate law firms are not "companies"

[4] As an example, Trench, Rossi e Watanabe Advogados, one of the top ranked firms by *Análise Advocacia 500*, has long had a formal relationship with Baker & McKenize – described as a

under Brazilian law and the OAB prohibits law firms with "mercantile forms or characteristics," new models of corporate law firms often operate very much like businesses, particularly as they respond to market demand by adopting corporate management structures.[5]

Because of these tensions, a gap has emerged between rhetoric and reality within the corporate law sector. On the one hand, there is evidence that suggests law firms are seeking to adopt more sophisticated, professional, and global forms and practices. On the other hand, these new models often butt up against, and have to operate within, more localized Brazilian culture, norms, and regulations. As such, part of the story outlined below is a continual tension between continuity and change. In other words, of critical interest is whether corporate law firms in Brazil are less directly replicating the Anglo-American model of corporate legal practice, than borrowing and adapting global standards in ways that are consistent with local contexts.

II THE IMPACTS OF GLOBALIZATION AND MARKET GROWTH

Análise Advocacia 500 estimates that more than 30,000 law firms are registered in Brazil.[6] In terms of absolute numbers of lawyers, the Brazilian legal market is the third largest in the world with 872,396 lawyers registered as of January 2014. This is surpassed only by the United States (1.26 million lawyers as of 2013) and India (1.26 million as of 2011).[7] Overall, there are almost 900,000 lawyers in Brazil, with almost half of them registered in the São Paulo (263,474, or 30 percent of the total) and Rio de Janeiro (137,694, or 16 percent) bars.[8]

"strategic partnership" on their website. Reflective of the depth of this relationship, the global chair of Baker & McKeznie's tax practice is based in Brazil and maintains formal affiliations (e.g., partnership, e-mail addresses) with both firms. For more on foreign firms in Brazil, see Chapter 6 on regulation.

5 Law firms in Brazil are not legally considered "companies," based on the OAB's Provision No. 112/2006 and on Law No. 8.906 of July 4, 1994 – the Statute of Legal Practice of OAB – especially in article 16 (which prohibits the operation of law firms that present mercantile forms or characteristics). For more on the regulation of the profession, see Chapter 6.

6 The *Análise Advocacia* 500 has been published annually in December since 2007 and contains information and rankings drawn from surveys of legal directors/general counsel of the largest companies in Brazil.

7 The OAB maintains a continually updated online listing of the total number of registered lawyers in Brazil. Among other things, it contains state-by-state and gender breakdown. It is available at: www.oab.org.br/institucionalconselhofederal/quadroadvogados.

8 As this book was going to press, the numbers of lawyers in Brazil had increased significantly. As of March 2017, just over 1 million lawyers were registered in Brazil. Just under 48 percent of registered lawyers were women and just over 52 percent were men. The São Paulo and Rio de Janeiro bars again represented the highest percentages.

TABLE 2.1 *Number of lawyers by number of law firms*

No. lawyers	No. law firms
1 to 10	54
11 to 20	90
21 to 30	54
31 to 40	41
41 to 50	13
51 to 60	10
61 to 70	8
71 to 80	10
81 to 90	11
91 to 100	7
91 to 100	7
101 to 200	17
201 to 300	12
301 to 400	7
401 to 500	1
501 to 600	0
601 to 700	1
More than 700	1
N.I.	30

Source: Sample of 367 produced by the authors.

The corporate sector in our database includes 367 firms. As Table 2.1 and Figure 2.1 show, ten of the firms surveyed have 301 or more lawyers (3 percent of the sample). Twenty-nine firms have between 101 and 300 lawyers (8 percent). Forty-six have between 100 and 51 lawyers (12 percent). The rest of the firms in the sample are more medium and small sized, with 108 (30 percent) having between fifty and twenty-one lawyers, and the remaining 144 (40 percent) have twenty lawyers or fewer.

Figure 2.2 shows the rapid rise of the corporate sector in the 1990s after the economy was opened and privatization began. In the 1990s and 2000s, more firms were added (194) than had been created in the entire period prior to 1900 (136). Put differently, of the 364 firms in our sample, more than half (53 percent) were founded since 1990.

Although the majority of Brazil's corporate law firms were formed in the years following the global shift in the 1990s, a different pattern emerges when looking at the country's most important firms in the sector. Table 2.2 lists Brazil's thirty-eight most admired law firms as ranked by *Análise Advocacia*

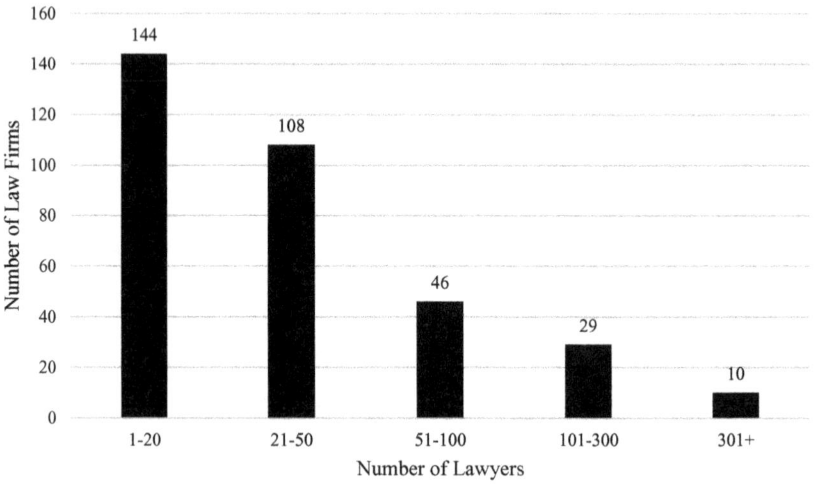

FIGURE 2.1 Number of lawyers by number of law firms.
Source: Sample of 367 produced by the authors.

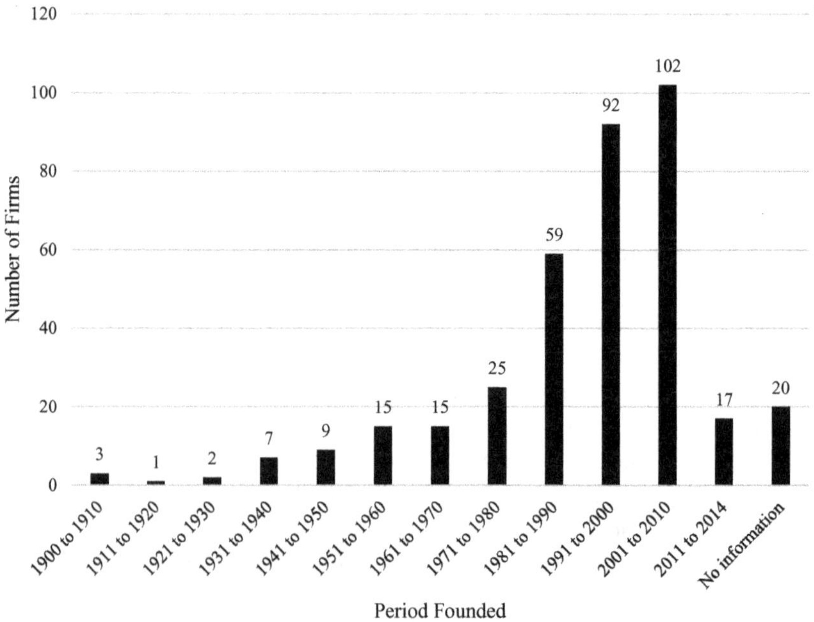

FIGURE 2.2 Year of the founding of corporate law firms by decade.
Source: Sample of 367 produced by the authors.

TABLE 2.2 *Thirty-eight most admired law firms in Brazil, 2016*

Rank	Name of firm	Founded	No. lawyers	No. partners	No. non-partner lawyers	Change from 2015
1	Pinheiro Neto Advogados	1942	407	86	321	26
2	Machado, Meyer, Sendacz e Opice Advogados (Machado Meyer Advogados)	1972	343	53	290	18
2	Mattos Filho, Veiga Filho, Marrey Jr. e Quiroga Advogados	1992	424	72	352	67
4	Siqueira Castro Advogados	1948	853	73	780	−169
5	Demarest Advogados	1948	277	62	215	9
6	Barbosa, Müssnich, Aragão (BMA)	1995	286	57	229	16
7	TozziniFreire Advogados	1976	550	80	470	94
8	Trench, Rossi e Watanabe Advogados (Baker & McKenize)	1959	309	59	250	16
9	Lobo & de Rizzo Advogados	2007	94	19	75	2
10	Veirano Advogados	1972	236	51	185	−9
11	Lefosse Advogados	1987	108	20	88	−5
12	Leite, Tosto e Barros Advogados	1991	144	29	115	4
13	Souza, Cescon, Barrieu & Flesch Advogados (Souza Cescon Advogados)	2001	213	35	178	9
14	Bichara Advogados	2001	155	15	140	4
14	Lacaz Martins, Pereira Neto, Gurevich & Schoueri Advogados	1992	110	64	46	11
14	Souto, Correa, CESA, Lummertz & Amaral Advogados	2013	65	65	0	20
14	Stocche, Forbes, Padis, Filizzola, Clápis, Passaro, Meyer e Refinetti Advogados	2012	120	20	100	27
18	Chediak, Lopes da Costa, Cristofaro, Menezes, Côrtes, Rennó, Aragão Advogados (Chediak Advogados)	2011	63	63	0	3
18	Peixoto & Cury Advogados	1948	134	14	120	2
18	Santos Neto Advogados	1992	40	5	35	−1
18	Tauil Chequer Advogados (Mayer Brown)	1992	149	35	114	25
22	De Vivo, Whitaker e Castro Advogados	1997	89	7	82	15
22	Felsberg Advogados	1970	119	19	100	4

(*cont.*)

TABLE 2.2 *(cont.)*

Rank	Name of firm	Founded	No. lawyers	No. partners	No. non-partner lawyers	Change from 2015
22	Lee, Brock, Camargo Advogados	2003	412	80	332	15
22	Mattos Engelberg Advogados	2016	94	14	80	n/a
22	Viseu Advogados	1994	100	10	90	21
27	Arruda Alvim & Thereza Alvim Advocacia e Consultoria Jurídica	1960	50	16	34	0
27	Azevedo Sette Advogados	1967	318	33	285	56
27	Bitelli Advogados	1987	18	2	16	−4
27	Cândido Albuquerque Advogados Associados	1981	49	9	40	
27	Décio Freire & Associados	1992	502	9	493	−1
27	Dias Carneiro, Flores, Sanches, Turkienicz, Amendola, Waisberg e Thomaz Baston Advogados (DCA Advogados)	2002	69	11	58	0
27	Koury Lopes Advogados	2002	95	31	64	6
27	Lobo & Ibeas Advogados	1974	67	37	30	−6
27	Martinelli Advogados	1997	310	11	299	5
27	Rayes & Fagundes Advogados Associados	1998	126	8	118	3
27	Trigueiro Fontes Advogados	1993	174	31	143	15
27	Vella Pugliese Buosi e Guidoni Advogados	2005	71	10	61	0

Source: Análise Advocacia 500 (2016).

500 in 2016.[9] Two important characteristics of the Brazilian corporate legal market are evident from this list. First, eight of the eleven most admired firms (listed as the top ten in Table 2.2 because two firms are tied for second) were founded well before the onset of globalization in early 1990s (Mattos Filho, founded in 1992, and Lobo & de Rizzo Advogados, founded in 2007, being the exceptions). Indeed, the top rank firm, Pinherio Neto, is also the oldest firm on the entire list, being founded in 1942. By contrast, nineteen of the remaining twenty-seven firms on the list were formed since 1990, with firms older than this date accounting for only three of the firms ranked eleventh to twenty-second (a total of fifteen firms including those tied in the rankings).

[9] Rankings are a composite of individual practice area rankings in which the firm with the firm with highest average across all practice area rankings earns the top spot and so on. For more, see *Análise Advocacia* 500 (Análise 2016).

This pattern provides an important qualification to the portrayal of Brazil's large corporate law firms as being a "new" phenomenon. To be sure, the size and importance of Brazil's emerging corporate legal sector has its origins in the country's shift to privatization and open markets in the period following the end of military rule. But the origins of many of the law firms that have been most successful in taking advantage of these opportunities date back to well before this period. This continuity is a testament to the ability of an important segment of Brazil's traditional legal elite to transition its social, economic, and political capital from the older style of law practice, dominated by appearances before the country's high courts and issuing opinions on technical issues of legal interpretation, to the new style of transactional and business focused lawyering increasingly demanded by foreign and domestic clients since the 1990s. Although as is discussed below, while not all of these traditional "notables" made this pivot, the fact that a significant number did distinguishes Brazil's preglobal shift elite from their counterparts in India who ran successful law firms during the colonial period of British Raj but whom were unable to translate this first mover advantage into sustained success once India underwent its global shift in the 1990s (Wilkins et al. 2017). As indicated in Chapter 1, and as Wilkins and Khanna demonstrate in detail in Chapter 4 comparing the role of in-house legal departments in Brazil and India, one plausible explanation for this difference ties between Brazil and United States during the period in which early Brazilian law firms such as Pinheiro Neto were getting their start.

The second aspect of the Brazilian large law firm sector evident from Table 2.2 is the relationship between the size of a law firm's partnership and its ranking from clients. Thus, the ten top rank firms have an average of sixty-one partners per firm, with only one having fewer than fifty partners. By contrast, outside of the top ten, the average number of partners drops to just twenty-five per firm, with only four firms having more than fifty partners – even though several of the firms outside of the top ten have as many or more total lawyers (Azevedo Sette Advogados, 318 total lawyers but only 33 partners; Décio Freire & Associados, 502 total lawyers but only 9 partners; Martinelli Advogados, 310 total lawyers but only 11 partners) than those ranked at the top of the list. Although our data does not allow us to say definitively why this correlation exists, once again the Indian experience may be instructive. As Wilkins, Nanda, and Fong found when studying that country's legal market, one of the factors that made it difficult for law firms that had been started during the period of the British Raj to transition to India's new market economy was their unwillingness to make new partners, causing many talented lawyers to leave these traditional firms for others that they believed to be more "modern" and egalitarian (Wilkins et al. 2017). These defections in turn fueled an increasing perception by clients that firms that were dominated by a small (and often aging) cadre of partners would be unable to provide them with a consistent quality of "partner level" service. Given the dynamics of the Brazilian legal market discussed below, it is plausible that a similar dynamic is at work in this country as well.

Both of these features of Brazil's contemporary corporate legal market underscore both how much has changed since 1990, and how much of that change continues to be based on uniquely Brazilian features of the country's legal market. Prior to the 1990s, the typical Brazilian corporate law firm was relatively small. A handful of lawyers joined together to form a firm, in many cases led by a "notable" – a lawyer who was well known in the community based on the notable's legal knowledge and skill. These notables used their intellectual and social capital, often built on family connections, academic positions, and publications of doctrinal texts, as the basis to form a law firm. The firms were informally managed with clients developed through social contacts and the reputation of the leading partner – often the notable. The firm's practice areas were focused on the lead lawyer's expertise.

There were some exceptions to this model, particularly among the small legal sector that catered primarily to foreign corporations. There you could find larger firms offering a fuller range of services, more professional management, and emphasis on the firm's brand, as opposed to just the notable. In some cases, these firms were founded by expatriates with experience in large law firms in the United States who settled in Brazil, or by Brazilians with overseas experience (Krishnan et al. 2014). It is important to note, however, these even these firms were small by today's standards.

All this began to change during privatization, which created whole new areas of law affecting business. For example, the telecommunications sector had long been a state monopoly, however in the 1990s was privatized and subjected to new forms of regulation, including the creation of the regulatory agency called the Agência Nacional de Telecomunicações (ANATEL).[10] Because of this, companies were suddenly faced with a new legal regime. This created a huge demand for lawyers who had both knowledge of the new telecom laws as well as international expertise. Similar changes happened in other legal fields. In each case, and as the economy grew, the demand for sophisticated corporate legal services increased. And this generated new competition between law firms. For instance, the old gentleman's agreement

[10] For a detailed discussion of the transformation of the telecom market and regulation, see Chapter 10 by Sa de Silva and Trubek.

against poaching lawyers from other firms eroded as the market became more competitive.

It is important to note that although firms grew substantially during this period and began to resemble global full-service firms, the 1990s and 2000s also saw the rise of boutique law firms offering specialized corporate expertise, for instance around initial public offerings, venture capital, and private equality. According to our interviews, firms often refer to themselves as "boutique" as a single of prestige and to differentiate themselves from generalist law firms, which are often associated with impersonal services. According to 2016, *Análise* data of just over 500 firms, 41 percent of firms in the sample classified themselves as "boutique," compared to 46 percent as "abrangente" (generalist/comprehensive) or 13 percent as "full service" (59 percent overall).[11]

III CHALLENGES FACING NEW-MODEL CORPORATE LAW FIRMS AND THEIR RESPONSES

By the time we completed our primary research in 2014, the corporate law sector had grown substantially and taken on a definitive shape. The traditional business law firm model that dominated the sector until the 1980s had largely been replaced by larger, more professionalized, and internationalized entities. In this section, we provide a profile of the sector and examine the challenges it faces. We look at three primary issues: (1) the nature of the clients and the services they demand; (2) the impact of internationalization, including the growing importance of international knowledge and the role played by foreign law firms; and (3) the challenge of managing these new form law firm, and the tension between its operational practices and Brazilian law and custom.

A *Client Demands for Greater Sophistication and New Styles of Lawyering*

The changes in the corporate law market occurred in part due to changes in client profiles as restructured in-house legal departments created new

[11] In the study, we classified firms as either full-service or boutique. This classification is similar to the triple classification used in the ranking of *Análise Advocacia* 500, e.g., full-service, generalist/comprehensive, and boutique. For this publication, a full-service firm has the capacity to serve clients without outsourcing any legal services. A generalist/comprehensive firm is able to meet clients' demands in the key areas of law. And finally, boutiques are highly specialized firms with work focused on a small number of areas. Given the difficulty in differentiating between the activities performed by full-service firms and comprehensive firms, this paper uses a dual classification, which includes the generalist category (or full-service) and the boutique category.

expectations for service and new demands for expertise. Today the major clients of most major Brazilian corporate law firms are large domestic companies, including state-owned enterprises and foreign corporations operating in Brazil. Clients are also foreign companies seeking entry into the Brazilian marketplace. Over the past twenty years, we have seen major changes in the role of in-house counsel, including the mix of legal services that are handled internally and those that are outsourced. In subsequent chapters in this volume, Oliveira and Ramos (Chapter 3) and Wilkins and Khanna (Chapter 4) document these changes in the Brazilian in-house legal sector, and compare them with both the "in-house counsel movement" in the United States and developments in this sector in India, from the perspective of general counsels the newly empowered legal departments they now lead. In this chapter, we document this transformation from the perspective of the new generation of Brazilian corporate law firms that have sought to serve these increasingly sophisticated internal counsel, both in domestic Brazilian companies and the growing number of foreign multinational companies (FMNCs) operating in the Brazilian market.

These changes, which are occurring worldwide, have had dramatic impacts on both the demand for legal services of Brazil's corporate law firms as well as the type of work that is given to them. In a study examining this dynamic in the US context, Chayes and Chayes note that "the status, organization, and business of the traditional elite law firm [were] substantially altered in both substantive emphasis and in the nature of client base by the new prominence of corporate counsel" (Chayes and Chayes 1985, 278). David B. Wilkins, in a study on the changing role of the global general counsel, buttresses this point, arguing that, "The transformation of law firms is brought about by the transformation of the clientele" (Wilkins 2012).

Therefore, while the seeds of this "new-model lawyering" can be found as far back as the 1960s in a few specialized and elite firms, it took the market openings of the 1990s and the changed demands from domestic and foreign corporate clients those openings brought with them to spread this type of lawyering style throughout the bar (Trubek 2011). Our interviews confirmed this view. In the words of one of our interviews:

> Companies have changed a lot because they have become globalized... [and they] began to face global competition. In previous days... the internal legal department took care of simpler matters, and if there was a more complex issue, an outside law firm handled it. It was the holder of legal knowledge. Not today. Companies have a very qualified legal department – the highest-quality lawyers – and people with expertise in management,

> administration, corporate culture. This sophistication of companies created a need for law firms to follow this trend. (managing partner of a full-service firm with 201 to 250 lawyers)

Indeed, law firms quickly realized that they failed to follow this trend at their peril. As another respondent noted, the expansion and restructuring of corporate legal departments in the recent decades has fundamentally changed the relationship between companies and outside firms. Traditionally, most large Brazilian companies had long-standing relationships with their lead outside law firm, often cemented through personal relationships between founders and other senior company executives and the lawyers they hired. Today, in the words of this informant, the relationship is much more "arm's length and transactional" with increasingly sophisticated general counsels attempting to break up these long-standing relationships and induce more competition among providers. Although as Wilkins and Khanna note, relationships with important law firms in Brazil continue to be more important than this respondent's comments might lead one to believe – as they report, Brazilian GC's terminate important law firm relationships relatively infrequently, and are less likely to do so than GCs in the United States or India (Wilkins and Khanna, Chapter 4). It nevertheless clear that the balance of power between GCs and law firms in Brazil has shifted significantly in recent years.

In this new world, Brazilian law firms are required to provide far more sophisticated legal services than they were expected to offer in not-so-distant past. As one respondent graphically summed up the change:

> When a doctor always has the same kind of patient and the patient becomes more sophisticated, the doctor has to become more sophisticated as well, otherwise the patient will know more than the doctor. If he really knows more than the doctor, he will certainly consider whether to hire him or... someone smarter. This revolution in the world of law comes via legal departments of companies that have had a fascinating boost in quality. (managing partner of a full-service office with 201 to 250 lawyers)

The latest data from *Análise* confirms this observation. In the magazine's 2016 edition, 85 percent of the legal executives surveyed noted that a firm's ability to offer "technical-legal expertise" was a very important factor their hiring decisions. Only a firm's reputation was rated higher, with 90 percent of legal executives viewing it as very important in hiring decisions.

This demand for increasingly sophisticated and specialized expertise, however, sometimes has clashed with the more traditional training lawyers receive in Brazilian law schools. As another respondent noted:

> The main challenge for lawyers is to stop looking at the past and try to look forward – to keep up with their client. In a sense, you have to forget all that training you have had. Forget all the education you had that told you to look back at the way things were. (founding partner in a full-service firm with 51 to 100 attorneys)

The transformation of the in-house legal departments also created new client expectations. For instance, clients began requiring that corporate law firms provide answers quickly – response time became of utmost importance. Clients also expected that their law firms offer solutions in line with the company's business need. As one interviewee noted, "You are expected to know each client's business extensively. The client today expects more and pays less" (founding partner in a full-service firm with 151 to 200 lawyers). As the interviewee notes, cost also increasingly became critical concerns. As case-in-point, according to 2016 *Análise* data, 82 percent of legal executive respondents reporting that being "flexible" on price was very important in their hiring decisions.

The combination of these new client expectations required new kinds of lawyering. According to some respondents, to efficiently provide solutions, lawyers can no longer prepare lengthy and wordy legal opinions full of Latin terms, as was common in traditional Brazilian firms. Today, they must have a detailed knowledge of the company's business, know how to analyze cost spreadsheets, be financially literate, foresee conflicts, and analyze risks – all at the same time and all in an extremely efficient manner. One interviewee noted:

> Lawyers are no longer those guys sitting behind a desk writing legal opinions in Latin. In order to become a businessman, attorneys have to sit down and understand the client's business and suggest solutions. They have to know what a financial return is, what interest rates are, what economic viability is. They participate in setting up the business with the client. They have to be a . . . mixture of a businessman with legal training. (managing partner in a full-service law firm)

The growth and power of in-house legal departments also gave company legal executives greater responsibility in establishing fees. Contemporary Brazilian legal executives frequently have the autonomy and responsibility to manage their own budgets. Therefore, they are often more cost-conscious when hiring a law firm as the high cost of hiring outside firms, directly impacts company bottom-lines. As the managing partner of a mid to large-sized firm put it,

> What the client cannot have is a surprise at the end. Today, the general counsel is not only a manager of external law firms, but he [or she] has to be profitable for his company. He [or she] also has his own financial pressures. (managing partner in a full-service law firm with 201 to 250 lawyers)

A founding partner of a full-service firm with 151–200 lawyers agreed, noting that, "In previous days the legal department of companies had no budget. Today, the legal director has a budget equal to that of all his peers."

The underlying point is that changes on the demand side – new types for corporate clients led by legal executives who themselves were becoming more powerful within their corporate hierarchies – necessitated changes within law firms. As clients demands for more professionalized, sophisticated, efficient, and cost-effective service became commonplace, lawyers and law firms had to respond.

B *The Internationalization of Law Firms*

As more foreign investors and multinational corporations entered the Brazilian market, Brazilian corporations started investing abroad. And, because of that, international rules, like the Trade-Related Aspects of Intellectual Property Rights (TRIPS) agreement, began to impact Brazilian law and lawyers directly. Once again, domestic firms needed to be able to work with new legal issues and new client demands. One major response of Brazilian law firms to these needs was to increase the internationalization of the sector. To explore these developments, we looked at three areas: (1) the relationship between domestic Brazilian corporate law firms and foreign law firms; (2) efforts to attract foreign clientele; and (3) support given to lawyers to pursue educational training abroad, including LLMs and internships/*secondments* in foreign law firms.

1 Domestic Law Firms Enter International Networks

Few domestic Brazilian law firms have branches abroad and no Brazilian firm has a truly global presence. Although a few have established formal ties with foreign firms, most Brazilian firms prefer looser affiliations that they mobilize based on the needs of specific projects and transactions. Moreover, recognizing the importance of international connections, most firms prefer to be part of global networks of independent law firms, such as Lex Mundi and Interlex, which are aimed at networking and mobilizing global experience rather than forming formal, exclusive ties with specific foreign law firms. The majority of our interviewees stated they were part of nonexclusive alliances that guarantee firm's independence. One interview noted:

> Since we have extensive international experience, we are familiar with many [foreign] law firms. So, instead of forming an association in which you are tied to those people, we prefer to choose whom we work with [based on] the case. (founding partner of a full-service law firm with 51 to 100 attorneys)

According to the 2012 edition of *Análise Advocacia 500*, of the 224 Brazilian law firms listed as the most prestigious, 70 percent said they either have considered, or would consider, some form of partnership with a foreign firm. If we look at the sixty-five firms the survey has consistently ranked as "elite," 55 percent claim to have received a proposal from a foreign firm to enter into a formal partnership or alliance, or were actively pursuing such a partnership at the time of the publication. Of the thirteen firms we interviewed in 2014, however, none had a formal partnership with a foreign firm. The interviewees consistently said that when they do work with foreign firms, it is typically an on-demand, case-by-case basis. As one interviewee noted:

> We have a very strong relationship with many foreign law firms, especially American ones, but also European, German, [and] Norwegian [firms]. But we do not have a specific partnership. We have always avoided that. To be a partner with one would close many doors for us. It makes no sense for the office to have a relationship with just one office. (founding partner in a full-service firm with 201 to 250 lawyers)

The interviewee went to give an example of past experiences forming a formal partnership:

> In 2004, we even had something like this, a partnership with a Chilean firm and an Argentine firm . . . but we realized in the end that it did not produce many results, there was no volume of exchange or relationship, no cultural exchange, no business that made sense for you to focus on.

Indeed, as the Brazilian economy expanded rapidly in the first decade of the twentieth century, many Brazilian law firms began to lose interest in expanding to other legal markets altogether, instead focusing all of their energy on the Brazilian market itself. As the founding partner of a full-service firm put it:

> In 2005, 2006, Brazil began to get sexy. Therefore, what is a good client these days? The Brazilian client. Because Brazil has a lot more work than abroad. Do foreigners still pay more? Yes. Except that for each foreigner,

you have five hundred Brazilians. In this sense, today, I cannot waste time going abroad to prospect with the number of Brazilian clients on the market. (founding partner in a full-service office with 151 to 200 lawyers)

As indicated above, because we ended our primary data collection for this study in 2014, we cannot say whether this respondent or others who we interviewed are taking a different approach to international expansion now that the Brazilian economy has slowed considerably. We suspect, however, that the results are likely to be mixed, since even if foreign markets now look more attractive to Brazilian law firms, these firms may have fewer resources to pursue these opportunities. The same is likely to be true with respect to the relative attractiveness of the Brazilian market to foreign law firms. The next section explores what our data tells us about how this aspect of globalization is impacting Brazilian corporate law firms.

2 Foreign Law Firms Start to Set Up Offices in Brazil

As the Brazilian economy opened and started growing in the late 1990s and early 2000s, foreign law firms began establishing themselves in Brazil. As the founding partner of a large Brazilian firm put it, "Many of them [foreign law firms] operate in Brazil. They are practicing law. Making money. [A] lot of [foreign lawyers] are living here in São Paulo and Rio de Janeiro" (founder partner in a full-service firm with 301 to 350 lawyers). Another Brazilian lawyer noted:

> Capital markets accelerated in Brazil [in the 2000s], and this caused a series of phenomena. First, the strengthening of Brazilian companies, capitalization of Brazilian companies, family businesses suddenly turning into large companies, suddenly becoming the target of major acquisitions. But apart from all this, foreign law firms are looking at the Brazilian market and seeing the maturing of companies and saying, "Now I have a market to sell to." With this, we saw a massive influx of the entry of foreign law firms in Brazil since the 2000s. We have around twenty-four or twenty-five foreign law firms here. Some have come and gone, but you still have over twenty offices that continue rendering services. (managing partner in a full-service law firm with 201 to 250 lawyers)

According to *Análise Advocacia 500*, the first foreign firms arrived in 1997 when Linklaters (UK) and White & Case (US) both opened offices. In 1998, Clifford Chance (UK) opened a branch in São Paulo. Cuatrecasas, Gonçalves Pereira (a Spanish and Portuguese firm) opened a branch in São Paulo in 1999. Shearman & Sterling (US) installed a branch in São Paulo in 2004. And, between 2007 to 2013, eighteen additional foreign firms opened branches in Brazil.[12] Of the twenty-three foreign law firms with branches in Brazil as of 2014, thirteen were founded in the United States, seven in the United Kingdom, one in Bermuda (Conyers Dill & Pearman), one in Spain and Portugal each, and one (Hogan Lovells) is jointly based in the United States and the United Kingdom. Of this total, nineteen have opened branches only in São Paulo. Two have branches only in Rio de Janeiro. One has a branch in São Paulo, Rio de Janeiro, and Vitoria. One has a branch in São Paulo and Rio de Janeiro. Based on these figures, one sees both the importance of São Paulo as the commercial center of the country as well as the comparative strength of US firms in the legal market. As is discussed below (and as is extended on in Chapter 6 on regulation), the actual market share and influence of these firms is strongly impacted by the rules through which these foreign firms can operate.

Under the OAB's Provision No. 91/2000, lawyers in a "foreign" firm – defined as one whose shares are held by foreigners – are only allowed to serve as "consultants" on foreign law. As such, foreign lawyers working in foreign firms cannot advise companies on Brazilian law or appear in court (for more on the regulation of foreign lawyers, see Chapter 6). Foreign lawyers can register with the OAB if (1) they are qualified in the law they wish to practice, (2) they have a residence visa in Brazil, (3) their home-country grants reciprocal treatment to Brazilian lawyers, and (4) they are in good standing. Once the registration is approved, the lawyer will need to take an oath of respect to the Brazilian Federal Constitution and the ethics of the legal profession. The license to practice consultancy on foreign law is valid for three years and renewable for successive three-year terms. Foreign firms with offices in Brazil may also hire Brazilian lawyers, but, like foreign lawyers, these lawyers are limited to dealing with issues involving foreign law. In such cases, a Brazilian lawyer cannot hold a license to practice Brazilian law by the OAB, even if he or she has graduated from a Brazilian law school and passed the bar exam.[13]

[12] These firms are Clyde & Co.; Mayer Brown; Proskauer Rose; Allen & Overy; Conyers Dill & Pearman; Skadden, Arps, Slate, Meagher & Flom; Holman Fenwick Willan Consultants; Gibson, Dunn & Crutcher; Simpson Thacher & Bartlett; Chadbourne & Parke; CMS Cameron McKenna; DLA Piper; Milbank, Tweed, Hadley & McCloy; Cleary Gottlieb Steen & Hamilton; Davis Polk & Wardwell; Jones Day; and K & L Gates, Hogan Lovells (Análise 2013, 46).

[13] With respect to the activities of foreigners or Brazilians who had training outside of Brazil, article 8, paragraph 2, of Law 8906/94 establishes the requirements for admission, including "revalidation" by the Ministry of Education (MEC) as well as the Brazilian Bar Association. As the Ministry of Education is typically slow in validating diplomas, the OAB may, on a temporary basis, grant the professional who passes the bar exam authorization to practice law in Brazil.

It is important to note that, per Article 1°, §1°, I and II of the OAB's Provision no. 91/2000, because none of these "consultants" can practice Brazilian law, technically speaking they do not compete for clientele or operations that require the application of Brazilian law. Some interviewees believe that this rule is clear, well-articulated and works in ensuring an appropriate distribution of work between the foreign firms who operate in Brazil and national law firms. For instance, the founding partner of a large Brazilian law firm told us,

> The large companies, as well as the ones that have never performed services here, always hire Brazilian firms. We do the same thing when we operate in a New York office. We perform counseling on Brazilian law for American companies. (founding partner in a full-service firm with 251 to 300 lawyers)

Another founding partner, again from a large firm, said:

> The majority [of foreign firms in Brazil] are taking care of international affairs as consultants in foreign law, which is allowed under an OAB provision. They are counseling in this area, and it seems to be very successful. There is nothing to complain about. We coexist very well with those who respect the law. They always work in partnership with several Brazilian firms. (founding partner in a full-service firm with 301 to 350 lawyers)

There is however, far from uniform agreement on this point. Several lawyers we interviewed believe that while rules limiting foreign law firms and lawyers to doing non-Brazilian legal may be there in theory, in practice foreign firms are taking a substantial part of the corporate legal work in Brazil even when they partner with Brazilian law firms. The following complaint is typical of those we heard:

> They are not allowed to compete, but they compete anyway. In fact, most of the foreign law firms work with Brazilian law, if indirectly. Some are obvious – even open. Others are a bit more discreet, servicing only part of the process and afterward going to a Brazilian firm to give an opinion. But they really did all the work... because not all the work is necessarily law practice. It is the work that is behind the opinion. So, they do all the work, charge by the hour, and in the end only ask [a Brazilian firm] for counsel. [Foreign firms] really do get the bulk of the work. (founding partner in a full-service firm with 201 to 250 lawyers)

The different views between these interviewees illustrates the gap between theory and practice. Even though the regulatory body, the OAB, has attempted to establish clear limitations regarding the operations of foreign firms, nothing prevents these entities from doing the lion's share of the work, including the strategic planning, thereby accumulating most of the billable hours. The work is then approved by their Brazilian partners, who may merely sign petitions, issue legal opinions, and act as agents in the courts, leaving Brazilian firms out of the most important, highest value, and most complex strategic decision-making processes.

Another interviewee noted that foreign firms may have advantages not enjoyed by domestic firms, no matter how sophisticated or internationalized they may be:

> A fact of life is that foreign firms are already here. They are working here. They are competing with us. This is serious and there are implications. First, [these firms] are financed by international corporations, so they have little concern if they're spending too much here in Brazil because they have a global budget. Therefore, the first thing is the unfair and evidently illegal *funding*. Besides this is the phenomenon of worldwide clients. The client, for example a bank, is a worldwide client of an international firm. These guys come to Brazil and have a great chance of picking up the bank's work here in Brazil. Of course, this is particularly true in friends such as M&A, capital markets, and so forth. But I think it is a serious phenomenon that we have to face. (founding partner of a full-service firm with 151 to 200 lawyers)

Indeed, some respondents went so far as to characterize the financial advantages of international law firms as a kind of "dumping" that gives these entrants a significant advantage over their Brazilian counterparts:

> You have some law firms that are still really practicing their own homeland law, which is what Provision no. 91/2000 allows. But others buy a Brazilian office and take advantage of the fact that many Brazilian lawyers have a license from New York or London to practice law and say, "No, these people are foreign lawyers." Even more aggressive law firms come to Brazil and take ten lawyers from here, fifteen from there, twenty from there, offering higher salaries, which are totally incompatible with the Brazilian market, because they have a strategic plan – the plan being, "Look, I'm going to lose money in Brazil for a year or two, but as I have a global platform, so I can support myself." It's almost a kind of dumping. [Foreign offices] that practice Brazilian law . . . are fighting me for the same domestic work. (managing partner of a full-service firm with 201 to 250 lawyers)

The reference to "buying" a Brazilian law firm in the above quotation has proven to be particularly contentious in recent years. Although as indicated above, most Brazilian law firms have chosen not to form exclusive alliances with foreign firms outside of Brazil, some have chosen to do so inside the country with an international firm that has one or more offices in Brazil. This has led to complaints from some Brazilian firms who consider it unfair competition. The issue has been taken up by the OAB, leading to proposals for detailed regulation that would outlaw every possible kind of joint venture or alliance between a Brazilian law firm and an international law firm operating in Brazil. After an extensive debate, the OAB decided not to issue new regulations, instead issuing an opinion construing existing law noting that the association between foreign law firms and Brazilian lawyers is lawful under Provision no. 91/2000 only if it is temporary and restricted to consultancy on foreign law. Any type of litigation by foreign lawyers or law firms is forbidden. Violations of these rules by both Brazilian lawyers and foreigners admitted as "consultants on foreign law" are subject to the administrative jurisdiction of the OAB, with foreigners being subject to criminal prosecution under Brazilian law for the "illegal practice of lawyering." This regulatory debate is examined in detail in Almeida and Nassar later in this volume, and it is not our intent to provide a full exposition here (see Chapter 6). Instead, we simply want to emphasize that even after OAB's ruling the contest between domestic and foreign law firms in Brazil continues – and is likely to continue for some time, depending in large part upon the strength of the Brazilian economy. The extent to which Brazilian law firms are likely to do well in this competition will depend in part upon how well these firms are able to identify and recruit talented lawyers who have the kind of education and experience demanded by global clients.

3 Brazilian Firms Invest in International Education and Experience

Faced with increasing demands from their clients and competition from foreign law firms, domestic Brazilian law firms have started to heavily invest in international training and experience for their lawyers. As numerous studies have found, the scale and intensity of lawyer mobility around the world has reached unprecedentedly high levels with large number of attorneys seeking global legal training in foreign universities – largely American and British – as well as looking for internships or *secondments* in foreign firms (Silver 2006, 2011; Liu 2013).

The majority of the lawyers we interviewed considered international training essential for career advancement, and firms offer incentives for attorneys to complete a master's program, such as an LLM, at a foreign university.[14] As one respondent stated:

[14] A foreign LLM does not automatically imply recognition of the LLM as a master's degree in Brazil. Instead, to be recognized, a foreign LLM must comply with certain requirements, checked on a case-by-case basis, such as the existence of a dissertation and the fulfillment of credits.

> Nowadays [a foreign LLM] is almost a prerequisite for you to be considered a qualified professional. It is highly valued because when someone leaves a firm, goes to an international exchange [program], and then starts to look for a position, many opportunities arise . . . because he speaks English and has international experience and was part of an internship program. [The person] is more mature. (founding partner in a small, specialized firm with up to ten lawyers)

But as the market matures, even a foreign LLM may not be sufficient in and of itself. Instead, as another respondent suggested, while foreign LLMs are the new standard for most lawyers in the corporate law sector, matching them with international internships, such as with a foreign law firm, is also important.

> The LLM is also becoming something of a standard for us as well as [speaking] English. In the old days, it was: Oh, you speak English? Today, it is: What do you speak besides English? Very soon it will be: What do you speak besides English and Spanish? Because you have to really have more experience, more skills. Today, especially in certain business areas, an international master's degree is vital. If you can . . . then work in a foreign firm as well, I think that will give you a very good background from a personal, educational, and professional point of view. (managing partner in a full-service firm office with 201 to 250 lawyers)

This trend is apparent with many firms publicizing the fact that their lawyers have academic and professional experience abroad. Some have internal committees and funding programs aimed at lawyers who are interested in specializing and improving their knowledge in institutions and firms abroad. A master's degree abroad, previously seen as taking away valuable hours of a dedicated professional from the firm, has turned into a prerequisite in a complex and globalized world.

Finally, in the wake of the demands of a globalized world, the legal services sector in Brazil, especially in corporate law, requires staff to be fluent in foreign languages. Many of the respondents highlighted the fact that speaking a second language is a minimum requirement for lawyers in their firms. As a managing partner of a large firm put it, "Here in the office everyone speaks at least two languages [and] everyone has [an] international education" (manager partner in a full-service office with 251 to 300 lawyers). Indeed, this point of view was also prevalent in the more mid-sized firms, with the founding partner of one saying,

> Speaking other languages is vital. Here in the office, four languages are spoken: English, German, Spanish, and French . . . And it is not only knowing the language. We are less interested in a lawyer who speaks French, than in

a lawyer who speaks French and has lived and worked in France because he or she understands the culture and . . . can do the translation. Knowing the culture – their way of thinking [about] the legal system – is very important. (founding partner in a full-service firm with 51 to 100 lawyers)

C *New Policies and Practices*

The past two decades have brought about a revolution in the management and governance of Brazilian's most prominent corporate law firms. As these firms have grown and coped with demands for greater sophistication and internationalization, they outgrew their older, more traditional and informal management methods. As such, they sought to create new structures, systems, and policies better attuned with market demands. To some degree they were influenced by global models, but the firms also responded to local customs and rules, including regulations over business structures. To look at this, we examine developments in six substantive areas of law firm management and organization: (1) governance and management, (2) branding, (3) career paths, (4) remuneration, (5) technology and client management, and (6) regulation and market realities.

1 Governance and Management Structures

To ensure effective operation, sustainability, and efficient delivery of services, some Brazilian firms have embraced new management philosophies and more formal governance systems. We use "management" in the broadest sense, encompassing a firm's operations, objective and strategies for achieving them, and internal control (Di Miceli 2010, 62).[15] For law firms, management includes defining objectives, creating and consolidating the strategy of its brand, creating innovative products, employing new technologies, keeping track of operations, and developing strategic planning and internal policies.

Although there are some concerns about the implementation of more formalized management models in Brazilian firms, overtime firms realized that to provide the high levels of service clients were demanding and minimize risks (e.g., conflicts), the establishment of governance and management standards was necessary (Análise 2011, 18). Proper management included several

[15] To understand the term *management* as ex ante planning and adjusting the plan to meet the company's objectives and mission, see Sanvicente (1979). For management as an act performed by those to whom decision-making powers are assigned (by means of different hierarchical levels), see Ansoff (1977). For a bibliography specialized in aspects of law firm management, see Mayson (2007).

actions, including (1) transparent, swift, and efficient communication with clients; (2) career planning and internal controls aimed at implementing meritocratic criteria for advancement; (3) time management procedures to monitor the services provided; and (4) setting up appropriate decision-making systems in line with the size and complexity of the firm.

Increasing customer service, reducing costs while increasing efficiency, and implementing new technologies (e.g., case management software) were aimed at meeting client expectations. Indeed, to help with these issues, law firms started bringing in management consultants to assess, and therein change, structures, and operations. As the managing partner of a mid to large-sized firm told us, "We hired a consultant to assess how our finance system and information technology was doing, and from there we created our branding and label with a company" (managing partner of a full-service firm with 201 to 250 lawyers). The founding partner of a similarly sized firm echoed that sentiment, saying, "[The consultant was hired] about eight years ago or so, and continues there today, doing research among lawyers, partners, staff attorneys, clients, and office staff on . . . the level of satisfaction or dissatisfaction" in the firm (founding partner of a full-service firm with 251 to 300 lawyers).

It should be noted that though the majority of Brazilian corporate law firms have sought to professionalize management and governance systems, no single model has emerged. For instance, larger firms tend to have a well-defined governance structures, including management committees and executive boards. In addition, these firms also tend to have both managing partners and dedicated staff whose duties include general administration, human resources (HR), information technology (IT), and finance. By contrast, smaller law firms may not always have such professional governance structures or organized administrative frameworks (e.g., dedicated HR or IT professionals). In these smaller firms, the managing partner often decides everything, from hiring personnel to managing administrative costs (Análise 2011).

Thus, while there is no single management model or administrative system followed by all law firm, there are some common denominators, particularly for mid to large size firms. One widely followed model is a governance body for each practice area plus an overall firm system that can include a steering committee, a board, and a general assembly. The founding partner of a large firm noted:

> Each sector has a boss whom we call a department head. These department heads are on a steering committee, which is led by a CEO. The CEO and department heads are responsible for taking care of the day-to-day business

> in the office. Alongside the steering committee is the office's council, which consists of nine people elected for a term of two years. The council is the supreme body, which decides the office's strategic issues and approves the budget. The council deals more with the general office policies as if they were shareholders in the business. The general assembly is held to approve the office's financial statements and appoint new partners or remove partners. It has never happened, but it also has the ability to remove partners. (founding partner of a full-service firm with 301 to 350 lawyers)

Some firms also have a board of directors that takes care of strategic issues and acts parallel to the administrative committees that are focused on more specific issues such as information technology (IT) and human resources (HR). One respondent described the system in a large full-service firm:

> We have a board of directors consisting of seven partners, who have a term of two years which may be renewed. We try to renew the council partially . . . to ensure a certain historical continuity as well as a continuity of vision. Therefore, people can be reelected, and it is good that some of them be reelected. We have a steering committee consisting of three partners and three professionals, one in the IT field and another in HR and administration, and another in the financial area, and on the managing committee you have a managing partner. The fifty-five partners elect the board members, and the council elects a managing partner. And the managing partner chooses the steering committee. (manager partner of a full-service firm with 201 to 250 lawyers)

Another managing partner notes,

> Our model is that there must be an election every two years to mandate who is in the administration for the council and for the board of directors. They are elected by the partners and, once on the board, you have a strategic discussion for the office. We have a five-year strategic plan . . . It is hard work. Then every year you make small course corrections, because you are subject to the market, to what happens. In the end, the firm is not an island. With written governance, a functioning strategic plan approved, the council thinks about strategy within those parameters. They cannot deviate completely from what the strategic plan proposed, or even the executive board's proposals, which has a slightly lower realm of influence with respect to strategy. (managing partner in a full-service firm with 201 to 250 lawyers)

The firm's prestige also seems to be an important factor in determining management systems. For instance, while most prestigious firms tend to have managing partners who are lawyers, they also tend to have a professional manager who often is not a lawyer. For instance, of the 200 most prestigious law firms in the country, two out of every three – around 66 percent – have a manager who is not a lawyer (Análise 2011). To be clear, the role of these professional managers varies. In about 50 percent of the firms, the professional manager participates in the decision-making process. The managing partner from a mid to large size firm remarks, "There is an executive committee of three of whom two are partners and one is not a lawyer. He is a professional. He was a CFO" (managing partner of a full-service firm with 201 to 250 lawyers). In other firms, however, the professional manager performs only administrative and controller-specific duties (Attuy and Stychnicki 2011, 21). As the founding partner of a small to mid-size firm told us, "We have an administrator who takes care of administration. He is an engineer. He looks after the day-to-day administration, but not the management. Management is a legal matter, and he is not a lawyer" (founding partner of a full-service firm with 51 to 100 attorneys).

2 Establishing the Brand

Traditionally, the reputation of Brazilian law firms was based on the reputation the senior partner (or, in some cases, a few partners). However, the rise of the corporate legal sector and the growth in the number of law firms and lawyers created very real challenges to this model. Firms could no longer rely on the reputation of one or two notable lawyers. To compete for clients, they needed to start developing brands. At the same time, however, law firms faced an OAB ban on formal advertising and marketing. Because of these regulatory barriers, they were limited to strengthening their firms' brands through informal means, including having their lawyers become public players in the media and in the market.

In *Análise Advocacia* 500, experts emphasized market-positioning and brand-building strategies as among the most critical strategies that need to be implemented by firms. There are some indications that firms believe that they are doing a good job. For instance, sixty-five of the most prestigious law firms surveyed reported that they believed they knew how to nurture their brands. At the same time, however, the magazine also found that only 44 percent of law firms reported having a marketing director and only 36 percent said they had a human resources director. Among the firms that are in the second, third, or fourth generation of ownership, an overwhelming 87 percent chose to keep the name of the founding partners on the door, perhaps in an attempt build off of long-standing name recognition (Secco 2012, 27).[16]

[16] In an interesting comparison, Indian firms seem more split on this issue. For example, the newly formed Cyril Armachand and Shardul Amarchand, formed out of the breakup of

Brazilian firms are also grappling with how to institutionalize clients. On the one hand, clients are often known to say "we hire lawyers, not law firms." And there is data that shows that clients often move with their lawyers should the latter switch firms (Coates et al. 2011), although that data also shows that relationships at the firm level are also still important in the United States. Not surprisingly, many of Brazilian respondents, particularly from larger firms, stated that they are attempting to build bands that emphasize the firm, not individuals partners. The goal is to therefore link clients to the firm.

3 Recruiting and Retaining Talent

At the heart of any law firm is the need to attract, develop, and retain the best lawyers. As Brazilian law firms have confronted the challenges of globalization, they have had reevaluate their traditional approaches to this key issue:

Not surprisingly, all the law firms that we interviewed claimed to have claimed to have systems in place to accomplish this goal, although responses varied according to firm size and the degree of professional management. Notwithstanding this variation, all the firms we interviewed make a concerted effort to select lawyers for their professional skills. This is because firms have begun to organize and see themselves as macrostructures detached from any one individual. They seem to prefer to spread a positive image of general excellence in the marketplace to establish a strong brand, instead of just counting on attracting clients via individual partner or associate attributes. As one respondent put it: "In the end, you have to reinforce the brand and not a partner. This is the objective criteria that any organized office has to have, strengthening the brand, and from there forth the brand will build the clientele. It is not a partner that will build clientele" (founding partner of a full-service firm with 351 to 400 lawyers).

Notwithstanding this general convergence, in older and larger law firms, career paths tend to be more formal with set criteria for promotion. But even in these firms, subjective elements of "values" and "fit" play a critical role. The following descriptions about making partner in three top law firms

Amarchand Mangaldas, doubled-down on their founder's names. However, other Indian top Indian firms are explicitly moving away from family and personal ties. For instance, J Sager Associates now formally goes by JSA in an attempt move beyond founder Joydi Sager. Similarly, new firms, like Trilegal and Economic Law Practices, are shunning individual names all together in an attempt to break free from personality-driven practices. For more on this, see Wilkins et al. (2017).

underscores the continuing importance of these subjective elements in Brazil's top law firms:

> Becoming partner . . . is the deliberation of the partners, which analyzes the lawyer's employee profile until that moment, and then the partners establish what those requirements are. It is usually client satisfaction, office representation capacity, working capacity, performance as a lawyer, ability to lead, group work capacity. (founding partner of a full-service firm with 251 to 300 lawyers)

> Basically, what we are looking for are people who are more aligned with the goals of society, whom we think will be good partners in the broad sense, not only in the financial sense. (managing partner of a full-service firm with 351 to 400 lawyers)

> This evaluation (for partner) has what we call adherence to values. This adherence to values must be understood not . . . in the sense of purely ethical value, moral, these things, but the office values. (managing partner of a full-service firm with 251 to 300 lawyers)

There is some evidence, however, that Brazilian firms below this top level are moving toward a more objective system for promotion. As the founding partner of a general service firm with 51–100 lawyers described his firm's process: "Our evaluation system evaluates about twenty characteristics, with different weights, and then you have grades at the end . . . and who receives the vote of two-thirds of the partners becomes partner" (founding partner of a full-service firm with 51 to 100 lawyers).

Regardless of the degree of formality and objectivity surrounding the partnership promotion process, our respondents made clear that most Brazilian firms have moved away from many of the traditional practices that characterized these institutions prior to Brazil's global shift in the 1990s, but have yet to embrace the neo-Cravathist practices that now dominate law firms in the United States. Thus, contrary to the traditional veneration of "notables" with strong ties to the academy, most Brazilian managing partners we interviewed stated that they place little weight on a lawyer's affiliation with a prestigious academic institution when making hiring or promotion decisions. At the same time, these same partners also claimed not to place great weight on a lawyer's existing client base or ability to attract new business when making hiring or promotion decisions. The only exception was for relatively new firms seeing to establish their position in the marketplace.

In addition to creating more formal criteria for making partner, several Brazilian firms we interviewed have also created formal antinepotism policies that prevent lawyers who are married to each other from staying in the firm. In these firms, if one spouse become partner, the other spouse (usually the woman) must leave the firm. Similarly, several firms have created mandatory retirement policies as a way of ensuring that the team has up-to-date knowledge and skills. As one respondent stated: "After a lawyer is made partner, he reaches his maturity as a partner after fifteen years of partnership, and our rule is that at sixty-five you need to return your quotas. Either you retire as a partner, and then, if the firm wishes you to continue working, you go back to being just a lawyer with lower payment" (partner manager in a full-service office with 201 to 250 lawyers). As several respondents made clear, there is a critical need for such policies considering the danger that senior partners will refuse to leave, thereby stunting the future growth of the firm – or worse. In the words of a typical managing partner: "The firm needs some updating, needs to modernize. We cannot stop in time. Then we saw several examples of firms that closed down because the founders and older partners wanted to stay there" (founding partner in a full-service office with 301 to 350 lawyers).

Finally, law firms are recognizing that they need to change the way that they recruit talent. Traditionally, Brazilian firms have relied on hiring law students as interns, training them while they are still in school, and then bringing the best of the interns into the firm as associates. Several firms, however, are beginning to take a more proactive approach, participating in job fairs both in Brazil and abroad.[17] Nevertheless, hiring lawyers from the pool of interns currently working at the firm continues to remain the preferred method of recruitment even for top law firms.

4 Compensation and Job Structures

Because law firms don't have a standardized model of management, the interviews did not allow us to identify a single remuneration model. All the law firms analyzed had similar hierarchical categories (partner, associate/senior, midlevel and junior, and trainee) but possessed important variations in the distribution between partners and associates and in the existence of lawyers who are salaried contract employees governed by the CLT (Consolidation of Labor Laws) system.

[17] Some Brazilian firms began to participate in LLM job fairs in the United States, such as the fairs organized by New York University (www.law.nyu.edu/sites/default/files/upload_documents/Job%20Search%20Handbook.pdf) and Columbia University (http://web.law.columbia.edu/career-services/employers/recruiting/interview-programs/llm-interview-program), both held in New York City, where Brazilians firms are present and are on the list of prospective employers. In this same vein, only at the undergraduate level, the FGV School of Law in São Paulo organizes an internship fair to place students in professional internships and to bring firms closer to students and future professionals. The fair presents the innovations and specializations introduced in the training of future attorneys at FGV DIREITO SP. For more information on the FGV internship fair, see http://direitogv.fgv.br/feira-estágios.

Only two respondents claimed to use a structure in which all associates and trainees are under CLT, with only partners having capital shares and voting power.[18] Others mentioned different categories of members, such as junior partners and service partners.[19] Some lawyers may be partners in the firm's bylaws for tax planning purposes only but do not have voting rights or partner status.

With regard to the distribution of quotas for partners and the allocation of voting rights among partners, there was also no model adopted uniformly. However, most respondents adopted the system of one vote per partner.[20] The proportion of variable and fixed remuneration of partners and associates did not follow a standardized system. Most firms interviewed, however, adopted a model in which most of the early-career attorneys' remuneration was based on a fixed salary, with a variable fraction or bonus increasing as they progress toward partnership.[21] As to distribution of the variable remuneration among partners, the respondents mentioned several different criteria, many of which

18 "Everyone here is hired under the CLT (as an employee), except for the partners. It is not only a CLT firm – the office is very paternalistic; they have private pensions [in which] we put R$1 for every R$1 that the employee contributes. There is an extensive health insurance plan extended to the family, of which the firm pays 100 percent" (managing partner of a full-service firm with 351 to 400 lawyers).

19 "You come in as an intern, then you become a lawyer. You may spend six years in this position, and then you become a junior partner, [and] then you are included in the articles of association. At this point you have differentiated payment, but you still do not have a vote, which is a main feature. Six years as an attorney, maybe four years as a junior partner, then you are elected to active partner, a voter" (managing partner in a full-service office with 201 to 250 lawyers); "The only difference in being a full partner from those others [service partners] is the right to vote, a full vote, and they earn a residual [profit from the firm]. The others [service partners] . . . do not receive the residual profit and the right to vote is limited. So we say, these [service partners] are not really partners as they do not have a vote; they have no political power but are partners in practice. They receive results; they receive everything accordingly. However, they are paid according to this variation" (founding partner in a full-service office with 51 to 100 attorneys).

20 Comments from interviewees included: "Each partner has a vote" (founding partner in a full-service firm with 201 to 250 lawyers); "A specialized consultant in the area of organizing and restructuring firms was hired. Nowadays each partner has a quota and a vote" (founding partner in a full-service firm with 251 to 300 lawyers); "All votes are equal, and the president of the General Assembly, who is the partner who brings in the most revenue, has the power of veto" (founding partner in a full-service office with 151 to 200 lawyers).

21 "It varies a lot, but I would say this: in large law firms, the variable remuneration of lawyers who are not partners is tied to the number of hours they work. This is the big matter. For those who become partners, it is a mixture of hours with a fixed percentage of participation" (founding partner in a boutique office with up to ten lawyers); "We have always had a culture of variable remuneration – that is to say, fixed but variable. Up to a certain level, especially junior lawyers, they only have fixed remuneration and once they become 'full lawyer,' they receive a combination of fixed and variable payments" (managing partner in a full-service office with 251 to 300 lawyers).

were based on the stage in their career plan and on their productivity.[22] Attracting clients as a relevant factor in distributing variable remuneration among partners was mentioned in only one interview.[23] It shows a changing pattern in law firms regarding the importance of attracting new clients: in the past, attracting clients used to be crucial to increasing the partners' bonus, but now the fee for attracting clients is not the main part of the partners' remuneration.

5 Information Technology and Client Management

Technology was once seen primarily as a support tool to help make actual legal work more efficient by facilitating court filings and drafting routine documents and procedural motion (Mayson 2007, 5).[24] Now technology is used to help manage the firm itself. As a case-in-point, examining the sixty-five most prestigious law firms since 2007, almost 80 percent have an IT director on their staff (Secco et al. 2012, 22). Moreover, an estimated 4,000 firms have implemented some sort of case management software. Examining the 200 most prestigious law firms from the 2011 edition of *Análise Advocacia* 500, almost all reported having a lawsuit management system (Attuy and Stychnicki 2011, 24–25). A small portion can produce performance indicators that contribute to strategic business planning. It should be stressed that, however, that apart from a few very advanced firms, most have not yet formed information management systems that cross-reference financial data, customer profiles, and hours worked to provide a complete performance overview of the firm.

Virtually all our interviewees stressed how much technological advances have changed the way law is practiced in Brazil, acknowledging that technology is one of the pillars of a properly functioning firm. As the managing

22 "Here we have a very aggressive remuneration system. We distribute one-third of our profits annually to nonpartners. And it depends a bit on your assessment and a bit on where you are in your career path" (founding partner in a full-service office with 151 to 200 lawyers); "[The different strata of partners are paid in accordance] with productivity and contribution in terms of work... at the moment of paying bonus, we take into account these contributions of productivity and other work that was performed" (managing partner in a boutique office with 51 to 100 lawyers).

23 "We have client credit – when the partner brings in a client, he receives a percentage of that client's billings. But all of this is summed up into his account to see how much he will receive in the end. It is one of his remuneration components" (managing partner in a boutique office with 51 to 100 attorneys).

24 After a few legislative changes have been put effect with respect to the adoption of electronic media for the practice of procedural acts (e.g., Law 11.419 of December 2006). This legislation created several different techniques and tools to enable the digital practice, transmission, communication, and storage of procedural actions (Sica 2012, 72).

partner of one mid to large-sized firm put it, "How do you reinvent your business? It takes constant upgrades – access to technical resources and an efficient IT personnel behind it all" (managing partner of a full-service firm with 201 to 250 lawyers).

Technology is also reshaping the relationship between law firms, lawyers, and clients. For instance, the use of e-mail forced many lawyers to adapt to a new method of communicating with their clients, including being prepared to answer e-mails succinctly, quickly, and at all hours. Noting the massive changes since the mid-twentieth century, a founding partner of a small to mid-size firm told us:

> [Prior to the digital revolution,] communication was very difficult. International phone calls were expensive, so you conducted correspondence via telex. Fax did not exist. There was none of that... Then you wouldn't work with a computer. You worked with typewriters. It was a much harder and much slower world. The client would send you a letter asking questions and you answered with a letter solving questions. Last year, I did not sign any letters! We communicate only by e-mail – quickly. Today is a world with a completely different dynamic. We had lawyers who relearned how to work. (founding partner of a full-service firm with 51 to 100 attorneys)

Indeed, technology is likely to play a larger role in reshaping the practices of large law firms in Brazil in the coming years than it has in the past. In the United States and other developed legal markets, "disruptive innovation" in the form of big data, artificial intelligence, and machine learning, and predictive analytics are already being used many large law firms – and even more by corporate legal departments (Wilkins 2015; Center on the Legal Profession 2015). As other chapters in this volume demonstrate, these innovations are also being introduced in Brazil as companies seek to find ways to more efficiently handle "mass litigation" and other kinds of routine legal work (see Chapter 5 on JBL and Chapter 4 on routine legal work). As these innovations spread, they are likely to have as much – or more – of an impact on the practices of Brazil's large law firms as the introduction of computers and e-mails described in the quote above.

6 Regulation and Market Realities

There is a fundamental contradiction between the legal structure governing Brazilian law firms and the realities that these organizations face in today's marketplace. Put simply, while the law says that law firms cannot be considered as corporations, the market demands that they operate as such. However, despite the formal legal structures, firms have found ways to meet market demands. Brazilian law recognizes two types of business organizations: mercantile entities/companies (including corporations and limited liability partnerships) and simple societies. Companies can be entrepreneurial and have a business element. Simple societies are not permitted to engage in either activity, except in very specific circumstances.[25] The law also separates intellectual, scientific, literary, and artistic professions from activities of a business nature. As a result, lawyers, artists, and doctors are excluded from the "company" category and instead are required to work together as "simple partnerships."[26] Examples of simple societies include: cooperatives (via Civil Code Article 982), certain companies engaged in the agricultural and pastoral activity (not including agricultural industries, because the activity of transforming, proper of industries, already gives them the business company condition), and law firms (Civil Code Article 966 combined with Article 15 of Law 8.906/94) (Campinho 2013, 430).

It is important to note that the law does allow certain professionals to operate as a company – for instance, doctors in a clinic or artists in a gallery can use the company form and thus operate entrepreneurially and use business methods.[27] This option, however, is not open to law firms due to OAB rules. More specifically, article 16 of the OAB statue regulating law firms forbids partnerships among lawyers because they present "commercial characteristics or

[25] More specifically, article 982 of the Brazilian Civil Code establishes that "excluding the exceptions mentioned, a partnership is considered a company when its objective is to carry out business activities subject to registration (article 967); and others will be considered simple partnerships." Brazilian law firms are formed and regulated according to (1) articles 15 to 17 of Law 8.906 of July 4, 1994 ("Statute of Legal Practice and the Brazilian Bar Association–OAB"); (2) articles 37 to 43 of the General Regulations of the Brazilian Bar Association; and (3) Provision no. 112/2006 of the Federal Council of the Brazilian Bar Association.

[26] According to legal doctrine, these entities are not established for the practice of medicine or law, but are societies of means, constituted to facilitate the professional practice of partners or persons entitled to both. As Gonçalves Neto writes, "Even law firms, whose record is made exclusively in OAB, ... are not set up to perform the legal profession but for guiding performance and income earned in the provision of their lawyers' legal services. In any case, all partnerships related to the performance of a liberal profession have the peculiarity of not exercising the activity for which the license is required; they are societies aimed at means, formed to facilitate the professional practice of members or persons entitled to both" (Gonçalves and de Assis 2011, 46–47).

[27] Article 966 of the Brazilian Civil Code states: "A businessperson is one who is engaged professionally in economic activity organized to produce or circulate goods or services ... A businessperson is not one who exerts an intellectual, scientific, literary, or artistic profession even with the help of assistants or employees, *unless the profession constitutes an element of a company.*"

structures."[28] According to the same statute, law firms are also prohibited from registering in the Civil Registry of Legal Entities and in the Board of Trade. They are, nonetheless, required to register before OAB's sectional council. Thus, the law indicates that law firms cannot be established as entrepreneurial and business ventures, and therefore are exclusively established as simple societies under the special "law firm" category.[29] Given this, partners assume unlimited financial liability for the firm's debts (Campinho 2013).

This legal structure is arguably at odds with the perceptive of many corporate lawyers in the sector. Several respondents expressed this disjunction vividly. For example, a managing partner in a large, full-service firm said of a law firm:

> It is a business. No doubt. And what if you do not face it as a business? You have a company, with its specificity, with its needs. Our shareholders are at the same time workers because partners are always working. Therefore, you become a shareholder and you continue working and are assessed on your work. But you have to manage. Today we have 650 people. That's not a small number. But you have to adapt to modern times, including servicing clients efficiently. For the client to see that you cost less and do more – that will keep everyone in-house happy. It is a company, there is no doubt. (managing partner of a full-service office with 201 to 250 lawyers)

A founding partner of a smaller firm echoed a similar sentiment, telling us:

> With the increase in [the] market, professionalizing firms . . . have become companies. Nowadays, major firms are companies where you earn a salary, the guy makes a profit, and when you become partner, you have to have a certain performance and bring in a certain amount of money. This is no longer a partnership. It is a capitalist business with results and everything else. (founding partner of a full-service firm with 51 to 100 lawyers)

[28] Article 16 states, "The following are not allowed to register, nor may they operate: law firms that are commercial in form or characteristics; adopt a DBA name; undertake activities foreign to the practice of law; include a partner not registered as a lawyer or completely prohibited from practicing law. §1. The business name shall have the name of at least one lawyer responsible for the partnership and may be of a deceased partner, given that such a possibility was established in the original charter. §2. The licensing of a partner to perform an activity that is incompatible with the practice of law on a temporary basis shall be recorded in the partnership registration and shall not change its charter. §3. It is forbidden to register before public notaries and boards of trade companies that include legal services, among other activities."

[29] With respect to the transformation of attorney partnerships, the OAB/SP Commission on Law Partnerships has issued an opinion stating that such transformations are only possible if the law firm "abandons its identity as a legal office to be registered as a company."

To be sure, some respondents pushed back against the idea that corporate law firms in Brazil are really nothing more than businesses. For some respondents, law firms cannot be compared with companies due to the importance of the intellectual capital of a firm and the unlimited liability of the partners. As one managing partner commented:

> I think there is a fundamental limit there. I think it is and will always be a partnership of people, because capital is irrelevant. If a law firm wishes to be successful, it cannot accept or allow an investment partner. Partners must be people who genuinely work with and contribute to the business. There is no capital in the monetary sense; there is the intellectual capital that each partner brings. This is a significant difference between a company and a law firm. (managing partner of a full-service firm with 351 to 400 lawyers)

For other respondents, law firms should not be considered companies because of the culture of rendering legal services as a means of achieving justice. Notwithstanding these dissenting views, however, it is clear that there is a significant tension between the legal treatment of law firms as "simple societies" and the increasing commercialization of Brazil's corporate law firm sector.

At present, this tension is managed in part through gaps in the applicable regulatory structure. Thus, the fact that legislation does not consider law firms in Brazil as "companies" does not mean that control structures cannot be created to ensure that law firms are not mismanaged. In this sense, many respondents stated that despite not being companies in the legal sense, they possess structures that in fact make them work like business organizations.

Nevertheless, the legal form imposed on Brazilian firms does have certain important features that affect their operations and structures. Unlike what has occurred in many other countries, Brazil has not changed its traditional rules regarding lawyer accountability.[30] As a result the liability of partners in all Brazilian law firms is personal, subsidiary, and unlimited, which causes many law firms to take out insurance for this liability.[31] Damages caused to clients

[30] By comparison, when describing the Anglo-American model that has spread around the world, Liu writes: "In the age of globalization, limited liability partnership (LLP) has become a popular new model of law firm management, in which one partner is not liable for another partner's misconduct or negligence, to control the risks of global mergers and expansion. While the international offices of large Anglo-American firms usually adopt the LLP model, most elite domestic law firms in emerging economies still use the traditional or bureaucratic models" ("Elite Law Firms in Emerging Economies," GLEE Project Topic Paper, 2).

[31] There is no specific rule that limits the liability of partners with respect to a company's debt. Article 17 simply sets down the rule for damage caused to clients by lawyers in the exercise of the activity. Therefore, because the law firm is a kind of simple society, it is subject to article 1023 of the Civil Code that determines the following: "If the company's property does not

by acts or omissions in the practice of law are also unlimited. Lawyers, in turn, have subsidiary and unlimitedly liable for damages and may also be subject to disciplinary liability.[32] This is an important difference between law firms and companies, which in Brazil have limited liability. As a result, Brazilian law firms cannot technically go bankrupt, since partners remain fully liable for all of the law firm's debts.[33] Finally, because law firms are not businesses, the association type they use is subject to a differentiated system of tax on services (ISS).[34]

Although the regulatory divide between law firms and companies continues to shape the practices of Brazilian law firms, we predict that the disconnect between the formal legal rules and the reality on the ground is likely to continue to increase in the coming years. Even though they cannot be established as companies, law firms have been able to respond to market demands by creating structures that increasingly resemble an enterprise-level organization. For example, as law firms move to create a brand, old distinctions built into the company versus partnership dichotomy are left behind. As firms continue to attempt to build themselves up as consolidated units, these efforts will often be at odds with legal and regulatory interpretations as to what the real character and purposes of law firms are and ought to be. Future research will be needed to understand the implications of this growing tension between the law on the books and the law in action for law firms, regulation, and for Brazilian society.

IV CONCLUSIONS AND CHALLENGES FOR THE FUTURE

This study has aimed to provide an overview of the corporate law firm sector in Brazil and its main characteristics, examining how it has transformed to adapt to the new opportunities and challenges brought by globalization and

cover its debts, partners are accountable for the surplus, in the proportion of their participation in social losses, except if there is a concurrent liability clause."

32 In this sense, the law firm itself is fully responsible for damages. However, if it cannot handle it, the lawyers are responsible for recovering the damages.

33 According to article 1 of Law 11.101/2005 (Recovery Act for Business and Bankruptcy), "this law regulates the legal recovery, extrajudicial recovery of the businessperson and of the company filing for bankruptcy, hereinafter referred to as simply the debtor."

34 Law firms pay the ISS on an annual fixed amount calculated considering the number of professionals working in the partnership, and not the percentage of revenue (as in other partnerships), as established in article 9°, § 1° and 3° of the Law Decree 406/68. There was a legal ruling on this issue, with decisions from the Brazilian higher courts that recognize the acceptance of the decree on the ISS by the Federal Constitution of 1988 (RE 236 604-PR), not having been revoked by the Complementary Law 116/03 (Resp no. 713 752/PB and Resp no. 1016. 688/RS). The value is determined by each municipality.

the economic liberalization that began in the 1990s. The expansion of corporate law firms and the change in the profile of services they provide has helped to transform a closed and parochial legal market into one that is more competitive and sophisticated, and in which the practice of law is more responsive to international standards.

These changes have occurred within a sector accustomed to acting along traditional logics, revealing important contradictions. On the one hand, corporate law firms have experienced an increase in competitiveness resulting from the growth of the Brazilian economy and the concomitant increase in the demand for sophisticated corporate legal services. On the other hand, there are still numerous OAB regulations, including on minimum fees, advertising, and marketing activities, as well as broader rules with respect organizational form, that continue to constrain how Brazil's large law firms respond to this new demand. Although allowing law firms to become companies is not without opposition, our interviewees, particularly those representing larger-sized firms, repeatedly expressed a desire to develop marketing and branding strategies more aligned to a Brazilian "company" than those that traditionally governed Brazilian "law firms." In the eyes of these respondents, solidifying the firm's image as a unified brand is critical in today's competitive environment, even if this means substituting a more client-centric and institutional approach that may appear to come at the expense of the older, more personalized and relationship based methods that typified the Brazilian approach to the practice of law prior to the 1990s. Consistent with this view, we found that larger corporate law firms usually have more defined governance structures, including a managing partner and internal administrative functions, such as IT, HR, and billing, often lead by dedicated personnel, many of whom are not lawyers. Indeed, in some cases, the firms had a professional with a business degree who worked with the managing partner and was responsible for the administrative and bureaucratic tasks. These firms also normally had a set of managing bodies, including councils and practice committees. Unlike these larger firms, we found that the smaller firms that we studied tended to place the decision-making authority in the hands of their founding partners. Although we therefore found that larger and smaller firms differ in terms of their use of nonlawyers in firm management, the core principle of lawyer-control remains. Thus, regardless of size, in all the law firms we interviewed the managing partner had a legal background.

Larger firms were also more likely to have formalized requirements for career progression, although once again there was considerable variation across our sample. Thus, several of the largest firms purported to have a "lock-step" system, by which they meant that there were a series of requirements for a lawyer to become a partner, with periodic assessments to determine payments, bonuses, and promotions. Even with respect to this core feature, however, there was no standardized management model, nor was there a single model for structuring remuneration. All the corporate law firms that participated in the interviews had similar hierarchical categories – partners, senior associates, midlevel associates, junior associates, and trainees. That being said, there were significant variations in how compensation was distributed among partners and whether or not the associates were salaried employees registered under the Brazilian labor laws (CLT).

Although our study therefore revealed important differences between larger and smaller offices, it is not clear whether these differences will continue to be as pronounced in the future given the predictions that many respondents in both larger and smaller firms are making about the future direction of the Brazilian corporate legal market. To get the participants to reflect on future trends, we ended our interviews by asking these law firm leaders to reflect on the challenges Brazilian firms will face in the coming years. Although respondents offered a wide variety of answers, several respondents predicted that there would be a trend toward the creation of more specialized boutiques and medium-sized law firms which would compete effectively with larger full-service firms to provide sophisticated services in Brazil's increasingly complex legal environment. The following comments by the founding partner of a small firm offers important insight into why this might be the case.

> The tendency is to consolidate it into specialized small law firms because the sectors are becoming increasingly complex, with a larger number of companies in each sector. As the number of companies grow, the relationship with the different public agencies becomes more complex as there are many public agencies interfering with every activity. So, it is not just the regulatory agency, but also the Executive Branch. You have the city hall and its offices, the state agencies. It is a much more complicated thing. (founding partner of a specialized firm with up to ten lawyers)

Another founding partner of a medium-sized firm echoed these sentiments:

> Large companies tend to use medium-sized law firms. Large companies, in a way, got a bit tired of large law firms. With large firms, due to the workload and the amount of people and everything else, you must standardize the procedures. So this will change the market because it means more medium-sized firms will be on the front line that serve those large clients. That did not exist ten years ago. It was unthinkable. (founding partner of a full-service firm with 51 to 100 lawyers)

Only time will tell whether this shift toward smaller and more specialized law firms comes to pass, or whether as some other respondents predicted, the Brazilian market will be transformed by the reduction or elimination of existing restrictions against the entry of foreign law firms into the Brazilian market. These trends will undoubtedly be affected by broader trends in the Brazilian economy, as well as the global economy generally. For example, when we conducted our interviews in 2014, respondents believed that compliance and infrastructure were likely to be the fastest growing areas of practice in the coming years, with alternative methods of dispute resolution such as arbitration and mediation also being important areas ripe for expansion.[35] It is unclear whether these areas will become more or less important now that Brazil is struggling to pull itself out of recession – just as it remains to be seen whether foreign law firms will have more or less interest in emerging economies such as Brazil now that the US economy is pulling itself out of its own economic doldrums. Thus, a main conclusion of our project is that much more needs to be done to understand the growth of the corporate law sector in Brazil. We hope that future research will build on our study, looking more deeply into some of the issues we have examined and engaging into a comparative analysis to see how Brazil compares with other emerging economies.

REFERENCES

Análise. 2008. *Análise Advocacia 500*. São Paulo: Análise Editorial.
2010. *Análise Advocacia 500*. São Paulo: Análise Editorial.
2011. *Análise Advocacia 500*. São Paulo: Análise Editorial.
2012. *Análise Advocacia 500*. São Paulo: Análise Editorial.
2013a. *Análise Advocacia 500*. São Paulo: Análise Editorial.
2013b. *Executivos Jurídicos e Financeiros*. São Paulo: Análise Editorial.
2016a. *Análise Advocacia 500*. São Paulo: Análise Editorial.
2016b. *Executivos Jurídicos e Financeiros*. São Paulo: Análise Editorial.
Ansoff, Igor. 1977. *Estratégia Empresarial*. São Paulo: McGraw-Hill.
Attuy, Gabriel, and Vivian Stychnicki. 2011. "Seis práticas para conduzir escritórios como empresas." *Análise Advocacia 500*. São Paulo: Análise Editorial.
Calmon, Petrônio. 2008. *Comentários à lei de informatização do processo judicial: Lei n° 11.419 de 19 de dezembro de 2006*. Rio de Janeiro: Forense.
Campinho, Sergio. 2013. "Sociedades simples e empresárias: necessidade de uma revisão de conceitos." In *Reflexões sobre o projeto de Código Comercial*. Edited

[35] 41 percent of the respondents in the *Análise Advocacia 500* (2012, 32) mentioned environmental law as the most prominent area. Following were infrastructure, arbitration, digital law, and petrol and gas. According to this publication, this reflects the level Brazilian economy and its new demands and priorities.

by Fabio Ulhoa Coelho, Tiago Asfor Rocha Lima, and Marcelo Guedes Nunes. São Paulo: Saraiva.

Center on the Legal Profession. 2015. "Disruptive Innovation in the Legal Services." *The Practice* 1 (2): N.P.

Chambers & Partners Legal Publishers. 2011/2013. *Chambers Latin America: Latin America's Leading Lawyers for Business*. London: Chambers & Partners.

Chayes, Abram, and Antonia H. Chayes. 1985. "Corporate Counsel and the Elite Law Firm." *Stanford Law Review* 37 (2): 277–300.

Coates, John, Michele DeStefano, Ashish Nanda, and David Wilkins. 2011. "Hiring Teams, Firms, and Lawyers: Evidence of the Evolving Relationships in the Corporate Legal Market." *Law & Social Inquiry* 36 (4): 999–1031.

Di Miceli, Alexandre. 2010. *Governança corporativa no Brasil e no mundo*. Rio de Janeiro: Elsevier.

Englemann, Fabiano. 2011. "O Espaço Jurídico Brasileiro e as Condições de uso do Capital Internacional" (unpublished paper assigned by the author).

Galanter, Marc, and Tom Palay. 1991. *Tournament of Lawyers: The Transformation of the Big Law Firm*. Chicago: University of Chicago Press.

Gonçalves, Neto, and Alfredo de Assis. 2011. "Sociedades para o exercício de trabalho intelectual." In *Temas de Direito Societário e Empresarial Contemporâneos*. Edited by Marcelo Vieira Von Adamek. São Paulo: Saraiva.

Krishnan, Jayanth K., Vitor M. Diasand, and John E. Pence. 2016. "Legal Elites and the Shaping of Corporate Law Practice in Brazil: A Historical Study." *Law and Social Inquiry* 41 (2): 346–370. http://ssrn.com/abstract=2534348.

Latin Lawyer 250. 2013. London: Latin Lawyer Magazine.

Liu, Sida. 2013. "The Legal Profession as a Social Process: A Theory on Lawyers and Globalization." *Law and Social Inquiry* 38 (3): 670–693.

Liu, Sida, and Hongqi Wu. 2014. *The Ecology of Law Firm Growth in China* (preliminary draft).

Mayson, Stephen. 2007. *Law Firm Strategy: Competitive Advantage and Valuation*. New York: Oxford University Press.

Oliveira, Fabiana Luci de, and Luciana de O. Ramos. 2015. "General (In-House) Counsels in Brazil: Career, Professional Profile and a New Role (March 18, 2015)" (research paper series 119, FGV Direito SP). http://ssrn.com/abstract=2580499 or http://dx.doi.org/10.2139/ssrn.2580499.

Pitchard, John. 2013. *The Legal* 500. London: Legalease.

Sanvicente, Anyonio Zoratto. 1979. *Administração Financeira*. São Paulo: Atlas.

Secco, Alexandre. 2012. "Fundador no comando." In *Análise Advocacia* 500. São Paulo: Análise Editorial.

Secco, Alexandre, Gabriel Attuy, and Vivian Stychnicki. 2012. "A elite da elite da advocacia brasileira." In *Análise Advocacia* 500. São Paulo: Análise Editorial.

Sica, Heitor Vitor Mendonça. 2012. "Comunicação eletrônica dos atos processuais: breve balanço dos cinco anos de vigência da Lei n° 11.419/2006." *Revista do Advogado* 32 (115): 69–76.

Silver, Carole. 2006. "Internationalizing U.S. Legal Education: A Report on the Education of Transnational Lawyers." *Cardozo Journal of International & Comparative Law* 14 (2): 143–207.

2011. "The Variable Value of U.S. Legal Education in the Global Legal Services Market." *Georgetown Journal of Legal Ethics* 24 (1): 1–57.

Trubek, David. 2006. "The 'Rule of Law' in Development Assistance." In *The New Law and Economic Development: A Critical Appraisal*. Edited by David Trubek and Alvaro Santos. New York: Cambridge University Press.

2011. "Reforming Legal Education in Brazil: From the CEPED Experiment to the Law Schools at the Getulio Vargas Foundation." In *Aventura e Legado no Ensino Juridico*. Edited by Gabriel Lacerda, Tânia Rangel, and Joaquim Falcão. Rio de Janeiro: FGV.

Wilkins, David B. 2015. "Law Firms." In *The International Encyclopedia of the Social and Behavioral Sciences*. Edited by James D. Wright. Oxford: Elsevier.

Wilkins, David B., and Mihaela Papa. 2012. "Globalization, Lawyers, and India: Toward a Theoretical Synthesis of Globalization Studies and the Sociology of the Legal Profession." *International Journal of the Legal Profession* 18 (3): 175–209.

Wilkins, David, Ashish Nanda, and Bryon Fong. 2017. "Mapping India's Corporate Law Firms." In *The Indian Legal Profession in the Age of Globalization*. Edited by David Wilkins, Vikramaditya S. Khanna, and David M. Trubek. Cambridge: Cambridge University Press.

3

In-House Counsels in Brazil

Careers, Professional Profiles, and New Roles

Fabiana Luci de Oliveira and Luciana Ramos

I INTRODUCTION

The title "in-house counsel movement" has been used since the end of the 1980s to describe what began as an American phenomenon entailing the numeric growth, increased prestige, and growing professional value afforded to lawyers working within company legal departments on the company's legal matters (Rosen 1989; Wilkins 2012). Rosen focuses on how corporate lawyers went from being "kept" counsel in the 1920s, to "tame lawyers" in the 1950s, to "in-house counsel" in the 1980s. Nor was Rosen alone in marking this transition. Beginning in the mid-1980s, scholars studying the legal profession began to note that inside legal departments, and the legal executives leading them, were increasingly valued within their companies and the legal profession as a whole.[1] Chayes and Chayes write:

> Not only have [in-house counsel] offices grown in size, but in importance as well. The general counsel sits close to the top of the corporate hierarchy as a member of senior management. There is a comparable increase in the importance and complexity of matters dealt with internally. (Chayes and Chayes 1985, 277)

Indeed, Chayes and Chayes found that legal directors in large US corporations were gaining relevance within internal corporate hierarchies as they began taking part in the strategic decision-making process of the company. Many were being integrated into higher levels in the corporate hierarchy as

[1] For the purposes of this paper, the terms "legal executive," and "legal director" are used interchangeably with the term "general counsel" (or GC), which is more common in the American context. Moreover, there is a degree of heterogeneity in the Brazilian context with respect to the exact title of the person leading the legal function (this is discussed in detail below). For the purposes of this chapter, the term "general counsel (GC)," "legal executive," and "legal director" are meant to signify the senior most lawyer in charge of the legal department.

members of management, with some even being included on the company's board of directors (Coates et al. 2011).

Early studies of the changing role of in-house counsel also showed that there was a trend to begin carrying out new types of legal services and implementing new methods when managing conflict. For instance, legal departments began performing new activities, such as preventive legal consulting by foreseeing potential conflicts by implementing long-term planning and establishing managing plans for litigation as well as managing legal services by outsourced law firms (Chayes and Chayes 1985, 200).

In the almost three decades since this initial work, David B. Wilkins has argued that this the trend of enhancing the value of in-house counsels in the United States and around the world is not over (Wilkins 2012). More specifically, he argues that the prestige of in-house counsel and, in particularly GCs, continues to rise. He notes, that in-house counsel increasingly interact with top company executives, including the board, when advising and solving legal needs in their companies. In-house counsel are also at the forefront of deciding what legal work will be done internally and what will be sent outside to external law firms. And, increasingly, legal directors are participating in strategic decisions by sitting on company boards (Coates et al. 2011).

Indeed, between the mid-1990s and the 2000s, GCs and the departments they lead have become even more in the United States due to changes in corporate criminal law which drew more attention to the rules of compliance. In-house counsel and legal directors began playing a central role in the decision-making structure of American companies, working both as key actors in the business and as guardians of the companies' reputations and values (Lipson et al. 2012; Wilkins 2012). As a case-in-point, the percentage of US legal executives who sit on senior management teams went from 47 percent in 2005 to 62 percent in 2010 according to Deloitte data (Lipson et al. 2012, 240).

Given this context of the expanding reach of GCs in the United States and other advanced market economies in the Global North, Wilkins poses the question whether the in-house counsel movement that began in the United States is expanding to the major emerging economies, particularly the BRICS (Brazil, Russia, India, China, and South Africa). Of critical debate is how the forces that are arguably pushing the in-house counsel movement global, such as globalization and the arrival of new models of lawyer, interact with local pressures, practices, and rules.

In this chapter, we examine the in-house counsel movement within Brazil.[2] Our purpose is to analyze who the legal directors of major companies in Brazil

[2] In the following chapter, Wilkins and Khanna compare the state of the in-house counsel movement in Brazil and India, based on a common survey administered to GCs in both countries. Where relevant we refer to some of their findings here.

are and what the department that they lead look like. In doing this, we focus on the period between 2008 and 2016, considering the effects of globalization on in-house counsel.[3] The chapter presents two central analyses: (1) how legal departments are internally structured, and how these structures changed over time, and (2) who is the typical legal executive within Brazil, and how this profile has changed over time. To help address these question, we follow Wilkins's six indicators of change:

1. the *size* of in-house departments
2. the *credentials and demographics* of the lawyers working inside these departments
3. the GC's relationship to, and degree of *control* over, outside counsel
4. the *internal standing, jurisdiction*, and *authority* of in-house lawyers
5. the *professional standing* of internal counsel vis-a-vis the profession as a whole
6. the participation and influence of GCs in public policy debates (Wilkins 2012, 2016)[4]

To do so, the research relies on primary and secondary data on the profiles of both company legal departments and their personnel, their legal executives. The secondary data was gathered and systematized using information available in the *Análise Executivos Jurídicos e Financeiros* magazine, largely from 2011 to 2013. This information was used to create the principal database we use in this paper containing 1,032 companies and 800 legal executives. We also incorporate data from *Análise Advocacia 500*, largely from 2013, which contains data on how GCs hire and terminate law firms.[5] The primary data was generated from semistructured qualitative personal interviews with legal directors and former legal directors from fourteen companies in several sectors of the Brazilian economy. All fourteen are part of the 1,000 largest companies in Brazil, according to the 2013 edition of the Brazil's newspaper *Valor Econômico*.

[3] The focus on the past six years, 2008–2016, is due to the availability of secondary data. Through our qualitative interviews, we attempt to look further backward to gain a more historical perspective.

[4] See Chapter 4 for more on these metrics of change.

[5] As this book was going to press, the 2016 edition of *Análise Jurídicos e Financeiros* and *Análise Advocacia 500* were released. Where and when appropriate, 2016 data are incorporated into the analysis and discussion. It should be noted that the various editions of *Análise* cited in this chapters (2008–2013, 2016) each contains slightly different samples, as is frequently the case in this sort of survey research. Nevertheless, in each case, the targeted respondents (e.g., legal department executives) are precisely the same. Moreover, the questions across the various editions are also very similar, allowing for comparisons across the entire period.

Our argument is that since the expansion of legal departments in Brazil, which began during the 1990s coinciding with the increased privatizing of companies and the opening of the Brazilian market to foreign capital, the profiles and careers of legal directors have undergone several transformations, culminating in more value and prestige being given to these professionals within their companies. These transformations have generated a series of implications for the country's corporate legal market, ranging from changing the criteria for hiring in-house lawyers to demands for more sophisticated legal services from their outside law firms. Thus, this chapter offers important insight into the extent to which the in-house counsel movement has indeed come to Brazil, and how this transformation has – and has not – taken place.

Our analysis is theoretically in tune with the research done by Nelson and Nielsen who identified several professional roles in-house counsel might play within their companies (Nelson and Nielsen 2000). These authors develop three ideal types to summarize the roles played by GCs in their sample: (1) in-house counsel as *cops*, who limit their work strictly to legal analysis; (2) in-house counsel as *counsel*, who combine legal counsel and with business thinking; and (3) in-house counsel as *entrepreneurs*, who prioritize the business goals and management of their companies, sometimes in detriment to legal analysis.

To be clear, these roles are not meant to be exhaustive and in-house lawyers may move between them based on circumstance and need. For instance, a GC may be dedicated strictly to the legal analysis of a contract in one instance all the while acting more as counsel in a more general sense. In this hypothetical case, the GC still plays the role of a "cop," but the core of his or her work is related to the role of "counsel." Among Brazilian legal executives, we sought to verify if and how these lawyers relate to these different roles, and their views on whether one is preferable to another.

The chapter is organized into three sections: Section II, the profile and career path of legal directors; Section III, the profile, structures, and work of the legal department as a whole; and Section IV, the work done by the legal executives and their views on their careers, importance, and prestige.

II WHO ARE THE LEGAL EXECUTIVES OF COMPANIES IN BRAZIL?

In the 1960s and 1970s, few domestic Brazilian companies had in-house legal departments. However, it was common for early multinational companies operating in Brazil to employ internal counsel. For example, Union Carbide, Goodyear, Cargill, Light, and Firestone all had at least some in-house legal capacity in the 1960s and 1970s. In these cases, legal directors most often took care of tax issues (e.g., taxes on the circulation of goods, imports, and exports), dealt with supplier and client contracts, and handled labor matters. For more complex and out-of-the-ordinary issues, external legal counsel was typically hired, mostly Brazilian firms (e.g., Pinheiro Neto or Demarest & Almeida) recommended by the head office.

It was only in the 1980s when legal directors began obtaining more autonomy to outsource services. Despite this autonomy, their participation in the strategic decision making in the company and on boards was still rare. During this period, most in-house counsel were male – if for no other reason than most of the graduates of Brazilian law schools were young men (see Chapter 8 for a review of legal education in Brazil).

By the end of the 1990s, more specialized legal services within companies had come to the fore due in part to privatization and the rise of more sophisticated and specialized demands. In general, our interviewees indicate that with growing globalization and the arrival of more foreign capital in Brazil, it became increasingly necessary for legal professionals working in the corporate world to have a more complete background. In particular, respondents cited a growing need for corporate specialization, including knowledge of business, accounting, and international law.

When we move forward to examine data from the period 2008–2016, although legal directors continue to be primarily male, the ratio of women occupying these positions is increasing gradually, rising from 31 percent in 2008 to 35 percent in 2013, to 37 percent in 2016 (Figure 3.1). Although the number of women at the top of Brazilian legal departments is therefore rising, barring a significant increase in the rate of growth during the last 8 years (less than 1 percent per year), the majority of legal directors in Brazil are likely to be men for quite some time.

Looking at this gender distribution, one of the interviewees from the banking sector stated that departments have seen more and more women in lower and intermediate positions (see below), but in management and director positions, men remain the majority. The male dominance is often attributed to mobility. As one interviewee put it,

> Of the eleven [management positions], we have four women. We have twenty-two local offices, which we call regional branches. Wherever there is a commercial director, there is a legal counterpart alongside. These people have been to many places. Mobility for a woman is a little more complicated than for a man. Often, women do not venture out and do not go as far in their career because of that. (male legal director, age 46–55, banking sector)

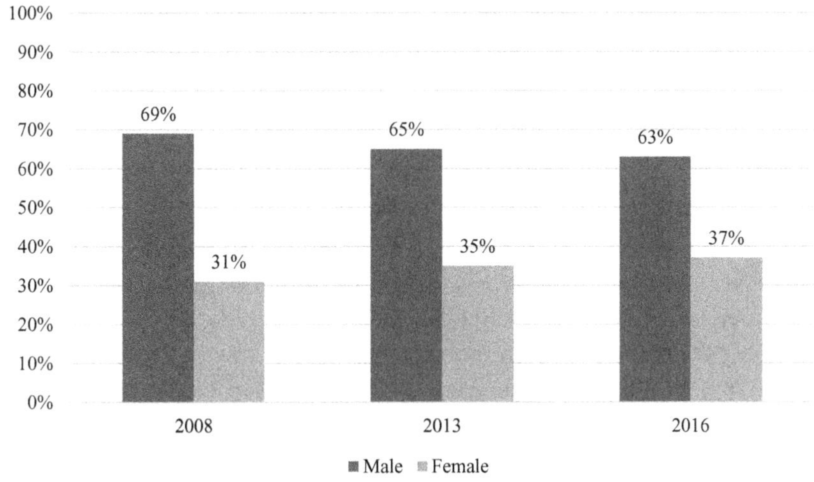

FIGURE 3.1 Gender breakdown of legal executives, 2008–2016.
Source: Análise Executivos Jurídicos e Financeiros (2008, 2013, 2016).

The fact that women in internal legal departments in Brazil have decreased chances for promotion because of their greater difficulty in accepting assignments that require them to relocate to other offices is consistent with research done on gender differences in promotion in the United States (Kanter 1977). With respect to age, 18 percent of legal directors are thirty-five years old or younger; 48 percent are between ages thirty-six and forty-five; 23 percent are between ages forty-six and fifty-five; only 11 percent are older than age fifty-six. The average age for the 800 executives in our sample is forty-three. These numbers are largely similar when compared to the 2016 *Análise* data on legal directors. The fact that more than two-thirds of legal directors remain under the age of forty-five is consistent with the fact that the position is still relatively new in many Brazilian companies.

With respect to educational background, the overwhelming majority of legal directors in Brazil majored in law. In our principal data set ending in 2013, the percentage of law majors was 98 percent. Interestingly, this percentage dropped to 85 percent in 2016 according to *Análise* data. This decline may be an indication of the growing importance of the "counselor" role in Nelson and Nielsen's typology, where GCs are expected to integrate legal and business advice, although the fact that only a small percentage of legal directors have formal training in a discipline other than law also underscores that this role may still be subordinate to that of a "cop" whose domain is primarily law. We return to this issue below.

In addition to being mostly trained in law, most legal directors received their training from a traditional law school in São Paulo, such as Universidad de São Paulo (UPS), Pontificia Universidade Catolica (PUC-SP), and Universidade Presbiteriana Mackenzie. The most recent *Análise* data confirms much of this trend – albeit with an important difference. Consistent with our principal data set, all five of the universities that graduated the most legal executives in the survey were located in São Paulo – 38 percent of the entire sample went to a São Paulo–based law school. However, 74 percent of legal executives reported going to a *private* university. Indeed, apart from USP, four of the five most frequently cited universities by legal directors in the 2016 sample were private. By comparison, only 60 percent of law firm partners in Brazil surveyed in the *Análise Advocacia 500* reported attending a private school. Moreover, this private law firm sample also had significantly more representatives from universities in Rio. It remains to be seen whether these differences also signal a shift toward the "counselor" role by highlighting a greater emphasis on the kind of specialized corporate and business skills that tend to be taught more in certain private universities than in traditional public ones (see Chapter 8 on legal education).

In terms of time since graduation from their primary undergraduate studies, 13 percent of legal executives graduated less than ten years ago; 49 percent finished school between eleven and twenty years ago; 27 percent between twenty-one and thirty years ago, and 11 percent gradated thirty-one years or more. The average time since graduation from undergraduate school was twenty years. These numbers are again largely similar when compared to the 2016 *Análise* data.

Virtually all in-house legal directors we interviewed had law degrees; however, this raises the question of what skills they most value from their education in their role as general counsel. Most interviewees pointed out that knowledge and abilities acquired at law school are important, but insufficient to carry out most of the duties required of legal directors. Many say that the knowledge acquired in university did not contribute to the "everyday life" of the profession, which encouraged them to seek out courses in other areas related to human resources, business, and project management, among others. It is also interesting to note that the answers show a relatively smaller importance placed on technical-legal knowledge as one advances in his or her career.

> When you work for a company and climb their corporate ladder, you leave a little behind, the technical part, and start to manage things based on experience, based on the team... because the company dynamic is quite fast-paced. (male legal director, age 36–45, telecommunications)

Interviewees also mentioned international experience as a key element to improving their management capacity and their performance in multinational companies. Knowing other cultures and speaking other languages are vital in a globalized world. Indeed, according to 2016 data, 97 percent of legal directors reporting speaking English and 40 percent Spanish. One of the professionals interviewed stressed the importance of academic and professional experience abroad, noting that the experience of studying and working in other countries was responsible for opening many doors in the corporate world.

> One thing I consider important for people working in a multinational company is international experience. You must travel abroad. You need to know how it works for various reasons – for your professional development, but also within the company. For you to operate globally, you must know how other cultures work. (male legal director, age 36–45, food sector)

Looking at international experience specifically, 20 percent of legal executives in our dataset reported studying abroad, 17 percent in business school and 83 percent in law school. Of these people, 37 percent studied for a master's degree (broadly defined), 32 percent for an LLM, 15 percent for a graduate certificate, 15 percent for an MBA, and just 1 percent for a PhD. 2016 numbers reflect a slight uptick in the percentage of those reporting studying abroad – of nine points to 29 percent – indicating the continued, and perhaps increased, importance of obtaining international training.

The most popular destination for education abroad is the United States, accounting for 44 percent of the total, followed by the United Kingdom with 13 percent (Figure 3.2). It is notable that both of these destinations have a common law, as opposed to civil law, tradition. This provides some evidence for the argument that Brazilian civil law is being influenced by common law insofar as leaders in the profession are being trained abroad in these traditions before returning home (Faria 2008). The other countries for international study are the Netherlands, Switzerland, Spain, France, Germany, and Portugal, followed by Japan, Canada, and Australia. Taking into account how young most legal executives are, most international experience is recent, dating from 2001 onwards. During this period, 69 percent studied abroad, with only 24 percent between 1991 and 2000 and 7 percent between 1979 and 1990.

Legal executives who study abroad do so at a wide array of institutions. As of 2013, the institution that garnered the most attendance from legal executives in our principal sample was The Hague Academy of International Law (12 percent), followed by UCLA and IIMD (9 percent each) (Figure 3.3). In the cases when interviewees had taken more than one course abroad, we

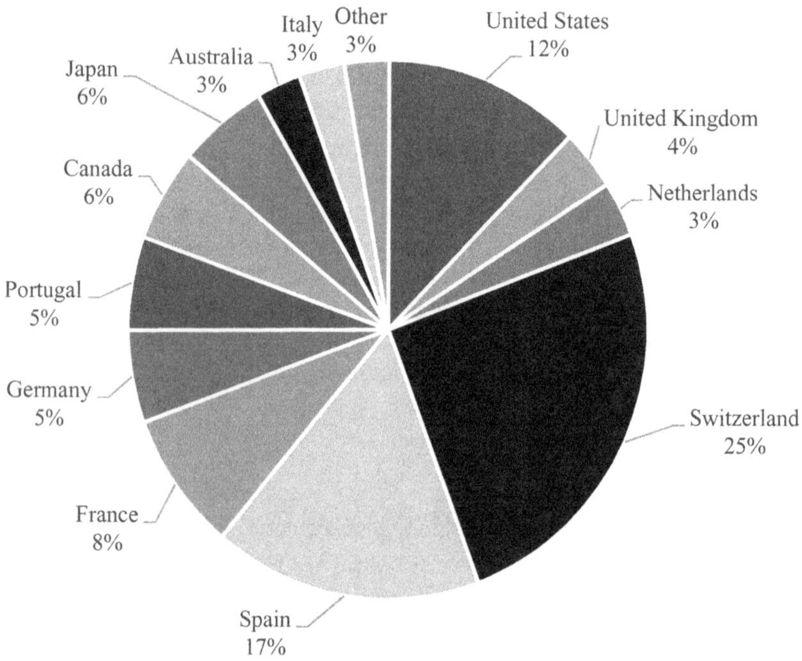

FIGURE 3.2 Countries where legal executives study abroad, 2013. *Source:* Data compiled from *Análise Executivos Jurídicos e Financeiros* (2013) from 206 executives who declared having studied abroad.

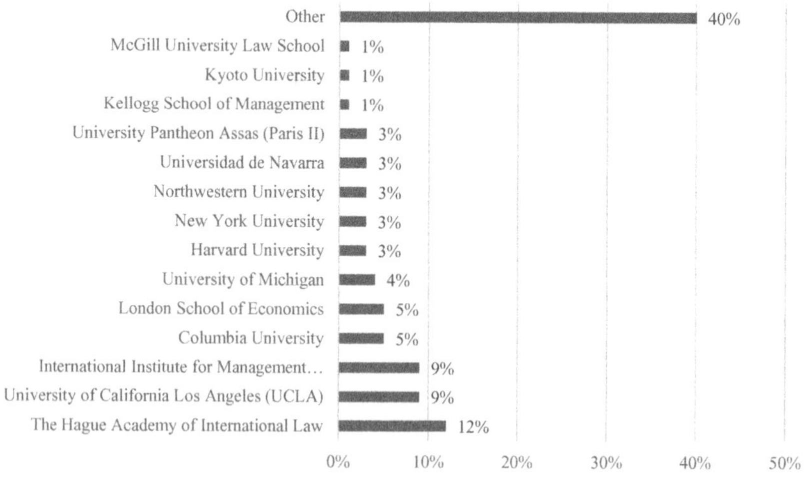

FIGURE 3.3 Institutions where legal executives study abroad, 2013. *Source:* Data compiled from *Análise Executivos Jurídicos e Financeiros* (2013) from 206 executives who declared having studied abroad.

registered the experience that they considered the most relevant to their background. There is some evidence, however, that the institutions where legal executives are studying has shifted over time. Thus, according to 2016 *Análise* data, Northwestern tops the list at 11 percent, followed by the London School of Economics and the University of Chicago at 9 percent. The top institution based on our 2013 sample, the Hague Academy of International Law, is not listed at all (the cutoff being 4 percent).

Although only 20 percent of the professionals in our principal sample have had experience studying abroad, almost all legal executives have some sort of graduate degree, even if it was acquired within Brazil. Indeed, 62 percent of general counsel have a *lato sensu* graduate certificate/degree – 30 percent have an MBA, 19 percent have a master's degree (including LLMs), and 1 percent have a PhD. These numbers changed slightly between 2013 and 2016. According to the 2016 *Análise* data, 82 percent of respondents reported having a postgraduate degree of some kind – a 20 percent increase from the 2013 number. 32 percent report having an MBA, which by and large conforms with the 2013 numbers. This overall pattern also confirms the importance of being able to integrate legal and business advice as outlined in Nelson and Nelson's "counselor" role.

Most of those interviewed indicated that their decision to further their education, whether through an LLM, MBA, or other graduate degree, was driven by a believe that their undergraduate legal education contained gaps when it came to working for companies. This was especially true with respect to the business perspective (business administration, human resources), or in specific areas of law, such as infrastructure, electronic law, intellectual property, new types of contracts, and environmental law.

Shifting the perspective from educational background to career histories, in our principal data obtained from 800 legal executives, most started at their respective company in the 2000s, with 40 percent starting between 2000 and 2007 and 33 percent between 2008 and 2013 (Figure 3.4).

For 720 of these legal executives, the date they took their current position is readily available. With that, it is possible to calculate how long they took to reach the position of legal executive. Approximately 30 percent of them started at their current company as the main legal executive, with the vast majority of them hired between 2008 and 2013. Half of them took up to two years to reach their current position. Overall, the average time for promotion to legal executive is 4.9 years (standard deviation of 6.9 years).[6]

[6] Of those interviewed, the longest time to ascend to the position of legal executive was forty-one years.

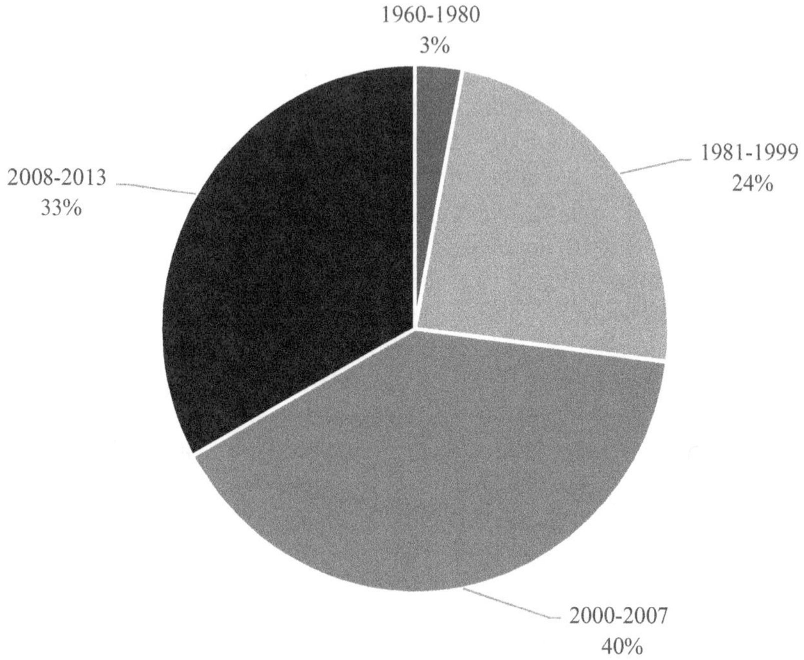

FIGURE 3.4 Period when legal executives started at the company, 2013.
Source: Data compiled from *Análise Executivos Jurídicos e Financeiros* (2013).

For some of these executives, we were able to trace their experience before they entered their current company. Prior to their current position, 37 percent had professional experience in other companies, 16 percent at law firms, and 4 percent in the government (Figure 3.5).[7]

Looking at job changes, between 2011 and 2013, 21 percent of companies changed their legal executive – or 217 of the 1,032 companies. Considering that the legal executive is normally the highest position in a company's legal department, this raises the question of where these individuals are going. In other words, this high turnover may indicate a search for advancement through a change of the career path (e.g., to business position). This is a hypothesis that would require more empirical evidence, but throughout the interviews, we saw indications of this trend. We do, however, have some evidence as to where legal executives prefer *not* to go to should they move away from a career in-house: law firms. According to the 2016 *Análise* data, 77 percent of the GCs Surveyed responded "no" to whether they would ever consider going to work for a law firm.

7 More than half of respondents (54 percent) did not offer information on their career path.

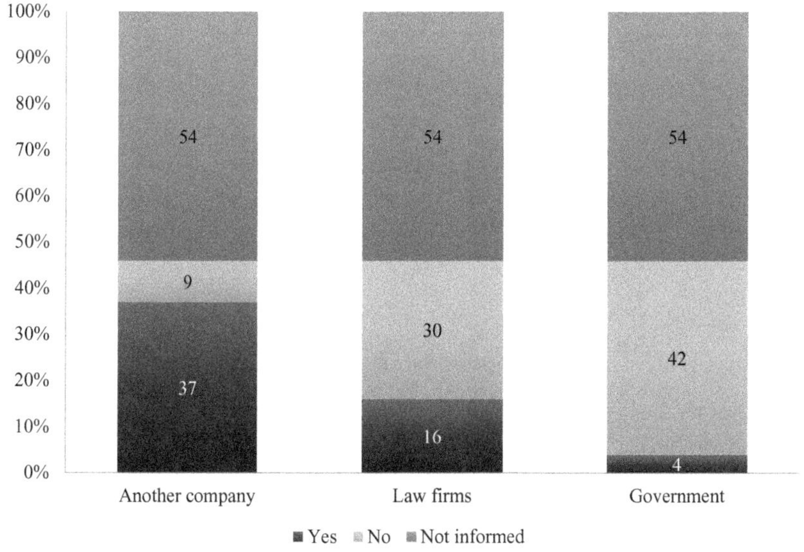

FIGURE 3.5 Prior experience of legal executives, 2013.
Source: Data compiled from *Análise Executivos Jurídicos e Financeiros* (2013).

III LEGAL DEPARTMENT STRUCTURE AND OPERATION

Of the 1,032 companies in our 2013 sample, more than half report having up to five lawyers in the legal department. The average size of a legal department is 11 lawyers, with a standard deviation of 29.2. As this number indicates, although the average size of the legal department in Brazil is relatively small, there are some that are quite large. Banks, for example, tend to have quite large legal departments, including Itaú, with 427 lawyers; Bradesco, with 421 lawyers; and Oi, with 150 lawyers.

These numbers have changed slightly based on the 2016 data. In looking at the sizes of some of the largest companies operating in Brazil, in 2016 Itaú reports having 450 lawyers (an increase of 23 from 2013), Bradesco 361 lawyers (a decrease of 60), and Oi 172 lawyers (an increase of 21). In looking at this 2016 data, it is important to stress that there continues to be a large variation in the size of in-house departments, even among the largest of companies. For instance, the difference in the number of lawyers between Itaú and Embraer (30 lawyers) – both major players in the Brazilian market – is 420 lawyers. This finding is similar to the US market, where research has found a large spread in the sizes of legal departments of the S&P 500 (Coates et al. 2011). It should be noted that in Brazil, the company with the largest legal department in the sample is the state-controlled Caixa Economica Federal with almost

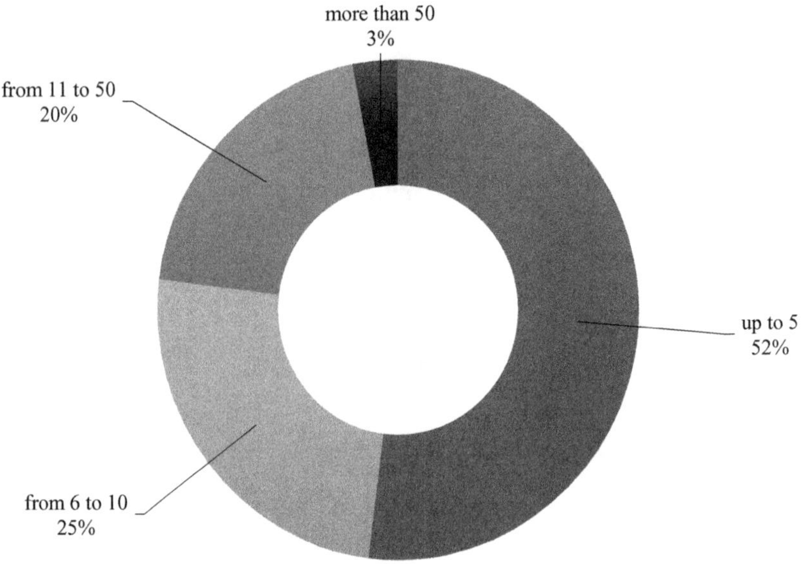

FIGURE 3.6 Size of legal departments according to the number of lawyers on the team, 2013.
Source: Data compiled from *Análise Executivos Jurídicos e Financeiros* (2013).

1,000 lawyers – a number that rivals even the largest US in-house teams and is more than double the size of the next largest, Itaú (Figure 3.6).

The gender distribution of in-house teams reflects one of the major shifts we observed during the course of our research on in-house legal department demographics. In 2008, in-house teams were predominantly male: on average, 66 percent of in-house lawyers were men. In 2009, this scenario began to radically change, with the percentage of men, on average, dropping 14 percent to 52 percent. In 2010, the percentage of men in Brazilian in-house legal departments dropped again, this time more slightly, to 51 percent. By 2011, the process of gender transformation was complete: on average, 51 percent of in-house teams were female. By 2013, the average percent of women on in-house teams was 54 percent (Figure 3.7). This data provides clear evidence that more female lawyers are entering in-house departments. On the other hand, whatever satisfaction this fact brings to advocates for gender equality in the legal profession must be tempered by the data presented above showing that men still dominate at the highest levels of those departments (Figure 3.1).

The average age of lawyers working within legal departments is thirty-seven years. Within that, 14 percent are younger than twenty-nine, 59 percent are between thirty and forty, 18 percent are between forty-one and fifty, and

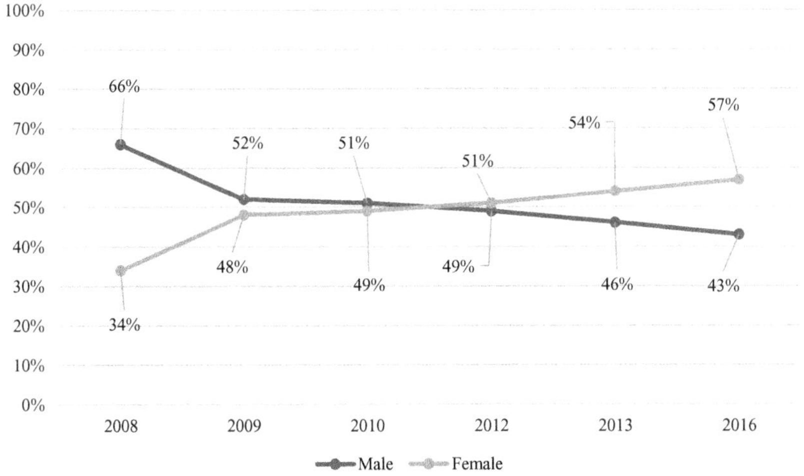

FIGURE 3.7 Percentage of male and female lawyers in legal departments, 2008–2016.
Source: Data compiled from *Análise Executivos Jurídicos e Financeiros* (2008–2016).

8 percent are fifty-one or older. Given these ages, the average time since graduation is twelve years. 18 percent graduated within the past five years, 28 percent between six and ten years ago, and 41 percent between eleven and twenty years ago. 13 percent graduated from law school more than twenty years ago. 68 percent have some sort of *lato sensu* graduate certificate degree, while 19 percent have an MBA and 8 percent have a master's degree of time type (including LLMs). These numbers largely hold steady in the 2016 data.

In terms of technical and support teams, in 2013 half of the legal departments had between one and three administrative employees. The average was ten nonlawyer employees (standard deviation of 42). Considering the whole team – lawyers and administrative staff – 30 percent of the departments have between one and five people, 29 percent between 6 and 10 people, 34 percent between 11 and 50 people, and 4 percent between 51 and 100 people, with 3 percent more than 100 people (Figure 3.8).

We next turn to departmental structure. In our primary research, interviewees offered at least two general models. In the first model, the legal department is organized around legal practice areas and areas of activity. in the second, there are further divisions, based on region, which are linked to the company's regional presence and market share.

One example of the first model is a company in the foodstuff industry, which structures divisions in terms of operational management (including

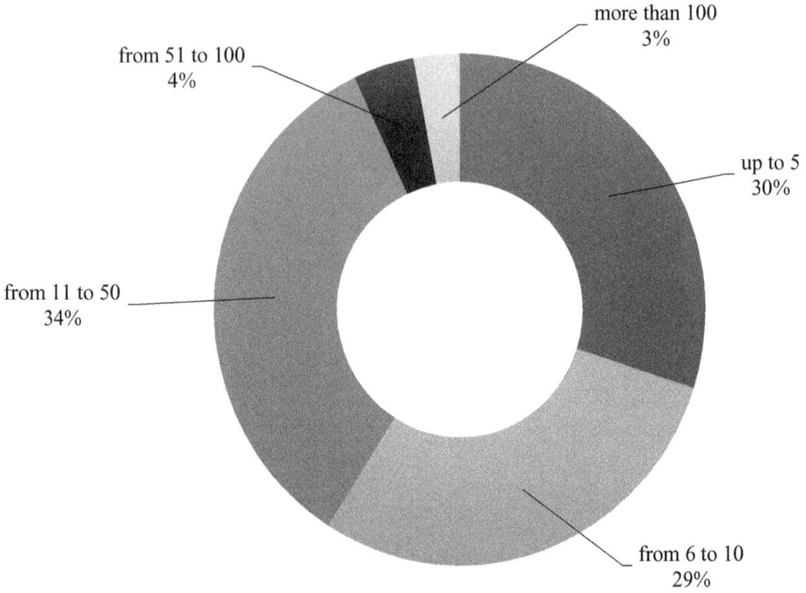

FIGURE 3.8 Total size of legal departments (total of lawyers and support team), 2013.
Source: Data compiled from *Análise Executivos Jurídicos e Financeiros* (2013).

civil, labor, criminal, and contracts); strategic corporate management (corporate); tax management; equity management (health surveillance, administration, and regulation); and ethics and compliance. Within this model, we found organizational structures that ranged from the simple to the complex. Among the simpler examples reported by an interviewee was a department organized into three areas: litigation, contracts, and corporate/consulting. Among the more complex, was a department structured around was tax, civil, commercial, environmental, labor, corporate, industrial property, compliance, and contracts, for which there was one management department for each of the nine branches who reported to the legal department.

With respect to the second model, which in addition to a "per area" structure establishes a regional subdivision, we identified a legal department with management departments across several states in the country reporting directly to the São Paulo headquarters.

In addition to organizational lines, another relevant aspect in understanding the functioning of in-house legal departments in Brazil is the l allocation of work between internal lawyers and external law firms and other providers, commonly referred to as the inside/outside split. From the interviews, we found that volume demands (e.g., litigation, consumer, labor), tax and

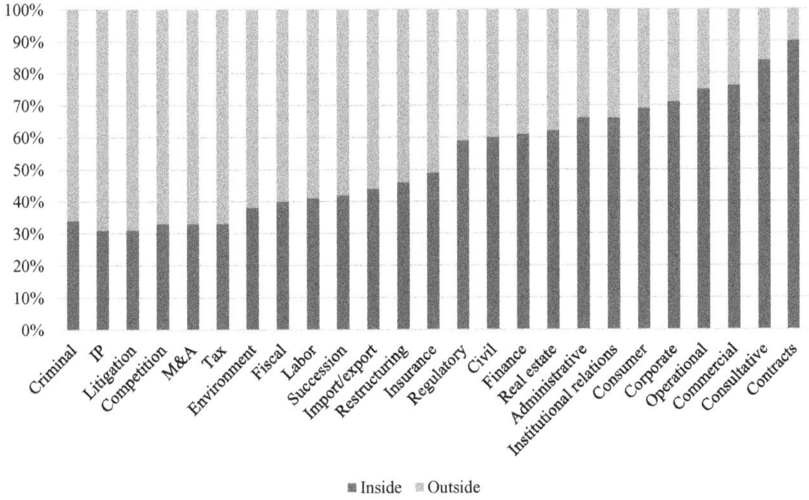

FIGURE 3.9 Distribution of in-house work versus outside work by practice area, 2016.
Source: Análise Executivos Jurídicos e Financeiros (2016).

fiscal, M&A, and specialized needs (criminal and intellectual property) tend to be outsourced. Demands related to the activities of the business, such as contracts, consulting, operational, corporate, commercial, and administrative, tend to be kept in-house (Figure 3.9). As one interviewee put it:

> Yes, we use outsourced services. We seek to preserve core business and to invest in in-house training to deal with the activities that are the core of the company – large-scale contracts in the area of supplying material, the corporate part, the labor part. Now, in labor law, for instance, we outsource what may be a more commonplace activity. Or when we need an opinion on specific legislation in another country, we also turn to [outsourcing]. We turn to [outsourcing] in high-expertise cases, in which either we do not have the experience here or the time required to reach that same level of expertise does not justify solving it in-house. But the activities that are very close to a recurring and vital activity for the company – selling products, purchasing materials – the aim is to invest and have professionals capable of handling these negotiations internally. (female legal director, age 36–45, transport sector)

One important difference we noticed from the 1960–1980 period to the period captured by our principal data set in 2013 is that tax law has become increasingly outsourced – 70 percent of companies now hire law firms or consultants for this type of work. Moreover, the companies that try to keep tax

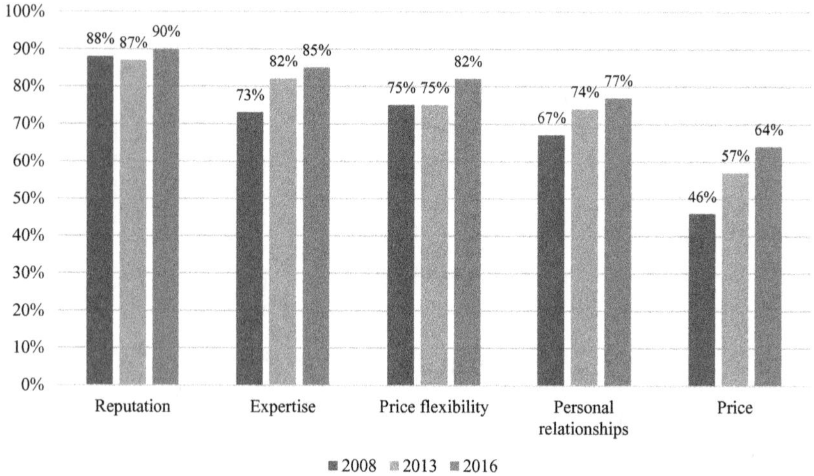

FIGURE 3.10 Hiring criteria for outside law firms (percentage reporting very important).
Source: Análise Advocacia 500 (2008, 2013, 2016).

internal often have a specific area to handle tax and other financial matters that may or may not be part of the legal department. Apart from this change, however, the pattern of which work is outsourced to law firms appears to have remained relatively constant, with companies continuing to keep the overwhelming majority of contractual matters in-house, which often constitute the bulk of the department's work.

Our research also provides some insight into the criteria that Brazilian companies use when outsourcing legal work.[8] *Análise Advocacia* 500, as related publication to *Análise Executivos Jurídicos e Financeiros*, interviews a selection of legal executives about the criteria they use for hiring outside law firms – and their reasons for terminating existing law firm relationships. Analyzing the publication's data between 2008 and 2016 underscores that legal executives appear to be placing increasing importance on three factors when deciding which law firms to hire to do the company's legal work: (1) price, (2) expertise, and (3) personal relationships (Figure 3.10).

This data above was corroborated by the perception of our interviewees, especially with respect to hiring law firms to handle litigation and everyday matters. In addition, however, interviewees in our primary research emphasized the law firm's reputation as one of the main criteria for outsourcing legal

[8] For a more extensive discussion of this issue, including how Brazilian GCs compare to their counterparts in India, see Chapter 4.

services. Importantly, respondents made clear that by "reputation" they not only meant the quality of the services provided by the firm, but also included the firm's integrity and ethics when performing its duties. The following comment from a female GC in the automotive sector is typical of how the Brazilian GCs we interviewed tied these two forms of reputation together.

> Obviously, quality is a very important aspect in the way this firm works, so there must be quality and very strict ethics concerning compliance, just like the demands of the company. If you have a specific subject, then the firm's expertise in that particular subject is also something to be weighed up. (female legal director, age 46–55, vehicles and auto parts sector)

Besides the quality of services provided and the ethics of the professionals when performing their duties, several interviewees mentioned that they also looked for law firm that had good local connections so that the firm would be able to keep a close eye on the company's matters in a particular jurisdiction, for example by easily attending hearings and other matters related to the case. As a result, in many cases GCs prefer not to hire the larger national firms, but instead will engage smaller offices that cover a specific part of Brazil, particularly with respect to handling the kind of "mass litigation" comprising tens of thousands of small individual actions spread across all states that company's in Brazil commonly face. As another interviewee stated:

> [The criteria for contracting is] the excellence of the firm in that area and that region. Let's assume there is an environmental issue in the state of Mato Grosso. I will not go after the best law firm in Brazil. I look for the best firm in environmental law in the state of Mato Grosso because that is where they know the regional institutions, where they know the rocky roads, where they will be able to articulate with the judge in question because they may be a local professor. So there isn't such a thing: "Let's hire the best environmental law firm to deal with this." This does not happen . . . exactly because of this [regional contracting], there are [no favorite firms]. (male legal director, age 36–45, food sector)

As one might expect, fees are another important factor when hiring. As one GC put it:

> Another important criterion is to have . . . a cost/benefit ratio. You work on a budget, so this is also part of the lawyers' role. (female legal director, age 46–55, vehicles and auto parts sector)

Data from *Análise Advocacia* 500 notes that cost can be a key driver in law firm selection. However, based on our qualitative interviews, it becomes clear that for more sophisticated matters cost is not they only driver. For such matters, the law firm's professional profile, as well as the reputations of the individual lawyers involved, were most likely to be noted as key considerations. Indeed, it was this latter consideration – the presence of a specific lawyer and his or her technical knowledge and expertise on the given subject – that was most often identified by respondents as the key justification for hiring a particular firm. It is important to note that this factor was used to justify hiring both Brazilian and international law firms. This importance place on the credentials of individual lawyers is consistent with one of the primary doctrines of the in-house counsel movement in the United States, where the mantra that "we hire lawyers not firms" has become accepted orthodoxy. However, as Coates, DeStefano, Nanda, and Wilkins document, law firm relationships are far "stickier" than these frequent pronouncements by US GCs would lead one to believe (Coates et al. 2011). As a result, one should be cautious about accepting similar statements from Brazilian GCs who operate in a market that has far fewer top law firm providers than their US counterparts. The following chapter by Wilkins and Khanna offers additional evidence for this skepticism when examining the hiring and termination decisions of Brazilian GCs in a representative sample of major Brazilian companies.

In addition to expressing a preference for lawyers with specific skills, there is also evidence that Brazilian GCs are also seeking greater specialization from their law firms as well. Thus in the five years between 2008 and 2013, we document a significant migration away from hiring full-service firms toward hiring more specialized firms (Figure 3.11). In addition to being consistent with the need for the general need for greater access to specialized expertise to cope with the increasing complexity of the legal matters Brazilian companies confront as a result of economic globalization, this result also supports the perception documented above that companies often keep general, less sophisticated matters in-house.

The search for more specialized law firms reveals that companies are looking for more individualized treatment and seek to establish longer-lasting partnerships based on a mutual trust. One of the interviewees shows why he has been searching for more specialized firms instead of resorting to full-service firms, particularly when complex and delicate matters are involved, such as M&A:

> Many larger firms turned out not to be partners. You start with the senior partner and then get moved to a junior associate – and we want special treatment. For instance, to be a part of the Administrative Council for Economic Defense, we use boutique law firms, because the treatment is personal, they

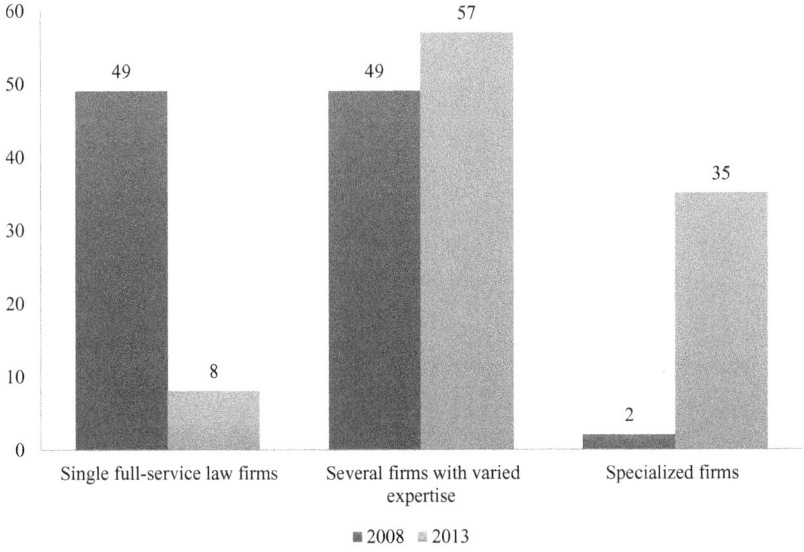

FIGURE 3.11 Types of law firms that companies prefer to hire.
Source: Análise Advocacia 500 (2008, 2013).

know the company in detail, we communicate just with a look. When they arrive at a meeting with the business area they already know the whole context. (male legal director, age 36–45, foodstuff sector)

Besides the criteria for hiring law firms, *Análise Advocacia* 500 also asked about the criteria GCs employ when deciding to terminate a law firm. Once again, this data revealed some important changes in the reasons given by GCs for terminating firms between 2008 and 2016.[9] While a drop in the quality of services provided by the law firm remained the main reason for terminating a law firm relationship, three other reasons were also frequently cited: cost, deterioration in partner relationships, and the loss of a key case (Figure 3.12). With respect to cost, in 2008, 37 percent of interviewees noted it was a key reason for terminating a law firm relationship. In 2013 that number rose to 51 percent, and by 2016 it was 53 percent. With respect to the importance of relationships with partners, in 2008, 77 percent of legal directors mentioned a deterioration in these relationships as one of the reasons to end a contract with a law firm. By 2016, that number had risen to 85 percent. Finally, in 2008,

9 In the following chapter, Wilkins and Khanna provide evidence about the frequency with which Brazilian GCs terminate important law firm relationships. As they indicate, this evidence underscores that important law firm relationships are more resilient than the spot contracting model espoused by many law firm GCs would lead one to believe.

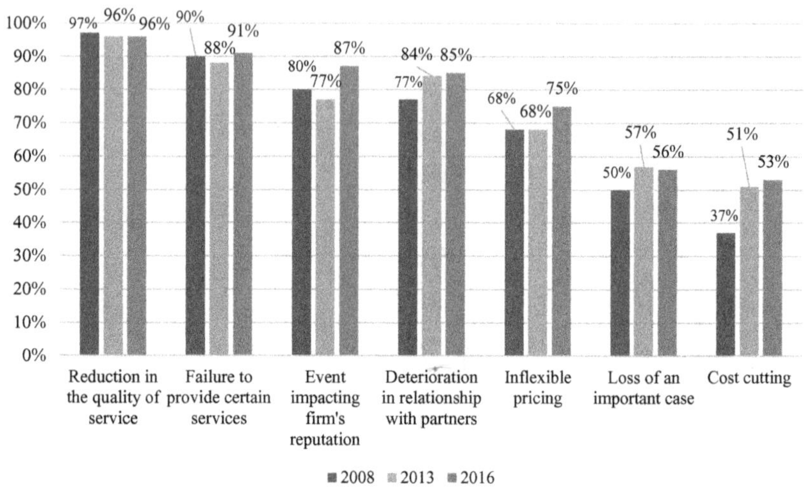

FIGURE 3.12 Reasons to terminate a contract with a law firm.
Source: Análise Advocacia 500 (2008, 2013, 2016).

50 percent of those interviewed mentioned the firm's loss of an important case as the reason to terminate the contractual relationship. In 2013 that number reached 56 percent. These increases suggest that results and client service are becoming more important to Brazilian GCs.

The 2013 and 2016 issues of *Análise Advocacia* 500 also offered new information regarding the criteria in deciding to terminate a law firm in the previous year. In 2013, 55 percent of the companies surveyed indicated that they had not ended any law firm relationships in the previous year. Of those that did, 26 percent reported doing so due to the poor quality of services; 5 percent due to the fees charged, 4 percent due to a damaged relationship with partners, and 10 percent for reasons not specified. 2016 *Análise* data is virtually identical across all cases. In the most recent sample, 52 percent of respondents reporting that they had not terminated a law firm over the last year. Of those who had done so, 25 percent reported that they had terminated for quality issues; 7 percent for damaged partner relationships; 4 percent for price; and 12 percent for other reasons. Interviewees were also asked about the current intention to terminate a relationship with a law firm. 69 percent said that they are not thinking about ending any current contracts. 17 percent said they might be considering ending the relationship due to the quality of services, 5 percent due to costs, 3 percent due to a damaged relationship with the partners, and 8 percent for other reasons. In that sense, almost 70 percent of the companies surveyed were not considering terminating a partner law firm.

Once again, this data provides an important qualification to the results presented above with respect to the reasons for termination. While Brazilian GCs clearly state that they are dissatisfied with issues such as partner relations and price, it appears that terminations happen relatively infrequently, and when they do, poor quality is most often the cause. The next chapter will return to this issue in the context of a comparative analysis of Brazilian and Indian GCs.

We also looked at what criteria companies use when hiring foreign firms. One of the expected impacts of globalization on Brazil's legal corporate market is growth in legal work for foreign law firms. Our research confirms that these firms are now an important part of the market. Thus, according to *Análise Advocacia* 500, in 2013, 40 percent of the companies reported that they had hired international law firms for work outside Brazil, with 30 percent noting that they had hired foreign law firms for work within Brazil. Although the 2016 numbers for those who reported hiring a foreign/non-Brazilian law firm for work outside of the country dropped 7 percentage points to 33 percent, the percent hiring foreign firms for work within Brazil held steady at 29 percent.

Based on our interviews, we identified that foreign firms are hired in situations involving mergers and acquisitions or when there are serious financial implications regarding the businesses' operations abroad. Moreover, multinational companies typically have their legal department and lawyers abroad deal with non-Brazilian questions with their Brazilian-based lawyers aiding with the more routine, Brazil-based matters. A series of interviews explained this process.

> We have had some operations in which the [company] hired a global firm. If you have some issue for which you might need legal assistance from another country, then we get in touch with our headquarters in the United States. (female legal director, age 46–55, vehicles and auto parts sector)

> Obviously, there are transactions that require counseling from foreign firms, and then you hire someone from abroad. But these are specific situations involving foreign legislation. There are no [*favorite*] law firms, so you go by the brand. You don't have a choice, because there is no other option. Until you establish a trusting relationship and get to know the local market, you are held hostage by the brand. (male legal director, age up to 35, energy and infrastructure sector)

> These are operations involving extremely high values, so all of this leads to choosing the best professionals. In these transactions, there are many interests involved. In general, the shareholders, the company's reputation,

> the company's image, the president, and the main executives are all involved. So, you look for someone who is a consensus in terms of trust, quality, reliability, and so on. I believe that on the whole planet most people based their decision on the lawyers' know-how – the experience not only of the firm but also of the lawyers involved in the operation and their availability. Sometimes when you are in a very aggressive market, you say, "Wow, something is happening there, but the person is busy with two other operations." (male legal director, age 36–45, tourism sector)

Hiring law firms, whether they are local or foreign, also depends on the budget. Few companies revealed the department's budget, but of those that did, the annual budget during our interview period (2014) varied between R$11 million and up to R$174 million.[10] The automotive, retail, and food sectors revealed budgets up to R$15 million per year. The highest overall average budget came from the banking sector at more than R$100 million.

Beyond the total budget, we were interested in knowing how costs in legal departments are divided between internal lawyers and outside counsel. Our interviewees stated that most of the budget is allocated toward hiring outside law firms – between 60 percent and 75 percent of the total. One interviewee noted: "One-fourth of my budget goes to the payroll and the other three-fourths are divvied up between outsourcing and general expenses" (male legal director, age up to 35, energy and infrastructure sector). A second noted, "I would say that 60 percent of the budget for service providers goes to these collaborators [outsourced lawyers], and 40 percent goes to the payroll – people hired here as employees" (male legal director, age 36–45, foodstuff sector). As Chapter 4 by Wilkins and Khanna indicates, data from a representative sample of Brazilian companies and FMCs operating in Brazil largely confirms this general observation. Nevertheless, it is important to note that the cost of legal services is sometimes budgeted outside of the legal department itself. In other words, some of our interviewees said that it is common for the business unit involved in a particular lawsuit to bear the expenses it generated. Thus, our primary data of interviews suggest a wide variety when it comes to how legal departments use their budgets. As such, it is not possible from this data to identify a pattern as the structure of the legal departments depends on the nature of the business and how expenses are managed.[11]

10 The following chapter provides more information about legal budgets from a representative sample of Brazilian and multinational companies operating in Brazil, as well as a comparison between these budgets and those from a representative sample of companies operating in India.

11 The more systematic data on this issue provided in Chapter 4 allow for a deeper exploration of this issue.

IV IN-HOUSE CAREERS: PERCEPTIONS OF PRESTIGE AND VALUE

How do general counsel perceive their role? There is a consensus among interviewees that there is the need for solid technical-legal knowledge, which is sine qua non for performing their duties. However, as the GCs we interviewed have progressed in their career and occupying a more predominant role in the management of business, respondents reported that in addition to technical-legal knowledge that they also needed series of other abilities, especially those related to strategic planning, risk management (compliance), leadership, and people management. In other words, from the perspective of most of those interviewed, their profile is more distant from the "cop" ideal-type articulated by Nelson and Nielsen, and closer to that of a "counselor" who integrates law and business advice (Nelson and Nielsen 2000). The role of entrepreneur – a participant in decision making that aims at increasing profit – actually appears in the discourse of only a few of our interviewees. However, the *aspiration* to play this role is present in the idealized future that many respondents would like to see for themselves and their company.[12]

Nelson and Nielsen's ideal standards were based on three aspects: (1) the extent to which the work of these professionals is limited to gate-keeping duties, with the more limited this role, the closer their profile is to the "cop" standard); (2) the scope of guidance and counseling offered, considering that the more restricted to legal counseling, the closer their role is to the "cop" standard; and (3) the nature of knowledge they claim to use in their work; again, the closer to the technical-legal background, the more aligned "cop" standard.

All professionals interviewed noted seeing a heightened value of lawyers within companies. This growing value, our respondents claim, applies both internally to their role within the company, and externally in terms of their standing in the legal community as a whole. One of the interviewees noted that a company that gives value to their legal department is safer, because it takes less risk and is able to better defend itself against external threats. One of the interviewees also pointed out the importance of compliance, not just in Brazil but worldwide, and that it is important for the legal department to work closely with the business units to build up and ensure ethical work and

[12] One of our interviewees (age 36–45, metallurgy and steel mill sector) claims that he wished the position of legal director in the company he works for was like the role of the *consigliere*, as portrayed in the novel *The Godfather* by Mario Puzo. The *consigliere* is a kind of consultant and advisor to the boss, who, in the book, has the additional responsibility of representing him in important meetings and actively participating in the family business. In the organizational structure, he is seen as the third most powerful and has the legitimacy to argue with the boss and oppose him when needed in order to maintain the good development of the business.

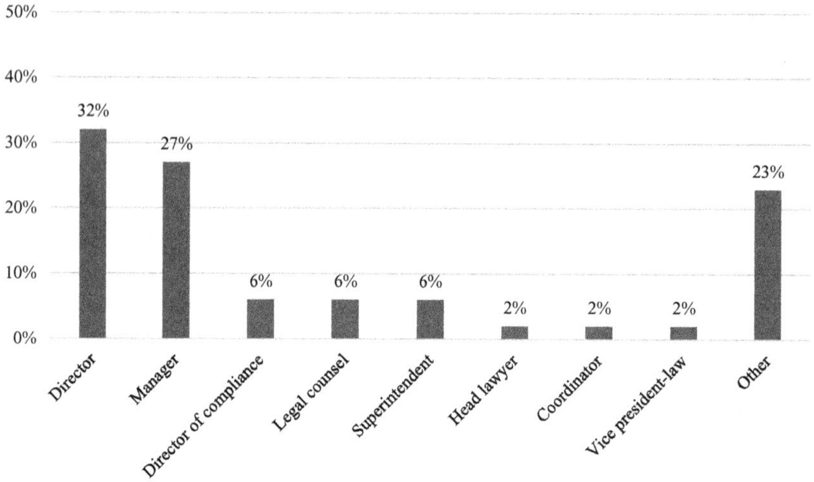

FIGURE 3.13 Titles of the company's main legal executive, 2016.
Source: Análise Executivos Jurídicos e Financeiros (2016).

compliance with rules. Indeed, 2016 *Análise* data found that 69 percent of companies surveyed had formal compliance programs, with 43 percent of these managed by the legal department. As in sometimes the case in the United States, 25 percent were managed as separate departments, with the balance being run out of another unit such as finance.

Some objective data indicates the increase of legal executive prestige. According to 2016 *Análise* data, 34 percent of those in charge of in-house departments identity as being directors or vice president. 27 percent reported being "managers" (Figure 3.13). The fact that almost two-thirds of legal executives hold one of these two titles is some indication of their importance within the corporate structure.

Indeed, analyzing this data over time, we see that senior legal executives who hold the position of director or vice president went from 23 percent in 2008 to 35 percent in 2012 and has held relatively steady ever since (Figure 3.14). Although this time comparison confirms that GCs have increased their status significantly since 2008, it also underscores that this increase may have hit a ceiling and that many companies in Brazil continue to regard their chief legal officer as a relatively low-level figure in the corporate hierarchy.

Evidence regarding the reporting structure for legal executives in sample confirm this general pattern. Thus, the percentage of legal directors who report directly to the company's main executive increased from 47 percent

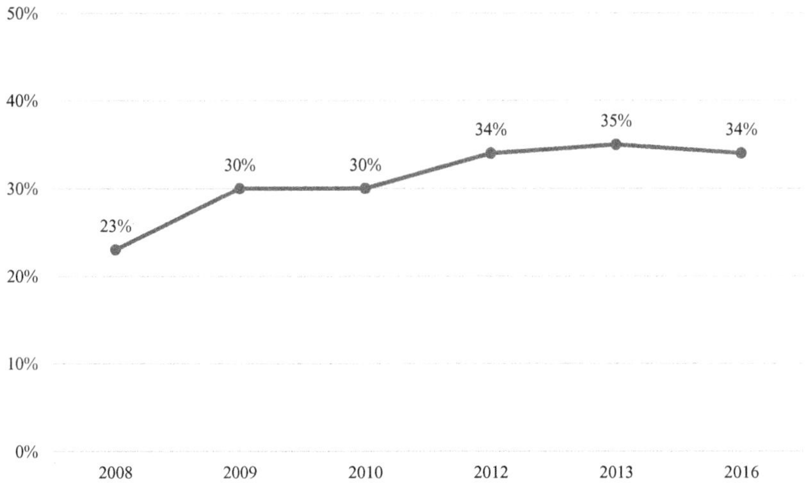

FIGURE 3.14 Percentage of legal executives who hold a director or vice president position, 2008–2016.
Source: Análise Executivos Jurídicos e Financeiros (2008–2016).

in 2008 to 64 percent in 2012, and has held steady since then (Figure 3.15). Once again, this steady state is almost identical to the percentage of GCs who hold a director or vice president title. It should be noted, however, that in 2016 22 percent of those in charge of legal reported directly to the board of directors, which may indicate an even higher level of prestige than those who report to the CEO.

Another indication of the increased status and responsibility of GCs by the in-house counsel movement is the range of functions that report to the legal department. Our research provides some evidence of these reporting-in relationships for Brazilian legal directors. According to the 2016 *Analise* data, 11 percent of legal departments are responsible for general administration, 10 percent for human resources, 9 percent for accounting, 8 percent for finance, 7 percent for sustainability, 5 percent for investor relations, 4 percent for communications, and 2 percent for marketing. In addition, 23 percent of the companies have a series of technical areas reporting to the legal department, such as billing (Figure 3.16). These numbers have not changed significantly since 2013.

Although these numbers indicate that Brazilian GCs are beginning to have important responsibilities in other parts of the company, the overall picture reaffirms that the legal function within many Brazilian companies remains focused on the law. This is just one more indication that Brazilian GCs still have a long way to go to catch their US counterparts who frequently oversee

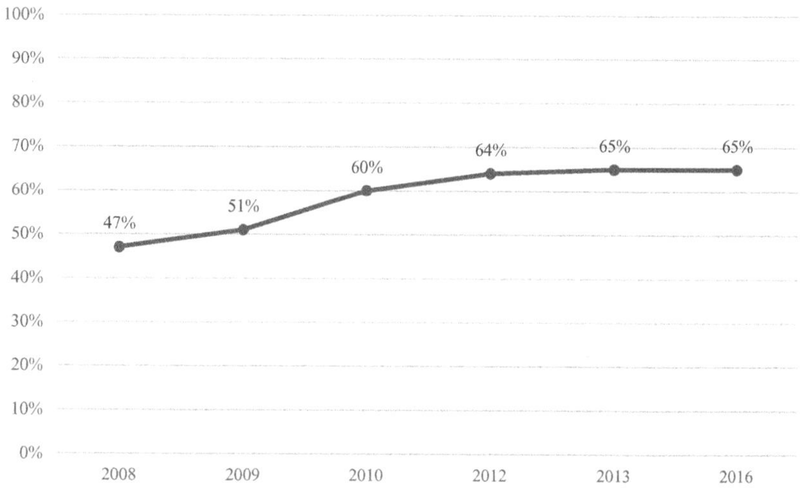

FIGURE 3.15 Percentage of legal executives who report to the company's main executive, 2008–2016.
Source: Análise Executivos Jurídicos e Financeiro (2008–2016).

a host of other functions, such as government relations, human resources, compliance, public relations, and corporate social responsibility, in this aspect of the in-house counsel movement (Wilkins 2012).

Brazilian legal directors have made more progress, however, on gaining control over the company's overall legal work. With respect to this core claim

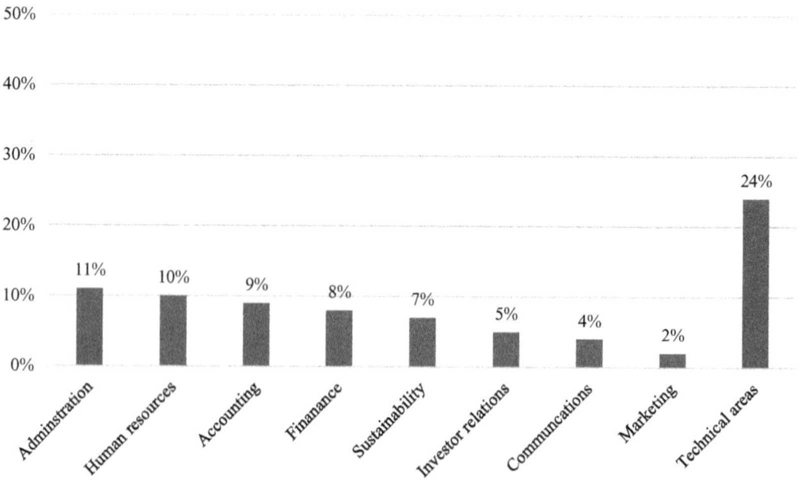

FIGURE 3.16 Percentage of legal departments to which other areas report, 2016.
Source: Análise Executivos Jurídicos e Financeiros (2016).

of the inside counsel movement, interviewees highlighted important changes in the legal director's role, particularly since 1990. Thus, several respondents pointed to the fact that companies are increasingly bringing inside legal services that used to be carried out by outside law firms. This trend is most commonly seen among the largest and most profitable businesses:

> Since I started working as an intern there were already legal managers and directors inside the company. I believe this is a trend [to bring legal services inside] began in the 1980s and 1990s. [To be clear] I am talking about more developed companies, larger companies, the more structured ones. (male legal director, age 36–45, tourism sector)

Based on interviews and secondary data, it is possible to clearly identify the transition of the lawyers' role in the company vis-à-vis the ideal types developed by Nelson and Nielsen (2000). When we look at the Brazilian situation, we can condense all three ideal standards into two company categories that distinguish themselves by the greater or lesser value the company's core business gives to their internal legal departments.

The first group comprises companies that consider the legal department a support area, which other sectors consult sometimes to solve specific issues. The role played by these legal departments is secondary, designed to manage litigation and to manage the process of hiring external law firms. Their legal directors are not usually called upon to participate in the strategic decision-making process pertinent to the company's business, and they do not participate in board meetings, not even informally. Thus, they would be seen as "cops," or even worse, as a necessary evil. Among the hundred largest companies from which we compiled our interview sample, this type of legal director is rare. However, when we look at the bulk of the 1,032 companies in our principal sample, we see that many companies still work under this archetype.

The transition from "cop" to "counselor" occurs as legal executives take on a more active and participatory role in business. To capture this change, one can consider the percentage of legal department leaders who report directly to the chief executive as well as the percentage of legal executives who hold a "director" position. The transition refers to the main role taken, and a legal executive can take on more than one of these roles simultaneously.

In contrast, the second category of companies assigns more relevance to the legal department. In this case, the in-house legal department works closely with the business units and is consulted on strategic decision making. The role of legal directors, therefore, takes on more importance when it comes to areas like product launches, M&A strategy, and/or the risks of moving into other regions or countries. Besides these new duties, legal directors report directly to the CEO and become executive directors. They are also frequently part of the board of directors.

In this second group, the key transition occurs when the legal director becomes part of the group in charge of making strategic decisions for the company, as demonstrated in other countries (Chayes and Chayes 1985; Wilkins 2012). By taking on larger responsibilities, legal directors became more valued and gain more clout in the decision-making process related to the company's core business. They are therefore seen as "advisors," who balance their duties in managing legal risks with the business's profile. They act both proactively, by preventing risks, as well as suggestively, by adding value to the business.

There is an important second transition, particularly seen in multinationals and larger companies, where those responsible for the legal department have gone from "advisor" to "entrepreneur," and have become more directly involved in the business as business partners. A legal director in the transport sector provides a clear example of this transition. When asked about her role and duties in the company, she emphasized how legal has become less of a "means area" and more of a "purpose area":

> If I compare the legal department [from 2004] to the current one, it is quite different. I felt a move closer to the business area, that is, understanding the business, understanding what the company goals are, and helping achieve them. We see a significant change in the lawyer's role, due to more acknowledgment of the role and the contribution the legal area can bring. And you start to think about the legal matter strategically, not only as the aftermath of specific situations. And it is an image that becomes clearer on how to better handle increasingly more complex conflicts, international legal cooperation among several organisms, in increasingly more restricted situations, that also force companies to take preventive measures almost as if carrying out supervision through the company. In the course of the years we have noticed that accurate legal knowledge and strategic knowledge of the goals, the actual vision of the economic scenario, allows you to follow, to anticipate, to make decisions more conscientiously. In the end, I believe there is a greater level of responsibility, especially on the legal professionals' part, toward the company's activities themselves. (female legal director, age 36–45, transport sector)

Although on the rise, this role is still foreign to most in-house counsels, especially if we consider the "entrepreneur" ideal-type. The fact that true "entrepreneurs" are rare among Brazilian legal directors is corroborated by the relatively low percentage of legal executives who participate in board of director meetings or take part in the decision-making process related to the company's core business. Of the 800 legal directors for whom we were able to collect information about these issues in our principal sample, only around 10 percent have taken on the "entrepreneur" role.

Regardless of the exact model, however, it is clear that legal departments in Brazil have come a long way from the days where they were considered at best a necessary evil and at worse largely irrelevant. Strengthening the ties of trust with other sectors of the company has given the legal department more importance inside the company. As one interviewee said:

> Until some time ago – some fifteen years ago – the legal department was considered a necessary evil. The arrival of foreign investors brought a new concept to the banks because you do not make any deals and you don't talk to anyone from abroad without a lawyer present. They may not say anything – usually they don't – but they are there, often just for compliance. And the bank began to see the need for better staff, professionals who are better prepared to accompany the bank's service. (male legal director, age 46–55, banking sector)

This change in the paradigm concerning the legal department job description is attributed to several factors, including Brazil's economic opening in 1990, the privatization of strategic sectors for the economy, as well as the arrival of compliance, which is often in charge of the legal department in companies. As a legal director put it:

> There has been a huge opening trend in the country, especially from the 1990s onwards. There were the privatizations at the end of the 1990s, then a boom in initial public offerings operations in 2003 and 2004 – really up to 2008 and the financial crisis. This brought huge growth, not only in the movement of the capital market but also in mergers and acquisitions. All this . . . has only helped to add value to this position – the legal director. Indeed, [not] only the legal director, [but] the company's legal department as a whole. (male legal director, age 36–45, tourism sector)

We also attempted to assess if there was any change the interviewees would like to see in their role within the company, and if so, what that change might be. Although many interviewees detected a trend of heightening the value given to their role, some still noted that they wanted more, suggesting a desire among legal directors to participate in the company's strategic decisions. This is particularly true with respect to operations that will be carried out by the company and that involve establishing practices of corporate governance and transparency.

Finally, we asked respondents to tell us their goals for the next phase of their careers given that within their current company they had reached the top of the legal ladder. Several respondents reported that they would be interested in moving over to the business side by becoming an executive in the company's management. However, in several cases those expressing this interest were doubtful whether they would be given the opportunity, since there were no lawyers among the company's top executives or on the board. Because of this, some suggested moving over to another line function where they could continue to advice the company, but in an area more closely connected to the company's core business. As one respondent put it:

> I have reached the top – from here there is nowhere else to go... [But] becoming an advisor to the company – even the name says so, general counsel – is much more important, regardless of the department I am in. I would like to go to other areas, for instance, human resources. I see myself working for human resources. In a couple of years, this is how I would plan it. But for now there is a lot to do here, a lot to organize, and to make sure it is ready for a successor. (female legal director, age 36–45, retail sector)

Others imagine taking on a specific operation within the company, or even becoming consultants in their own businesses.

> I have made it, but it is funny talking about the top. I see it as the end. I am 41. I don't think of myself as an old man, but... there aren't many places for me to go now. Depending on your age, being in this position is the celebration of a career. It is nice and has to be valued. There is even this friend of mine who was in the same position, not in a big company like [name of company], but a smaller one. He left the legal area completely and took on an operation. This is a path I think I can... take too if I stay in the company. Otherwise, you go back to private enterprise to start a firm or become a consultant. (male legal director, age 36–45, foodstuff sector)

Finally, we investigated whether the legal directors in our interview sample were involved in debates over public policy on behalf of their company. We initially asked our interviewees to use their own experience to reflect upon what key changes they would like to see in the Brazilian legal system and, based on that, their potential involvement as a legal director. The two topics that came up most frequently were reforms to tax and labor law. Interviewees mentioned the need to standardize the countless rules regulating the relationship between citizens and the treasury to avoid fiscal conflict between states and enable better quality control. Some interviewees also identified the sluggishness of the judiciary as one of the most problematic issues in the country, whether because the slowness to judge cases generates uncertainties or because some misuse the system to get rich. Others mentioned changes are to civil procedure rules and the commercial code.

In many of these companies, especially those in the banking and other regulated sectors, lawyers are working toward formulating proposals for legislative reforms. That being said, none of the legal directors interviewed mentioned being involved directly in the public policy debate over these issues. In other words, none of them take on an active and open legislating role, possibly because "lobbying" in Brazil is seen in a bad light. In the following chapter, Wilkins and Khanna examine whether some Brazilian GCs are more active in this area than those we interviewed (Chapter 4).

V FINAL CONSIDERATIONS

The study of in-house legal departments and the legal directors who lead these organizations is new in Brazil. Therefore, it is not possible to make comparisons between or references to other national studies on the subject. The works that establish a dialogue with this article are mostly North American studies.

The main conclusion we can draw about the Brazilian situation follows a trend previously identified in this foreign literature – the increasing value and prestige of legal directors inside companies, due to both the numerical growth of professionals working in legal departments as well as the duties taken on by legal directors. As we document, in Brazil this growth has occurred most intensively since the 1990s, precipitated, as indicated in Chapter 1 of this volume, by the privatization of many state-owned enterprises and the greater opening of the Brazilian market to foreign capital. At the same time, however, despite this heightened value, legal executives continue to express a desire for even more influence. This conclusion is based on three central elements: (1) the views of the legal executives interviewed in our primary sample, (2) data on the reporting lines of the legal executives in our principal data set, and (3) the hierarchical position of the legal department and legal directors within the companies in this data set.

As we indicated, many interviewees believe that there has been an important transformation of their role illustrated by the upgrading of their duties as counselors in the company's strategic decisions. For example, legal directors are now being called into board meetings to participate in the decision-making process related to the company's core business. To be clear, however, this position represents only a small group of legal executives. Based on the more generalized data analysis of 800 legal directors, only 10 percent can be placed in the role of "entrepreneurs."

Even though the "entrepreneur" standard may not be fundamental among legal directors, there has been a trend of professional growth inside companies based on the hierarchical position taken on by legal directors. First, data from 2008 to 2016 shows an increase in the number legal directors taking on the position of "director" or "vice president." Second, data shows that the internal promotion of legal directors is tied to whom they report. By 2016, 65 percent answered directly to the company's top executive with another 22 percent reporting to the board.

This all raises the question of why legal directors have gained more prominence inside companies in Brazil. Many interviewees identify economic growth, the increase in foreign capital entering the country, privatizations, the creation of new areas such as compliance, and gains in trust from other areas in the company as core reasons driving their increased value within their companies.

Moreover, consistent with the core tenets of the inside counsel movement, the increased prominence and sophistication of the legal director's role over the past few decades has fostered significant transformations in Brazil's legal market, impacting both the criteria through which companies hire in-house lawyers as well as legal education and lawyers' desire to develop abilities not provided in law schools. Both of these transformations directly influence the activities carried out by corporate law firms, which are now required to provide higher-quality and swifter law service – and better cost-benefit ratios because of the increased sophistication of their corporate clients (Chapter 2).

These same pressures, however, are reshaping the legal director's role as well. Economic globalization and the arrival of new sectors to the Brazilian economy have required law professionals working in the corporate market to acquire new legal and business knowledge. Indeed, these changes have been so great that t many legal directors we interviewed, most of whom had traditional legal backgrounds, noted that they have sought to improve their legal and business acumen through additional educational courses in the country and abroad.

The need for these new qualifications are a direct result of the greater responsibility given to legal directors and the diversification of legal departments. As we documented, these departments have taken on more duties internally, especially with respect to the everyday running of the business, such as contracts, consulting, operations, corporate, and administration. In general, legal departments outsource mass demands to law firms, involving labor and consumer litigation; tax litigation; very specific yet complex issues that require a lot of time from the team, such as mergers and acquisitions (M&A); as well as specific and specialized matters, such as criminal and intellectual property.

One can see these changes in the growth in the size of Brazilian legal departments over the period of our study. Before the 1990s, legal departments comprised just two or three lawyers, with almost all legal services being outsourced. Then, in an attempt to reduce costs, legal directors began bringing routine legal work inside the company. Today, our data indicates that mass litigation and more sophisticated legal matters are primarily given to law firms, whereas everyday legal services (e.g., contracts) are handled internally. In larger companies, especially those with international operations, the work legal executives have been doing toward fostering good corporate governance stands out.

When legal directors choose to hire law firms to handle a service, the main criteria they use are related to the firm's reputation (ethics and market recognition), fees, and, as revealed by some interviewees, the lawyer's profile and excellence, regardless of the firm he or she works for.

Finally, although most legal directors recognize the heightened value companies are giving to their roles, some claim that their position as a key element in the strategic decision-making process deserves to be strengthen. Others say that the board of the company should consider recommendations of legal professionals, which would offer even greater value to the legal department. The stature and prestige of legal directors promised by the in-house counsel movement in the United States and other countries is therefore still a work in progress in Brazil. Nevertheless, the trajectory toward greater importance for the role is strong, and there are likely to be further changes in this direction in the coming years.

Comparing the Brazilian scenario with the United States, using Nelson and Nielsen's (2000) three ideal standards identified in those responsible for the legal department, it is possible to find elements of this transition in Brazil. Thus, many legal directors are moving from solely occupying the role of "cop," perceived as a necessary evil involved in managing the business's legal risks, to the role of "counselor," balancing legal risk management, compliance, and business recommendation. The "entrepreneur," in turn, is still reserved for a small minority, but is desired by many.

We hope that these findings will prompt future research on these important actors. Among the main questions worthy of further investigation are as follows: (1) are OAB rules adequate to discipline the work performed by in-house lawyers and, if not, what should be done? (2) what are the main ethical dilemmas faced by in-house counsel and how are they solved on a day-to-day basis? (3) what happens to legal directors when there is a change in shareholder structure in the company or the main executive is replaced? and

(4) how do in-house counsel assess using arbitration in matters involving the company? These questions, stemming from the discoveries made by this first study, point to the need to set up an extensive research agenda that is in sync with the development of new work standards for legal professionals.

REFERENCES

Análise. 2008a. *Análise Advocacia 500*. São Paulo: Análise Editorial.

2008b. *Executivos Jurídicos e Financeiros*. São Paulo: Análise Editorial.

2009. *Executivos Jurídicos e Financeiros*. São Paulo: Análise Editorial.

2010. *Executivos Jurídicos e Financeiros*. São Paulo: Análise Editorial.

2011. *Executivos Jurídicos e Financeiros*. São Paulo: Análise Editorial.

2012. *Executivos Jurídicos e Financeiros*. São Paulo: Análise Editorial.

2013a. *Análise Advocacia 500*. São Paulo: Análise Editorial.

2013b. *Executivos Jurídicos e Financeiros*. São Paulo: Análise Editorial.

2016a. *Análise Advocacia 500*. São Paulo: Análise Editorial.

2016b. *Executivos Jurídicos e Financeiros*. São Paulo: Análise Editorial.

Chayes, Abram, and Antonia H. Chayes. 1985. "Corporate Counsel and the Elite Law Firm." *Stanford Law Review* 37 (2): 277–300.

Coates, John C., Michele DeStefano, David B. Wilkins, and Ashish Nanda. 2011. "Hiring Teams, Firms and Lawyers: Evidence of the Evolving Relationships in the Corporate Legal Market." *Law and Social Inquiry* 36 (4): 999–1031.

DeStefanto, Michele. 2016. "The Chief Compliance Officer: Should There be a New C in the C-Suite." *The Practice* 2 (5): N.P.

Engelmann, Fabiano. 2012. "Globalização e Poder de Estado: Circulação Internacional de Elites e Hierarquias do Campo Jurídico Brasileiro." *DADOS–Revista de Ciências Sociais* 55 (2): 487–516.

Faria, José Eduardo. 2008. *Direito e Conjuntura*. São Paulo: Saraiva.

Hackett, Susan. 2002. "Inside Out: An Examination of Demographic Trends in the In-House Profession." *Arizona Law Review* 44 (3/4): 609–619

Hendley, Kathryn. 2010. "The Role of In-House Counsel in Post-Soviet Russia in the Wake of Privatization." *International Journal of the Legal Profession* 17 (1): 5–33.

Kanter, Rosabeth M. 1977. *Men and Women of the Corporation*. New York: Basic Books.

Lipson, Jonathan C., Beth Engel, and Jami Crespo. 2012. "Who's in the House? The Changing Nature and Role of In-House and General Counsel." *Wisconsin Law Review* 2012 (2): 237–250.

Nelson, Robert L., and Laura B. Nielsen. 2000. "Cops, Counsel, and Entrepreneurs: Constructing the Role of Inside Counsel in Large Corporations." *Law and Society Review* 34 (2): 457–494.

Ranking Valor 1000. 2013. www.valor.com.br/valor1000/2013/.

Rosen, Robert Eli. 1989. "The Inside Counsel Movement, Professional Judgment and Organizational Representation." *Indiana Law Journal* 64 (3): 479–553.

Rostain, Tanina. 2008. "General Counsel in the Age of Compliance: Preliminary Findings and New Research Questions." *The Georgetown Journal of Legal Ethics* 21 (2): 465–490.

Wilkins, David B. 2012. "Is the In-House Counsel Movement Going Global? A Preliminary Assessment of the Role of Internal Counsel in Emerging Economies." *Wisconsin Law Review* 4 (2): 251–304.
2016. "The In-House Counsel Movement: Metrics of Change." *The Practice* 2 (4): N.P.

4

South by Southeast

Comparing the Development of In-House Legal Departments in Brazil and India

David B. Wilkins and Vikramaditya S. Khanna

I INTRODUCTION

By almost any measure, one of the most significant developments in the corporate legal services market in the United States over the past thirty years has been the growth in the size, stature, and influence of internal legal counsel (Heineman 2016; Wilkins 2012). This "in-house counsel movement," as the American legal scholar Robert Eli Rosen aptly labeled this transformation (Rosen 1989), has been based on three interrelated arguments: *economic value* (i.e., that handling legal work internally is more efficient than hiring outside law firms), *substantive expertise* (i.e., that because of their proximity to the business, in-house lawyers can give better advice than outside counsel), and *professional independence* (i.e., that because general counsel are better able to understand and protect the company's long-term interests and reputation than law firm partners that they are more likely to uphold the legal profession's traditional ideal of the "lawyer statesman" who counsels clients to conform their conduct to the public purposes of the legal system) (Kronman 1993; Heineman 2016).

By the turn of the millennium, internal lawyers in the United States had successfully deployed these arguments to transform themselves from "house counsels" to "general counsels" to "chief legal officers," with income, power, and prestige within their organizations equivalent to other members of the corporate "C" suite, and a pivotal role in shaping the structures, norms and practices of the legal profession as a whole (Coates et al. 2011). Although originally only an American phenomenon, during the first decade of the twenty first century the movement spread to the United Kingdom and Western Europe, playing a critical role in transforming the role of internal counsel in these jurisdictions as well (Saiko 2011; Wilkins 2012).

In the preceding chapter, Oliveira and Ramos present compelling evidence that some version of the in-house counsel movement has come to Brazil. Although there are important deviations from the role that inside lawyers play in the United States, the authors demonstrate that the GCs of Brazilian companies – often called legal directors – have increased their power and status across all six of the dimensions prior research has identified as hallmarks of the in-house counsel movement: (1) the overall size of the legal department, (2) the demographic and educational profile of in-house lawyers (particularly of the GC), (3) the degree of control over external law firms and other legal providers, (4) the prestige and authority of the GC within the company, (5) the status of in-house counsel within the legal profession as a whole, and (6) the participation and influence of GCs within wider debates over legislation and public policy (Wilkins 2012; see also Chapter 3 in this volume).[1]

In this chapter, we compare the Brazilian experience on these issues with prior research on the status of internal counsel in another important emerging economy: India (Wilkins and Khanna 2017). We do so on the basis of a survey of GCs conducted in both countries as part of an ongoing effort by the Harvard Law School Center on the Legal Profession to study the changing role of in-house lawyers around the world (Wilkins and Khanna 2017; Wilkins 2012; Coates et al. 2011). In Section III, we present the findings from the surveys we conducted of general counsels in Brazil and in India. In addition to documenting similarities and differences in how the in-house counsel movement is unfolding in the two countries, this section also highlights differences among companies within each jurisdiction, and the potential implications of these differences for the development of each countries' legal market. Finally, Section IV concludes by examining the implications of our findings for the overall development of the role of GCs in the Global South.

Before proceeding with our analysis, however, it is important to situate our findings about Brazilian and Indian GCs within a broader comparative analysis of the respective position of these two important emerging economies, and their historic and contemporary connection to the forces that produced the in-house counsel movement in the Global North. Section II therefore begins with these issues.

[1] As Oliveira and Ramos note, there is more heterogeneity with respect to the exact title afforded to the executive in charge of the legal department/function in Brazil While "legal director" is the most frequent designation, others include "legal manager" and "vice president-legal." For more on this topic, see Chapter 3 by Oliveira and Ramos.

II EMERGING ALONG DIFFERENT PATHS: A BRIEF HISTORY OF BRAZIL'S AND INDIA'S RELATIONSHIPS TO ANGLO-AMERICAN MODES OF THE PRODUCTION OF LAW

As indicated in Chapter 1, there is significant reason to believe that the processes of globalization – *economic globalization* and the growing integration of emerging economies such as Brazil and India into the wider global economy, the *globalization of knowledge* through formal and informal transfers of people and ideas between the developed and developing worlds, and the *globalization of governance* in the form of transnational regulation and organizations – are spreading a version of the Anglo-American Model of lawyering around the world. These forces are likely to be especially important in spreading the in-house counsel movement. For example, as economic globalization produces the "global shift" that leads countries such as Brazil and India to integrate their economies (more or less) into global markets, a growing number of multinational companies based in the Global North have set up operations in these increasingly important jurisdictions. As these investments increase in size and importance, it stands to reason that companies will want the same level of support and protection from their in-house lawyers operating in emerging markets as they receive from their GCs back home. Similarly, as the national – and increasingly multinational – companies based in countries such as Brazil and India seek to capture a greater share of the shift in economic globalization toward emerging markets, it is plausible that these companies will look to emulate the model of the general counsel used by the foreign multinational companies (FMNCs) with which they compete, particularly as these new world companies expand their own operations outside of their home markets.

The globalization of knowledge and governance are likely to reinforce this trend. Thus, as lawyers trained in the United States and other jurisdictions steeped in the in-house counsel movement are hired by companies based or operating in emerging markets one would expect to see them attempt to incorporate at least some of the movement's tenets into their new positions. The fact that many of these new in-house lawyers have joined professional organizations such as the Association of Corporate Counsel whose mission is to spread the movement's gospel is likely to reinforce this trend. Finally, there are reasons to think that the globalization of governance will drive home the value of this new model of in-house lawyering as the growing complexity and reach of national, regional, and global regulation place a premium on the ability to integrate law with business that GCs credibly claim to be able to deploy.

There is, however, certainly no guarantee that economic globalization, the globalization of knowledge, and the globalization of governance will necessarily produce sophisticated in-house counsel, let alone that the general counsel that do emerge from these new environments will look exactly like their US counterparts. However, there is a growing body of literature indicating that the processes of globalization are changing the role and function of in-house lawyers in many emerging economies (Wilkins 2012; Heineman 2016; Wilkins and Khanna 2017).

Nevertheless, there are likely to be important country-specific differences to the basic model. Brazil and India present a good laboratory to explore these differences. Notwithstanding their joint status as rising powers, there are significant differences among these superficially similar member of the BRICS quintet. It is reasonable to think that these differences will impact how the in-house counsel movement develops in each country. Three differences appear particularly salient to this discussion: economic structures, proximity and exposure to the "West," and the state of the legal profession. We review each in turn.

A *Economic Structures*

As indicated above, economic globalization is a major factor leading to the spread of the in-house counsel movement. Although this factor is clearly at play in both Brazil and India, the economies of the two countries nevertheless differ significantly. Since the 1990s, both countries have benefited greatly from economic globalization. However, their rates of economic growth have varied over time, with India's being far more robust recently than Brazil's. Indeed, India is now viewed as the shining star of the BRICS (Brazil, Russia, India, China, and South Africa) countries, and one of the most dynamic economies in the world (Nataraj 2016). In contrast, after soaring high for the first decade of the twenty-first century, Brazil's economy has faced numerous challenges in recent years, due initially to the slowdown in the commodities market (itself, in part, because of China's slowed growth) and more recently due to the country's tumultuous political crisis (European Central Bank 2016; BBC News 2016). These different rates of growth in different time periods plausibly affect how economic globalization is likely to shape the development of the in-house counsel movement in each country.

The structural character of the corporate sector also differs between the two economies. Although both countries have a significant number of family-owned businesses, companies with this structure have a far greater share of the Indian economy than they do in Brazil. As we documented in our study of Indian GCs, "business groups," as such promoter-owned businesses are referred to in India, account for nearly 49 percent of India's market capitalization, with business groups controlled by powerful families such as the Tatas, Mahindras, and Ambanis ranking among the largest and most important companies in the country (Wilkins and Khanna 2017). Brazil, by contrast, is home to some of the world's most powerful multinational companies, such as Vale, Embrar Air, and (until the recent scandals) Petrobras, making the country a leader among developing economies in outbound investment (Fundacao Getulio Vargas and Columbia Center on Sustainable Investment 2016). As we will see, these differences in the structure of the economy also affect the structure and functioning of in-house legal departments in the two countries.

Finally, India's population is much larger than that of Brazil, by about a factor of six, and its economy is arguably more varied. This greater size and variety may also impact the development of in-house legal departments as different companies and industries develop their own approaches to internal lawyering.

B *Proximity and Exposure to the "West"*

As indicated above, the inside counsel revolution began in the United States. It is therefore plausible that an emerging market's proximity and exposure to America, and to the Global North generally – whether in terms of business flows, educational connections, and/or cultural ties – increases that jurisdiction's likelihood of adopting key elements of the Anglo-American model of legal practice, relative to countries that have had less of this kind of contact. Both Brazil and India now have close economic ties with the United States and Western Europe. But a closer examination of the timing and extent of these ties highlight important differences.

These differences begin in each country's colonial history. Brazil gained independence from Portugal in the mid-nineteenth century. India's independence from the United Kingdom came nearly a century later in 1947. This greater period of colonial rule has left its mark on India, including on the development of the country's emerging corporate legal sector. For example, as Nanda, Wilkins, and Fong document, India's large–law firm sector can trace its roots back to the British Raj firms that played a key role in managing the country's economic relationship with England (Wilkins et al. 2017).

While the Big 5 law firms that developed in India during the 1990s were influenced by the United Kingdom's approach to corporate legal practice (even as these firms also sought to distinguish themselves from this older model in ways that Nanda, Wilkins, and Fong document, this same historical model provided very little precedent for in-house lawyers to have a significant role either within their company or in the profession generally) (Wilkins et al. 2017). There were no sophisticated internal lawyers in England during India's colonial period, and even as late as the 1990s when India's corporate sector began to develop in earnest, even the largest UK companies lagged considerably behind their US counterparts in embracing the tenants of the in-house counsel movement (Wilkins 2012). It is therefore not surprising that India's rising corporate elite, which continued to look to the United Kingdom for guidance in many fields including law, was slow to embrace the role of sophisticated internal lawyering.

Paradoxically, the fact that Brazil cut formal ties with Portugal at an earlier period may have left it freer to develop "new" models of legal practice that borrowed from the country's increasing ties to the United States, which due to its geographic proximity and economic power not surprisingly exerted considerable influence. And, by the time that Brazil's corporate sector began its rapid development in the 1990s, the American version of the in-house counsel movement was firmly underway. This process of transplantation (which, as we will see was only partial) has arguably been accelerated by the globalization of knowledge. Beginning in the 1950s, and accelerating throughout the 1960s and 1970s, Brazil deepened its ties with the United States as a growing number of the country's elite, including elite lawyers, opted to pursue graduate education (including LLMs and other advanced law degrees) in the United States, as opposed to in Europe where the prior generation of elite Brazilian lawyers had trained. By the 1980s and 1990s, these leading lawyers were being exposed to many aspects of the American Mode of the Production of Law, mostly through the "informal" curriculum of the job market and the legal press, including the growing importance of in-house legal departments. Although most of these lawyers went into Brazil's growing number of elite corporate law firms, as documented below some were eventually hired by multinational and Brazilian companies seeking to build more sophisticated internal legal capacity.

India's postcolonial legal elite, by contrast, was introduced to quite different legal models. As the GLEE project has documented elsewhere, India's transition to independence was dramatic, dominated by the ascension of a new elite that had been excluded from power during the colonial era (Gupta et al. 2017). Shortly after independence, India elected a socialist government committed to regulating virtually every aspect of the economy and effectively cut the country off from significant contact with the West. As a result, the country's reference points for the legal profession during this period came either from the United Kingdom's traditional approach, which valorized the practice of Barrister's in the High Courts, or the "new" approach to lawyering being created by the Soviet Union, India's friend and benefactor during this period. As Galanter and Robinson underscore, echoes of this postindependence period can still be found in the prominence of India's Grand Advocates (Galanter and Robinson 2017). One can also trace the low status of in-house counsel to Soviet practices, practice that continued in Russia long after that country had formally abandoned the command and control economy that shaped this approach to internal lawyering (Hendley 2001, 2010).

Although Brazil also experienced a certain amount of isolation during the period of military rule in the early 1980s, the degree to which the country was cut off from the West was far less severe than in India, allowing for much more interchange with the United States and others as the country developed its corporate hemisphere in the years following the return to civilian rule. The fact that the Association of Corporate Counsel, which was originally an American association but since 2003 has made it a priority to expand globally, has had a Brazilian chapter for several years but still does not have one in India underscores the degree to which India's corporate counsel sector continues to be relatively isolated from developments in the West. As we describe in more detail below, this solution is undoubtedly reinforced by the severe restrictions that India places on the entry of foreign lawyers (Wilkins et al. 2017).

Finally, India's relative isolation from Anglo-American corporate models, which tend to emphasize dispersed ownership and transparency, has also allowed India's traditional kinship and communal networks to play a far greater role in the economy in general, and the market for legal services in particular, than similar traditional social structures have played in Brazil. India represents a much older civilization than Brazil, and its social structures are therefore much more ingrained and resistant to change.[2] These networks both make possible and reinforce the dominance of promoter-driven capitalism described above. But as we saw in our research in India, the continued dominance of this underlying social structure also privilege a more relational and inward looking model of the company's chief legal officer that downplays the

2 This is not to say that traditional patterns of interaction and subordination play no role in the Brazilian economy and in the country's legal profession. As Bonilla demonstrates in Chapter 5, gender hierarchies remain potent in Brazil's contemporary corporate legal market, and there is significant evidence that racial and class hierarchies have proven even more resistant to change. For issues regarding Brazil and race (Adilson Moreira 2016). Nevertheless, it is widely understood that India's caste, clan, and communal networks are particularly powerful, and as we found in our research in that country, continue to pervade every aspect of economic life, including the corporate legal sector (Gupta et al. 2017).

importance of independence and legal expertise in a way that is at odds with core commitments of the in-house counsel movement (Wilkins and Khanna 2017). Brazil's greater openness to Western (particularly American) corporate investment, including investment in Brazil's emerging corporate legal services market through the presence of foreign law firms, is likely to make it more open to the American model of internally lawyering as well.

C *The State of the Legal Profession*

The Indian and Brazilian legal professions also have marked differences in structure and regulation. In India, most legal practice has historically centered around litigation and court procedures, and very few firms specialize in corporate law. As a result, until the mid-1990s there were no even moderately large corporate law firms or in-house departments. By contrast, in the 1960s in Brazil there was already one relatively large corporate law firm, Pinheiro Neto, and a few multinationals operating in Brazil even had significant in-house legal departments, including Union Carbide, Goodyear, Cargill, and Brazil Light (Chapter 3).[3] Once again, this reflects the heavy regulatory hand of the state in postindependence India during the so-called "License Raj," which both limited the scope for corporate law practice and placed strong restrictions on foreign investment. Apart from the period of military rule, Brazil was far more open to foreign trade and investment, and did not dictate commercial matters to nearly as great an extent as India.

Brazil's more open approach than India's to the entry of foreign lawyers in the intervening years is also likely to be relevant to the diffusion of the American model of in-house lawyering. As Chapter 6 on regulation in this volume documents, the Brazilian Bar Association or OAB has consistently allowed foreign law firms to open offices in Brazil, and even to hire Brazilian lawyers, so long as they don't practice Brazilian law. Although the boundary delineated by this restriction has proved contentious over the years, there are currently several foreign law firms operating in Brazil, the overwhelming majority of which are based in the United States (Chapter 2). India, by contrast, is one of the last countries to bar foreign law firms from having any formal presence in the country (Singh 2017). Although these restrictions have not stopped global law

[3] As one of the editors of this book recalled, when he had to find a law firm to help him with a major loan transaction while serving in Brazil as an AID official in the 1960s, he engaged Pinheiro Neto because they closely resembled the New York law firms that he was familiar with in the United States. See also Oliveira and Ramos, Chapter 3, reporting that in the 1960s and 1970s, multinationals operating in Brazil typically hired Pinheiro Neto and Demarest Almeida for "more complex and out of the ordinary issues."

firms (primarily from the United Kingdom) from serving the Indian corporate market by "flying in and flying out" to meet clients and close transactions, this difference in regulation is likely to further exacerbate the differences between the two countries with respect to the diffusion of Anglo-American corporate models.

As Chapter 2 on Brazil's corporate legal sector documents, the law firms that developed in the 1990s have adopted many of the managerial practices – formal and professionalized lines of authority, an emphasis on branding and business development, offering a full range of services but with an emphasis on mergers and acquisitions and other sophisticated corporate work – typical of neo-Cravathist firms in the United States. Consistent with the point made above about the globalization of knowledge, some of these firm were founded by expatriates with experience in large law firms in the United States who settled in Brazil, or by Brazilians with overseas experience (see Krishnan et al. 2016). The same has not been true with respect to India's first generation corporate law firms in the 1990s, which have been slow to adopt many of these neo-Cravathist practices and which continue to be run more as "family" business (Wilkins et al. 2017). Indeed as Krishnan documents, many of India's "second generation" corporate law firms established after 2000s were formed by lawyers who "peeled off" from the country's Big 5 law firms precisely because of their disappointment in the fact that these first generation corporate firms were failing to adopt key aspects of the Anglo-American model (Krishnan 2017).

Once again, these differences in the two countries' legal field plausibly affect the extent and timing of the potential diffusion of the in-house counsel movement. As with the differences in macroeconomic structure and proximity to the West discussed above, it is important to keep these regulatory issues in mind as we compare the results of our survey of general counsels in these two rising powers.

III CONVERGING ON THE IN-HOUSE COUNSEL MOVEMENT

In this Part, we present the results of our survey of GCs in Brazil and India. Section IIIA briefly sets the stage by providing a snapshot of the status of the in-house counsel movement in the United States circa 2007, along with the six factors that we will use to benchmark Brazil's and India's legal departments and to compare the two with each other. Section IIIB discusses our research methodology and presents an overview of the size and characteristics of the companies we surveyed in each jurisdiction. Sections IIIC–IIIG compare developments in Brazil and India along the five areas explored in our survey.

A *The Standard: In-House Legal Departments in Large US Companies*

As indicated above, the in-house movement originated in the United States and has arguably reached its fullest expression in the practices of large US companies. In 2006–2007, the Harvard Law School Center on the Legal Profession conducted a study designed to test some of the movement's claims, particularly with regard to how companies purchase legal services for "very important matters" (Coates et al. 2011). The study, entitled "The Corporate Purchasing Project," consisted of a series of in-depth interviews with GCs ($n = 44$) in three sectors – banking, pharmaceuticals, and energy – that have historically been significant consumers of legal services, and a survey of a large percentage of the GCs in S&P 500 companies ($n = 139$, or 28 percent). Together, these two methodologies provided a comprehensive and representative sample of the structures and practices of large US companies. Although the study's primary purpose was to test the effects of the decline in information asymmetry between companies and their outside law firms as a result of hiring sophisticated GCs, the study also collected a significant amount of qualitative and quantitative information on the general structure and practices of internal legal departments in the sampled companies. Based on this information, one of the study's primary authors subsequently identified six factors that can be used as a benchmark to assess the extent to which a given legal department has embraced the tenets of the in-house counsel movement (Wilkins 2012). They are as follows:

1. *size*, with many GC offices now rivaling the size of major law firms (Baker and Parkin 2006; Coates et al. 2011)
2. *credentials and identity*, with internal law departments becoming a premier employment destination for top associates and partners from large law firms, especially among women (Dinovitzer et al. 2012; Neil 2011)
3. *control over the legal function*, with inside lawyers now acting as the primary diagnostician of the company's legal problems, and the chief purchasing agent for outside legal services (Schwarcz 2008; Coates et al. 2011)
4. *expanded responsibility and membership in senior leadership*, with most GCs reporting directly to the CEO, overseeing functions adjacent to the legal department (e.g., public relations, government affairs, human relations, compliance), and serving on senior leadership teams with jurisdiction over strategy and other major corporate decisions (Morrison 2006; Coates et al. 2011)
5. *professional status*, with GCs increasingly viewed as equal – and in many respects dominant – members of the legal profession who exercise

significant authority over the profession's norms and practices (Wilkins 2012)

6. *influence over public policy*, with GCs in the United States exercising important influence, both individually and through collective action by the Association of Corporate Counsel and other similar organizations, over important public policy issues, both domestically and globally (Rostain 2008; Coates et al. 2011)

TABLE 4.1 *US in-house legal departments circa 2007*

Variable	US in-house movement
Size	Grown dramatically since the 1980s; large corporations have GC offices that rival the size of large outside law firms
Credentials and identities	Almost all are lawyers and members of the bar; a large percentage of in-house lawyers are female
Control over the legal function	Largely select outside counsel and manage the relationship.
Internal reporting relationships	Commonly report to the CEO
Linkages with the profession	Important players in the profession with increasing influence throughout
Role in public policy	Active role in public policy with regular interactions with government

Collectively these six changes provide empirical support for the economic, substantive, and professional claims made by in-house counsel in the United States, and increasingly in the rest of the Global North. Table 4.1 summarizes these findings.

In the prior chapter, Oliveira and Ramos rely on a mix of qualitative interviews and publicly available data to conclude that Brazilian internal legal departments now exemplify some – but certainly not all – of these characteristics (Chapter 3 in this volume). In this chapter, we extend this analysis by examining the results of a survey of large Brazilian companies that allows us both to further refine Oliveira and Ramos's analysis of the spread of the in-house counsel movement in Brazil, but also to compare the extent and character of this transformation with what is currently taking place in this sector in India.

B *Methods*

In 2011, the Center on the Legal Profession launched a major research initiative to extend and deepen the findings of the US Corporate Purchasing

TABLE 4.2 *Survey topics*

Background information
Company background
Description of the legal department
Job responsibilities of the general counsel
Legal department budget
Hiring legal department lawyers
Legal department policies
Legal needs
Hiring outside law firms
Terminating outside law firms
Legal work and needs
Career background and history of the general counsel
Demographics
General comments

Project by investigating the changing role of general counsel around the world. As part of this initiative, the Project on Globalization, Lawyers, and Emerging Economies (GLEE) developed a survey to determine whether the kind of changes we chronicled in the United States were spreading to emerging economies in Asia, Latin America, and Africa. (The Center is also planning to resurvey large US companies, to examine how these departments have changed since the GFC, and to conduct a similar survey in the United Kingdom and Western Europe.) The questionnaire is quite extensive – consisting of more than 100 questions – and is designed to provide a comprehensive picture of an in-house legal department's demographics, structure, and function. Table 4.2 sets out the topics covered.

GLEE began collecting data using this survey in both India and Brazil in 2014. (A similar survey is currently underway in China, and one will be launched in several African countries in 2017.) The survey targeted "large" users of legal services with the goal of collecting a representative sample of both domestic and foreign multinational companies (FMNCs) operating in each jurisdiction. Data collection ended in both countries primarily in 2015 (with a few surveys completed in 2016). As Table 4.3 demonstrates, the sample of participating companies in the two countries are similar with respect to the number of responding firms (sixty-three in Brazil; seventy-four in India), and virtually identical with respect to the percentage of the country's overall market capitalization that the surveyed firms represent (29 percent in Brazil; 27 percent in India). Moreover, both percentages underestimate the total value of the companies in each sample because a number of the responding firms, although quite large, are either privately held or not publicly traded

TABLE 4.3 *Sample compared to the market*

	Market cap of responding firms[a]	Market (BSE/BOVESPA)[a]	Percentage of sample/market capitalization	No. respondents
India	INR 1,668,000	INR 6,226,491.35	27	74
Brazil	BRR** 732,480,000	BRR 2,528,604,597	29	63

[a] Market cap information in Brazil from November 2016. Market cap information in India from November 2015. Data rounded to the nearest thousand.

on the Brazilian or Indian stock exchange respectively. As a result, our sample of companies represents an even greater share of each country's economic activity – and therefore, plausibly its market for legal services – than the above percentages would suggest. This is particularly true in Brazil, where only thirteen of our responding firms – all Brazilian companies – are listed on the Brazilian stock exchange. Yet, these firms represent an astounding 29 percent of the total market capitalization of the Brazilian exchange. As this percentage suggests, Brazil's capital market is highly concentrated (Antunes 2014), with significantly fewer listed firms than in India.[4] Given that we have another fifty firms in our Brazil sample, some of which are FMNCs with quite large presences in the country, it is clear that the surveyed firms account for a significant share of the Brazilian legal market.

Table 4.4 on ownership structures underscores that the two samples also contain a broad range of different kinds of companies, although it also highlights an important difference between the structure of the Brazilian and Indian economies alluded to above. As indicated in Section II, India's economy continues to be dominated by family-owned "business groups," the largest of which are among the most important companies in the country. Brazil, on the other hand, has fewer such companies, although family businesses remain important. At the same time, Brazil has a greater number of FMNCs than India, given the former country's relatively open stance toward foreign direct investment, as opposed to India's continued efforts to limit such investment in important sectors of the economy such as multibrand retail (*Economic Times* 2016). Our samples reflect these national differences.

[4] Brazil has approximately 350 publicly traded firms, compared to approximately 4,000 in India. Of course, some of India's firms are not traded with great frequency and, as we indicated above, India's population is nearly six times that of Brazil's. But these differences are important to keep in mind since they may affect the market in ways that are not fully captured by our data.

TABLE 4.4 *Ownership structure*

	Percentage of sample		No. firms		No. firms by type in market (%)	
	Brazil	India	Brazil	India	Brazil	India
Family/Business Group	22%	46%	14	34	30%	33%
Non-Family/Non-Business Group	24%	11%	15	8	53%	58%
FMNC	51%	26%	32	19	10%	6%
SOEs	3%	18%	2	13	7%	3%

22 percent of our Brazilian sample comes from family/business group owned businesses, which is roughly representative of the percentage of such businesses (30 percent) in the Brazilian economy. The percentage of business groups in our India sample (46 percent) is higher than the share of such companies in the Indian economy (33 percent). As we indicated in our prior analysis of the Indian general counsel market, we especially targeted such firms to give us greater insight into their role important role in the Indian economy, and because we hypothesized that such companies might use internal counsel in ways that were significantly different than other Indian firms. Similarly, 51 percent of our Brazilian sample is composed of FMNCs operating in that country, whereas only 26 percent of Indian firms surveyed fall into this category. Although both percentages are significantly greater than the percentage of FMNCs in each country, the relative weighting is correct. FMNCs make up a significantly larger share of the absolute number of companies in Brazil (10 percent) than they do in India (6 percent).

More importantly, the fact that even with such a large number of foreign firms, our sample still constitutes 29 percent of Brazil's stock market underscores that even without these FMNCs, we have captured a very large share of the Brazilian marketplace. Moreover, as we indicated, our research methodology targeted the largest users of legal services in each country. The fact that this strategy resulted in such a large number of FMNCs in Brazil therefore is likely to reflect the importance that these entities play in the Brazilian economy. Given that GCs in domestic companies are likely to get many of their cues about the tenets of the in-house counsel movement from their interaction with their counterparts in FMNCs, this difference is also likely to be reflected in the model's diffusion in Brazil as well. In any event, as we make clear in the survey, we asked GCs working in FMNCs in both jurisdictions to provide information only about their Brazilian or Indian operations respectively, so even with a significant representation of such firms in both samples we are still only capturing developments within each country. Throughout our analysis, however, we will distinguish between FMNCs and Brazilian domestic firms (of all types) to highlight any potential differences between the two groups.

There is, however, one sector where our sample of Brazilian firms is not representative. There are only two state-owned enterprises (SOEs) in our sample of Brazilian companies. Although both companies are among the largest companies in Brazil, the total number of such companies is too small to do any meaningful comparisons, either with other types of Brazilian companies, or with India's SOE sector, where our sample is more representative.

Given these sample characteristics, for most of what follows we restrict our analysis to a comparison between "domestic firms" and "FMNCs" in each jurisdiction, although we note where the underlying data suggests that these broad differences may be driven by the prevalence of "business groups" or "SOEs" within the particular market. The next five sections present our findings along the following dimensions investigated by the survey: the GC's background and career (Section IIIC); the size and organization of the legal department (Section IIID); the GC's job responsibilities and reporting requirements (Section IIIE); the relationship with outside firms and other providers (Section IIIF); and the GC's participation in public policy debates (Section IIIG).

C *The Man – or Woman – behind the Movement*

At the core of the in-house movement is a claim about the person who assumes the leadership role in the in-house legal department of the twenty first century. Tables 4.5 and 4.6 describe the backgrounds, credentials, and job histories of the responding GCs in Brazil and India. Both tables provide evidence that the in-house counsel movement has made in-roads in each jurisdiction, but also underscores some of the differences between Brazil and India suggested above.

Consistent with expectations, Table 4.5 underscores that GCs in both Brazil and India are an elite group. In both countries, these leading company lawyers come from high status backgrounds. Thus in each country, the GCs in our sample are overwhelmingly likely to come from families in which their father had at least a college degree (79 percent in Brazil and 74 percent in India). However, the Brazilian GCs in our sample arguably hale from even more elite backgrounds than their Indian counterparts, with 62 percent also having mothers who have obtained at least a college level education, compared to

TABLE 4.5 *Demographics and credentials*

	All		Domestic		FMNC	
	Brazil	India	Brazil	India	Brazil	India
Male GCs (%)	75%	89%	74%	89%	75%	89%
Age of GC (average)	42	48	41	49	44	47
LLM earned (%)	48%	24%	55%	14%	47%	32%
Mother's education (college+) (%)	62%	47%	65%	38%	59%	74%
Father's education (college+) (%)	79%	74%	71%	73%	87%	79%
No one in immediate family with legal education (%)	27%	53%	14%	53%	34%	53%
Current/former member of the Brazilian/Indian bar (%)	95%	59%	100%	56%	89%	68%
Never a member of the Brazilian/Indian bar (%)	5%	30%	0%	31%	11%	26%
Currently a member of another country's bar (%)	9%	4%	4%	2%	14%	5%

47 percent of GCs in India. Even more telling, 47 percent of Indian GCs come from families where there is at least one lawyer in the family, compared to 73 percent of the Brazilian GCs in our sample.

Perhaps most importantly of all for the core precepts of the in-house counsel movement, virtually all (95 percent) of the Brazilian GCs we sampled were currently or had at one time been members of the Brazilian bar – a percentage comparable to that found in the United States and other countries where the in-house counsel movement has firmly taken hold. By contrast, in India only 59 percent of GCs could claim this designation. Although this percentage is undoubtedly higher than it was for most of India's history, where

TABLE 4.6 *Job history of the general counsel*

	All		Domestic		FMNC	
	Brazil	India	Brazil	India	Brazil	India
Mean tenure of GC at firm (years)	6.41	9.74	6.39	9.96	6.44	9.06
Mean tenure of GC as GC (years)	4.40	5.35	4.23	4.90	4.56	6.71
GC promoted from within (%)	44%	39%	42%	42%	47%	38%
Previously worked at another company (%)	62%	57%	58%	55%	66%	63%
Previously worked at a law firm (%)	30%	11%	32%	9%	28%	16%
Previously worked at other (e.g., government) (%)	8%	26%	10%	31%	6%	11%

the person in charge of a company's legal matters often was qualified as a "company secretary" and not a lawyer, it nevertheless highlights that India has been slower than Brazil to embrace the in-house counsel movement's requirement that the GC should have professional status Nor are these differences explained by the higher percentage of FMNCs in our Brazilian sample. Across both foreign and domestic companies, Brazilian GCs come from more elite backgrounds and have more professional status than their Indian counterparts. Indeed, Brazilian GCs in domestic companies are more likely to have an LLM degree – 55 percent – than Indian GCs working in FMNCs – 32 percent.

The fact that Brazilian GCs are far more likely to be female further reinforces the conclusion that the in-house counsel movement has established deeper roots in this country than it has in India. Although nearly three-quarters of GCs in Brazil are men (75 percent), this is still significantly less than the nearly nine out of ten (89 percent) who are male in India. In addition to reflecting another core tenet of the in-house counsel movement – that internal counsel positions are attractive destinations for talented lawyers, especially for women – the greater representation of women in Brazil is also likely correlated with the fact that Brazilian GCs are five years younger on average than those in India. Taken together the greater prevalence of younger GCs, many of whom are female, is likely to lead Brazil's GCs to be more open to new ideas about the proper role of internal counsel.

A comparison of the career histories of Brazilian versus Indian GCs (Table 4.6) further reinforces this general pattern. For example, although Brazilian GCs are somewhat more likely to have been promoted from within then their Indian counterparts (44 percent Brazil; 39 percent India), Brazilian GC have occupied the GC seat for less time than their Indian counterparts (4.40 years in Brazil vs. 5.35 years in India), and spent considerably less time (6.41 years vs. 9.74 years) at their current employer. Together, these findings suggest that there may be more mobility in the Brazilian in-house legal market than in India, another sign of its maturity under the criteria of the in-house counsel movement.

More importantly, Brazilian GCs are far more likely to have worked at a law firm before assuming their current position than GCs in India (30 percent Brazil, 11 percent India). Indian GCs, on the other hand, are much more likely to have worked in positions other than law firms or in-house legal departments, such as government, during their careers (26 percent vs. 8 percent) than their Brazilian counterparts. These differences once again suggest that Brazil's in-house legal market is closer to the American model where GCs

TABLE 4.7 *Size of in-house department*

	All		Domestic		FMNC	
	Brazil	India	Brazil	India	Brazil	India
Average number of lawyers in country	30	29	33	33	27	16
Median number of lawyers in country	9	12	8	10	10.5	13.5
In-house lawyers who are women (%)	59%	32%	53%	32%	65%	32%
Increase in number of lawyers (past three years) (%)	65%	64%	45%	67%	82%	53%
Expected increase, next three years (%)	25%	66%	36%	67%	16%	63%
Number of nonlawyer professionals	38	7	63	7	14	8

frequently come from law firms, whereas the profile of Indian GCs reflects the legacy of the "License Raj" discussed in Section II. Indeed, when combined with the 62 percent of our sample of Brazilian GCs who had worked in another company before assuming their current position, it is clear that a large segment of top in-house lawyers in Brazil have had at least some relevant experience before assuming their current role.

D *The Legal Department*

A key signal of the growing prominence of in-house counsel in the United States has been the increase in the overall size of in-house legal departments, the budgets these departments control, and in the credentials and experience of the lawyers working within internal legal departments. Tables 4.7 and 4.8 present what our surveys revealed about these issues for Brazilian and Indian in-house legal departments.

With respect to overall size, Table 4.7 underscores that both Brazilian and Indian GC offices are relatively small compared to their US counterparts. Thus, the average number of lawyers stationed in-country in the legal departments of each country was thirty (Brazil) and twenty-nine (India), with the median number of lawyers being respectively nine and twelve.[5] These numbers are well below what we found in our survey of the legal departments of S&P 500 companies in the United States, where the average

[5] The survey also asked for the total number of lawyers employed by responding firms worldwide. For present purposes, we exclude lawyers outside of Brazil and India so as not to skew the comparison between the two countries due to the greater percentage of foreign multinationals in our Brazilian sample.

TABLE 4.8 *Budgets*

	Mean (USD)		Percentage change (%)		Range of budget of outside lawyers (%)	
	Brazil	India	Brazil	India	Brazil	India
All						
2009	6,690,000	2,957,000	–	–	51–60%	51–60%
2012	13,361,000	3,526,000	67%	18%	51–60%	51–60%
2014–2015	17,889,000	4,286,000	29%	19%	51–60%	51–60%
Change 2009–2015	–	–	91%	37%	–	–
Domestic						
2009	5,443,000	1,579,000	–	–	51–60%	51–60%
2012	6,801,000	1,820,000	22%	14%	51–60%	51–60%
2014–2015	9,066,000	2,199,000	29%	19%	51–60%	51–60%
Change 2009–2015	–	–	50%	33%	–	–
FMNC						
2009	7,936,000	259,000	–	–	61–70%	61–70%
2012	19,907,000	611,000	86%	81%	51–60%	51–60%
2014–2015	26,326,000	697,000	28%	13%	51–60%	51–60%
Change 2009–2015	–	–	107%	92%	–	–

Note: Budgets rounded to nearest thousand. All figures are pegged to the 2009 US dollar.

number of lawyers in-house was sixty-five with a median of thirty-five (Coates et al. 2011).

Although relatively small in absolute size, however, almost two-thirds of respondents in both Brazil (65 percent) and India (64 percent) reported that their legal departments had increased in size in the last three years. Interestingly, while GCs in both countries expected their departments to expand in size even further in the next three years, Indian GCs were more than twice as likely to report that they expected further growth in the next three years (66 percent) than their Brazilian counterparts (25 percent). This difference in expectations between Indian and Brazilian GCs about future growth in the legal department was true for all domestic companies, although in an analysis not reported here, almost three-quarters (74 percent) of Indian business group GCs expected to increase the size of their legal departments in the coming three years. This large percentage arguably reflects the fact alluded to in Section II that these departments may still be undersized relative to the size and growing global reach of India's Business groups (Wilkins and Khanna 2017).

It may also be part of a general pattern, also reflected in Table 4.7, that India's in-house legal departments are much more likely to employ a significant number of nonlawyers than their Brazilian counterparts. On average, more than half (56 percent) of those working in such departments in Brazil were nonlawyers compared to just 19 percent in India. Once again, this difference is consistent with the overall picture that Brazil's legal departments have internalized more of the ethos of the in-house counsel movement, perhaps because of the country's greater openness and proximity to the West.

Finally, the percentage of women employed in legal departments is significantly greater (59 percent) in Brazil than it is in Indian in-house counsel offices (32 percent). These percentages are consistent for both domestic companies and FMNCs, as well as with the publicly reported numbers in the legal magazine *Analise* reported by Oliveira and Ramos (Chapter 3). Although significantly higher than the percentage of female GCs reported above, Brazil's in-house legal departments are far more reflective of the overall representation of women in the legal profession than are those in India. This suggests that the new "scripts" that have allowed women to succeed in India's large–law firm sector (Ballakrishnen 2017) may not be operating in that country's in-house counsel sector. Only time will tell whether the greater percentage of women employed in the lower ranks of the legal departments of Brazilian companies will eventually be reflected in a greater percentage of female GCs in these organizations. For now, however, it is clear that Brazilian companies are closer to the US model of gender integration captured by the in-house counsel movement than comparable companies in India.

Table 4.8 examines the budgets across GC offices in Brazil and India. These numbers reveal dramatic differences between the overall size of the legal budgets in these two important emerging economies, and their relative increase over time. Consistent with the basic hypothesis that the in-house counsel movement is spreading in these two countries, both Brazilian and Indian companies experienced important increases in the size of their legal budgets in the period from 2009 to 2015. But this overall growth belies important differences in both scale, pace, and location. Thus, while Indian legal department budgets grew by 37 percent in constant 2009 US dollars during this period, the budgets of companies operating in Brazil in our sample grew by almost three times as much (91 percent) in percentage terms during this same period.

Moreover, when one compares the two country's legal budgets in absolute terms, the difference is even starker. On average, Brazilian legal departments in 2015 allocated over four times the legal budget as companies operating in India ($17,889,000 Brazil, $4,286,000 India). This difference in absolute legal spend is greatest for FMNCs operating in the two jurisdictions. Although FMNCs in each jurisdiction experienced comparable rates of growth in percentage terms during this period (107 percent Brazil, 92 percent India), the dollars allocated to the legal departments were radically different. In 2015, the average FMNC in allocated only $697,000 to the legal department – an amount equal to approximately one-third of the $2,199,000 that Indian domestic companies set aside for the legal department that same year. By contrast, the average legal department of an FMNC in Brazil had a budget of $26,326,000 in 2015, which was almost three times larger than the $9,066,000 that the average Brazilian domestic company set aside for the legal budget.

Unfortunately, given our research methodology we can only speculate about the reasons for these dramatic differences – differences that persist even if we exclude the highest spending firms in each jurisdiction. It is possible, for example, that some of the dramatic differences in overall legal spending between the two countries may have to do with some combination of the respective cost of procuring outside legal services (law firm rates were likely higher in Brazil than in India, particularly for associates and junior partners) and exchange rates (Brazil's Real was much stronger against the US dollar between 2009 and 2015 that the Indian Rupee, particularly during the first three years of this period when most of the growth in legal spend occurred). Moreover, the fact the legal budgets of all companies operating in Brazil in our sample grew by an average of 67 percent between 2009 and 2012 is likely linked to the rapid expansion of Brazil's economy during this period (Schineller 2012). Similarly the fact that Brazilian FMNCs dramatically outspent their Indian counterparts is likely due to Brazil's far greater openness to foreign investment than India's from 2009 to 2015, although for both countries the first three years of this period from 2009 to 2012 was where FMNCs really ramped up their legal budgets in both countries (86 percent Brazil, 81 percent India). The fact that Brazilian domestic companies consistently devote more resources to their legal departments than similar Indian companies, both in absolute terms in 2015 ($9,066,000 Brazil, $2,199,000 India) and in percentage growth over the period (50 percent to 33 percent) also is consistent with Wilkins and Khanna's finding in their examination of the Indian corporate counsel market that India's large promoter led business groups tend to devote less resources to their legal departments than similarly sized companies in other jurisdictions (Wilkins and Khanna 2017). It will, however, require future research of the kind that we hope this volume inspires to determine the root causes of these large disparities in legal department budgets definitively.

TABLE 4.9 *GC reporting structure*

	All		Domestic		FMNC	
	Brazil	India	Brazil	India	Brazil	India
Board (%)	8%	13%	10%	12%	6%	6%
CEO (%)	48%	39%	58%	44%	41%	29%
Global/regional GC (%)	22%	13%	13%	6%	34%	41%
CFO (%)	8%	12%	13%	12%	3%	6%

Finally, Table 4.8 indicates that legal budgets in both countries were evenly split between internal spending and spending on outside lawyers, and that these splits remained relatively constant over the six-year period under study. These results are consistent for both domestic companies and FMNCs, although in 2009 both Brazilian and Indian FMNCs sent an even greater percentage of their overall legal work (61–70 percent) to outside providers. This is consistent with the explanation presented above that these companies had very little legal infrastructure during this initial period and therefore had to rely more on outside firms. As these FMNCs built their own internal legal departments, the amount sent to outside firms declined in both countries to the steady state of 51 percent to 60 percent. We return to the kinds of work companies in both countries tend to send to external providers – and to which kinds of external providers – in Section IIIF.

E *Job Responsibilities and Reporting*

Tables 4.9 and 4.10 examine whether GCs are playing the kind of influential role within their organizations championed by the in-house counsel movement. We do so by tracking to whom the GC reports, who reports to the GC, and how much of their time GCs in the two jurisdictions spend on interacting with high-level figures inside their organizations.

Table 4.9 begins by examining a classic measure that organizational theorists use to gauge occupational power: to whom does a person report in the corporate hierarchy. One of the major goals of the in-house counsel movement was to have the GC report directly to the CEO (Rosen 1989). Our survey of US GCs underscored that by 2007, the overwhelming majority of top lawyers within companies had achieved this goal, with 89 percent reporting directly to the CEO (Coates et al. 2011). As Table 4.9 underscores, GCs Brazil and India have yet to achieve this broad-based level of success. Less than half of all GCs in each country (48 percent and 39 percent respectively) report directly to the CEO.

TABLE 4.10 *Relationships with internal players*

	All		Domestic		FMNC	
	Brazil	India	Brazil	India	Brazil	India
All lawyers report to GC (%)	49%	51%	45%	55%	53%	39%
Other functions or departments report to GC (%)	25%	35%	26%	33%	25%	40%
GC in charge of compliance (%)	91%	86%	100%	85%	92%	89%
Advising the board (frequently) (%)	62%	53%	58%	51%	66%	59%
Participating in senior leadership discussions (frequently) (%)	86%	64%	84%	60%	88%	76%
Counseling the CEO (frequently) (%)	86%	79%	87%	75%	84%	88%
Time spent on these activities increased/stayed the same (past three years) (%)	98%	98%	97%	100%	100%	93%
If increased, how much more time do you spend on these activities (%)	38%	40%	32%	38%	42%	45%

Not surprisingly, when we exclude FMNCs from this calculation, who often report to a global or regional GC, the percentage of those reporting to the CEO in each country increases, but it still remains well below what it is in the United States (58 percent Brazil, 44 percent India). Although some of those who don't report to the CEO instead report directly to the Board (10 percent Brazil; 12 percent India), as our research in India uncovered, this may signal that the GC has less power than might at first appear. Board members in domestic companies based in emerging markets like Brazil and India may have less respect for the GC's expertise and for legal concerns generally than is typically the case in more established markets such as the United States, particularly when those companies are family owned (Wilkins and Khanna 2017). Consistent with this hypothesis, in a finding not presented in Table 4.9, we found that a higher percentage of Brazilian GCs in family controlled companies report directly to the Board (21 percent) than in any other category of Brazilian company. The fact that we also found that an equal percentage (21 percent) of Brazilian GCs in family controlled businesses continue to report to the company's chief financial officer (CFO) – once again, the highest percentage of any group – further suggests that the same dynamic we found in India may also be occurring in Brazil. Indeed, the fact that 8 percent of all Brazilian GCs and 10 percent of those in India continue to report to the CFO underscores that many GCs in both jurisdictions have a long way to go before they realize this central tenet of the in-house counsel movement. As Oliveira and Ramos document, however, even these percentages represent a significant improvement in the GC's internal status in Brazil, and that many Brazilian legal executives expect their status and authority within the company to improve further in the coming years (Chapter 3).

The data presented in Table 4.10 about who reports to the general counsel, and the GCs primary duties, presents a similarly mixed picture. At a minimum, the in-house counsel movement argued that the GC should have full control over a company's legal function. GCs in both Brazil and India, however, have yet to achieve this goal. As Table 4.10 demonstrates, less than half of GCs in Brazil (49 percent) and just over half (51 percent) of GCs in India stated that all lawyers in their organization report directly to them.

Nor are GCs in these two jurisdictions frequently overseeing other functions in addition to legal. In the United States it is now quite common for GCs to have control over functions such as government affairs, public relations, and human resources in addition to the legal department (Heineman 2016). Only 25 percent of Brazilian GCs and 35 percent of those in India, however, reported having any similar responsibility. The only exception was compliance, where 91 percent of Brazilian GCs and 86 percent of those in India reported that they had responsibility for this area. Ironically, although many US GCs continue to oversee compliance, there is a growing tendency for this function to be separated from legal, often as a result of pressure from regulators (Heineman 2016).

Apart from direct oversight, Table 4.10 also suggests that GCs in Brazil may be more integrated into the company's senior management and business decision making than their Indian counterparts. Thus, with respect to "advising the board" (62 percent Brazil; 53 percent India), "participating in senior leadership discussions" (86 percent Brazil; 64 percent India), and "counseling the CEO" (86 percent Brazil; 79 percent India), Brazilian GCs report doing so "frequently" far more often than GCs in India. Once again, this difference which is similar across both domestic and foreign companies in both jurisdictions, is consistent with the hypothesis presented in Section II that Brazil's more open economy and proximity to the United States would lead to greater diffusion of the American model of internal lawyering where GCs are considered important members of the senior leadership team.

Finally, Table 4.10 documents that both Brazilian and Indian GCs overwhelmingly report (98 percent Brazil; 98 percent India) that their time spent on these activities has increased over the past three years, and by close to 40 percent in each jurisdiction (38 percent Brazil; 40 percent India). This suggests that both the *substantive* argument for increasing the status and authority of internal lawyers – that because of their greater proximity to the business, in-house lawyers can give better advice – and the argument from

TABLE 4.11 *Primary responsibilities of the GC*

	All		Domestic		FMNC	
	Brazil	India	Brazil	India	Brazil	India
Managing legal department staff (%)	98%	99%	100%	98%	97%	100%
Hiring outside lawyers/law firms (%)	98%	94%	97%	94%	100%	94%
Managing outside lawyers/law firms (%)	98%	92%	97%	91%	100%	94%
Company representative in public policy debates (%)	73%	68%	77%	58%	69%	94%
Compliance with domestic regulations (%)	92%	86%	97%	85%	88%	89%
Compliance with regulations arising out of cross-border interactions (%)	84%	77%	90%	72%	78%	94%
Contract design and negotiation (%)	94%	87%	90%	87%	97%	89%
Managing IP assets (%)	48%	72%	45%	70%	50%	78%
Designing or implementing corporate social responsibility policies (%)	44%	45%	39%	47%	50%	39%
Ensuring compliance with antibribery/similar policies (%)	79%	66%	84%	60%	75%	83%

professional independence – that GCs should be included in senior decision making because they are well positioned to look out for a company's long-term reputation and interests – may be taking root in both countries.

Table 4.11's description of the GCs primary duties in the two jurisdictions reinforces this overall narrative. As indicated above, GCs in both countries frequently do not directly oversee all the lawyers in their respective organizations. Nevertheless, the data underscores that managing the lawyers they do oversee is at the heart of their job, with 98 percent of Brazilian GCs and 99 percent of those in India citing managing the legal department as a core responsibility. The same is true for overseeing the hiring and functioning of outside counsel with the overwhelming percentage of respondents in both countries stating that this is also their primary responsibility (98 percent Brazil, 94 percent India).

The further one gets from these core legal functions, however, the less responsibility Brazilian and Indian GCs have – and the more divergence there is between prevailing practices in the two countries. In immediately adjacent fields with clear domestic legal implications, GCs in both countries appear to be playing an important role. For example, 92 percent of Brazilian GCs and 86 percent of those in India have important responsibility for ensuring the company's compliance with domestic regulation. Indeed, as we indicated above, the majority of GCs in both jurisdictions oversee this function directly.

Similarly, 94 percent of GCs in Brazil and 87 percent in India play a central role in the company's contract design and negotiation. With respect to compliance with regulations arising from a company's cross-border interactions, the percentage of GCs for whom this is a significant part of their responsibilities drops to 84 percent in Brazil and 77 percent in India. The percentage of GCs who play a central role in compliance with antibribery and other similar issues – many of which originate in foreign jurisdictions such as the United States or United Kingdom – is even lower, with only 79 percent of Brazilian GCs and 66 percent of those in India having these issues as an important part of their job description. The percentage of those with important responsibility for managing corporate social responsibility declines even further, with fewer than half (44 percent Brazil, 45 percent India) reporting that these issues are an important part of their jobs.

The only area where there is a significant deviation between the work allocated to Brazilian and Indian GCs is with respect to the management of the company's IP assets. While less than half (48 percent) of Brazilian GCs count this in their portfolio, nearly three-quarters (72 percent) of Indian respondents reported that this was an important part of their portfolio. Although once again our data does not allow us to answer the question definitively, one can speculate that this difference may have to do with the greater importance of IP assets to companies operating in India, where the tech sector plays a critical role in the Indian Economy (Singh 2014). The fact that GCs in both Indian domestic companies and FMNCs report having responsibility for this area at similar levels reinforces the suggestion that this related to an underlying characteristic of the Indian economy as a whole.

Overall, the trend reported in Table 4.11 is consistent with Oliveira and Ramos's central finding that GCs in Brazil have not yet adopted the "entrepreneurial" role that Nelson and Neilson reported as being prevalent among US GCs as early as the 1990s (Chapter 3). For both Brazilian and Indian GCs, there primary role is managing the legal function, with decreasing responsibility the further one gets away from this core area. Given this pattern one suspects that the relatively large percentage of GCs in both jurisdictions who report that representing the company in public policy debates (73 percent Brazil, 68 percent India) is also a part of their job description – including a surprising 94 percent of the GCs in Indian FMNCs – are primarily referring advocating for the company in legal debates, something that GCs in foreign companies operating in India may very well have been doing often given India's contentious debate over opening various sectors of its economy to foreign investment discussed in Section II. We will return to this issue in Section IIIG.

TABLE 4.12 *Legal work by type (all company types)*

	Percentage of legal work[a]		Percentage kept in-house	
	Brazil	India	Brazil	India
Civil liability/arbitration (%)	21–30%	31–40%	31–40%	41–50%
Criminal (%)	11–20%	11–20%	11–20%	31–40%
Consumer (%)	21–30%	21–30%	41–50%	41–50%
Commercial contracts (%)	41–50%	41–50%	41–50%	61–70%
Corporate securities (%)	21–30%	11–20%	41–50%	51–60%
IP (%)	11–20%	11–20%	41–50%	51–60%
M&A (%)	21–30%	21–30%	81–90%	41–50%
Competition (%)	11–20%	11–20%	61–70%	41–50%
Trade (%)	11–20%	11–20%	31–40%	41–50%
Finance and restructuring (%)	21–30%	21–30%	51–60%	41–50%
Regulatory compliance (%)	31–40%	21–30%	41–50%	61–70%
Labor (%)	31–40%	21–30%	61–70%	41–50%
Other (%)	11–20%	11–20%	21–30%	41–50%

[a] Last three years.

Nevertheless, the primary pattern noted by Oliveira and Ramos remains, with GCs operating more as "cops" who police the company's compliance with legal rules, and occasionally as "counselors" who integrate law with business, as opposed to "entrepreneurs" who see themselves as full business partners. Having said this, the data the uniformly higher percentage of Brazilian GCs with responsibility for functions at the intersection of law and business documented in Table 4.12 (with the important exception of managing IP assets) also underscores that Brazilian GCs have adopted more of the entrepreneurial element of the in-house counsel movement than their Indian peers.

F *Relationships with Outside Law Firms and Other Providers*

Arguably, the single most dramatic change inspired by the in-house counsel movement in the United States has been the shift in power between GCs and outside firms. As General Electric's longtime general counsel Benjamin W. Heineman Jr., one of the chief prototypes for the in-house counsel movement, has made clear, sophisticated GCs were brought in to "break up the monopoly" that outside law firms had traditionally enjoyed with their important clients, and to place internal lawyers firmly in charge of all legal purchasing decisions (Heineman 2016). Tables 4.12–4.14 and Figures 4.1–4.4

TABLE 4.13 *Outside legal work (all company types)*

	Domestic firms		Foreign firms		Other provider	
	Brazil	India	Brazil	India	Brazil	India
Civil liability/arbitration (%)	91%	83%	7%	31%	1%	28%
Criminal (%)	96%	90%	0%	60%	0%	63%
Consumer (%)	85%	89%	1%	23%	1%	13%
Commercial contracts (%)	75%	72%	33%	40%	8%	23%
Corporate securities (%)	72%	80%	26%	36%	0%	0%
IP (%)	96%	81%	2%	38%	2%	10%
M&A (%)	78%	74%	15%	47%	1%	5%
Competition (%)	81%	79%	29%	33%	1%	30%
Trade (%)	79%	79%	15%	46%	1%	50%
Finance and restructuring (%)	65%	78%	29%	40%	1%	7%
Regulatory compliance (%)	69%	79%	31%	28%	4%	26%
Labor (%)	81%	82%	11%	53%	2%	40%
Other (%)	32%	86%	1%	0%	0%	100%

TABLE 4.14 *Top three areas of routine legal work*

All	
Brazil	India
Civil liability/arbitration	Civil liability/arbitration
Commercial/contract	Criminal
Domestic	
Brazil	India
Regulatory compliance	Commercial/contract
Civil liability/arbitration	Civil liability/arbitration
Commercial/contract	Criminal
FMNC	
Brazil	India
Regulatory compliance	Commercial/contract
Civil liability/arbitration	Civil Lability/arbitration
Commercial/contract	M&A
Regulatory compliance	Commercial/contract

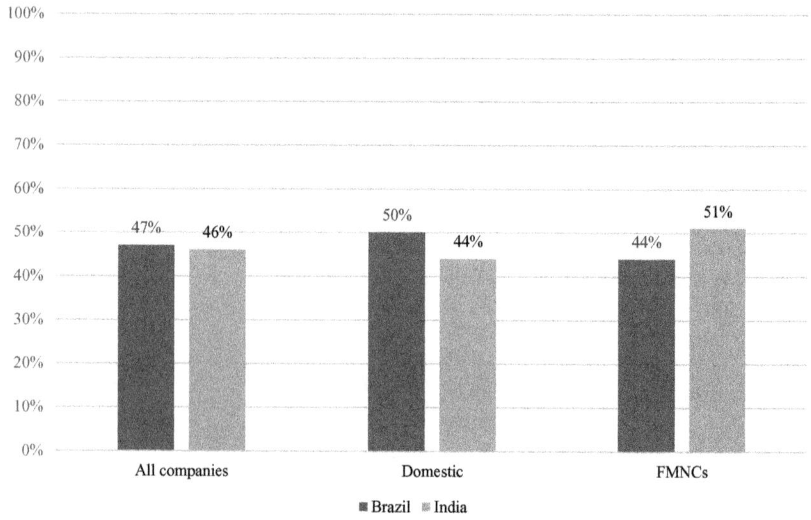

FIGURE 4.1 Percentage of legal budget spent on top three routine matters.

present what our survey results tell us about how far GCs in Brazil and India have been able to shift this balance of power.

In Section IIID, we saw that companies in both jurisdictions spend equal amounts of their total budgets on outside providers. Thus, in both countries 51–60 percent consistently went to outside providers across all company types

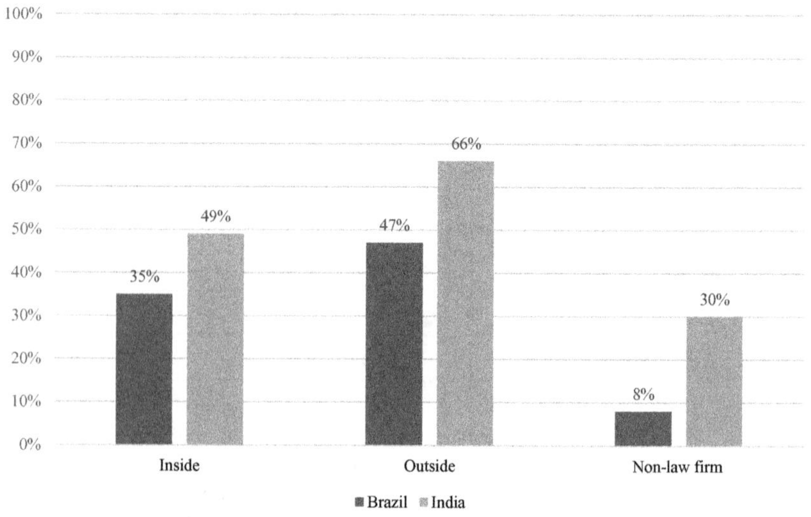

FIGURE 4.2 Breakdown of routine spending (all companies, top three areas).

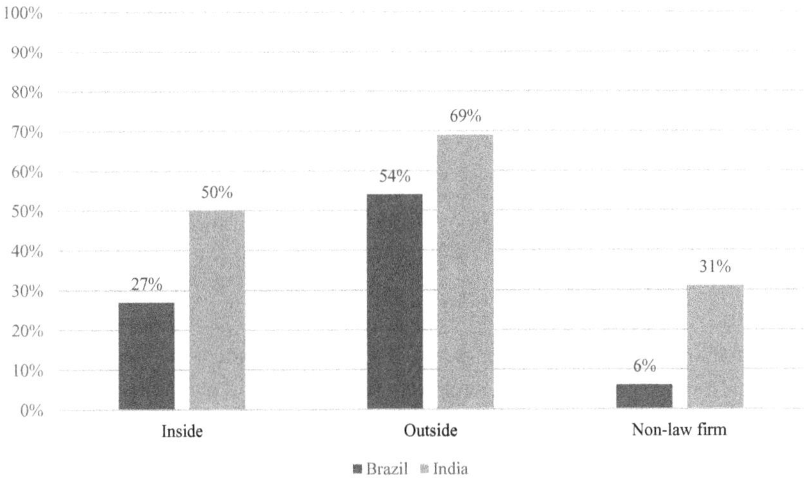

FIGURE 4.3 Breakdown of routine spending (domestic companies, top three areas).

and time periods, with the exception of FNMCs in both countries which sent an even greater share of work to outside providers (61–70 percent) in 2009. This overall similarity, however, masks some important differences between Brazilian and Indian companies about what kinds of work is sent outside and to which providers. Tables 4.12 and 4.13 document this variation.

Table 4.12 begins by looking at the kinds of legal work done by legal departments in each jurisdiction, and examines how much of that work is kept

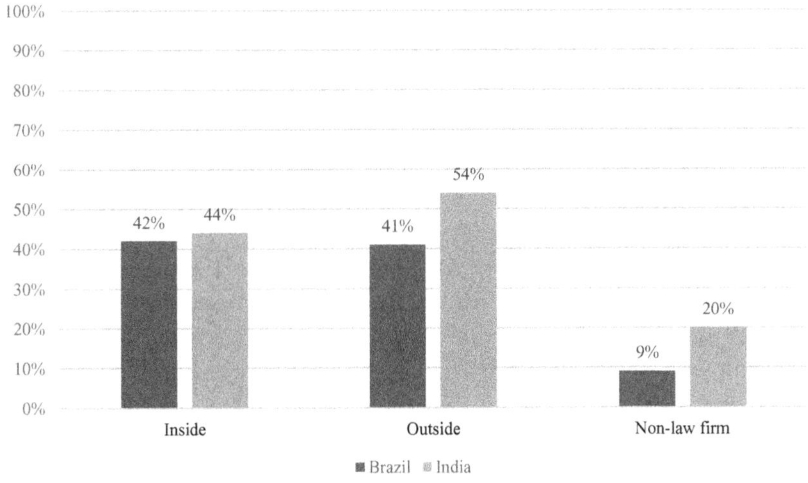

FIGURE 4.4 Breakdown of routine spending (FMNC companies, top three areas).

in-house to be done by internal lawyers. As the table underscores, there are broad similarities between the work of internal counsel in India and Brazil, but also some noticeable differences. Thus, in both countries, commercial contracts account for close to half (41–50 percent) of the work done by in-house legal departments over the last three years. Moreover, GCs in both countries keep a large share of this work in-house, although the percentage done internally in India (61–70 percent) is even greater than in Brazil (41–50 percent). In analysis not presented, we have determined that all of these ranges are relatively consistent for both domestic and FMNCs in the two jurisdictions. At the opposite end of the spectrum, very little of the work of internal legal departments in the two jurisdictions concerns matters involving criminal law, IP, competition, or trade, each accounting for only 11–20 percent of work done over the last three years. Interestingly, in all but competition law matters, Indian GCs also keep more of this lower occurring work in-house than their Indian counterparts. In competition law, Brazilian GCs are far more likely than their Indian counterparts to keep this work in-house (61–70 percent Brazil; 41–50 percent India). Once again, in analysis not presented here we determined that these results are also broadly similar for domestic companies and FMNCs in both countries.

The difference in how GCs in the two jurisdictions handle competition matters is particularly noteworthy in light of the even greater difference in the percentage of M&A work that is kept inside in the two countries. Thus, while legal departments in both jurisdiction have spent less than a third of their time (21–30 percent) on such matters in recent years, Brazilian companies keep virtually all such work in-house (81–90 percent) while Indian companies send more than half of it to outside firms (keeping 41–50 percent in-house). Moreover, in Brazil there are differences between the practices of domestic and foreign companies in this area. In results not reported, we found that FNMCs operating in Brazil were somewhat less likely than domestic Brazilian firms to keep M&A work in-house (71–80 percent for Brazilian FMNCs; 81–90 percent for Brazilian domestic companies). We did not find this difference between FMNCs and domestic companies, however, in India, where in results not reported here we found that both groups kept less than half (41–50 percent) of their work in this area in-house. Conversely, Indian internal legal departments are much more likely to handle regulatory compliance work (61–70 percent) than Brazilian legal departments (41–50 percent), a result in other analyses that we determined holds across domestic and foreign firms in both jurisdictions.

Collectively, these findings further support the conclusion that internal legal departments in Brazil are closer to the US model of the in-house counsel movement than their Indian counterparts. M&A and competition law tend to be the kind of sophisticated legal work that GCs in the Global North have argued that their departments are now capable of handling internally – although it should be noted that not even the largest legal departments in the United States tend to handle close to 90 percent of such work in-house. At the other end, regulatory compliance is often the kind of low-level task that GCs in the United States are increasingly trying to send to low-cost outside providers. Indeed, only with respect to labor matters is this general pattern reversed. Brazilian legal departments do a higher percentage of labor work (31–40 percent) than those in India (21–30 percent), and keep a higher percentage of that work in-house (61–70 percent Brazil, 41–50 percent India). Although labor matters are typically not considered high-end legal work, one suspects that the fact that Brazil's labor laws are both highly complex and highly restrictive makes matters of this kind a higher priority for Brazilian companies than they are in the United States.

In addition to differences in how much work is sent to outside providers, there are also interesting variations in the providers to whom legal departments in Brazil and India send this work. Table 4.13 documents these differences. Not surprisingly, the overwhelming majority of outside legal work in both jurisdictions is sent to domestic law firms. This is consistent across all kinds of legal work and company types. Notwithstanding this basic similarity, there are important differences between the outsourcing practices of legal departments in these two rising powers. Specifically, Indian companies are far more likely to send work to foreign law firms and to other non–law firm providers than their counterparts in Brazil. Although in analysis not presented here, this difference is reduced when we look only at FMNCs in the two jurisdictions (e.g., 38 percent of Brazilian FMNCs have used foreign law firms for commercial contracts as compared to only 17 percent of FMNCs in India), the overall pattern of Indian companies employing foreign law firms more than Brazilian legal departments remains even for this group. The differences are even starker with respect to non–law firm providers, with Indian legal departments employing these types of firms far more frequently than GC offices in Brazil, across all kinds of work and company types. Once again, this suggests both the greater overall sophistication of the Brazilian corporate legal market, where Brazilian law firms have had to compete much more directly with foreign law firms than similarly situated law firms in India, and the importance of legal process outsourcing and other alternative providers in the Indian legal market.

Similar patterns emerge when we restrict our focus to the "routine" legal work sourced by GCs in both jurisdictions. As indicated in Section II, the initial justification for the growth of in-house counsel in the United States was that it was cheaper to handle legal work "inside" than "outside." This argument was particularly compelling with respect to the kinds of routine legal matters that arise frequently for every company. As Section II also underscores, however, as the movement matured in the United States, GCs argued that the real value of internal lawyers was their ability to provide higher-quality legal advice as a result of their proximity to, and understanding of, the company's business. As a result, many GCs pushed to reverse the initial focus on cost-arbitrage and argued that more routine legal work should be pushed out to low-cost external providers (including an increasing percentage to LPOs and other non–law firm providers) freeing up internal lawyers to concentrate on more important matters where their greater understanding of the company's business would produce greater returns. As indicated above, there is evidence that Brazilian GCs have been more successful at taking more of this high value work in-house than their Indian counterparts. In this section, we examine the other side of this issue by examining how much of a company's legal budget is spent on routine legal work, and how that work is sourced, in order to gain additional insight into how far along this value curve internal legal departments in each jurisdiction have progressed.

We begin by looking at what percentage of each the legal work done by companies in each country is considered routine. Figure 4.1 presents our findings. It underscores that companies in both jurisdictions continue to spend close to half of their overall legal budgets (47 percent Brazil; 46 percent India) on routine legal work. This is relatively constant for both domestic and foreign companies in each jurisdiction. Moreover, as Table 4.14 indicates, the kind of routine legal work done by companies in both jurisdictions is also similar, although there are some interesting differences as well. In both jurisdictions, civil liability/arbitration matters constitute the most important segment of routine legal work. Given the high litigation rates in both countries, the fact that companies in each jurisdiction face a number of small claims is hardly surprising. Similarly, it is predictable that companies in each country would have a number of routine contract matters.

What is surprising is that these matters, which are second in Brazil (ahead of regulatory compliance, which is also a predictable source of routine work) is behind "criminal" matters for Indian legal departments – a matter that not only not present in the top three areas for Brazilian companies, but as Oliveira and Ramos document, are a small percentage of the work of Brazilian GCs (Chapter 3). Although further research is required to investigate why criminal matters rate so highly in the routine matters handled by Indian legal departments, we suspect (as one of us has observed in another context) that the notorious backlog in the Indian civil justice system may be an important cause. As many observers have noted, it can take decades – quite literally – for ordinary civil litigation to work its way through the Indian courts (Hazra and Debroy 2007; Krishnan 2010; Kumar 2012). As a result, litigants, including government regulatory authorities, often attempt to shoehorn what would otherwise be civil disputes into criminal charges, which while still delayed, are likely to get a far faster hearing than if the same issues were adjudicated civilly (Khanna and Mahajan 2016; Khanna 2017). This "criminalization" of the regulatory state is likely to have a particularly adverse effect on the kind of large companies we are studying here. It is therefore not surprising that in-house legal departments in India find themselves dealing with many more of these issues than their Brazilian counterparts.

The only exception to this general pattern are FMNCs in India, who report that their second largest category of routine legal work involves M&A. This suggests that the criminalization of the regulatory state is much more likely to adversely affect Indian domestics as opposed to FMNCs operating in that country, who for various reasons may be less subject to this kind of practice than the domestic Indian companies. It also suggests that much of the M&A work done by FMNCs in India is relatively small compared to what is happening in Brazil (where, as we saw above, a very high percentage of this work is done in-house but is not considered routine), and that big M&A in India is sent to outside law firms. Once again, this fits the general pattern of Brazilian GCs being farther along the continuum suggested by the in-house counsel movement. Interestingly, this gap is particularly true with respect to domestic companies, where only 27 percent of the budget of the average Brazilian company is spent internally on routine legal work, as compared to 50 percent of the budgets of Indian domestic companies. FMNCs in each country, are almost identical in this particular outsourcing policy, keeping approximately 40 percent of their work in-house.

Indian companies, however, also send a significant amount of their routine legal work to outside law firms (66 percent), which is appreciably higher than internal legal departments in Brazil (47 percent). But the biggest difference is with respect to non–law firm providers, where Indian companies once again send nearly a third of their routine legal work (30 percent) to less than 10 percent (8 percent) of the work sent out by Brazilian companies. This gap is consistent for both domestic and FMNCs in both jurisdictions.

Tables 4.15 and 4.16 examine one of the key ways that GCs in the United States exert their control over the hiring of outside law firms: the use of a list of "preferred providers." In the Center on the Legal Profession's prior survey of the legal purchasing decisions of large US companies, we found that

TABLE 4.15 *Hiring domestic law firms*

	All		Domestic		FMNC	
	Brazil	India	Brazil	India	Brazil	India
Use preferred provider list (%)	66%	81%	67%	77%	65%	94%
Number of firms on list	9.6	10.8	12.9	12.1	6.1	7.2
List made by GC (%)	90%	91%	94%	90%	87%	93%
List in 2010 (%)	38%	71%	31%	70%	46%	73%
Work to list (%)	75%	61–70%	76%	61–70%	75%	61–70%
Change since 2010 (same or more to list) (%)	50%	36%	50%	43%	50%	18%

80 percent of S&P 500 companies had such a list, which they used to source most – but not all – of their legal work (Coates et al. 2011). In qualitative interviews with US GCs, creating such a list was one of their primary tools for reducing the cost of outside legal services, primarily by pushing for volume discounts. In addition, many GCs also argued that reducing the number of law firms that they use, and concentrating most – but again, not all – of their legal work in these preferred providers also increased the quality of the services they received by encouraging law firms on the list to "know the company's business" (Wilkins 2012). Our data underscores that this aspect of the inside counsel movement has indeed come to Brazil and India, particularly with respect to the hiring of domestic law firms.

Table 4.15 documents that a substantial majority of GCs in Brazil and India (66 percent Brazil; 81 percent India) report that they currently use a list of preferred providers. Moreover, like their US counterparts, the overwhelming majority of respondents (90 percent Brazil; 91 percent India) report that they are primarily responsible for putting the list together. And, again consistent with the practice in the United States, GCs in both countries send the majority (75 percent Brazil, between 60–70 percent India) – but not all – of their outside legal work to law firms that are on the list. These results are similar for domestic and foreign companies operating in both jurisdictions.

TABLE 4.16 *Hiring foreign law firms: use preferred provider list*

	All	Domestic	FMNC
India (%)	49%	42%	69%
Brazil (%)	53%	46%	61%

Although the two countries are therefore broadly similar, and similar to what we see in the United States, the use of preferred providers appears to be more firmly established in India, where 71 percent of respondents reported that they already had such a list in 2010, and 36 percent reported that they were sending as much if not more work to the firms on the list in 2015 as they did in 2010. Although the percentage of Brazilian companies employing such a list in 2010 was significantly lower (38 percent), the fact that this percentage has nearly doubled (to 66 percent) in five years, and that these GCs now send 75 percent of all outside legal work to companies on the list – with 50 percent reporting that they were sending as much or more work to firms on the list as they did in 2010 – underscores that this aspect of the inside counsel movement is now firmly established in Brazil as well.

Table 4.15 demonstrates, however, that the use of preferred providers is still primarily a feature of the domestic legal markets in both countries. Only 53 percent of Brazilian companies report using a preferred provider list when hiring a foreign law firm, with only 46 percent of domestic companies having this practice. The percentages are even lower for India, where 49 percent of Indian companies report employing such a list for foreign firms, with only 42 percent of domestic companies reporting this practice. This result suggests that the power of GCs in both jurisdictions – particularly those in domestic firms (FMNCs in both countries are more likely to have a list of foreign preferred providers, which may be connected to one employed by their parent company) – is largely confined to their home market, although the fact that nearly half of those in our sample report using a preferred provider list for foreign firms also underscores that their authority over such matters may be on the rise.

Of course, even when a company has a list of preferred providers, the GC still has to determine which firm to hire from the list, or to give the work to another law firm not on the list that might be better suited for the task. This decision is particularly freighted for the work that the GC considers especially important. We therefore asked respondents to recall the last time they hired a domestic law firm for "very significant work," and to tell us how they picked which firm would be given this choice assignment. Figures 4.5–4.7 present our results.[6]

[6] We also asked respondents about the last time that they hired a "foreign" law firm for a very significant matter. The results are broadly similar to what we report here for domestic firms, e.g., reputation, relationships, and prior results dominate all other factors in these hiring decisions as well. We note in additional footnotes where there are significant differences in how GCs in the two jurisdictions handing the hiring of domestic versus foreign law firms that provide insight into the primary analysis presented in text.

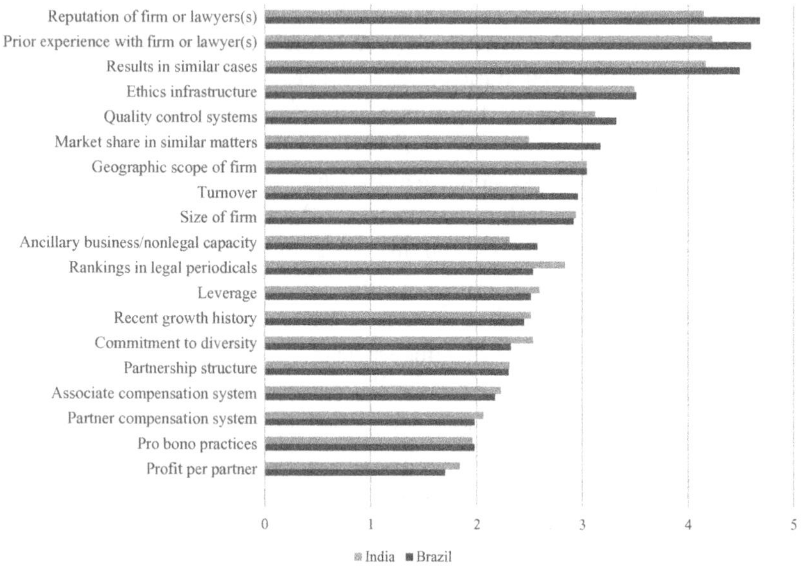

FIGURE 4.5 Factors influencing hiring domestic law firms (all company types). Chart based on a 5-point Likert scale, with 0 representing "not at all important" and 5 representing "very important."

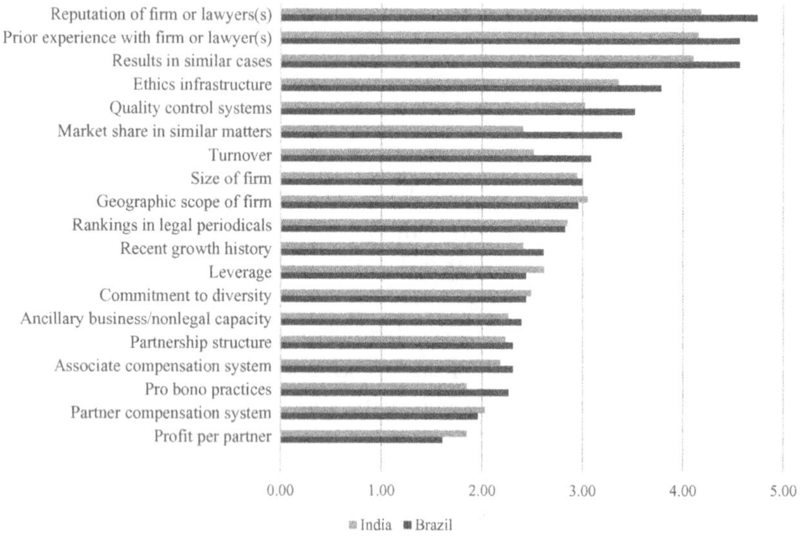

FIGURE 4.6 Factors influencing hiring domestic law firms (domestic). Chart based on a 5-point Likert scale, with 0 representing "not at all important" and 5 representing "very important."

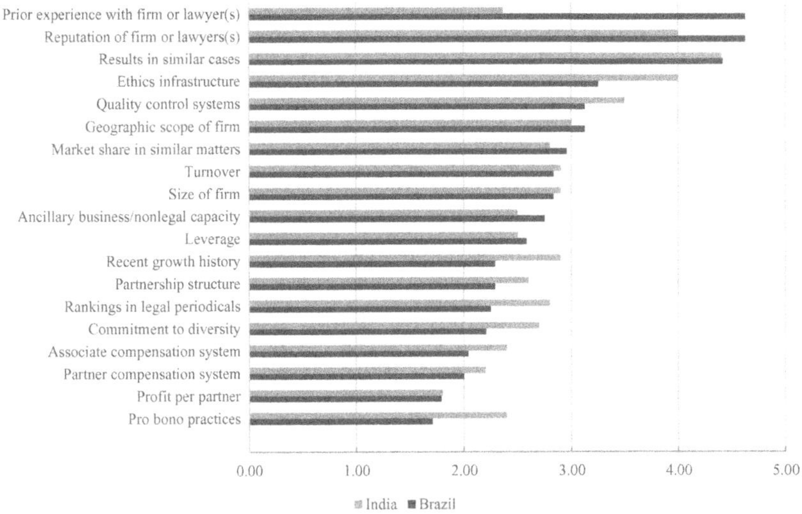

FIGURE 4.7 Factors influencing hiring domestic law firms (FMNC). Chart based on a 5-point Likert scale, with 0 representing "not at all important" and 5 representing "very important."

From a cursory examination of the data, it is clear that three factors dominate all others in law firm hiring decisions in both countries: reputation, results, and prior experience. These factors are the only ones that GCs in both jurisdictions consistently rates as "very important" when hiring domestic law firms for very important matters. The pattern is very similar to what we found in our research of US GCs, where these three factors also dominated all other considerations in hiring law firms for very significant matters (Coates et al. 2011).

Even with respect to these critical factors, however, there are some interesting differences between the two jurisdictions. For example, Brazilian GCs were even more likely than their Indian counterparts to identify reputation, prior results, and prior experience as driving their decision when hiring domestic law firms. Interestingly, this divergence appears to be primarily driven by Indian FMNCs who reported paying far less attention to their prior experience when hiring Indian law firms (2.4 out of 5.0) than GCs in similar companies in Brazil reported relying on reputational factors when hiring Brazilian firms (4.6 out of 5.0).[7] Indeed, for Indian FMNCs this factor, which

[7] Respondents were asked to rank the importance of nineteen factors in the hiring of outside law firms on a 5-point Likert scale, with 0 representing "not at all important" and 5 "very important." Scores were averaged across the responding companies to determine overall scores. In

was also ranked at the top in our study of US GCs, is ranked third from the bottom of our list of our list of factors for hiring domestic law firm. Although it is possible this difference is due to the fact that the GCs of FMNCs operating in India have less prior experience hiring India's top law firms, this explanation seems unlikely give the degree to which a few large Indian law firms continue to dominate the legal market in that country (Wilkins et al. 2017). Instead, we suspect that it may reflect the unevenness of the quality of many of these top Indian law firms, particularly outside of the most senior named partners in these organizations, a complaint that both authors of this chapter have heard frequently expressed by GCs in India during our research in that country. The fact that GCs of FMNCs (and indeed of all companies) in Brazil continue to place great weight on their prior experience when hiring domestic Brazilian law firms is consistent with such unevenness being less of a concern in that jurisdiction – which, in turn, is consistent with our hypothesis that the overall level of sophistication is higher in Brazil's corporate legal market than in India.[8]

When we look outside of these top three considerations, we also see important similarities between Brazil and India, but also important differences, both between these two jurisdictions, and between both countries and the United States. Thus, for GCs in both Brazil and India "ethical infrastructure" was the fourth most important factor in hiring domestic law firms between reputation, relationship, and prior experience. In the United States, by contrast, this factor ranked significantly lower, behind considerations such as firm size, and a law firm's commitment to diversity as only "somewhat important" to GCs (Coates et al. 2011). This heightened interest in a law firm's ethics likely reflects the heightened risk associated with doing business in jurisdictions where unfortunately regulatory noncompliance and even outright corruption unfortunately remain far too prevalent.

Our data also suggests, however, that domestic companies and FMNCs in the two jurisdictions may be responding to this risk in different ways. Although FMNCs in India are far less likely to rely on reputation when hiring local law firms, they are far more likely than their Brazilian counterparts to be concerned with a law firm's "ethical infrastructure," as well as the related issue of "quality control systems," Conversely, Brazilian domestic companies are

this example, 2.4 represents a point between "somewhat important" and "important" and 4.6 between "important" and "very important."

[8] Interestingly, in research not presented here, when hiring foreign law firms these differences between Brazil and India disappear, with GCs in both jurisdictions placing equal – and equally great – reliance on reputation. Whatever worry that Indian FMNCs have about the consistent quality in Indian law firms appears to disappear when hiring firms based outside of India.

more likely to care about these factors (as well as a firm's "market share" and "turnover") when hiring local Brazilian law firms than Indian domestic companies are when hiring local law firms in their country.

Once again, our methodology does not allow us to explain these differences definitively. However, other research suggests that different actors may have differing perceptions about how to respond to ethical risk in the two jurisdictions. As Oliveira and Ramos highlight in their chapter on the Brazilian corporate counsel market, Brazilian corporates are sensitive to the dangers of being embroiled in issues of regulatory noncompliance or even corruption (Chapter 3). Although recent events suggests that many companies were not as careful as they should have been, the high priority that our respondents gave to ethics issues when hiring Brazilian law firms suggests that at a minimum legal directors in this country want to ensure that their law firms have systems in place to guard against these dangers. Our research in India, on the other hand, suggests that Indian corporates and their primary law firms often share important communal bonds that may – for better and for worse – make them less concerned about these issues. FMNCs operating in India, on the other hand, are likely to have fewer of these communal ties and therefore may be more conscious of the attendant risks than their domestic counterparts. As we stated above, however, only time and further research will determine whether these broad attitudes explain the differences we see in our data.

Finally, in addition to asking about hiring, the survey also queried respondents about when they terminate the law firms they are using for very significant work. As indicated in Section II, one of the hallmarks of the in-house counsel movement in the United States has been the claim that GCs have "broken up" the long-standing relationships between companies and outside law firms by frequently switching legal providers to obtain the best service and price. However, as CLP's survey of large US companies demonstrated, the reality is more complex. Although GCs have moved away from the bilateral monopoly relationships that companies traditionally had with their top outside law firms, this does not mean they are switching important law firm relationships as frequently as a "spot contracting" analogy implies. Instead, the data indicated that important law firm relationships change relatively infrequently, with only 31 percent of GCs reporting that they had terminated one of their preferred providers in the preceding three years, and 48 percent stating that they had done so only "once or twice" (Coates et al. 2011).

Table 4.17 documents that GCs in Brazil and India exhibit similar patterns about the frequency with which they terminate law firms that are among their preferred providers, along with important differences between the two jurisdictions. As the data indicates, GCs in Brazil look very similar to those in the

TABLE 4.17 *Termination of "important" law firm relationship*

	All		Domestic		FMNC	
	Brazil	India	Brazil	India	Brazil	India
Yes, many times (%)	4%	2%	8%	2%	0%	0%
Yes, few times (%)	23%	8%	27%	8%	17%	8%
Yes, once or twice (%)	43%	28%	46%	22%	35%	54%
No (never) (%)	32%	62%	17%	68%	48%	38%

United States. Overall, 32 percent of Brazil's GCs report having terminated an important law firm relationship during the last three years, a percentage almost identical to the 31 percent that we found in the United States. Indeed, when combined with the 43 percent of Brazilian GCs who report having done so only "once or twice," the total of companies in Brazil who are willing to disrupt such relationships relatively frequently (27 percent) is actually larger than their US counterparts (21 percent). Nor are the Brazilian results being driven by the greater percentage of FMNCs in our Brazil sample. To the contrary, nearly half (48 percent) of Brazilian FMNCs report not having terminated an important law firm relationship during the relevant period – a percentage far greater than we found in our sample of large US companies in 2007. Instead it is Brazilian domestic companies who appear more willing to disrupt their law firm relationships, with only 17 percent stating that they had not done so in the last three years, and more than a third (36 percent) reporting that they did so relatively frequently.

This pattern, however, is reversed for India. Almost two-thirds (62 percent) of all Indian firms report that they had not terminated an important law firm relationship during the last three years, with Indian domestic companies reporting an even higher percentage (68 percent). As opposed to Brazil, FMNCs in India were less likely (38 percent) than their Brazilian counterparts (and far less likely than GCs in Indian domestic companies to report not having terminated such a relationship in the relevant period, although when combined with the 54 percent who reported doing so only rarely, it is clear that such relationships are still far "stickier" in India than they are in either the United States or Brazil). Once again, this provides further support for our hypothesis that the in-house counsel movement has obtained much greater traction in Brazil than it has in India.

G *Role in Public Policy*

Table 4.18 presents the surveys' findings about the extent to which GCs in Brazil and India participate in debates over public policy and the regulation

TABLE 4.18 *Relationships with the bar and government (percentage reporting frequently or very frequently)*

	All		Domestic		FMNC	
	Brazil	India	Brazil	India	Brazil	India
Comment on pending legislation (%)	40%	46%	39%	43%	41%	53%
Interact with agency officials (%)	43%	34%	39%	32%	47%	41%
Speak out on public policy issues on behalf of the company (%)	13%	27%	10%	25%	16%	35%
Participate in debates over the regulation of the legal profession (%)	14%	28%	23%	28%	6%	29%
Participate in any trade group organizations (%)	35%	35%	48%	30%	22%	53%
Percent change in time spent on participation on politics and legislative matters (%)	53%	95%	59%	96%	49%	94%

of the legal profession. As Benjamin W. Heineman underscores, the fact that GCs in the United States are now seen as playing a critical role in shaping public policy, both internally within their own organizations, and externally in important centers of power in the profession and in society, provides potent proof of the in-house counsel movement's ultimate claim that these lawyers are equally – if not more – entitled to the status of independent professional as their peers in outside law firms (Heineman 2016). As Heineman concedes, even in the United States not every company has embraced this last tenet of the in-house movement, and there is considerable evidence that this aspect of the GCs role has been even slower to emerge elsewhere in the Global North, particularly in Europe where many GCs still do not have full professional status (Wilkins 2012; Heineman 2016). It is therefore not surprising that our data indicates that Brazil and India have been slow to adopt this role for GCs as well.

GCs in Brazil and India do appear to be playing an important role in managing their company's interactions with the legislative and executive branches of government. Thus, 40 percent of Brazilian GCs and 46 percent of those in India report that part of their duties is to comment on pending legislation. Similar percentages also report interacting with government officials, although in this case Brazilian GCs are more likely to report doing so than their Indian counterparts (43 percent to 34 percent). The fact that less than half of GCs in both jurisdictions report participating in even these core aspects of the public policy process reinforces the conclusion drawn above that these internal departments are still viewed more as a legal function than their US counterparts. Only participation in trade or industry groups rises to similar levels in both countries (35 percent Brazil; 35 percent India). With respect to the two other public policy areas we inquired about – speaking out publicly on behalf of the company on public policy issues and participating in debates over the regulation of the legal profession, just over a quarter of Indian GCs (27 percent and 28 percent respectively) reported that they took part in these activities, with the percentage of Brazilian GCs so reporting (13 percent and 14 percent respectively) even lower. Once again, these numbers reaffirm the conclusion that GCs continue to play a primarily legal role in both jurisdictions, and that whatever speaking out that they are doing as the "company's representative" as documented in Table 4.12 is likely primarily on legal issues, as opposed to broader matters of public policy.

However, like their US counterparts in the 1990s, this limited role may be able to change. Thus, over half (53 percent of Brazilian GCs, and an astonishing 95 percent of those in India, report that their work in these areas had increased significantly in the last three years). Although given their current engagement with these issues, this is a testament to how little these matters were considered a part of a GC's portfolio in the past, it also underscores that there is a strong trend toward embracing this last aspect of the in-house counsel movement, particularly in India. Only time will tell whether GCs in either country are able to attain the status that their US counterparts have in the public policy realm.

IV CONCLUSION: THE STATE OF THE IN-HOUSE COUNSEL MOVEMENT IN BRAZIL AND INDIA

In 2012, one of us asked the question "is the in-house counsel movement going global?" (Wilkins 2012). The evidence presented in Section III provides strong evidence that the answer to this question is a resounding yes with respect to Brazil and India. As Table 4.19 summarizes, across all six metrics the survey data demonstrates that GCs and in-house legal departments are becoming increasingly powerful players, both in their overall corporate structures and in the legal profession as a whole. In ways that were largely unthinkable as little as twenty-five years ago, in-house counsel have become important players in the legal services markets in Brazil and India, mirroring many of the developments that have taken place in the United States and other parts of the Global North.

At the same time, however, the data also underscores that this is not simply a story of the diffusion of the US model – nor are Brazilian and Indian companies at the same point in their respective development in embracing the model's tenets. Consistent with the factors identified in Section II, the survey

TABLE 4.19 *United States, India, and Brazil in comparison*

	US model	India post-2000	Brazil post-2000
Size	Increased dramatically since 1980s; large corporations have GC offices that rival the size of large outside law firms	Increased dramatically	Increased dramatically
Credentials and identities	Almost all are lawyers and members of the bar; a large percentage of in-house of female	Elite backgrounds; still, few are members of the bar	Elite backgrounds; much more likely to be members of the bar than in India; majority in-house teams are women
Control over the legal function	Largely select and manage outside counsel	Most GCs now have substantial influence in selecting and managing outside counsel	Most GCs have substantial influence in selecting and managing outside counsel
Internal reporting relationships	Commonly report to the CEO; most if not all lawyers report to the GC	Fewer than half of GCs report to the CEO and only half of lawyers report to the GC; frequently advise top corporate players	Fewer than half of GCs report to the CEO and only half of lawyers report to the GC; growing role in advising top corporate players
The profession	Important players in the profession with increasing influence throughout	Influence in profession is increasing; still suspend bar membership (if have it) when enter in-house department	Influence in profession is increasing, particularly through growth of in-house counsel professional organizations
Public policy	Active role in public policy with regular interactions with government	Increasing role interacting with government, though not yet as pervasive as in the United States	Increasing role interacting with government, though not yet as pervasive as in the United States or India

data suggests country-specific differences with respect to the precise contours of the inside counsel movement – differences likely driven by factors such as the jurisdiction's overall economic condition, exposure to the "West," the state of the legal profession, and other local factors. As a result, Brazilian and Indian in-house legal departments will not only differ from the US model, but also from each other due to their unique historical, economic, political, and social circumstances. These local contextual factors are likely to play a similarly important role in the diffusion and translation of the in-house counsel movement into other emerging economies in Asia, Latin America, and Africa. Thus, like many other aspects of the evolving corporate legal services market, the ultimate answer to the question Wilkins posed in 2012 is more likely to be "glocalization" than "globalization," as diffusing global models interact with particular local practices and norms (Silver et al. 2009).

Moreover, as these new models of in-house lawyering evolve in jurisdictions such as Brazil and India, they will also inevitably be shaped by the kind of "disruptive innovation" that is already reshaping the legal profession in the United States, including the role of internal lawyers. Ironically, the scholar who first documented the rise of in-house counsel in the United States was among the first to also raise questions about the in-house counsel movements continuing viability.

In an article published in 2002, Rosen revisited many of the legal departments he had studied for his initial article chronicling the in-house counsel movement and found that several of "those that had been transformed in the 1980s and whose inside counsel were management's trusted advisors, have been re-engineered" in a manner that significantly altered their work – and more importantly, their self-image. In response to management's demand that they demonstrate their value to the company, Rosen argues that many legal departments have been redesigned to integrate in-house lawyers into functional project teams within the organization to work more closely with business units. Indeed, some observers have gone even further in forecasting the demise of the core premises of the in-house counsel movement. Building on the growth of "smart" technology that is increasingly allowing companies to develop process-based solutions to many standard legal problems, Larry Ribstein argues "in-house lawyers ultimately may find their own power eroded by products and services that replace customized legal advice with standardized technology" (Ribstein 2012, 311). As a result, Ribstein claims, "in-house legal departments" may be replaced "by law-trained people dispersed throughout the organization" (311). Although perhaps not signaling "the end of lawyers," as another prominent commentator highlighting the growing importance of information technology to legal practice has posited (Susskind 2008), this replacement of "lawyers who have been inculcated with traditional professional norms to business people with legal expertise" nevertheless poses a significant challenge to the fundamental tenets of the in-house counsel movement (Ribstein 2012, 330).

Needless to say, it is far from clear whether the trend toward the broader integration of law into "business solutions" – a model that one of us has documented is currently being championed by the Big Four accounting firms who now actively competing with both law firms and in-house legal departments to handle the legal needs of global companies (Wilkins and Esteban 2017) – or the general forces of "disruptive innovation" currently sweeping over the legal services industry (Susskind and Susskind 2017) will undermine the critical role that GCs now play in the US corporate legal market. And even if these forces do significantly alter the role of internal lawyers in the Global North, as we have seen the translation of these new norms and practices to the legal markets of Rising Powers such as Brazil and India will likely not be a straightforward process of diffusion. Nevertheless, any investigation of the evolving role of in-house counsel in emerging economies will have to take these critiques seriously. Indeed, given that we might expect companies in emerging economies such as Brazil and India to be under even greater pressure to produce "business solutions," and even more open to incorporating new technologies – technologies that have, after all, contributed significantly to the rise of these countries as important economic powers – it is certainly possible that corporations in these jurisdictions may be even more willing to experiment with commercially focused "smart" solutions that allow them to reduce legal headcount while increasing business-friendly results than their more established counterpart.

There are, however, forces likely to push in the opposite direction. As we indicated at the outset, the growing complexity of the global legal, political, and social environment in which companies in emerging markets such as Brazil and India increasingly operate is likely to put a premium on gaining access to the kind of integrated business and legal advice that in-house lawyers claim to offer. How the increasingly sophisticated lawyers who fill these positions in companies around the world respond to this imperative is exactly the kind of research we hope to inspire by this study.

REFERENCES

Antunes, Anderson. 2014. "The 20 Companies That Own Brazil." *Forbes*, January 23. www.forbes.com/sites/andersonantunes/2014/01/23/the-20-companies-that-own-brazil/#189e54812ec9.

Baker, George, and Rachel Parkin. 2006. "The Changing Structure of the Legal Services Industry and the Careers of Lawyers." *North Carolina Law Review* 84 (5): 1635–1682.

BBC News. 2016. "What Has Gone Wrong in Brazil?" August 31. www.bbc.com/news/world-latin-america-35810578.

Ballakrishnen, Swethaa. 2017. "Women in India's 'Global' Law Firms: Comparative Gender Frames and the Advantage of New Organizations." In *The Indian Legal Profession in the Age of Globalization*. Edited by David Wilkins, Vikramaditya S. Khanna, and David M. Trubek. Cambridge, MA: Cambridge University Press.

Coates, John C., Michele DeStefano, David B. Wilkins, and Ashish Nanda. 2011. "Hiring Teams, Firms and Lawyers: Evidence of the Evolving Relationships in the Corporate Legal Market." *Law and Social Inquiry* 36 (4): 999–1031.

Dinovitzer, Ronit, Robert L. Nelson, Joyce S. Sterling, and Bryant G. Garth. 2012. *After the JD 2: A Longitudinal Study of Careers in Transition, 2007–2008*. Ann Arbor, MI: Inter-university Consortium for Political and Social Research.

Economic Times. 2016, "'Not Yet,' Says Nirmala Sitharaman on FDI in Multi-brand Retail." September 8, 2016. http://economictimes.indiatimes.com/industry/services/retail/not-yet-says-nirmala-sitharaman-on-fdi-in-multi-brand-retail/articleshow/54048468.cms.

European Central Bank. 2016. "What Is Driving Brazil's Economic Downturn?" www.ecb.europa.eu/pub/pdf/other/eb201601_focus01.en.pdf.

Fundacao Getulio Vargas and Columbia Center on Sustainable Investment. 2016. "Leading Brazilian Multinational Enterprises: Trends in an Era of Significant Uncertainties and Challenges." January 20. http://ccsi.columbia.edu/files/2013/10/EMGP-Brazil-Report-2015-Jan-27-final.pdf.

Galanter, Marc, and Nick Robinson. 2017. "Grand Advocates: The Traditional Elite Lawyers." In *The Indian Legal Profession in the Age of Globalization*. Edited by David Wilkins, Vikramaditya S. Khanna, and David M. Trubek. Cambridge: Cambridge University Press.

Gilson, Ronald. 1990. "The Devolution of the Legal Profession: A Demand Side Perspective." *Maryland Law Review* 49 (4): 869–916.

Gupta, Arpita, Vikramaditya S. Khanna, and David B. Wilkins. 2017. "Overview of India and the Indian Legal Profession." In *The Indian Legal Profession in the Age of Globalization: The Rise of the Corporate Legal Sector and Its Influence on Lawyers and Society*. Edited by David B. Wilkins, Vikramaditya S. Khanna, and David M. Trubek. Cambridge: Cambridge University Press.

Hazra, Arnab Kumar, and Bibek Debroy (eds.). 2007. *Judicial Reforms in India: Issue and Aspects*. Delhi: Academic Foundation.

Heineman, Ben. 2016. *The Inside Counsel Revolution: Resolving the Partner-Guardian Tension*. New York: Ankerwycke.

Hendley, Kathryn. 2010. "The Role of In-House Counsel in Post-Soviet Russia in the Wake of Privatization." *International Journal of the Legal Profession* 17 (1): 5–34.

Hendley, Katheryn, Peter Murrell, and Randi Ryterman. 2001. "Agents of Change or Unchanging Agents? The Role of Lawyers within Russian Industrial Enterprises." *Law and Social Inquiry* 26 (3): 285–715.

Khanna, Vikramaditya. 2017. "Can Two Wrongs Make a Right? Insights from the Development of the Home Mortgage Market in India." Draft.

Khanna, Vikramaditya, and Kartikey Mahajan. 2016. "Anticipatory Bail in India: A Novel Way to Address Misuse of the Criminal Profess." In *Research Handbook on Comparative Criminal Procedure*. Edited by Jacqueline Ross and Steven Thaman. New York: Edward Elgar.

Krishnan, Jayanth K. 2010, "Globetrotting Law Firms." *Georgetown Journal of Legal Ethics* 23 (1): 57–102.

Krishnan, Jay, and Patrick Thomas. 2017. "Being Your Own Boss: The Career Trajectories and Motivations of India's Newest Corporate Lawyers." In *The Indian Legal Profession in the Age of Globalization: The Rise of the Corporate Legal Sector and Its Influence on Lawyers and Society*. Edited by David B. Wilkins, Vikramaditya S. Khanna, and David M. Trubek. Cambridge: Cambridge University Press.

Krishnan, Jayanth K., Vitor M. Dias, and John Pence. 2016. "Legal Elites and the Shaping of Corporate Law Practice in Brazil: A Historical Study." *Law and Social Inquiry* 41 (2): 346–370.

Kronman, Anthony T. 1993. *The Lost Lawyer: Failing Ideals of the Legal Profession*. Cambridge, MA: Harvard University Press.

Kumar, Vandana Ajay. 2012. "Judicial Delays in India: Causes and Remedies." *Journal of Law, Policy & Globalization* 16 (4): 16–22.

Moreira, Adilson. 2016. "Discourses of Citizenship in American and Brazilian Affirmative Action Court Decisions." *American Journal of Comparative Law* 64 (2): 455–504.

Morrison, Reese. 2006. "What's the Difference between General Counsel and Chief Legal Officer?" *Law Department Management Blog*, March 22. www.lawdepartmentmanagementblog.com/law_department_management/2006/03/whats_the_diffe.html.

Nataraj, Geethanjali. 2016. "India Takes the Lead in BRICS." East Asia Forum, October 8. www.eastasiaforum.org/2016/10/08/indias-takes-the-lead-of-brics/.

Neil, Martha. 2011. "Some Corps Cut Costs by Hiring Law Grads to Work In-House Instead of Using Big Law Associates." *ABA Journal*, August 11. www.abajournal.com/news/article/some_corps_cut_costs_by_hiring_attorneys/.

Nelson, Robert, and Laura Nielsen. 2000. "Cops, Counsel, and Entrepreneurs: Constructing the Role of Inside Counsel in Large Corporations." *Law and Society Review* 34 (2): 457–494.

Ribstein, Larry. 2012. "Delawyering the Corporation." *Wisconsin Law Review* 4 (3): 306–322.

Rosen, Robert Eli. 1989. "The Inside Counsel Movement, Professional Judgment and Organizational Representation." *Indiana Law Journal* 64 (3): 479–553.

2002. "We're All Consultants Now: How Change in Client Organizational Strategies Influences Change in the Organization of Corporate Legal Services." *Arizona law Review* 44 (2): 638–682.

Rostain, Tanina. 2008. "General Counsel in the Age of Compliance: Preliminary Findings and New Research Questions." *Georgetown Journal of Legal Ethics* 21 (2): 465–490.

Saiko, Mari. 2011. "The General Counsel with Power." http://eureka.sbs.ox.ac.uk/4560/1/General_Counsel_with_Power.pdf.

Schineller, Lisa. 2012. "Brazil's Economic Success Is Based on More Than Demand for Natural Resources." *American Quarterly*, Summer. www.americasquarterly.org/node/3811.

Schwarcz, Steven. 2008. "To Make or to Buy: In-House Lawyering and Value Creation." *Journal of Corporation Law* 33 (3): 497–575.

Silver, Carole, Nicole De Bruin Phelan, and Mikaela Rabinowitz. 2009. "Between Diffusion and Distinctiveness in Globalization: U.S. Law Firms Go Global." *Georgetown Journal of Legal Ethics* 22 (4): 1431–1471.

Singh, Navikar. 2014. "Information Technology and Its Role in India's Economic Development: A Review." April. https://pdfs.semanticscholar.org/28a6/77544c835eaaf20392b411540cfdcc725caa.pdf.

Singh, Rahul. 2017. "Festina Lente or Disguised Protectionism? Monopoly and Competition in the Indian Legal Profession." In *The Indian Legal Profession in the Age of Globalization: The Rise of the Corporate Legal Sector and Its Influence on Lawyers and Society*. Edited by David B. Wilkins, Vikramaditya S. Khanna, and David M. Trubek. Cambridge: Cambridge University Press.

Susskind, Richard. 2008. *The End of Lawyers: Rethinking the Nature of Legal Services*. Oxford: Oxford University Press.

2013. *Tomorrow's Lawyers: An Introduction to Your Future*. Oxford: Oxford University Press.

Susskind, Richard, and Daniel Susskind. 2017. *The Future of the Professions: How Technology Will Transform the Work of Human Experts*. Oxford: Oxford University Press.

Wilkins, David B. 2012. "Is the In-House Counsel Movement Going Global? A Preliminary Assessment of the Role of Internal Counsel in Emerging Economies." *Wisconsin Law Review* 4 (2): 251–304.

Wilkins, David B., and Esteban Maria Jose. Forthcoming. "The Integration of Law into Global Business Solutions: The Rise, Transformation, and Potential Future of the Big Four Accountancy Networks in the Global Legal Services Market." *Law & Social Inquiry*.

Wilkins, David B., and Vikramaditya S. Khanna. 2017. "Globalization and the Rise of the In-House Counsel Movement in India." In *The Indian Legal Profession in the Age of Globalization: The Rise of the Corporate Legal Sector and Its Influence on Lawyers and Society*. Edited by David B. Wilkins, Vikramaditya S. Khanna, and David M. Trubek. Cambridge: Cambridge University Press.

Wilkins, David, Ashish Nanda, and Bryon Fong. 2017. "Mapping India's Corporate Law Firms." In *The Indian Legal Profession in the Age of Globalization*. Edited by David Wilkins, Vikramaditya S. Khanna, and David M. Trubek. Cambridge: Cambridge University Press.

5

Globalizing Processes for São Paulo Attorneys

Gender Stratification in Law Firms and Law-Related Businesses

Maria da Gloria Bonelli and Camila de Pieri Benedito

I INTRODUCTION

In the discourse on globalization of professions, scholars frequently refer to globalization in the singular, as if it were a unidirectional phenomenon by which professionals in northern-based countries export expertise to professionals in southern-based nations, which import advances in knowledge that circulate throughout the global network of professional power structures (Dezalay and Garth 2002). But when we look at how these processes have played out in the Brazilian legal profession, we see there are variable impacts and multiple directions, producing new local practices using models generated in other social contexts, often adapted from specific legal cultures. Inversely, we also see how professionals who cross borders take with them methods employed at home to meet the specific interests of clients that migrate or have transnational mobility.

This chapter aims to analyze two aspects of these globalizing processes in the profession, showing how the forms of global homogenization they produce leave enough space for coordinated fragmentation of the world, placing differences and inequalities in a new order without eradicating them (García Canclini 2014). In this sense, a country with social disparities such as those in Brazil reproduces this stratification in the legal profession, which is characterized both by gender stratification and by transformation of the meaning professionals attribute to globalization in accordance with their relative positions within the social hierarchy, manipulating and negotiating those meanings on a local level.

The first aspect of globalization's fragmenting effect is that it is not restricted solely to law practiced by law firms that deal with business clients outside the country, or in association with large-scale foreign offices and partners, reducing the globalizing effect to the professional elite who travel internationally.

Globalization impacts other segments of legal practice, including those not usually classified as being of "excellence" or conducted by renowned names in the legal field, but rather performed by professionals who offer specialized services in the mass-litigation field. Influenced by global ideas of specialization and organization, this mass-litigation segment of the profession has also been integrated into a global market and organized along business lines.

The globalization experienced by large-scale corporate law firms in São Paulo, whose expertise includes internationalization and cross-border transactions in specialized areas, such as environmental law, digital law, imports and exports, financial transactions, business contracts, and infrastructure and regulation, differs from the globalization that sets the tone for litigation en masse practiced by legal companies that hire attorneys to take on rote work. The process of outsourcing mass litigation from corporate general counsel offices to specialized mass-litigation firms started in the United States in the 1980s following the litigation explosion. In Brazil, this occurred in the 1990s as the economy grew, more foreign corporations entered the market, and litigation soared. Possibly influenced by foreign models, corporations outsourced this work to specialized law firms, which created unique models mixing legal practices with business methods.

The second aspect of globalizing processes refers to contrasts permeated by social differences and inequality. It is incorrect to reduce transnational effects to a uniform process with similar results everywhere. Such processes not only reproduce inequalities between men and women in private life, transposing them to their careers and stratifying the profession based on gender (Thornton 1996; Schultz 2003; Feuvre and Lapeyere 2005; Bolton and Muzio 2007; Kay and Gorman 2008), but also create new opportunities for such professionals that can become part of the internationalized legal elite (Ballakrishnen 2012), especially when they share a masculine view of professionalism (Bonelli 2013).

This is shown by the study of the fragmenting aspects of global law practices on gender and diversity in the law firms in São Paulo that shows how these new forms of organizing legal work, which mirror transnational models, have led to broader inclusion of women on technical teams while maintaining gender stratification. Although the ideology of professionalism emphasizes autonomy and neutrality of knowledge, reinforcing the belief that the differences in gender and sexuality do not matter in the face of technical capacity, it is acknowledged the world over that career opportunities are established because of visible aspects like gender, even when trying to remove them.

II METHODOLOGY

This investigation employs a multimethod approach, bringing together quantitative and qualitative data. In the former we analyze law firms that are members of the Center for Studies on Law Firms (CESA), an organization of the large Brazilian corporate law firms, using information taken from websites for CESA law firms in São Paulo. In the latter we rely on semistructured interviews and observation of gender relations in some of these firms, as well as a case study from JBM Advogados, the largest mass-litigation firm in the country.[1]

We consider that the large-scale corporate firms in CESA, as well as the very different mass-litigation firms, illustrate the stratification and fragmentation of globalizing processes. CESA's members are renowned in the legal field, and JBM is establishing itself among the professional elite based on its success in managing litigation en masse on behalf of companies. The organization of both types of practice reflects the hybridism brought on by globalizing processes, whether it is to produce and distinguish expertise by adding value to the client's business or to displace the predominating concept of professionalism in favor of a market-based rationale in mass litigation.

In these very different practices, we can see the differentiation that occurs when women enter a predominantly male legal field. We show the gender breakdown in CESA member firms in terms of the positions held by professionals as well as the role of women in JBM. With this, both the choice of methodology and the fieldwork are in accordance with the debate on the two processes being discussed: the fragmentation caused by globalization with a range of impacts on the professional market, and gender-based stratification.

Data on the gender breakdown in the São Paulo law firms helped classify professionals as partner or associate. Of the 385 law firms in São Paulo that were CESA members at the time data was collected, there was information on the website for 198 of them; still, many did not specify the positions of the professionals within the firm, referring to them merely as part of the "team." We found classifications as partners and associates for 3,321 attorneys (864 for the former, 2,457 for the latter). This data was organized and placed in charts, which will be presented in the next section.[2]

[1] JBM leads the segment in the market, facing competition from other offices that operate in a similar fashion, including selling its model to other massified legal practices.

[2] The subjective meanings for gender relations in CESA member law firms were analyzed in Bonelli, based on qualitative interviews and observation (Bonelli 2013). Because of space restrictions, these aspects will not be addressed in this chapter.

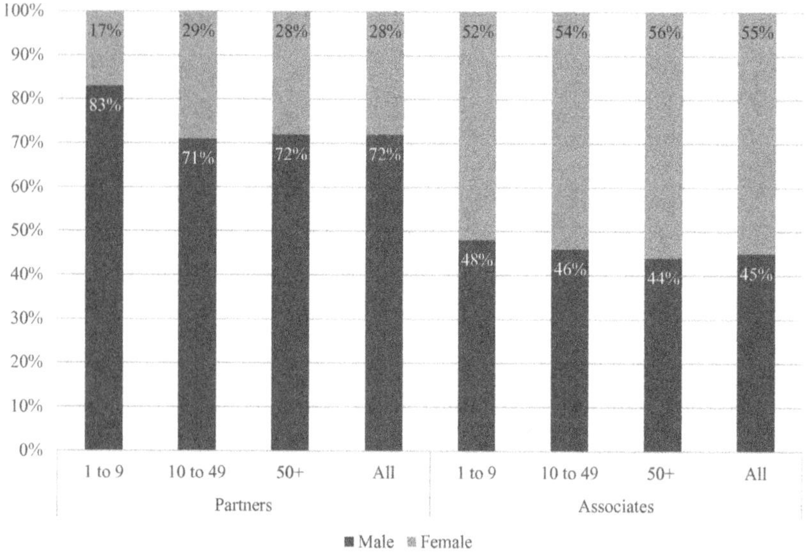

FIGURE 5.1 Breakdown of partners and associates in the law firms that are CESA members, per office size and gender.
Source: Bonelli (2013).

For the JBM Advogados case study, besides documents and information provided by the office, nine semistructured interviews were conducted with professionals operating in the Bauru office, where the firm's headquarters are located. Seven female attorneys were interviewed, as was one male attorney and one female operational manager. They had all been born in the neighboring region or had some long-standing ties with the city, having studied law in one of the private colleges there. Their ages ranged from twenty-nine to thirty-nine years, most were single, and none had children.

III SÃO PAULO LAW FIRMS THAT ARE CESA MEMBERS

Empirical studies on legal practice in law firms indicate that globalizing processes that internationalize professions have an impact on the opportunities for women in professional teams. We found that large-scale Brazilian corporate firms copy more closely the homogenizing model of global firms, in which female participation has blossomed. The larger firms proved to be more open to incorporating female professionals both as partners and as associates. Figure 5.1 presents data on this gender breakdown per the size of the office.

The smaller firms look more like the traditional style of legal practice,[3] mostly under the command of male attorneys, incorporating female attorneys in the less prestigious positions within the career, which entail the more rote/mundane services.

In large-scale firms (with more than fifty attorneys) and medium-sized offices (between ten and fifty attorneys), females make up close to 30 percent of the partners, which is the most valued position, with leadership roles, high-level expertise, corporate clients, and networks of contacts. In the individual or small offices, male partners surpass the 80 percent mark, with female partners at 17 percent. The gender-based stratification among associate attorneys varies less per the size of the office. Most are female professionals, which confirms that men are more represented in the higher positions and that progress within the career differs according to gender.

Studies on professional placement of female attorneys in other countries reveal standards that are quite different:

> International comparisons reveal significant differences in terms of the kind of law firm women find themselves in. For instance, in Germany they are more likely to be sole practitioners; in Japan it is small law firms that provide the most posts for women lawyers; and in Canada women are just as likely to be practicing on their own as they are to be working in large law firms. (Schultz 2003, xlii)

In this sense, the Brazilian case only strengthens the idea presented above that female participation in law depends on national differences, even though it is a phenomenon resulting from globalizing processes. In Brazil, the large-scale and medium-sized law firms promote female attorneys to partner, in contrast with the traditional Brazilian small law firms, which close the doors to females when it comes to partnership.

As can be seen in Figure 5.2, both male and female attorneys at CESA member law firms seek the model of expert specialization. Some 61 percent of male and female partners and 52 percent of female and male associates invested in professional development, either in postgraduate continuing education diploma courses (*lato sensu*) and other short-term courses, or in master's and doctoral degree programs (the latter to a lesser extent and mainly taken by males). Such education generates merit-based distinctions that weigh heavily in law firms that work internationally and that tend to place the

[3] Traditional legal practice refers to liberal work, in family firms or with very few professional peers, litigating to defend their clients' interests in court.

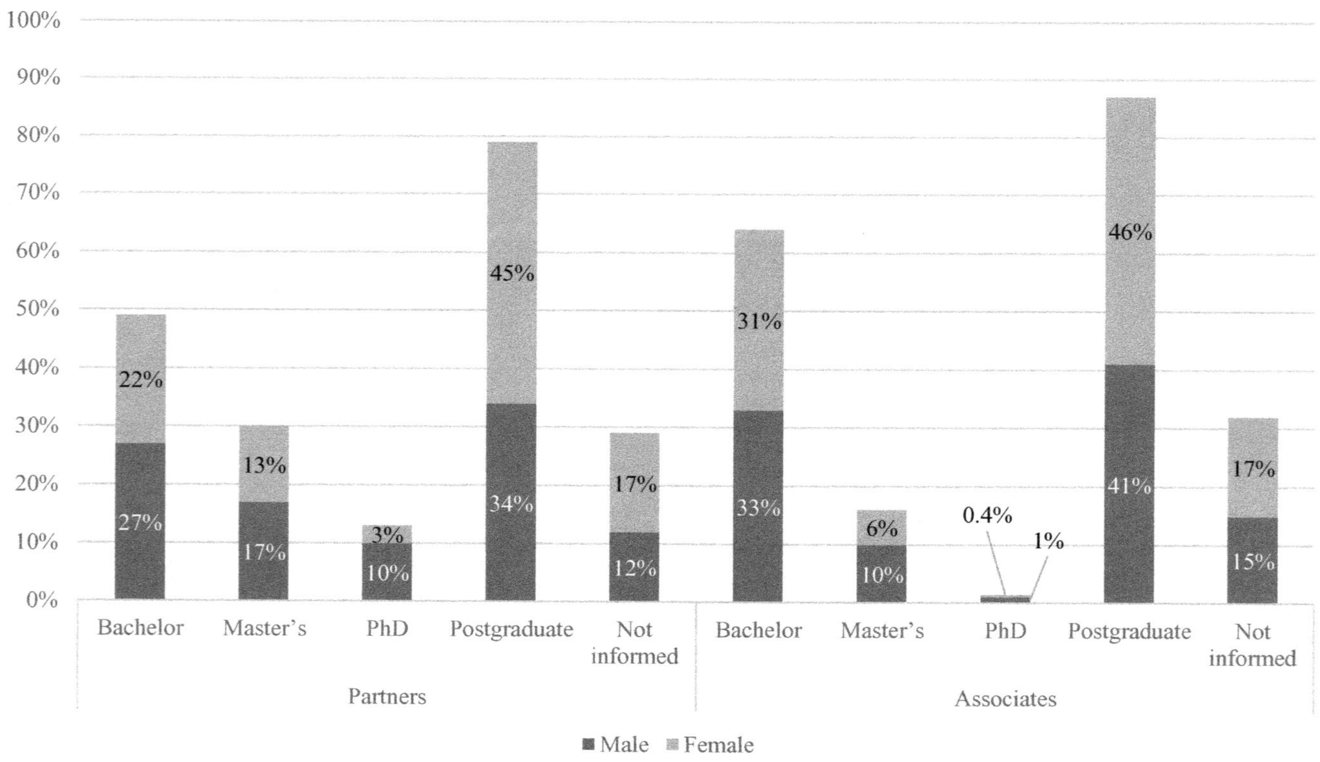

FIGURE 5.2 Breakdown of partners and associates in CESA member law firms, per level of schooling and gender.
Source: Bonelli (2013).

academic qualifications of their main team on their websites as proof of their excellence.

This is another characteristic that differentiates professionals in globalized law firms from those in local firms: in the large firms, the individual drive to attain competences is equal for both genders, instead of more specialization for males, as seen in other research (Bergoglio 2007; Gastiazoro 2007; Bonelli et al. 2008). Such investment, however, has uneven results, disproportionately guaranteeing more advances for male attorneys who are made partner than for female attorneys. Emulating the legal practices of large-scale global firms and the need for capable professionals who can confidently transit across and between the boundaries of civil and common law, Portuguese and English and other foreign languages, the large-scale law firms not only place higher value on expertise but also foster the inclusion of women and promote advances in their careers. In this vein, differences become clearly visible in the professional legal market.

If one of the impacts of globalizing processes was the capacity to bring about the stratified inclusion of women in the professional private legal market, making it possible for a number of them to progress in their career to the point of becoming partners on the basis of expertise and a corporate client base, we also noticed the opposite standard that massified legal education has helped promote: higher numbers of female students coinciding with Taylorism of the professional practice and the fact that activities are becoming more rote.

When organizing legal work, the traditional model links "liberal" work – typical in a small law firm, with predominately white, heterosexual males educated in generalist private schools who have knowledge on the specifics of local case law and little international experience or expertise. The ways that globalization mixes with this local standard result in hybrid structures in which autonomy and specialized professionalism blend together with corporate and business ideals, as well as a focus on several demands made by corporate clients that stretch beyond legal knowledge; within this market rationale there is the stratification of the career, salary standardization, and downgrading work for some lawyers, with law graduates taking on work usually performed by paralegals and legal assistants.

The ideal of professionalism – in which expertise is used to render services of excellence, without subjecting such diagnostics to political or economic interests, or that of clients – has given way to corporate needs. A system of peer-based relations, which was the usual way to organize this kind of work, has given way to hierarchical structures, producing the professional elite and oceans of hired attorneys, while recent law graduates take on paralegal positions until they pass the Brazilian Bar exam. Each one of these levels faces the effects of globalizing processes in their activities, whether it is in the advent of this new position whose practitioners – mostly women – expect to perform it temporarily until they enter the legal field; the creation of massified law firms, specialized in high-volume litigation with a flow of operationalized lawsuits as if on a conveyor belt; or the stratification of law into partners, associates, and contract lawyers.

IV CONSTRUCTING LEGAL COMPANIES THROUGH LITIGATION EN MASSE: JBM ADVOGADOS AND GENDER STRATIFICATION

JBM's website declares that, for the fourth consecutive year, the 2013 Annual Law Awards deemed it the largest law firm in the country in terms of numbers of attorneys. JBM was founded in 1997 by Mandaliti Advogados, a small law firm that, in 2008, merged with the São Paulo firm Demarest e Almeida Advogados. The merger was made possible by José Edgard Cunha Bueno Filho (J. Bueno) and the brothers-partners Reinaldo and Rodrigo Mandaliti.

JBM specializes in corporate litigation en masse. Headquartered in the city of Bauru, it has twenty-six affiliate offices in Brazil, which handle 15,000 hearings a month, 150,000 due diligence operations, and 18,000 lawsuits.[4] JBM is an office focusing specifically on mass litigation that deals with a large number of lawsuits on a daily basis within a framework referred to as a "conveyor belt" on the basis of an assembly line and automated production in Fordism – along with a sector that is specialized in quality. JBM is a law firm that sees itself as an extension of the companies it renders services to, emphasizing organizational values instead of a rationale of professionalism and diversified expertise. Most of its attorneys carry out repetitive work, which does not require specialized qualifications; the predominating law school generalist education is sufficient for this work.

In March 2014 the Bauru headquarters had 535 legal operators, of which approximately 65 percent were women. With a structure quite different from those of other law firms, which have both partners and associates, JBM employs both female and male attorneys under the regular labor laws (known as the Consolidation of Labor Laws, or CLT), much like companies do with regular workers, negotiating wages with the trade union. In terms of the ideal, JBM partners distance themselves from the predominating rationale of occupational professionalism, under the standardized value of generating cohesion within the group. They share the corporate viewpoint and that

4 Data taken from an interview with José Edgard Bueno in Consultor Jurídico. See www.conjur.com.br/2013-out-06/entrevista-jose-edgard-bueno-socio-fundador-jbm-advogados.

of organizational professionalism, whose discourse is aimed at disciplining bodies and work.

According to Evetts these two structures to organize work on the basis of knowledge can be systematized into: (1) *occupational professionalism*, which is related to not only the discourse constructed within a professional group but also the authorized collegiate, the ability to have discretion in work, occupational control of work, the trust placed in the practitioner by clients and employers, the practitioners that operationalize controls, and finally the professional ethics monitored by institutions and associations, falling into the Durkheim model of moral communities; and (2) *organizational professionalism*, which refers to not only the discourse of control used more often by administrators in work organizations but also the structures of rational-legal authority, standardized procedures, hierarchical frameworks of authority and decision-making power, managerialism, and finally rendering accounts and outside methods of regulation, establishing targets, and supervising performance, falling into the Weberian model of organization (Evetts 2012, 7).

The organizational hierarchy at JBM Advogados and the respective gender breakdown at the headquarters in Bauru can be seen in Figure 5.3.

The city of Bauru, where most of JBM's legal operators are concentrated, is situated in the midwest region of São Paulo state, some 326 kilometers from the capital city of São Paulo. Bauru has two public university branches (USP and UNESP) and some other colleges, of which four – from the private sector – offer a BA in law: the Toledo Educational Institution (ITE), the Integrated Colleges of Bauru (FIB), the Sacred Heart University (USC), and Universidade Paulista, from where many of the attorneys, both male and female, who work for JBM have graduated.

Legal petitions are drafted only at three of JBM's branches, known as the "Head Branches."[5] In the other affiliates, employed attorneys receive lawsuits they must defend in hearings, as is described by an interviewee from one of the Head Branches:

> They do not draft petitions – they go to hearings; they work out in the field, on the streets, in the courtrooms. Here we are more... on the intellectual side, and there they... get down to the nitty-gritty, go to hearings, these sorts of things. Everything comes from here [and] goes to the affiliates. Here we have hearings as well, but the lawsuits are drafted here because here we have an entire infrastructure: we have a section to correct petitions, we have someone who writes them, we have someone who corrects them. It is impossible

5 The "Head Branches" are in the cities of Bauru, São Paulo, and Ribeirão Preto.

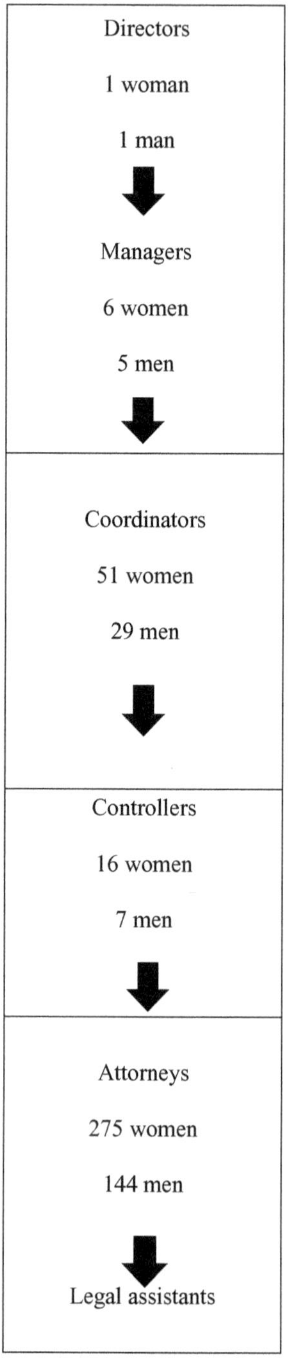

FIGURE 5.3 Flowchart and the breakdown of gender in legal positions.

to do this in all the affiliates. (interview with an attorney at the company for more than five years)

The infrastructure at the office in Bauru is significant. In the building where the legal division is located, on Avenida Getúlio Vargas – one of the city's main avenues – approximately 540 employees are spread across four floors (ground, first, second, and third floors), and there are long tables with computers where the attorneys and legal assistants work.

Each table is responsible for one client, and that is where legal assistants, level 1 attorneys, level 2 attorneys, two controllers, and one coordinator work. The coordinator maintains direct contact with the client and receives feedback on services rendered, while the controllers provide assistance to the coordinator, helping him or her tutor the attorneys and legal assistants who draft the petitions. Besides the tables – which are divisions that represent and work for specific clients – there is also the Quality Division, which is responsible for correcting the lawsuits. Hierarchically above the coordinators are the managers, establishing a bridge between the services rendered at the long tables and the board of directors.

The hierarchical structure and the standardized production of lawsuits, which are controlled by managers and are not in a collegiate framework in which peers take on legal cases as per their expertise, distinguish organizational professionalism from occupational professionalism. Law firms specialized in litigation en masse for their clients build their public reputation, in contrast to the law firms that exhibit indicators showing the professional excellence of their teams. On JBM's website, only five male attorneys are presented by name and accompanied by their respective professional qualifications. Work done by women is not seen as specialized and is reserved for activities in operationalization and supervision areas. The company's management sees these positions in the light of conventional wisdom, in which feminine culture is more practical and disciplined to carry out more rote tasks, showing less insubordination and working for lower salaries. On the other hand, in this office, the expertise related to higher abstract knowledge and discretionary autonomy is concentrated on five professionals.

Fragmented homogenization caused by globalizing processes in Brazil's legal practice has been made easier through gender discrimination. In the mass-litigation model, which incorporates massified work in law firms by taking on professionals who took a law course at educational institutions that themselves provided massified education, we can see a strong presence of females (65 percent) compared to the percentage of attorneys enrolled at the Brazilian Bar Association in São Paulo (OAB-SP), which is 45 percent females. In the elite corporate model of internationalization of expertise, professionals are empowered when they circulate in transnational networks in countries from both the north and the south (Dezalay and Garth 2002), producing the new legal elite comprising mainly male partners of large-scale law firms, but including female partners on a smaller scale. Even though the masculine viewpoint on professionalism and on exclusive dedication to the law firm predominates in such progress, global processes also provoke deviations in gender-based barriers and in the values that guide professional action.

On the one hand, there is the JBM model, whose legal operators are rooted in a local context, receiving the basic salary as agreed upon by the lawyers' trade union; on the other hand, in the international circulation scenario, there is an agenda promoting diversity and gender identification in elite law firms. An example of this other model is the 2009 event organized by the partners at Pinheiro Neto Advogados, which was proposed by the Committee on Women in the Profession, of the New York City Bar Association, to discuss the report titled "Best Practices for the Hiring, Training, Retention and Advancement of Women Attorneys."

The event brought together about 120 women from law firms and corporate legal departments in São Paulo, constituting an audience made up of the female legal elite. The aim, based on the report, was to help improve legal practices in Brazil by reducing gender inequality among male and female attorneys while building new visions on professionalism and gender difference.

Five years after the event, some impact has been made by internationalization, notably in the increasing number of female partners in medium-sized and large-scale firms. The law firm Machado, Meyer, Sendacz e Opice Advogados, for the second year running, was presented with the Euromoney Award for being the best office in terms of gender diversity and policy in Latin America.

The homogenization of the imagined globalization established a new order for inequalities in the legal field, but did not eradicate them. It produced a hierarchy of opportunities for female professionals coming from remote social origins: while most of them undergo massified professionalization processes, others become part of the professional elite seeking equal treatment for both genders (García Canclini 2014).

V JBM AND DISCOURSE REFERENCES IN THE INDUSTRIAL MODEL

The word *company* appears quite often in the attorneys' and partners' discourse, which reveals they have identified with JBM. The industrial universe gave us mass production, mechanization, conveyor belts, and Fordism, which are now present in the ideology of professional services. JBM adapted to the business process outsourcing (BPO) model, segmenting its activities into three different groups: a company focused on recovering credit and billing carried out by Concilig; a company in charge of technology, information services, HR, and accounting, carried out by Finch Soluções; and the legal attributions left to JBM proper. According to J. Bueno in an interview to Conjur, in 2013, Finch provides services to several companies and law firms. The market rationale is summed up by the journalist holding the interview:

> Systems and methods are so important to JBM's operations in the market that, in the middle of this year, the office was split, placing attorneys on one side and the technology team on the other. Finch Soluções was born. The new business began with 550 collaborators in twenty-seven affiliates, taking with it the data expertise that JBM had collected over the five years of existence and through the 18,000 lawsuits that it receives every month. Today it deals with close to 320,000.
>
> Finch renders services to JBM itself, to the law firm's clients, and to other law firms. Its annual turnover is R$45 million, which seems to please the attorney José Edgard Bueno. A master at conducting these two orchestras, accompanied by his partner Reinaldo Mandaliti – at Finch, there are two other partners – Bueno is not a fan of ties, prefers jeans to suits, and constantly uses the term the "industry of law." He wants to break the taboo concerning the so-called mercantilization of law, an expression that sends shivers down the spines of attorneys due to the OAB restrictions. (Consultor Jurídico 2013)

This corporate structure and JBM's mass production were also presented in the magazine *Exame*, in 2011, and were described as follows:

> The entranceway to JBM, downtown Bauru, in the interior of São Paulo state, opens up to a 2,000m² room with high ceilings, like a shed. There, gondolas are lined up like those in a supermarket, each one with dozens of work stations, where more than four hundred employees, side-by-side, are glued to the screens of their computers.
>
> These professionals have targets to meet: they need to attend a specific number of customers before their shift ends. Among the most common terms used throughout the day are workflow, checklist, team management, quality control, result indicators. It is only when visitors take a few steps back that they can see, on the silver plaque in the hallway to the elevators, that this is not a telemarketing center or something like that.

> "J. Bueno and Mandaliti – Law Firm" it reads. It is the largest law firm in the country in terms of numbers of attorneys. It is also – most certainly – the most nonconventional law firm working in Brazil today.
>
> The main reason for this is its field of operations. JBM is the first office in the country specialized in what lawyers refer to as "litigation en masse." This means that their attorneys take care of tens of thousands of small cases that target large companies – mainly labor cases and consumer law.
>
> To organize the slew of lawsuits their legal departments have to deal with, companies hire law firms – which, to handle the work, are organized like veritable sausage factories of law. JBM alone manages more than 230,000 lawsuits. And, according to its partners, will turn over close to 110 million reais in 2011. (Moschella 2011)

However, the internal interpretation of JBM's work is quite different from that shown above. Mass production, mechanization, and Fordism gain meanings that oppose those used in the article, as they are understood as positive qualifications of the services the group provides. When the interviewees[6] were asked about the article, they were quite disappointed with the derogatory image used to describe the company's work:

> The use of this term? I don't know where this came from, because it matches nothing... "sausage factory"... because if you wanted to talk about something mechanized, I think he used a very misleading term because there is no connection between the term and the type of work we do. No connection. If he wanted to say Fordism, perhaps, it would be a more intelligent word to use – Fordism, which is the mechanization of work, and our work is quite mechanized. But "sausage factory"? I don't know where he got that. (interview with an attorney at JBM for more than five years)

> There really is a mass flow of work – others might say conveyor belt, even mechanization – but when you work like this, there is study, there is an effort, but when the magazine said "sausage factory," it gives the impression that it is anybody, drafting any old thing. (interview with a female attorney, at JBM for more than five years)

And there is a viewpoint that puts the depreciative aspect of mass production into perspective:

6 It is important to clarify that during this research, there was some difficulty in obtaining authorization from the JBM human resources department to conduct the fieldwork, which, after several attempts at contact, provided names and a schedule to hold the interviews.

> JBM is a mass production office because we work with banks. Most of our clients are banks; that is, they are boring matters – the bank is always accused of being wrong; it is always the bank that incorrectly sent someone's name to the blacklist. Or it is a mechanized office in the sense that there are always mechanized arguments for specific types of lawsuits, but it does not mean the whole office runs like this. JBM is not solely en masse. JBM has consultation, special cases. There are sectors that the client requests to which the client forward the lawsuit he wants to file; he himself is accusing someone. So, most of the office is a mass production office that runs this production line – someone registers the lawsuit, another one requests a copy, the other drafts the answer, the other accompanies the lawsuit, the other drafts the appeal, another one does this, another does that, and so forth, until the case is closed and we return the case to the client. (interview with a female attorney at JBM for more than five years)

One of the managers at the headquarters in Bauru, who believed the article could have a negative effect on the office's reputation, became quite positive after receiving new clients who were interested in the specific way the office was run:

> I truly believe that it benefited the company. It caused quite a ruckus; people were upset with the situation. But in terms of market – and here I mean the professional side – this episode opened up some doors for us, because some companies were interested in our business, in our products, seeing how they were conducted and offered. So, amazing as it sounds, something that was quite negative became positive, and we gained three or four more new clients at the office. I think the term ["sausage factory"] was useless and unnecessary – they had "X" number of ways to talk about an office of this size, and the structure it has – but I think the press . . . you can sell yourself well when you sell a term that gives an impression, a bad impression, a good impression, I don't know, but one that generates some . . . media. The magazine wants to sell! So they use the term for this, to draw the public's attention. That's the only reason. (interview with a female coordinator at JBM for more than five years)

Taking the unidirectional viewpoint on the global law model, partner J. Bueno, in the aforementioned interview, affirms that perceptions on high-volume litigation are expected to change, because JBM represents a new way to conduct law in Brazil, which fits in well with the changes the market and globalization are imposing on legal practice. For him, the numbers of partners and associates should be revised, justifying his hiring new attorneys as salary-based workers with labor rights:[7]

> Very few offices have attorneys registered under CLT. The Brazilian Bar Association established the associate or partner structure according to the amount of work done. The structure of partners working under this quota system has been accepted by case law, and there are not many legal problems. Meanwhile, the associate quotas, which is what most offices use, case law has not accepted. When an attorney files a labor suit against his office, registered employment is legally recognized. Most of the market works with associates; many have no employment regime whatsoever. This needs to be looked into, because, on the one hand, attorneys are not protected and, on the other, this establishes unfair competition. In a procured estimate, one law firm may not have everyone working under registered employment and, thus, has a natural advantage over the firms that have to cover CLT surcharges. The practical consequence of this is that the price of the former will be much better for that potential client. In our profession, a large part of our overhead is labor. This is a huge disadvantage. We have to change this. It is so ridiculous that we have a rule established by the OAB – the associate attorney concept – but which is not accepted by the judiciary system. (Consultor Jurídico 2013)

JBM's attorneys work forty hours a week and receive benefits, such as an annual paid OAB membership, private health plan, and travel and meal allowances. The floor salary at the Bauru headquarters is less than R$2,000 (US$835) per month, while the floor salary established by the Attorneys Trade Union in São Paulo was R$2,130 and the general minimum wage for the state of São Paulo was R$810 a month.

Most of those working at the headquarters also live in Bauru or in surrounding cities, traveling every day to get to work. The turnover of attorneys is high because many, as part of their career plans, move to places where salaries are higher, as happens in the city of São Paulo, where more specialized services than just the conveyor belt system are offered. Some male and female attorneys from neighboring cities choose to work from home, thus justifying the

[7] Hiring workers with set salaries establishes boss-employee type relationships for rendering professional services. Under this structure, workers have rights guaranteed by the Consolidation of Labor Laws (CLT) and a floor salary due to trade union agreements. These rights are costlier for employers, as there are twelve monthly salaries, thirty days of paid vacation time, and Brazil's bonus, but mandatory, thirteenth salary, as well as a severance fund payment for time in service and Social Security. Several professionals work in law firms on a regular basis in conditions quite different from those with set salaries. They work as associate attorneys and do not have these rights; law firms do not cover these costs.

option to remain in their cities of origin due to the difficulty in paying rent and bills in the city of Bauru on a limited salary.

One of the interviewees mentioned that many colleagues, when considering the work at the firm, feel like factory workers and not attorneys:

> I've heard people say: "Here, I am not an attorney; I am a factory worker, because I sit here, I have to fulfill my quota,[8] and I am not treated like an attorney." So people end up subjecting themselves to this because they have no other option. It is difficult. Here, they call you a service provider. You are not an attorney. So you do five years of college [law school], and you do not have a floor salary that is correct. (interview with a female attorney at JBM for up to five years)

The interviewee expressed her interest in finding a better job where she would be recognized as an attorney. Another aspect she lamented was the level of stress from living in one city and working in another, a routine she opted for because she believes her salary is not enough to cover the cost of living in Bauru itself. According to her, JBM is able to treat their employees better, and this could boost their reputation as a mass-litigation firm when compared to other offices in the legal field.

Another professional mentioned her plans to leave JBM; however, she attributed her problems with leadership at work to herself, which stymie any chance for promotion within the company. Because of this, she is studying to pass a recruitment exam for some banks. Male and female attorneys who have been at the office for some time, or who have managed to get some kind of internal promotion, had more positive opinions about their work relations at the JBM headquarters in Bauru.

VI WOMEN IN MASS LITIGATION: PERCEPTIONS FROM FEMALE ATTORNEYS AT JBM

At JBM Advogados, there is a strong presence of female legal staff, in an environment whose discourses are closer to organizational professionalism. Does the company prefer to recruit females? Data seems to suggest it does for litigation en masse. As we saw in the introduction, our argument is that globalizing processes in the professional world are fragmenting, producing homogenization without eradicating differences and inequalities. This type of

8 This refers to the conveyor belt structure, in which the process is not attributed to an attorney but rather treated as a fragmented flow so as to increase productivity. There is a system in which services are distributed on a daily basis. Thus, attorneys do not continue with the work they did the day before, nor do they know what is to come.

professionalism blends the profession and bureaucracy, standardizing hierarchical practices based on gender.

According to one female manager, the profile the firm tends to hire is the recently graduated youth, which is justified by the belief that they do not have any "attorney habits" in a profession seen as complicated and quite often "not so teachable." This is how she sees the work of women who adjust the best they can to the work. Today, they are changing things slightly and trying to attract more experienced and educated people.

Meanwhile, in the opinion of the interviewees, the reasons that women are more strongly present is due to their own world rather than to corporate initiatives. They attribute this to (1) the number of female university students available in the city coming from the four undergraduate law courses offered in Bauru; (2) the fact that JBM is a newer firm, which increased its staff numbers when there was already a large number of women for legal services; and (3) the merit they have for taking on staff and internal promotion.

> In the past there were more men working here, and today this is no longer an issue. The legal careers are usually public positions, so there is no way of eliminating a man or a woman, but they are . . . We are actually dominating the field; we are getting there. If the numbers are not the same, they are very close. As there is no discrimination, [JBM] does not hire a person because she is a woman or because he is a man, but rather because of his or her competence, on the basis of what happens in the job interview. There is a four-stage selection process. There is no discrimination against men or women. It is how you perform, your experience. (interview with a female attorney up to five years at JBM)

> I am not sure if in the past it was more difficult for women because the mentality was that they had to stay at home, taking care of the children, and today that's not the case; that doesn't exist anymore. Perhaps, in the future this number may level out, maybe. Today, it is easy to get into an office similar to ours here, and for you to get into a legal career like this. So maybe in the future this will level out, I don't know. Maybe. (interview with a male attorney more than five years at JBM)

The expectation that gender-based opportunities will level out over time appears not only in interviewees' opinions but also in the conventional wisdom and sociological approach to gender within the legal profession. Several studies show that time is not a decisive factor in helping level out numbers, with disparities and gender differences consistently abounding in the professional area, even in countries that implemented affirmative action aimed at women several years ago. With this, combining theoretical perspectives seems to be more appropriate when trying to understand the distances between men and women in the legal field, bringing together theories on gender-based discrimination, unequal structural conditions, and human capital (Kay and Gorman 2008).

In the interviews, mention was made of the fact that working in an office with such strong female presence works as an energy boost, with female attorneys feeling at ease in a space with female colleagues and leaders, including with a board of directors as a reference, as described in this interview:

> It is a great office to work in. There are some people who say otherwise, but they don't leave and I think it's an office that seeks to speak with you every day. [Name of the female attorney], who is a friend of the owners, became a director. She has been here since the beginning, so I think that women, when attributed with a task, manage to achieve more than men. I think, on this issue, I was being a feminist, but I think it is true – we delve deeper, we go further, we are more intense with what we do. This is why sometimes I prefer to work with women. (interview with a female attorney, up to five years at JBM)

The female interviewees also highlighted other positive aspects about having female attorneys at the office, such as (1) they believe women in leadership positions are more receptive to problems involving family and sickness, (2) they feel more respected and excited about work, and (3) they carry out their work with more dedication and enthusiasm:

> As there are plenty of women, we feel great because we understand that women have their own dynamics, timing, things they want to do. There are many pregnant women, who have children, who are on maternity leave, so they are used to thinking about this. (interview with a female attorney, more than five years at JBM)

> When we are given a task, we do more than just the task here; at least, I am like this. Women do not like to be the center of gossip, and the office here is run by large names. As I am a coordinator, I prefer to work more with women because I think women go further, they are more into detail. Men do not. Men are broader: "Ah, but I did that," "You did not include that, dear," "No, but it'll do." Women are different. Women go into the smallest detail. That's it. (interview with a female coordinator up to five years at JBM)

> But women themselves, they have a more persistent profile, you know? So, in my experience I see men and women, and I think women have more relationship problems, but in terms of work they are more persistent, they

> stick with it, they are warriors. Men are less so. Women insist more; they are more committed. (interview with a manager, more than five years at JBM)

> So, some values are changing because before, I thought that certain companies did not hire women because of maternity leave, because they prefer to hire men, to avoid paying surcharges and in the future having to pay leave. But today, women are conquering their own space, because women are more sensible, especially in the legal field. 60 percent of the prep courses comprise women. A female judge is more sensible that a male justice; for example, a female judge in family law, for example, who is to rule on a case, is much better than a male judge. They are more sensible, more human. So, a bus company, for example, is hiring more women than men. Women are taking the jobs. Here at JBM, my sector has a female manager and coordinator. There are no male leaders. (interview with a female attorney, up to five years at JBM)

We can see that the viewpoints based on the essentialism of gender differences,[9] understood as the nature of men and women and often used to establish gender stratification in the workplace, are constructed as a positive attribute within the discourse of female attorneys. At JBM, the reference to gender appears as a resource to obstruct the professional space in which women work (Bolton and Muzio 2007). While they are able to make headway in the mass-litigation area, these practices feed the essentialism of gender and make the deconstruction of such inequalities more and more distant.

VII FINAL CONSIDERATIONS

This text sought to emphasize that the homogenization caused by global processes within the legal field has a fragmenting effect instead of a unidimensional outcome. This allows for the local reestablishment of meaning, forming a hybrid mix between organizational structures and the rationale of work, as well as fostering unfair opportunities when including women in the profession. The cases analyzed focused on law firms that were CESA members who were stratified in terms of gender, especially in partner and associate attorney positions, highlighting work that is separated into mass or elite structures and the inclusion of gender differences. Internationalization has had a more

[9] Feminist theory rejects essentialism and maintains that gender difference is socially constructed. Essentialism assumes that there is a fixed masculine and feminine essence, thereby transforming what are really small body differences and culturally produced distinctions into permanent and unchangeable characteristics. This biological approach creates an obligatory and linear relationship between sex, gender, desire, and sexual practices prescribed in the dominant heterosexual culture. Such a hegemonic and binary vision contrasts the respective roles of men and women in society and justifies existing gender hierarchies (Scott 1986; Butler 1990).

significant impact on the entry of women both into elite positions and nontraditional legal positions.

Concerning the JBM Advogados case specifically, which does not correspond to the traditional model for the Brazilian law firm market but in some ways is inspired by law firms using organizational standards, our analysis addressed how it came to be, separating itself from the professional world of law moving into the corporate universe, taking on standards aimed at cutting costs to become more competitive in the mass-litigation market. For such, the reference used is that of a production line, with turnover and cheap labor, blending the industrial model with the rationale of bureaucratic organizations and a discourse of professionalism, merging the frontiers together between free competition and market reserves, between autonomy and hierarchy, between rote tasks and specialization. This office is not alone in the process of melding serial production with legal services, and the "massification" of legal services in other smaller firms has become apparent, accompanied by the increasing participation of women in high-volume, rote litigation suits.

The globalization of law provides the foundation on which JBM sustains its disputes in the legal field for broader approaches to practices that surpass the frontiers between the legal profession and corporate business. A similar battle, however, from the opposing side has been brought to the fore by CESA in relation to the national barriers against using foreign expertise in law firms. Both influence the meaning of globalizing processes in the legal world.

Even though JBM holds a high-flying position at the top of the professional hierarchy, it has arrived there through en masse law services, which makes its legitimacy vulnerable in terms of the prestige attributed by the elite known and established in the world of excellence, as required by CESA. In contrast with the specialized international language that has taken the spotlight in law (common law, civil law, home office, jobs, controllers, sole practitioner, partner, associate, BPO, workflow, checklist, feedback, etc.) are the images produced by expressions such as "sausage factories," industry, assembly lines, and mechanization, revealing the competition within the segment to establish how law is carried out at law firms in Brazil, the symbolic disputes to monopolize prestigious positions, and the discourse employing imagined models of singular globalization to tip the scale (in their favor) in such clashes.

REFERENCES

Ballakrishnen, Swethaa. 2012. "Breaking Bad: Gender Inequality in the Indian Legal Profession and the Advantage of New Institutional Frameworks" (paper presented at the International Conference on Law and Society, Honolulu, June 5–8).

Bergoglio, Maria Inés. 2007. "Llegar a sócia? La movilidad ocupacional em las grandes empresas jurídicas: analísis de gênero" (paper presented at the II Congreso Socio-Jurídico de Oñati, País Basco, July 18–20).
Bolton, Sharon C., and Daniel Muzio. 2007. "Can't Live with 'Em; Can't Live without 'Em: Gendered Segmentation in the Legal Profession." *Sociology* 41 (1): 47–64.
Bonelli, Maria da Gloria. 2013. Profissionalismo, gênero e diferença nas carreiras jurídicas, Edufscar/Fapesp.
Bonelli, Maria da Gloria, Luciana Gross Cunha, Fabiana Luci de Oliveira, and Maria Natália B. Silveira. 2008. "Profissionalização por gênero em escritórios paulistas de advocacia." *Tempo Social* 20: 265–90.
Butler, Judith. 1990. *Gender Trouble: Feminism and the Subversion of Identity*. New York: Routledge.
Committee on Women in the Profession. 2006. "Best Practice for the Hiring, Training, Retention, and Advancement of Women Attorneys." New York: New York City Bar. www.nycbar.org/images/stories/pdfs/BestPractices4WomenAttorneys.pdf.
Dezalay, Yves, and Bryant Garth. 2002. *The Internationalization of Palace Wars: Lawyers, Economists, and the Contest to Transform Latin American States*. Chicago: University of Chicago Press.
Evetts, Julia. 2012. "Professionalism: Value and Ideology." *Sociopedia.isa*. available at http://www.sagepub.net/isa/resources/pdf/Professionalism.pdf.
Feuvre, Nicky Le, and Nathalie Lapeyere. 2005. "Les 'scripts sexués' de carrière dans les professions juridiques en France." In *The Feminization of the Professions, Thematic Issue, Knowledge, Work and Society*. Edited by Mirella Giannini. London: Bloomsbury.
García Canclini, Néstor. 2014. *Imagined Globalization*. Durham, NC: Duke University Press.
Gastiazoro, Maria Eugenia. 2007. "Gender Differences in the Legal Profession" (paper presented at the 2007 International Conference of Law and Society Association, Berlin, July 25–27).
Kay, Fiona, and Elizabeth Gorman. 2008. "Women in the Legal Profession." *Annual Review of Law and Social Sciences* 4 (2): 299–332.
Moschella, Alexandre. 2011. "A Salsicharia do Directo no JBM." Exame.com, April 25. http://exame.abril.com.br/revista-exame/a-salsicharia-do-direito/.
Schultz, Ulrike. 2003. "Introduction: Women in the World's Legal Professions: Overview and Synthesis." In *Women in the World's Legal Professions*. Edited by Ulrike Schultz and Gisela Shaw. Oxford: Hart.
Scott, Joan W. Gender. 1986. "A Useful Category of Historical Analysis." *American Historical Review* 91 (5): 1053–1075.
Thornton, Margaret. 1996. *Dissonance and Distrust: Women in the Legal Profession*. Melbourne: Oxford University Press.

6

The Ordem dos Advogados do Brasil and the Politics of Professional Regulation in Brasil

Frederico de Almeida and Paulo André Nassar

I INTRODUCTION

This chapter explores regulation of the legal profession by the Brazilian Bar Association (Ordem dos Advogados do Brasil, or OAB) in the context of the rise of the corporate law firm sector. We show how the OAB responded to several challenges created by the emergence of new organizational forms and new styles of lawyering.

OAB regulations played an important role in the growth of the corporate law firm sector. As Brazilian lawyers began to adopt corporate law firm models from the United States and other countries, the OAB was faced with a new entity that operated differently than the traditional Brazilian law offices. These "new-model" firms were relatively large, highly specialized, organized in a hierarchical fashion, and profit seeking. Although there were concerns that this "commercialized" approach to law practice was at odds with the principles of professionalism, the OAB created a regulatory framework that accommodated the new model, allowing the corporate sector to grow substantially in the 1990s and early 2000s.[1]

The rise of the corporate sector created a new actor in OAB politics. The OAB had been dominated by two groups: the traditional elite of prestigious lawyers, who had dominated the profession since the beginning, and the OAB's organizational elite, who occupied important posts within the OAB and were responsive to the great mass of members. With the rise of the corporate law firms, a third elite entered the picture: large-firm business lawyers.

This chapter explores the interaction of these three elites as the OAB dealt with two issues that arose as a result of globalization and the rise of the corporate sector: (1) business and traditional lawyers wanted the approval of pro

[1] For data on the growth of the sector, see Chapters 2, 3, and 4 of this volume.

bono practice and (2) leading business leaders wanted alliances between foreign law firms and Brazilian firms to be outlawed. We show how the struggles over these issues played out through the interaction of these groups within the complex federal structure of the OAB.

A *The OAB and the Challenges of the 1990s*

The OAB was created in the period of corporatism, a political system that brought many social groups under the control of the state.[2] It was delegated the exclusive authority to organize and control the practice of lawyers. Membership is mandatory for all lawyers. Although created by the state and originally part of a system of state control of civil society, over time the OAB achieved considerable autonomy and self-governance capacities. By the end of the 1970s, the OAB was considered one of the most important Brazilian civil society organizations. This was in large part due to the central role it played in the struggle against the military regime (Bonelli 2002; Almeida 2005, 2010; Taylor 2008). Today it is still one of the most prestigious and politically powerful organizations in Brazil.

By the 1990s, the OAB was facing two major challenges. The first was a massive increase in the number of lawyers, which started as early as the 1960s due to the expansion of legal education (Almeida 2005). The second was the opening of the national market to the global economy and the concomitant pressures for different kinds of legal services and new ways of conflict resolution.

The bar, once an exclusive and small group of professionals, became a large group composed of lawyers from different social origins, headed by professional elites (Almeida 2010). "Old-style" lawyering, based on independent, solo professionals and family firms specializing in litigation, was being replaced by big law firms that offered a diverse set of legal services, focused on business matters, and employed an advisory, preventive law approach (Cunha et al. 2007). Of course, the legal profession did not change completely, nor did old-style lawyers become extinct. Rather, newer professional patterns coexisted with traditional ways of lawyering.

Those changes in the social and economic profile of lawyers put new pressures on the regulatory capacities of the OAB. Brazilian bar leaders faced a long list of challenges. They needed to oversee the working conditions of lawyers employed by the big law firms, ensure minimum conditions so that independent professionals could survive in a competitive labor market,

[2] For a discussion on corporatism, see Schmitter (1974). For an analysis of the creation of OAB under corporatism, see Bonelli (2002).

regulate foreign law firms acting in Brazil, preserve lawyers' monopoly of the practice of law, regulate new practices and demands brought by a globalized economy, and preserve the idea that lawyers are *not* business professionals despite the existence of a competitive, money-intensive legal services market.

Can we find a pattern in the regulatory interventions of the OAB? Who are the relevant political actors when the OAB seeks to control the major law firms and their practices in the market of legal services? How are professional rules enforced throughout the internal organization of the OAB?

To identify and understand the politics of the professional regulation by the OAB, this chapter analyzes recent and controversial regulatory issues, focusing on their historical, economic, and political aspects. The two main issues this chapter explores – the regulation of foreign firms and their relationship to Brazilian firms and the rules governing pro bono practice – embody the main economic, political, and symbolic conflicts created by the internationalization of the Brazilian legal services market and generated by the arrival of the American law firm model, the increasing commercialization and sophistication of legal practices, the debate on the proper role of lawyers in a modern society, and differing opinions about the role of the OAB itself as a professional regulatory authority. Because São Paulo is the major center for corporate law, these issues naturally involved the São Paulo State Bar. But because the OAB is a national institution, the regulatory battles also involved the national level and were affected by the dynamic between local and national interests and professional politics.

II PROFESSIONALISM, POLITICAL ACTORS, AND FORMAL INSTITUTIONS

The creation of a new model of the organization of legal services, based on specialization in large profit-seeking firms, was the first step in the increasing commercialization[3] of the legal profession in Brazil. Although this commercial aspect of the big law firm is well known, and well accepted, in the United

[3] We use the concept of commercialization in a scientific, sociological sense, according to the analysis of big law firms performed by Galanter and Palay (1994), mentioned above. It is important to stress the difference between a sociological sense and a common sense of the idea of commercialization: in a common sense, commercialization is understood as a distortion of the profession and of the professional ideal of the public role of lawyers; however, as we will show here, commercialization in a sociological sense is an economic and organizational trend of the profession, and the political regulation of the professional practice is a process of accommodating that trend, according to the power and interests of the different sectors of the professional community, which means the renovation of the professional ideal and its official discourses.

States and in England,[4] the main difference in Brazil is that all the professional regulation by the OAB is still based, in theory at least, on the idea of the *public role* of lawyers and practice as a *noncommercial* activity, directly related to access to justice and enforcement of constitutional rights. As we will show here, this tension between a *public role–based* approach to regulation of the legal profession and increasingly commercial activity in the corporate law sector explains many of the political aspects of the two controversial regulatory issues we studied.

This tension is related to the very concept of "profession": an economic and political group, representing a specialized occupation, with autonomy for the self-government of its own activities, justifying monopoly of the market by the expertise and the public function of professional work (Rueschemeyer 1964, 1977, 1986; Freidson 1996, 1998; Bonelli 2002; Cummings 2011; Mather 2011). It relates to the core of what Scott Cummings (2011) calls "a fundamental paradox of the legal profession." According to him,

> as professionals, they [the lawyers] are accorded wide discretion to define their own standards for admission and rules of conduct in order to promote craft expertise and quality service. In exchange for this privilege, lawyers are expected to embrace a set of public values – a code of "professionalism" defined by a commitment to competence, independence, and public service – distinguishing them from "mere" commercial actors. They are asked, in short, to be "public citizens" with a special obligation to promote the "administration of justice." This dual status – in the market, but above it; diligent servants of clients, but also special guardians of the "public interest" – raises our expectations of lawyer conduct. (1)

Globalization and the rise of the corporate sector created a need for new regulations of these new organizational firms, especially with lawyers hired under contract and the very specific structures created by the newest big law firms. Although the political processes that brought those new rules are described and analyzed in other works (Bonelli 2002; Almeida 2005), it is important to understand how the most recent regulatory issues were affected by the regulations that accompanied the growth of the modern Brazilian big law firm starting in the 1990s.

4 Although the conflict between the public role of lawyers and the commercial aspects of their services is also present in the United States and Britain, the professional regulation in those countries admits, by different means, the commercial aspects as acceptable. More than that, lawyers in those countries "are permitted – and indeed encouraged – to make money, often lots of it" (Cummings 2011, 1). That is the case, for example, of advertising in US legal marketing, and also the recent decision to allow British law firms to search private, nonlawyer investors by IPO, such as industry and service companies do.

During the 1970s and 1980s, the OAB regulated the situation of lawyers working for big firms on a contractual basis. This was a new form of employment relation for professionals brought about by the growth of the number of lawyers and the diversification of the structure of law firms. The idea of lawyers employed by firms under contract and subject to hierarchical control within the firms seemed at odds with the principle of professional autonomy. To protect their rights, Brazilian bar leaders were asked to represent the concerns of employed lawyers, almost like union leaders.

The rise of the contract lawyer is a phenomenon directly connected to the rise of the modern Brazilian law firm (*sociedade de advogados*), characterized by the hierarchical relations between major partners and associated lawyers, and between those lawyers and those hired on contract. It also brings with it the idea of the property of a law firm being owned by the major partners. Those characteristics forced the OAB to face new regulatory demands very different form the well-known patterns of independent lawyer practice (*advogado autônomo*) and the traditional law office (*escritório de advocacia*), a horizontal, informal association between independent lawyers sharing the same office and its costs.

According to Galanter and Palay (1994), the rise of the American big law firm is the result of the commercialization of legal practice, under pressures for standardization, continuity, and specialization of legal services. This novel model of legal organization introduced a new division of labor between partners, associated lawyers, and contracted lawyers, and led to high levels of revenue and profit.

That is why Galantér and Palay use the idea of the big law firm as a "law factory" when they analyze the impact of the rising of the American big law firm during the 1930s:

> The "factory" metaphor caught not only the instrumentalism but the systematization, the division of labor, and the coordination of effort introduced by the large firm. Commentators also felt that the metaphor expressed something about those firms that was profoundly at odds with professional traditions of autonomy and public service. What bothered critics was not efficiency, but what they viewed as the total commercialization associated with it. (Galanter and Palay 1994, 907)

In this sense, the organizational pattern of law firms based on major (capitalist) partners and contracted (working) lawyers for a large-scale production of legal services is the same as the modern capitalist production, as it was analyzed by Karl Marx:

> Capitalist production only then really begins, as we have already seen, when each individual capital employs simultaneously a comparatively large number of labourers; when consequently the labour-process is carried on on an extensive scale and yields, relatively, larger quantities of products. (Marx 2013, 397)

As Dezalay and Garth (2002) have shown, the model of the American large law firm had a strong influence in Latin American countries starting in the 1970s. By the 1990s, major domestic firms had taken shape, and business lawyers had improved their practice, expertise, and social networks. In Brazil and elsewhere in Latin America, these large domestic firms began to serve as key intermediaries among foreign capitalists, and the business and political elites in national economies seeking legal solutions to the debt crisis looked toward the opening of national markets and the favoring the privatization of public companies. According to Dezalay and Garth:

> The business law firm is a key agent and product of the Americanization of the legal landscape. The proliferation and growth of business law firms appears to be the most successful or even the only successful legal transplant from the north into the south. This success is even more striking because of the strong European legal tradition – or legal culture – in Latin America, which assigned a marginal role to lawyers who were identified with business. The story of success goes even further, since it appears not only that these business law firms in the south have become the key agents for the entry of multinational conglomerates into their territory but also that business lawyers have become recognized as a legitimate part of the legal elite. (Dezalay and Garth 2002, 198)

The first Brazilian big law firms (such as Pinheiro Neto Advogados) were born before the 1970s, but the model spread as a new pattern for law offices during the 1990s.[5] The modern Brazilian big law firms are not as big as their American equivalents, but they have many similarities to the original model: large organizations, rationalized on a large scale, offering full service or sets of highly specialized and sophisticated professional services.[6]

5 For an analysis of Pinheiro Neto's trajectory, see Dezalay and Garth (2002).

6 If we consider taxation regimes, the practice of law in a law firm (*sociedade de advogados*) is more economical than as an independent lawyer practice or in a traditional law office. On the one hand, Brazilian corporations pay two corporate income taxes: Imposto de Renda de Pessoa Jurídica at 15 percent over their incomes and Contribuição Social sobre Lucro Líquido (CSLL) at 9 percent over the profits. On the other hand, individuals pay income tax at progressive rates up to 27.5 percent. There is also a service tax (Imposto Sobre Serviços, or ISS) charged at a fixed rate based on the amount of practitioners associated at the firm. Since the

In Brazil, the firm model (*sociedade de advogados*) was first regulated by the Statute of Lawyers in 1963. Some internal rules of the OAB also ruled law firms until the new Statute of Lawyers (1994) was created. Although that law brought few innovations (Ferraz 2002; Giacomo 2002), it successfully conciliated the role of the business lawyers as legal advisors and the traditional role of lawyers as litigators (Bonelli 2002). This was a real achievement, especially considering that national regulations – such as in France until the 1990s – were not able to maintain lawyers as a unified group or have a single regulation for litigators and advisors.

By the 1990s the business law firms were becoming important political actors. The role was aided by the Center for Studies on Law Firms (Centro de Estudos das Sociedades de Advogados, or CESA), a civil association founded by the major law firms in Brazil in 1983. The CESA is responsible for political representation and for dialogue between the OAB and the major Brazilian law firms on regulatory issues. In 1992 the CESA achieved an important goal when the São Paulo State Bar Association created a permanent commission on law firm issues (Giacomo 2002). Some years later, the Federal Council of the OAB also created a similar commission, in which the partners of large law firms found a formal space for political representation in the OAB.

By making official and legitimate a new model for the organization of legal services based on large-scale, profit-seeking organizations providing specialized and sophisticated services and operating on hierarchical lines, OAB regulation signaled institutional and regulatory acceptance of an increasing process of commercialization of the legal profession in Brazil. Regulatory acceptance of this model gave considerable economic advantages for law firm partners; it also produced new political actors – the big law firms themselves – who are strong economic players that can act to increase their power and block legal reforms that might restrict the range of their business. Thus the evolution of professional regulation by the OAB is an example of path dependence: "social processes that exhibit positive feedback and thus generate branching patterns of historical development" (Pierson 2004, 20–21). By recognizing the new model and empowering the new business law elite, the OAB guaranteed continued tension between a "public role-based" and an "anticommercial" approach to regulation of the legal profession and the increasingly commercial activity performed by the big law firms. As we will see, this played out in the two regulatory debates we examine.

ISS is a municipal tax, its rate varies in each city. In São Paulo, for example, law firms pay approximately R$800 per year per lawyer. On the other hand, individual lawyers pay an ISS at 5 percent over service value.

A *Legal Elites as Political Actors*

Professional regulation by the OAB is the result of silent struggles and public deals between the *traditional elite* of lawyers (traditional, prestigious lawyers), the OAB's internal *organizational elite* of lawyers (bar leaders), and the new *business law elite* (business lawyers and major partners of big law firms). Although so far deals among these different groups of lawyers have preserved professional unity within the OAB and surrounding its rules (Bonelli 2002), the tension is getting intense as commercialization of the legal profession increases.

According to an extensive sociological literature, each group of lawyers carries their own professional ideology and their own professional identity, which are the results of their social trajectories and positions in the legal field (Dezalay 1991; Dezalay and Trubek 1996; Dezalay and Garth 2000, 2002; Engelmann 2006a; Bourdieu 2007). Dezalay and Garth (2002) show that the rise of the business lawyer as part of Latin American legal elites can be explained by two factors: (1) the influence of American business law, which was transplanted through law and development projects[7] and local lawyers with contacts and personal experiences in the United States and (2) the opening of national economies to American companies and investors. According to the authors,

> In Brazil those who occupied the most elite positions in law, politics, and business, especially those located in cosmopolitan Rio, typically spoke French, were not sympathetic to the United States, and had relatively little contact with the United States prior to the law and development initiatives in the 1960s. They served international interests, but their focus was much more on Europe. In the Brazilian context of law firms, therefore, which was consistent with what we have seen more generally in Brazil, this situation allowed the construction of new hybrids out of different sectors of the relatively diverse and competitive elite. (Dezalay and Garth 2002, 201)

Our research shows that there are, at least, three main political groups acting in OAB regulatory issues. The first are the *traditional elites*, represented by those lawyers from the "traditional field of law" (Engelmann 2006a), with connections to the political field and substantial prestige because of their professional and academic capital and their family inheritance. The second are the *organizational elites*, represented by OAB leadership. This elite

[7] The Law and Development Movement exposed Brazilian lawyers to US legal ideas and practices through educational programs including the experimental CEPED project at FGV in the 1960s and 1970s (Lacerda et al. 2012).

builds organizational capital by assuming formal positions at bottom-level and middle-level OAB institutions. They are supported and responsive to the large constituency of lawyers who typically engage in less sophisticated ways of lawyering than large-firm lawyers. The third are the *business law elites*, represented by business lawyers from the internationalized field of the legal profession, characterized by substantial symbolic capital derived from international and business connections as well as substantial economic resources.

Table 6.1[8] compares different members of those three elite groups. The individuals selected were all involved with the regulatory conflicts, and their trajectories show different structures of symbolic capital represented by their professional experiences, academic titles, and family and political connections.

Traditional elites are characterized by their family status, professional trajectories relatively distant from business law, investments in an academic carrier and the achievement of high university positions, and low participation in the internal or corporative issues of the OAB. Organizational elites have more internal OAB political capital, represented by the assumption of leading positions in the hierarchies of the OAB, which confirms the hypothesis of a more endogenous selection of bar leaders and the power of the constituency in the internal politics of the OAB. Finally, business law elites have the power of their economic capital (i.e., of their clients and their law firms) – they do not have any distinguished set of family, political, academic, or corporative capital – and also by the symbolic capital of their international connections, foreign degrees, and alliances with global actors. The trajectories represented in the table are obviously illustrative, and the examples of Carlos Miguel Castex Aidar and Orlando Di Giacomo show how an individual member of a group of elites can circulate between different elites.

B *Formal Institutions as Points of Interaction*

To fully understand the regulatory struggles and outcomes, it is necessary to understand the institutional organization of the OAB. Institutions like the

[8] The data on the trajectories were collected from different sources, especially from the official biographies available on the websites of the law firms and also from data that are publicly known (such as family connections and professional activities). We assume that both the absences of and the insistence on certain information in public, official biographies are important data themselves, because they show how life experiences are selected, informed, and valuated throughout the construction of the public images of the elites; that is why the absence of certain data does not necessarily mean the objective absence of that type of life experience, as it can mean that the experience itself is not important enough to distinguish that individual from other individuals in the same social field. For an analysis of public biographies and the sources for studying legal elites, see Almeida (2010).

TABLE 6.1 *Illustrative trajectories of life of members of the elite*

Elite group	Elite member	Family symbolic inheritance	Professional trajectory	Academic trajectory	Political trajectory	Recent corporative trajectory at OAB
Traditional elites	Miguel Reale Jr. (supporter of pro bono)	Son of Miguel Reale, an important Brazilian philosopher and jurist; former professor, dean, and president at University of São Paulo	Criminal lawyer; partner at Miguel Reale Júnior Law Firm, a *boutique* law firm specializing in criminal law; defendant of political prisoners during the military regime	Law degree, master's and PhD in law from University of São Paulo Law School, where he was also a professor of criminal law	Former minister of justice (federal government), secretary of justice (São Paulo state government), secretary of public safety and secretary of public administration (São Paulo state government); member of several commissions and committees (federal and state government)	None
	José Carlos Dias (supporter of pro bono)	Son of Theodomiro Dias, former chief justice of São Paulo State Court of Justice	Criminal lawyer; major partner at Dias e Carvalho Filho Lawyers, a boutique law firm specializing in criminal law; defendant of political prisoners during the military regime	Law degree from University of São Paulo Law School	Former minister of justice (federal government) and secretary of justice (São Paulo state government); member of several commissions and committees (federal and state government)	None

Oscar Vilhena Vieira (supporter of pro bono)	Son of José Oswaldo Pereira Vieira, former chief general of police (São Paulo state) and national secretary of public safety (federal government)	Human rights and public interest lawyer; former public attorney (São Paulo state); founder of Conectas Human Rights (NGO)	Law degree from Catholic University of São Paulo, master's in law from Columbia University, master's and PhD in political science from University of São Paulo; former professor of constitutional law at Catholic University of São Paulo; dean and professor of constitutional law at FGV Law School	None	None
Carlos Miguel Castex Aidar (president of the São Paulo State Bar when the Pro Bono Institute was founded)	Son of Henri Aidar, lawyer, former secretary chief of staff at São Paulo state government; president of São Paulo Energy Company (public company); president of São Paulo Soccer Club (soccer team)	Sports lawyer; partner at Aidar SBZ Lawyers, a small-sized law firm; president of São Paulo Soccer Club	Law degree from Mackenzie Presbyterian University; specialist on civil procedural law of Catholic University of São Paulo; professor at both universities	Member of the Commission of Studies on Sport Law at the Ministry of Sports (federal government); former legal consultant of the Minister of Sports (federal government)	President and secretary general of the São Paulo State Bar

(*cont.*)

TABLE 6.1 *(cont.)*

Elite group	Elite member	Family symbolic inheritance	Professional trajectory	Academic trajectory	Political trajectory	Recent corporative trajectory at OAB
Organizational elites	Luís Flávio Borges D'Urso (president of the São Paulo State Bar during the discussion on foreign law firms)	Son of Umberto Luiz D'Urso, lawyer	Criminal lawyer; partner at D'Urso and Borges Associated Lawyers, a small-sized law firm	Law degree from United Metropolitan Schools; master's and PhD in law from University of São Paulo; professor at United Metropolitan Schools	Former member of the National Council of Public Safety and the National Council of Criminal and Prison Policies	President of the São Paulo State Bar for three times, where he was prior director for cultural affairs; head of the Young Lawyer Council; head of the Academic Development Center; member of the Commission on Professional Rights and Prerogatives; member of the Sectional Council
	Marcos da Costa (president of the São Paulo State Bar; suspended all the restrictions to pro bono practices)	None	Business lawyer; partner at Costa e Duque Bertasi Associated Lawyers, a small-sized law firm	Law degree from United Metropolitan Schools; specialist on business law at Mackenzie Presbyterian University	None	Several positions at the São Paulo State Bar: former financial director; member of the Sectional Council; member of the Commission on Professional Rights and Prerogatives; member of the Tribunal of Ethics and Discipline; member of Commissions on Institutional Relations with the Public Defense Office and the State Court of Justice; member of the Commission on Informatics at the Federal Council

	Orlando Di Giacomo (CESAS's founder, supporter of pro bono, and objector of foreign law firms)	None	Business lawyer; partner at Demarest & Almeida Lawyers, one of the twenty major law firms in Brazil	Law degree from Catholic University of São Paulo	None	Member and president of the Commission on Law Firms; president of the Special Commissions on Legal Practice Defense Against Professional Interference, and on State Law Revision and Consolidation; member of the Commissions on Internal Elections, Judicial Modernization, Professional Prerogatives, and Professional Market Defense
Business law elites	Antonio Corrêa Meyer (objector of law firms)	None	Business lawyer; partner at Machado Meyer Sendacz Opice, one of the ten major law firms in Brazil	Law degree from University of São Paulo Law School	None	None
	Luís Salles Freire (former president of CESA and objector of foreign law firms)	None	Business lawyer; partner at Tozzini Freire Lawyers, one of the ten major law firms in Brazil	Law degree from University of São Paulo Law School; master's in comparative law of New York University; extension course on business at FGV Business School		

(cont.)

TABLE 6.1 *(cont.)*

Elite group	Elite member	Family symbolic inheritance	Professional trajectory	Academic trajectory	Political trajectory	Recent corporative trajectory at OAB
	None	None				
	Ivan Tauil (supporter of foreign law firms)	None	Business lawyer; partner at Tauil & Chequer Lawyers, a medium-sized law firm associated with the British law firm Mayer Brown	Law degree from Fluminense Federal University; master's in constitutional law and theory from State of Catholic University of Rio de Janeiro	None	None
	Eduardo Cerqueira Leite (supporter of foreign law firms)	None	Business lawyer; partner at Baker & McKenzie, an American law firm that kept for decades a partnership with Trench Rossi Watanabe, one of the twenty major law firms in Brazil	Law degree from University of São Paulo; master's in comparative jurisprudence from New York University	None	None

Sources: Miguel Reale Júnior Advogados (2014); Dias e Carvalho Filho Advogados (2014); Escola de Direito de São Paulo da Fundação Getúlio Vargas (2014); Aidar SBZ Advogados (2014); Costa e Duque Bertasi Advogados Associados (2014); Migalhas (2012); Machado Meyer Sendacz Opice Advogados (2014); Tozzini Freire Advogados (2014); Tauil and Cherquer Advogados (2014); Baker and McKenzie (2014); Análise Editorial (2012).

OAB can be considered points of interaction in which actors, values, and interests are confronted and defined. According to Ellen Immergut:

> Constitutions and political institutions, state structures, state interest group relations, and policy networks all structure the political process. Consequently, political demands and public policies are not shaped by the neutral and convergent exigencies of modernization. Rather, political economies – like political systems – are structured by dense interactions among economic, social, and political actors that work according to different logics in different contexts. (Immergut 1998, 17)

The OAB is a national organization legally responsible for controlling the profession in Brazil. It has a federal structure, with twenty-seven sectional councils (and sectional presidencies), one for each Brazilian state or territory, and a Federal Council (with a national presidency). In each state, lawyers elect the sectional president, the Sectional Council, and three federal councilors. The Federal Council is made up of the national president, eighty-one federal councilors – three from each Sectional Council – and former presidents of the Federal Council. The latter do not have the right to vote on the Council. An electoral college formed by the eighty-one federal councilors elects the national president. In each federative unit, the Sectional Council also includes subsections (city sections), with their own presidents. The Statute of Lawyers is a federal law that organizes the profession but is enforced by the sectional councils – especially by the Sectional Commissions on Ethics. The Federal Council can review sectional decisions and carries out federal regulation of the legal profession by internal administrative rules (*provimentos*, *resoluções*, *portarias*, and *instruções normativas*).

Every sectional council has a Tribunal of Ethics and Discipline (Tribunal de Ética e Disciplina, or TED). The TEDs have jurisdiction over ethical issues and disciplinary misconduct through administrative disciplinary processes. If a lawyer is found guilty of misconduct, the TED can apply the following penalties: censure, suspension, disbarment, and fine. Each Sectional Council defines the composition and form of appointment to the TED. To serve as a judge on the TED, a lawyer has to have a reputation for exceptional ethical conduct. Lawyers appointed to the TED serve a three-year term.

The OAB's organization can be divided between *bottom-level* institutions (the constituency and the subsectional Commission of the Presidents), *middle-level* institutions (the Sectional and Federal councils, and thematic commissions), and *high-level* institutions (the sectional presidencies and the national presidency). The bottom-level institutions are the locus of representation of basic professional interests and demands, often related to the labor market, material conditions of work, and other economic issues (Almeida 2005). They usually represent the interests of the great majority of lawyers who are not part of the high-powered, competitive world of the elite business law firms. The high-level institutions are responsible for the standardization of professional rules and regulatory decisions through the Federal Council but also for the political representation of professional interests and ideology (by the national president) (Taylor 2008); these high-level institutions are the arenas where professional elites act and interact nationally. The middle-level institutions (the sectional councils of the OAB) are responsible for the effective enforcement of national rules and decisions (by the Sectional Council and the Sectional Commissions on Ethics) but also for political representation of professional interests and ideology (the sectional president). They represent the local professional elites. In their formal role, the middle-level institutions are pressured by the bottom-level interests on the one hand and affected by the power high-level review of local decisions on the other.

III THE STRUGGLE OVER REGULATION OF FOREIGN LAW FIRMS

If the opening of the national economy during the 1990s triggered the rise of the modern, large, hierarchical Brazilian law firm (Cunha et al. 2007), it also attracted foreign lawyers and law firms to Brazil and led to regulatory debates about their role.

The OAB's Federal Council enacted an internal rule (Provimento n. 91/2000) that states that foreign lawyers can act in Brazil only in very restricted ways. Basically, the OAB allows foreign lawyers to act as advisors on foreign law (not on Brazilian law, just on their "native" law). The lawyers can associate among themselves and create law firms that provide that type of restricted legal service. This rule does not say anything explicit about association between Brazilian and foreign lawyers or law firms.

Since the late 1990s many foreign law firms came to Brazil to work alone or in association with Brazilian law firms, despite the restrictions imposed by federal law and the internal regulations of the OAB. These firms tend to concentrate on "new" legal areas. Instead of the traditional litigation path, which is outlawed, foreigners act mainly in arbitration, antitrust, capital markets, energy, oil and gas, M&A, project finance, infrastructure, and intellectual property. The following chart shows the increasing number of foreign law firms with branch offices in Brazil since 1997 and its subtle decrease after 2011, but increase in 2013 (Figure 6.1).

All these law firms are based in the Southeast of Brazil, primarily in São Paulo, with a few in Rio de Janeiro. Looking at the origin of these firms,

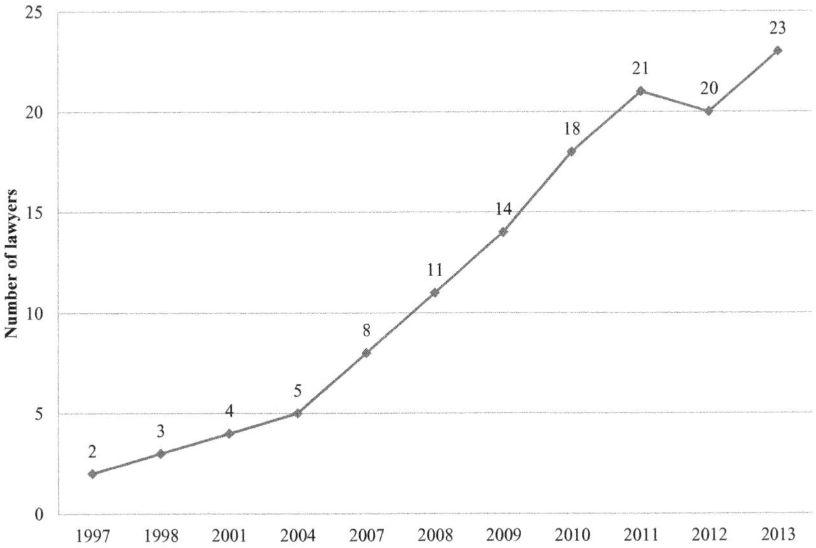

FIGURE 6.1 Foreign law firms in Brazil.
Source: Análise Editorial (2011, 2013). Graph by the authors.

the most frequent countries are the United States and the United Kingdom. Figures 6.2 and 6.3 show the distributions of foreign firms in Brazil and their native country.

In a survey reported in *Análise Advocacia* 500 of the 224 firms ranked most admired (a specialized annual review that ranks Brazilian law firms in terms of size, incomes, and prestige), 70 percent reported that they have searched for, or at least analyzed, the possibility of a "partnership" of some kind with a foreign law firm (Secco 2012, 8).

The legal profession in Brazil is regulated both by federal legislation (a federal law called The Lawyers and Bar Association Statute) and by internal rules created by the Federal Council of the OAB. Each Sectional Council has autonomy to enforce federal rules (by their Commission on Ethics) and to create new rules, but those rules cannot conflict with the national ones. A national Commission on Ethics, at the Federal Council of the OAB, is responsible for national guidelines for the enforcement of federal rules by sectional councils.

In 2011 the Tribunal of Ethics and Discipline of the São Paulo Sectional Council stated that the association between Brazilian and foreign law firms is not allowed by the OAB's national rules and imposed a penalty of censure on a Brazilian law firm. The Brazilian firm appealed before the Federal Council, which raised the penalty to suspension.

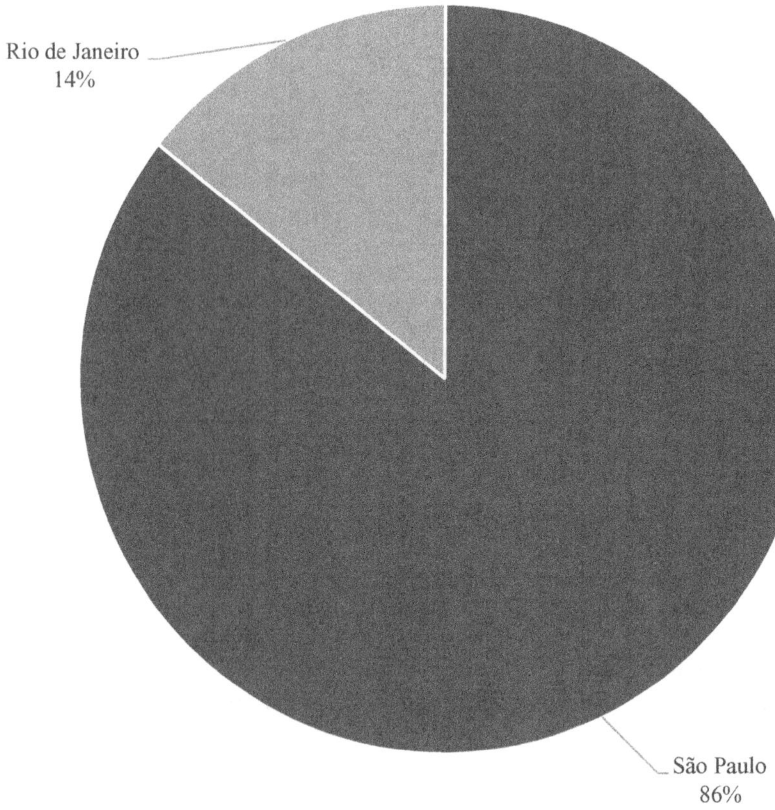

FIGURE 6.2 Location of branch offices in Brazil.
Source: Análise Editorial (2011). Graph by the authors.

The statement of the São Paulo Sectional Council on foreign law firms was approved by the XXI Brazilian Conference of Lawyers, an official meeting organized by the Federal Council of the OAB. The Federal Council's Commission on Ethics also punished some law firms that maintained various kinds of alliance with foreign firms. After that, both the OAB's Commission on Foreign Affairs and the Federal Council stated that the association between Brazilian and foreign law firms is prohibited by Provimento 91/2000.

In early 2011 the CESA made a formal request to the São Paulo Sectional Council for a ruling on the legality of the associations between Brazilian lawyers or law firms and foreign lawyers or law firms set pursuant to Provimento 91/2000. The São Paulo Sectional Council reaffirmed its opinion on the unlawfulness of any type of association between foreign and Brazilian lawyers. Since Provimento 91/2000 is a federal rule, the inquiry was submitted

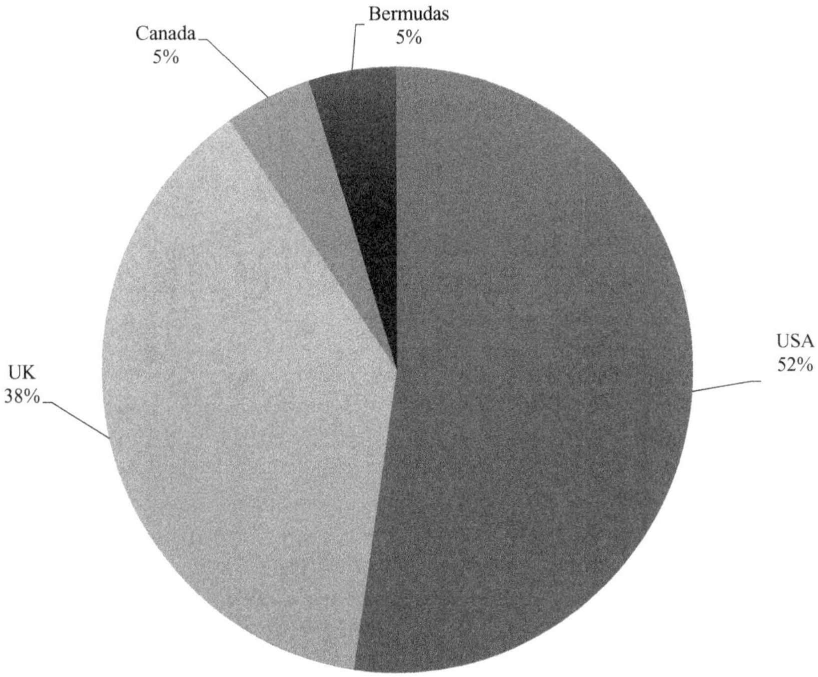

FIGURE 6.3 Origin of the law firm.
Source: Análise Editorial (2011). Graph by the authors.

to the Federal Council by request of the national president of the OAB. At this point, a new question emerged: because Provimento 91/2000 does not explicitly address the issue, some saw the need for a specific rule to regulate this issue.

The National Commission for International Affairs requested Carlos Roberto Siqueira Castro, a federal councilor from Rio de Janeiro and partner of a large law firm founded in 1948, to propose a draft of an administrative rule (*provimento*) to regulate the associations between Brazilian lawyers or law firms and foreign lawyers or law firms. The draft explicitly forbade any type of association between Brazilian lawyers or law firms and foreign lawyers or law firms, but it allowed foreign law firms established in Brazil to provide legal service as "advisors on foreign law" under Provimento 91/2000 as well as all other foreign firms. The draft was accompanied by an extensive report about the Brazilian market of legal services, including a comparative overview of regulation for foreign lawyers in different countries.

The report contended that all the following would be a violation of the Statutes of Lawyers: (1) use of the same building or address in Brazil, even on different floors of the same building; (2) misusage of logos, brandings, social name, or any type of visual identity; (3) usage of terms such as *in cooperation with* or *associated with*; (4) usage of same pattern of commercial cards, papers, portfolios, e-mails, website, software, marketing material, and all other types of cross-references; (5) hosting of events, even about foreign law or foreign investments in Brazil; and (6) sharing of database, IT, clients lists, management, invoicing, and HR policy.

The Siqueira Castro report claimed that restrictions on foreign lawyers were necessary to avoid the commodification of legal practice, already far along in other countries. The report explicitly says:

> These tremendous transformations in international lawyering and the structuring of law firms, in the wake of corporate and market models already taken over by England and Australia, tend to put into practice an authentic process of "marketization without borders" of the legal profession. The legal services are transformed into "commodities," freely traded and perhaps securitized as future receivables subject to the risk of the business. Even rights and subjective interests, individual and collective interests, filled by the lawyers of those countries and the lawsuits in which they are channeled, eventually could be transformed into mere assets of these law firms tuned into publicly traded company subject, and as such appropriable and subject to financial and commercial exploitation for all types of investors. (Castro 2012, 45, translated)

Ivan Tauil, partner of a Brazilian law firm associated with the second largest law firm (by revenue) in the world (Mayer Brown), says that the dispute is really about market share of legal services in Brazil.

> The real threat is the unregulated expansion of southeastern law firms that still establish hierarchical relationships with the rest of the Brazilian lawyers (center–periphery, metropolis–colony, developed–undeveloped), expanding to other regions of the country as if lawyers from there did not know or could not operate the corporate law and serve corporate clients . . . Those who are against international associations (held by less than half a dozen of Brazilian law firms) are law firms seeking to change the "Cause of National Lawyers," which is nothing but a fight for customers, which, far from threatening the foreigners involved, is fought exclusively by Brazilian lawyers who have different views regarding the development of the professional activity. (Tauil 2011, translated)

Under the same inquiry, in May 2012, federal councilor Welber Barral submitted another draft of the *Provimento* to the Federal Council. This draft differed considerably from Siqueira Castro's proposal because it allowed Brazilian and foreign law firms to associate when its purpose is (1) to provide a joint service to a common client, (2) related to organizational aspects, or (3) to represent common clients on third-party jurisdictions (Ordem dos Advogados do Brasil 2012).

By a majority decision, led by federal councilor Marcelo Zarif, from Bahia, the Federal Council found that a new *provimento* was not needed and concluded that the associations between foreign law firms and Brazilian lawyers are lawful under Provimento 91/2000 but only if they are temporary and restricted to consultancy on foreign law. Any type of litigation by foreign lawyers or law firms is forbidden. Infringements by Brazilian lawyers and foreigners admitted as "consultant on foreign law" are subject to the administrative jurisdiction of the OAB; foreigners operating in Brazil and not admitted through OAB procedures can be criminally prosecuted for "illegal practice of lawyering."

Some *obiter dicta* in the opinion about the *essence* of lawyering say a lot about the self-perception of lawyers. Lawyering is said to be "a public activity" and that it is "very especial . . . in Brazil because of its constitutional status" and that "it is not only inconvenient but also constitutionally impossible to make any concession to the practice of foreign lawyering on the national ground."

It is worth noting that for the first time the number of foreign lawyers in Brazil declined in 2012 after five years of rapid increase. While we cannot say this was the result of the Federal Council ruling, it is clear that it was a sign of growing resistance to foreign presence. The ruling was followed by the dissolution of some formal alliances. In early 2013, Lefosse Advogados formally announced the end of a long-term partnership with Linklaters, started in 1997. Lefosse refers to the decision as the decisive reason for the breakup, given that the OAB explicitly forbids permanent association between Brazilian and foreign lawyers. Thus it decided to terminate the joint operations with its British partner (Vasconcellos 2013). Since then, Linklaters operates alone in Brazil as "consultants on foreign law."[9] Other alliances, however, were maintained.[10]

IV PRO BONO PRACTICE

Globalization can be understood as cultural and symbolic as well as economic and political. The diffusion of the American model law firm in Latin America includes features that may be adopted for reasons that are as much cultural

9 It is important to note that while permanent and visible alliances are now threatened, most Brazilian corporate firms retain close relations with international firms and engage in ad hoc alliances (for more, see Chapter 2).

10 This issue is discussed at length in Chapter 7.

and symbolic as economic (Dezalay and Garth 2000, 2002). This occurred in Brazil in what would seem like the secondary issue of pro bono practice.

Pro bono is a tradition of the legal profession in the United States strongly encouraged by law schools, law firms, and bar associations. But pro bono practice as an organized activity for lawyers was introduced in Brazil only in the 1990s by the same major law firms that founded the CESA (Almeida 2005). In this sense, the Brazilian Pro Bono Institute (Instituto Pro Bono, or IPB), founded to promote this idea, can be considered as the "social" arm of the CESA.

While business law elites pushed for pro bono, development of the field and the creation of the IPB were also supported by traditional elite lawyers and human rights lawyers from different generations, such as Miguel Reale Jr., Belisário dos Santos Jr., and Oscar Vilhena Vieira.[11] The alliance between business lawyers and the traditional elite human rights lawyers is a key factor to explain the outcome of the struggle over regulation of pro bono practice by the OAB.[12]

It is no accident that pro bono practice grew fastest in the São Paulo state, where most business lawyers and big law firms are located. The growth of pro bono in large law firms became a major issue because it was seen as a threat to the livelihood of low-level, generalist, and relatively poor lawyers. To understand this issue, you have to understand the status of public defenders in São Paulo. The Brazilian Constitution guarantees free legal aid for the poor. While some states met this obligation by creating state public defender offices, São Paulo initially chose a different route. Rather than create a state agency, São Paulo relied on a judicare approach in which the legal aid unit of the OAB coordinated the work of individual lawyers who were paid by the state government. Even after the creation of the São Paulo's Public Defense Office, in 2006, the OAB kept offering alternative legal aid to guarantee assistance to people that was not covered by the state agency's services.

The money paid by the São Paulo state government for this service was responsible for the professional survival of a large number of poor lawyers in a saturated market of legal professionals (Almeida 2005). In this sense, the OAB considered pro bono practice as a threat: bar leaders were afraid of unfair competition between the free legal services that might be offered by specialized big

[11] For an analysis of the life trajectories of some of those traditional elite lawyers, see Table 6.1.

[12] It is important to understand the introduction of the pro bono practice in Brazil in a historical perspective, which considers other ways of similar practices in Brazil, such as *popular lawyers*, *cause lawyers*, and *public interest lawyers*, most of them kept by traditional lawyers, public institutions, or lawyers of social movements. To understand these Brazilian experiences, see Fabiano Engelmann (2006b), Oscar Vilhena Vieira (2008), and Fabio Sa e Silva (2012).

law firms and the services provided by low-level, generalist, and poor lawyers and paid for by the state government.

After the creation of the IPB, the Commission on Ethics of the São Paulo State Bar started prosecuting a number of lawyers who were practicing pro bono assistance. The Commission on Ethics argued that pro bono practice represents unfair competition between lawyers. The major law firms, some traditional elite lawyers, and the IPB fought back, seeking to protect this practice. As a result of these negotiations, in 2002 the State Bar issued a new internal rule that allows the pro bono practice but only for advisory services, offered for free to nongovernmental organizations (NGO) with no resources to pay a lawyer. Free work for individuals was banned.

The struggle inside the São Paulo State Bar over pro bono practice did not attract national attention as it was seen as a local problem by both the leaders of other state bars and the Federal Council. With that compromise solution in 2002, the issue lost most of its explosive potential, and pro bono lawyers could act in a relatively free way, protected both by the indifference of the Federal Council and by a type of "gentlemen's agreement" that allowed the pro bono in limited situations.

However, in 2012 an "external" actor, the Federal Public Prosecutor's Office in São Paulo, started an extra judicial proceeding to investigate regulation of the practice by the São Paulo State Bar after a representation made by anonymous citizens. Issues were raised concerning the possibility that the limitations imposed on pro bono violated both the constitutional right of citizens to legal assistance and the constitutional freedom of professional practice (Canário 2013; Procuradoria da República no Estado de São Paulo 2014).

The Federal Public Prosecutor's Office in São Paulo organized a public hearing on the issue, to which the IPB, the State Council of the OAB, and many lawyers and legal scholars were invited. The sectional president of the OAB did not attend, and no one represented the OAB at the hearing; in his response to the invitation, the sectional president argued that regulatory issues should be treated by the Federal Council (despite the fact that there was no regulation on that issue at the national level, and only the São Paulo and the Alagoas state bars had regulations on pro bono practice).

All lawyers and law scholars at the hearing – including Gilmar Mendes, justice of the Brazilian Supreme Court, and Flávio Croce Caetano, secretary of judicial reform of the Ministry of Justice – defended pro bono practice with no restrictions, as was intended since the beginning by the IPB, i.e., the complete legal assistance to both poor individuals and NGOs (Canário 2013). In a very emotive statement, criminal lawyer and former minister of justice José Carlos Dias said:

> I feel shame about the position of OAB/SP [São Paulo State Bar] against the pro bono practice. At the same time, I feel myself very emotive, because after fifty years of lawyering, I can ask for the blessing of the Public Prosecution Office, because of the shame I feel today as a lawyer. I cannot believe that it is forbidden to the lawyer the exercise of freedom. (quoted by Procuradoria da República no Estado de São Paulo 2013)

After the hearing, the Federal Public Prosecutor's Office in São Paulo made an official statement, recommending that the Federal Council of the OAB cancel any existing restrictive regulations and allow the complete freedom of pro bono practice by lawyers; it also stated that if the OAB should not accept that recommendation, it would initiate a judicial proceeding to enforce the constitutional rights to legal assistance and freedom of professional practice. On June 17, 2013, after the Federal Public Prosecutor's Office repeated that recommendation, the Federal Council finally informed all the sectional councils that all the restrictions on pro bono practice were suspended pending further regulation.

Initial response to the suspension was varied. Some firms kept doing pro bono as they usually did before; others firms thought this new situation was more uncertain.[13] However, on June 2015, the Federal Council of the OAB finally approved pro bono practice including individual representation and with no restrictions, and indicated that formal regulation of the matter will be included in the new Code of Ethics, which is being prepared by the OAB (Ordem dos Advogados do Brasil 2015a). In December 2015 the Federal Council published a new formal rule (Provimento n. 166/2015) that allows pro bono practice with minor restrictions: a quarantine of three years before a lawyer can offer new paid services to a pro bono client; a prohibition to link pro bono services to any electoral or partisan activity or organization; and a prohibition to use pro bono practice for marketing or self-promotion purposes (Ordem dos Advogados do Brasil 2015b).

V CONCLUSION

Our research sought to understand the political context in which new rules of professional regulation were created and to identify the political actors who influenced the final result. We also sought to show how those rules and political processes can be understood in relation to globalization, the growth of the Brazilian market for legal services, and other regulatory interventions of the OAB. Finally, we were concerned with the interaction

[13] These data can be found in Chapter 7, which presents a more detailed analysis of the pro bono practice in Brazil.

between actors, institutions, and interests in different regulatory issues and contexts.

The negotiation between the Pro Bono Institute and the OAB in the regulation of pro bono practice created an alliance between the traditional and business law elites – both supported free legal aid for both groups and individuals as a social responsibility of the legal profession. They were opposed by the OAB organizational elites and the majority of lawyers the bar leaders represented who were concerned that free legal services would undermine the lucrative legal aid market.

The issue of foreign firms created a different set of alliances. The business law elites were split on the issue. Some business law firms, probably seeing benefits for themselves, favored formal relationships between foreign and Brazilian firms, while the majority of business law elites were opposed. Traditional elite lawyers who weighed in on the issue had mixed opinions. Representatives of the traditional elite – such as Sepulveda Pertence (former justice of the Brazilian Supreme Court), Adilson Abreu Dallari (professor at the Catholic University of São Paulo), and Carlos Ari Sundfeld (former public attorney of the São Paulo State and professor at the Catholic University of São Paulo and FGV Law School) – issued formal opinions that opposed some of the proposed restrictions but accepted others.

In both cases, the institutional design of the OAB helps explain the political processes and results described above. The conflicts generated by tension between the traditional model of lawyering and the model developed by the large, internationalized law firms tended to be more intensive in São Paulo because of its immense and dynamic market for legal services. It is no surprise that the regulatory issues first surfaced in the São Paulo State Bar, including its Tribunal of Ethics and Discipline and the Sectional Council.

Because state-level regulation is subject to scrutiny at the federal level, however, it was always possible for parties to try to move the conflict to the Federal Council. The decision to try to move to a higher level, and the responses at that level, vary with the nature of the rule in question and the interests of officials at the federal level in the issues raised.

In the case of pro bono, the power of the coalition composed by traditional elites and business law elites in defense of that practice was strong enough to create a solution at the local level that both sides accepted. So the issue remained within São Paulo, and the Federal Council did not take note of the matter until 2013, when an external actor – the Federal Public Prosecutor's Office – forced the Federal Council to look at the issue. Once the Federal Council was seized of the matter, under threat of judicial action and with constitutional issues on the table, it responded quickly by suspending restrictions followed by the announcement that all types of pro bono would be allowed and a new Code of Ethics prepared to regulate the matter. Although through external intervention the issue finally reached the federal level, the long period in which pro bono remained a local matter shows that issues can remain at that level unless and until there are strong political interests in moving them to the Federal Council.

In the case of the foreign law firms, there were such interests. The move to the federal level in this case was a strategy of Brazilian law firms already associated with foreign law firms. They sought to move the conflict to an arena where decision makers were less directly interested in the outcome. The fight over these alliances was highly localized in São Paulo (and to a lesser degree in Rio de Janeiro) and meant little to the bar in other states and territories.[14] That made the federal level look attractive to the groups seeking to legitimate the alliances. Another reason the issue could not be contained at the state level was that, unlike the pro bono case, no agreement could be reached at the local level that left everybody happy. In this case, the strongest political actors in São Paulo (traditional elites and business law elites) were divided internally on the issue.

The final federal ruling on foreign firms, which stated that a new regulation was not necessary, can be considered as the way the Federal Council found to decide the conflict by not deciding it in a decisive and specific manner. The ruling left substantial ambiguity about what was and wasn't allowed. While some Brazilian law firms ended their association with foreign law firms after the Federal Council's statement, other partnerships were kept, probably under the understanding that there was no significant regulatory change that explicitly prohibited the existing partnerships.

In conclusion, we have tried to show that the politics of professional regulation in Brazil can be explained by the interaction of several factors. The first is the power of the main political actors, who have their respective resources of economic and symbolic power. The second is the institutional design of the OAB, which tends to let intensive conflicts stay at the local level as far as possible while at the same time reducing the relative power of certain local actors when issues do reach the national level. The third is path dependence, the inheritance of previous choices, as in the case of the regulatory acceptance of the capitalist law firm that injected a powerful new actor into the system and influenced the outcome of subsequent efforts to preserve traditional models and markets.

14 Similar issues in which local struggles were met with indifference at the national level occurred during the 1980s when the São Paulo State Bar tried several times to take to the national level its resistance against the creation of a Public Defense Office in São Paulo, but it faced the indifference from the leaders of other state bars, who argued that it was a local problem (Almeida 2005).

REFERENCES

Aidar SBZ Advogados. 2014. http://aidarsbz.com/.

Almeida, Frederico N. R. de. 2005. "A advocacia e o acesso à justiça no estado de São Paulo (1980–2005)" (master's dissertation, Faculdade de Filosofia, Letras e Ciências Humanas, Universidade de São Paulo, São Paulo).

2010. "A nobreza togada: as elites jurídicas e a política da justiça no Brasil" (PhD thesis, Faculdade de Filosofia, Letras e Ciências Humanas, Universidade de São Paulo).

Análise Editorial. 2011. *Análise Advocacia* 500. Análise: São Paulo.

2012. *Análise Advocacia* 500: Análise: São Paulo.

2013. *Análise Advocacia* 500: Análise. São Paulo.

Baker & McKenzie. 2014. www.bakermckenzie.com/.

Bonelli, Maria da Glória. 2002. *Profissionalismo e política no mundo do direito: as relações dos advogados, desembargadores, procuradores de justiça e delegados de polícia com o Estado*. São Carlos: EdUFSCar/Sumaré.

Bourdieu, Pierre. 2007. *O poder simbólico*. Rio de Janeiro: Bertrand Brasil.

Canário, Pedro. 2013. "Advogados se voltam contra Resolução Pro Bono da OAB-SP." *Consultor Jurídico*, February 23. www.conjur.com.br/2013-fev-23/grandes-nomes-advocacia-voltam-resolucao-pro-bono-oab-sp.

Castro, Carlos Roberto Siqueira. 2012. "Associação/cooperacção entre escritórios brasileiros e firmas estrangeiras de advocacia: proposta de provimento ao Conselho Federal da Ordem dos Advogados do Brasil." http://s.conjur.com.br/dl/proposta-siqueira-castro-advogados.pdf.

Costa e Duque Bertasi Advogados Associados. 2014. www.costaduquebertasi.adv.br/.

Cummings, Scott L. 2011. "Introduction: What Good Are Lawyers?" In *The Paradox of Professionalism: Lawyers and the Possibility of Justice*. Edited by Scott L. Cummings. New York: Cambridge University Press.

Cunha, Luciana Gross Siqueira, Maria da Glória Bonelli, Fabiana Luci Oliveira, and Maria Natália B. Silveira. 2007. "Sociedades de advogados e tendências profissionais." *Revista Direito GV* 3 (2): 111–138.

Dezalay, Yves. 1991. "Territorial Battles and Tribal Disputes." *Modern Law Review* 54 (6): 792–809.

Dezalay, Yves, and Bryant Garth. 2000. "A dolarização do conhecimento técnico-profissional e do Estado: processos transnacionais e questões de legitimação na transformação do Estado, 1960–2000." *Revista Brasileira de Ciências Sociais* 15 (43): 163–176.

2002. *The Internationalization of Palace Wars: Lawyers, Economists, and the Contest to Transform Latin American States*. Chicago: University of Chicago Press.

Dezalay, Yves, and David Trubek. 1996. "A Reestruturação Global e o Direito – a internacionalização dos campos jurídicos e a criação dos espaços transnacionais." In *Direito e Globalização Econômica – implicações e perspectivas*. Edited by José Eduardo Faria. São Paulo: Malheiros.

Dias e Carvalho Filho Advogados. 2014. www.diascf.com.br/.

Engelmann, Fabiano. 2006a. *Sociologia do campo jurídico: juristas e usos do direito*. Porto Alegre: Sergio Antonio Fabris.

2006b. "Internacionalização e ativismo judicial: as causas coletivas." *Lua Nova* 69: 123–146.

Escola de Direito de São Paulo da Fundação Getúlio Vargas. 2014. http://direitosp.fgv.br/.

Ferraz, Sérgio. 2002. "Capítulo I." In *Sociedade de Advogados*. Edited by Sérgio Ferraz. São Paulo: Malheiros.

Freidson, Eliot. 1996. "Para uma análise comparada das profissões: a institucionalização do discurso e do conhecimento formais." *Revista Brasileira de Ciências Sociais* (31): 141–154.

1998. *Renascimento do profissionalismo: teoria, profecia e política*. São Paulo: EDUSP.

Galanter, Marc, and Thomas Palay. 1994. "The Many Futures of the Big Law Firms." *South Carolina Law Review* 45 (5): 905–930.

Giacomo, Orlando. 2002. "Capítulo VIII." In *Sociedade de Advogados*. Edited by Sérgio Ferraz. São Paulo: Malheiros.

Immergut, Ellen M. 1998. "The Theoretical Core of the New Institutionalism." *Politics & Society* 26 (1): 5–34.

Lacerda, Gabriel, Tanya Rangel, and Joaquim Falcão. 2012. *Aventura e Legado no Ensino do Direito*. Rio de Janeiro: FGV.

Machado Meyer Sendacz Opice Advogados. 2014. www.machadomeyer.com.br/.

Marx, Karl. 2013. *O capital: crítica da economia política*. Vol. I. São Paulo: Boitempo.

Mather, Lynn. 2011. "How and Why Do Lawyers Misbehave? Lawyers, Discipline, and Collegial Control." In *The Paradox of Professionalism: Lawyers and the Possibility of Justice*. Edited by Scott L. Cummings. New York: Cambridge University Press.

Migalhas. 2012. "Orlando Di Giacomo Filho, primeiro presidente do Cesa, falece em SP." www.migalhas.com.br/Quentes/17,MI163807,51045-Orlando+Di+Giacomo+Filho+primeiro+presidente+do+Cesa+falece+em+SP.

Miguel Reale Júnior Advogados. 2014. www.miguelrealejr.adv.br/.

Ordem dos Advogados do Brasil. 2012. *Limites éticos da cooperação e associação entre sociedades de consultores estrangeiros e sociedades brasileiras de advogados. Proposição nº 49.0000.2011.002723-1/COP. Relator: Conselheiro Federal Marcelo Cintra Zarif*. Brasília: Conselho Federal da OAB.

2015a. "OAB aprova advocacia pro bono no Brasil." www.oab.org.br/noticia/28512/oab-aprova-advocacia-pro-bono-no-brasil.

2015b. "OAB edita provimento que regulamenta a advocacia pro bono." www.oab.org.br/noticia/29076/oab-edita-provimento-que-regulamenta-a-advocacia-pro-bono.

Pierson, Paul. 2004. *Politics in Time: History, Institutions, and Social Analysis*. Princeton, NJ: Princeton University Press.

Procuradoria da República no Estado de São Paulo. 2014. "OAB suspende proibição à advocacia pro bono em todo o país." www.prsp.mpf.mp.br/prdc/sala-de-imprensa/noticias_prdc/19-06-13-2013-oab-suspende-proibicao-a-advocacia-pro-bono-em-todo-o-pais.

Rueschemeyer, Dietrich. 1964. "Doctors and Lawyers: A Comment on the Theory of the Professions." *Canadian Review of Sociology and Anthropology* 1 (1): 17–30.

1977. "The Legal Profession in Comparative Perspective." *Sociological Inquiry* 47 (3/4): 97–127.

1986. "Comparing Legal Professions Cross-Nationally: From a Professions-Centered to a State-Centered Approach." *American Bar Foundation Journal* 11 (3): 415–446.

Sá e Silva, Fabio de. 2012. "Lawyers and Governance in a Globalizing World: Narratives of 'Public Interest Law' across the Americas" (PhD thesis, Northeastern University, School of Public Policy and Urban Affairs, Boston).

Schmitter, Phillippe C. 1974. "Still the Century of Corporatism?" *The Review of Politics* 36 (1): 85–131.

Secco, Alexandre. 2012. "O mercado desafia seus paradigmas." In *Análise Advocacia 500–Anuário 2012: os escritórios e advogados mais admirados do Brasil pelas maiores empresas*. São Paulo: Análise Editorial.

Tauil, Ivan. 2011. "Associação com escritório estrangeiro não é uma ameaça." *Consultor Jurídico*. www.conjur.com.br/2011-out-11/escritorios-estrangeiros-brasil-nao-sao-ameaca-contrario.

Tauil and Chequer Advogados. 2014. www.tauilchequer.com.br/.

Taylor, Matthew MacLeod. 2008. *Judging Policy: Courts and Policy Reform in Democratic Brazil*. Stanford, CA: Stanford University Press.

Tozzini Freire Advogados. 2014. www.tozzinifreire.com.br/.

Vasconcellos, Marcos de. 2013. "Decisão sobre bancas estrangeiras gera fim de parceria." *Consultor Jurídico*, January 24. www.conjur.com.br/2013-jan-24/decisao-oab-bancas-estrangeiras-gera-fim-parceria-escritorio.

Vieira, Oscar Vilhena. 2008. "Public Interest Law: A Brazilian Perspective." *UCLA Journal of International Law and Foreign Affairs* 13 (1): 219–262.

7

Doing Well and Doing Good in an Emerging Economy

The Social Organization of Pro Bono among Corporate Lawyers and Law Firms in São Paulo, Brazil

Fabio de Sa e Silva

I INTRODUCTION

Since the 1990s, corporate law practices in countries like Brazil, India, and China have gone through a great transformation. As these economies were opened to global capital, corporate lawyers and law firms and in-house legal departments in the business sector grew in number, adopted new organizational forms and styles of practice, and gained influence in the profession and those societies in general.

The literature suggests these changes should go beyond the strict provision of services to businesses. Contribution to the public good, especially via pro bono work – free legal services to the poor and disadvantaged – should be a feature of that changing corporate bar (Dezalay and Garth 2002a; Dezalay and Garth 2002b; Halliday and Osinsky 2006; Trubek and Santos 2006; Cummings and Trubek 2008; Garth and Dezalay 2012). Yet, assessments of pro bono in Brazil are less than optimistic. Reports from India and China are also discouraging (Dong, forthcoming; Gupta 2017). In all three countries, pro bono seems to lag behind other developments in the corporate legal hemisphere and comparable experiences in the world. By examining the social organization of pro bono in São Paulo – the largest market for corporate law services in Brazil – this chapter seeks to address this puzzle and add to the broader debates underlying this volume.

The chapter is divided into six sections, including this introduction. Section II details the mentioned puzzle of underdeveloped pro bono in a globalizing legal profession. Section III outlines the research design and methods used to address such puzzle. Section IV reports the research findings by describing four dimensions in the development of pro bono work among São Paulo corporate lawyers and law firms in São Paulo: (1) pro bono's promotion, (2) resistance to pro bono, (3) pro bono's rationalization, and (4) pro bono's endurance and radicalization. Section V describes the most contemporary events in such story. Finally, Section VI builds on the preceding findings and accounts to make more general points relevant to theory and research on law, lawyers, and globalization.

II THE PUZZLING PICTURE OF PRO BONO IN EMERGING BRAZIL

The history of the US legal profession shows a slow but steady process wherein private lawyers assimilated the provision of pro bono work as a matter of professional responsibility. Despite an old rhetoric of progressivism among bar leaders and legal scholars, the profession was generally indifferent – and even hostile – to the idea of serving those who could not afford legal representation. Lawyers resisted solutions like contingency fees and use of federal resources to fund legal aid. "Pro bono" referred only broadly to what lawyers could do "in the public interest" (Lochner 1975; Cummings 2004; Rhode 2005; Granfield and Mather 2009).

This began to change in the 1980s, when the American Bar Association (ABA) Code of Professional Responsibility established a minimum amount of hours per year that every lawyer should provide free of charge to people of limited means or to charitable organizations (Lochner 1975; Cummings 2004; Rhode 2005; Granfield and Mather 2009). Within three decades, US lawyers doing pro bono, largely within big corporate law firms (Boutcher 2010; Cummings and Rhode 2010; Galanter and Palay 1995; Granfield and Mather 2009; Sandefur 2007), became responsible for impressive amounts of legal services for the poor nationwide (Cummings 2004; Rhode 2005; Sandefur 2007; Granfield and Mather 2009).

This remarkable change has been the subject of a growing body of literature. According to these studies, investments on pro bono were neither accidental, nor due to greater altruism among US lawyers. Rather, pro bono succeeded for being satisfactory to those who provide it, functional to their employing organizations, and beneficial to the profession at large. Some authors, for example, have stressed the positive association among engagement with pro bono, career satisfaction, and sociodemographic variables like race, gender, professional socialization, and political values (Wilkins 2004; Granfield 2007a; Granfield 2007b; Cummings and Sandefur 2013). Others have argued that pro bono matured in law firms as it helped the firms meet some major organizational demands, such as training first-year associates and retaining young talents (Cummings 2004; Granfield and Mather 2009; Boutcher 2010; Cummings and Sandefur 2013). Finally, others have claimed that firm investments in pro bono have helped legal professionals sustain social and political legitimacy, especially when federal funds for free legal assistance to the poor have been severely cut back (Rhode 1998, 2005).

Additional works have suggested this pro bono trend should spread beyond the US borders, particularly in the case of emerging economies like Brazil, India, and China. In general terms, the idea that private lawyers can work for the public good would help legitimize the economic order these countries have become participants, in which demands for increased corporate power come with requirements for corporate social responsibility (Shamir 2010, 2011; Garth and Dezalay 2012). Moreover, engagement with pro bono is in sync with a growing consensus on the rule of law, which embraces concerns with rights enforcement and political accountability as much as with property rights, freedom of initiative, and predictability for business transactions (Dezalay and Garth 2002a, 2002b; Trubek and Santos 2006; Cummings and Trubek 2008; Halliday and Osinsky 2006). In more concrete terms, as these economies become more open, their legal professions should be more exposed to practicing styles and organizational forms from the global north, especially the United States. For example, several organizations have made international cooperation in pro bono their core business, like PILNET,[1] the Pro Bono Institute,[2] the International Bar Association,[3] the Cyrus R. Vance Center for International Justice,[4] and New Perimeter.[5] Exchanges with these

[1] "With seed funding from the Ford Foundation, PILnet was established in 1997 as the Public Interest Law Initiative in Transitional Societies at Columbia University (PILI) to promote the use of law as a tool to serve the interests of the whole of society rather than those of a powerful few... In 2007, PILnet became an independent non-profit organization (then the Public Interest Law Institute) and established a New York office" (PILNET 2015).

[2] According to the PBI website, the organization as "Founded in 1996, the Pro Bono Institute (PBI) is a Washington, DC–based nonprofit organization. With an unparalleled depth of knowledge, resources, and expertise, PBI is a respected resource for all things pro bono... By providing expert consultations and technical assistance; educational programming; and local, national, and global pro bono convenings, [PBI's] goal is to constantly improve and enrich pro bono service" (Pro Bono Institute 2015).

[3] According to the IBA website, "The International Bar Association (IBA), established in 1947, is the world's leading organization of international legal practitioners, bar associations, and law societies. The IBA influences the development of international law reform and shapes the future of the legal profession throughout the world... It has considerable experience in providing assistance to the global legal community" (International Bar Association 2015).

[4] The Cyrus R. Vance Center for International Justice (Vance) "advances global justice by engaging lawyers across borders to support civil society and an ethically active legal profession. [It has] two principal approaches to fulfilling [its] mission. [It provides] legal representation to civil society organizations... [It also builds] the capacity of the legal profession to pursue pro bono practice, ethics, and diversity through [its] Program on Strengthening the Legal Profession" (Cyrus R. Vance Center for International Justice 2015).

[5] According to its website, the "New Perimeter is a nonprofit organization established by global law firm DLA Piper to provide pro bono legal assistance in underserved regions around the

and other players should help make pro bono more widespread among professionals in the global south.

But despite these predictions, the advancement of pro bono in Brazil has proven slow. For example, in 2011, a survey on pro bono in Latin America conducted by *Latin Lawyer* and the Vance Center found that Brazil had "the biggest deterrents" in those surveyed.[6] The survey report stated:

> Brazilian firms have not been able to do the same level of pro bono work as in [other countries in the sample]. Some 40 percent of firms say 25 to 50 percent of their lawyers did pro bono work in 2011, but no firms said more of their lawyers did that amount, and one-third said less than 25 percent of their lawyers did pro bono work. Furthermore, just 20 percent of respondents said their lawyers had reached the PBDA target of 20 hours a year per lawyer. (Latin Lawyer and Cyrus R. Vance Center for International Justice 2012, 21)

In the 2013 edition of this survey, *Latin Lawyer* and the Vance Center reiterated that "the majority of Brazilian firms . . . report low levels of engagement among their lawyers" (see Figure 7.1). Moreover, they stressed that the Brazilian corporate legal sector provided very modest support to pro bono promotion: "The Instituto Pro Bono reports that only four of its forty-five law firm members and one of four corporate legal department members make financial contributions, which vary from $2,000 to tens of thousands of dollars per organization" (Latin Lawyer and Cyrus R. Vance Center for International Justice 2014, 20).[7]

Studies about India and China report different circumstances but similar results (Dong, forthcoming; Gupta 2017). In all three countries, engagement with pro bono seems to fall behind the development of other aspects of corporate legal hemisphere or comparable experiences in the world. How has this disconnection arisen and remained over time? Where might the links between the corporate bar and pro bono have been missed? What possibilities can we envision for pro bono work in the Brazilian corporate bar in the years to come? Finally, what implications does this all have for theory and research on law,

world to support access to justice, social, and economic development and sound legal institutions. [It was] founded in 2005 as a result of [the] firm's commitment to support legal advancement worldwide." (New Perimeter 2015).

6 *Latin Lawyer* magazine presents itself as "the definitive business law resource for Latin America." In addition to producing news articles about business opportunities and legal developments in the region, *Latin Lawyer*'s work involves "research and benchmark," which result in the publication entitled *Latin Lawyer 250: Latin America's leading guide to business law firms*. (*Latin Lawyer* 2015).

7 Instituto Pro Bono, henceforth IPB, is a clearinghouse and advocacy center for pro bono work in Brazil.

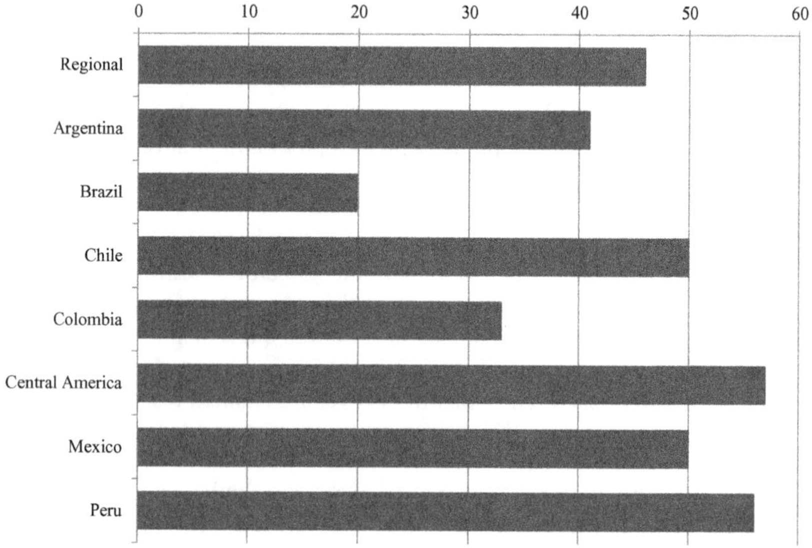

FIGURE 7.1 Percentage of Latin American firms whose lawyers averaged twenty hours or three cases pro bono in 2012.
Source: Latin Lawyer and the Cyrus R. Vance Center for International Justice (2014).

lawyers, and globalization? These are some of the questions this chapter seeks to illuminate.

III RESEARCH DESIGN AND METHODS

This chapter relies on empirical research on the social organization of pro bono work in São Paulo. Following similar works in the sociology of the legal profession (Nelson and Trubek 1992; Seron 1996; Heinz and Laumann 1994; Cummings 2004; Granfield 2007b; Boutcher 2009; Boutcher 2010; Cummings and Sandefur 2013), I sought to understand how pro bono work has been structured, delivered, and conceived amid the operation of larger social forces. In particular, I focused on two arenas (Nelson and Trubek 1992) in which these forces tend to come together. The first was law firms and in-house legal departments (Lochner 1975; Sarat and Felstiner 1995; Seron 1996; Mather et al. 2001; Levin 2008). The second was the more general legal field – the space formed by varied legal professionals struggling to set the terms of what legal work is, the results of these struggles constituting the limits and hierarchies of the field (Bourdieu 1986; Dezalay and Garth 2002b; Dezalay and Madsen 2012; Garth and Dezalay 2012).

TABLE 7.1 *Arenas of inquiry and research techniques*

Arena	Subjects involved	Research techniques	Sampling strategy
Legal field	• Pro bono activists • Independent specialists • Bar leaders • Public defenders • Prosecutors	• Reviews of previous studies • Analyses of available documents • Observation in public events related to pro bono work in Brazil • Interviews	• Several qualitative sampling techniques, given the iterative process of field research (Marshall 1996)
Firms and in-house legal departments	• Lawyers or partners at firms (10, N = 33) • General counsels (2, N = 4)	• All of the above plus semistructured interviews	• Purposive, with maximum variation (Trost 1986; Marshall 1996)

The core of the data collection occurred between 2011 and 2013. In addition to reviews of previous studies, I relied on several ethnographic techniques. I analyzed documents about the history of pro bono work in São Paulo, conducted direct observation in public events related to pro bono work in Brazil and Latin America, and did qualitative interviews with corporate lawyers and other participants of the Brazilian legal field, like public defenders, prosecutors, bar leaders, pro bono activists, and academics.[8]

After preliminary analysis of corporate lawyers and law firms doing pro bono work with the IPB, I purposely selected a sample of lawyers from ten firms ($n = 33$) and two in-house legal departments ($N = 4$) for the interviews component (see Table 7.1). The sample included partners and pro bono managers from law firms, as well as general counsels from in-house legal departments.

Efforts were made to include firms with a range of sizes and tradition in the São Paulo corporate law market. Some of the attorneys worked for law firms that had been in business for decades, while others worked for firms that were just taking shape. Six of the firms had over 100 lawyers; the other four ranged from 20 to 100 lawyers.

Interview protocols included questions on the history of pro bono in Brazil and within the firm or legal department, procedures used for selecting and conducting pro bono cases, and the interviewee's opinion about the challenges to pro bono development in the country. Interviews took an average

[8] To validate the results, these were presented and discussed with key subjects and peers and the compiled stories were closely followed through mid-2015.

of one hour. Records were anonymized, coded, and analyzed along with the rest of the data produced during fieldwork. The results pointed out to a multistaged story, which I report in greater detail next.

IV PRO BONO AMONG CORPORATE LAWYERS AND LAW FIRMS IN SÃO PAULO: A MULTIDIMENSIONAL STORY

Findings from the empirical research resulted in a story of four dimensions. The first dimension involves different forces in the São Paulo legal profession coming together to promote pro bono. Chief among these forces were lawyers with US training and socialization and concerns with the rule of law, who returned to Brazil and presented the local legal community with the notion of pro bono. But other forces were also important, like corporate clients, traditional legal elites, bar leaders, and corporate law firms and in-house legal departments.

The second dimension involves growing resistance to pro bono. Although that resistance came from many sources, the core of it resulted from disputes for shares at both the high and the low ends of the São Paulo legal market. In these disputes, pro bono was attacked as a tactic of unfair competition. To mediate these disputes, bar officials sought to regulate pro bono and restricted it to transactional work for nonprofits. But while this regulation limited corporate lawyers' ability to incorporate pro bono into their everyday lives, their willingness to challenge the bar waned over time. Some corporate law firms backed off as they needed help from the bar to curtail foreign competition.

The third dimension involves pressures to rationalize of pro bono work at the corporate bar. This resulted in the adoption of more objective protocols for selecting, conducting, and evaluating provision of pro bono.

The fourth dimension involves pro bono surviving such hostility. The bar's restrictions enabled pro bono promoters to raise support from other sectors of the profession, like public defenders and NGO lawyers, bringing more diversity to the pro bono movement. As a result, IPB became involved in new forms of legal activism, including more radical initiatives such as litigation before the Supreme Court in controversial issues like affirmative action.

This section addresses these dimensions, as it follows.

A *Promoting Pro Bono*

The inauguration of the IPB in 2001 embodies modern efforts to disseminate ideas and practical models for pro bono in Brazil. That event brought together different forces – global and local – which prompted the legal profession and the corporate bar in São Paulo to provide free legal services to those in need in a more systematic way. In this section, I examine how this process occurred.

1 Rule of Law and Corporate Social Responsibility: Global Drivers of Pro Bono

A chief force behind IPB was that of an emerging legal elite bearing US legal training and socialization and committed with the global dissemination of pro bono and the rule of law. Oscar V. Vieira, the current dean of Fundação Getúlio Vargas law school in São Paulo, is an example of this category.[9] Vieira had always believed that Brazilian legal professionals should do more to help the poor and disadvantaged. However, only after he pursued a Master of Laws at Columbia Law School and worked with the US public interest law community he could translate these beliefs into feasible action. The notion of pro bono was central in this move.

Vieira quickly saw an opportunity to implement his evolving ideas as he went back home. In 1997, as a human right law professor and the executive director of ILANUD, a United Nations organization focused on reforming criminal justice in Latin America, Vieira discovered that young people at juvenile courts were lacking legal defense. He gathered law students and elite lawyers from São Paulo to research on and respond to that issue. "That was a modest project," said he, "but very inspirational for what I did next on pro bono."

Years later, indeed, when Vieira was leading Conectas Direitos Humanos, a human rights NGO supported by entities like the Ford Foundation and the Open Society Institute, he organized various meetings of elite lawyers in São Paulo to promote pro bono. These meetings featured Daniel Grunfeld, the then-executive director of the Public Counsel Law Center in Los Angeles and

9 Vieira's father was close to Alberto Franco Montoro, a progressive politician and São Paulo state governor from 1983 to 1987. Vieira combined legal training from the Pontifical Catholic University of São Paulo School of Law and advanced studies in political issues. He received a Master's (in 1991) and a PhD (in 1998) in political science from the University of São Paulo, "Where (he) learned that the end of the military regime would not necessarily be the beginning of democracy and the rule of law in Brazil" (Estadao Educacao 2011). Vieira also completed a Master of Laws in 1995 at Columbia University School of Law, where he established an organic relationship with public interest lawyers and organizations in the United States, including the Ford Foundation and the Open Society Institute. "At that time I became sure I was never going to leave the university…but I only would be able to stay at the university if I could match together teaching and researching with professional and political activities geared to reforming institutions and further the rule of law," he explained to a journalist (Estadao Educacao 2011).

Ellen Chapnik, a law professor from Columbia. The IPB was established as a result of these meetings (Fuchs 2004; Vieira 2008).

Professionals like Vieira encountered a favorable time to advance their ideas. Sympathy to pro bono existed among other members of the bar, namely corporate lawyers and law firms with growing exposure to foreign cultures of work and trends of corporate social responsibility. The years around IPB's inauguration had been fertile for legal businesses involving foreign investors and multinationals. As the bar imposed regulatory restrictions to foreign firm entry, Brazilian corporate lawyers faced a much promising scenario. Yet, they knew they had to have a strategy to attract the global clientele and appear as trustworthy partners locally. As a step in that direction, firms set up a think tank called Centro de Estudos de Sociedades de Advogados (CESA) or the Center for Studies on Law Firms, which should help them increase their knowledge about foreign clients' expectations. Moreover, firms decided to embrace pro bono and IPB, which they learned would resonate well with their target-audience. As a scholar specialized in the Brazilian legal profession said, "CESA was these firms' intellectual branch; with IPB, they saw the chance of having a philanthropic branch as well" (Interview 5). Hence, after the meetings Vieira organized, leading CESA associates agreed to join and support IPB.

At this point, however, other global trends were driving law firm attention to pro bono. Needing to develop corporate social responsibility (CSR) projects, businesses already settled in Brazil looked to members of the corporate bar for help. For example, when a mid-sized law firm lawyer accounted for her experience with pro bono, she said:

> It begins with clients who want to form a non-profit to support a CSR project. Sometimes we take these as routine services, although we tend to charge lower fees because of the purpose involved... Other times we do it pro bono... There are many non-profits that grow out of small projects our corporate clients support... Things that initially no one knows that are going to work, until there comes a time when the company's CSR sector looks at them and says: This is already too big, it must walk by itself... And the market demands this from our clients. Many of them... have developed good reputation because of successful CSR projects they have supported.[10]

[10] Some of these CSR projects I came across involve, for example, supporting musical education for children living in favelas or training programs for juveniles from poor areas in São Paulo. Lawyers helped structure these projects via tax planning and incorporation of nonprofits.

Pro bono could meet this demand, figures like Milu Villela – an elite social entrepreneur linked to the financial sector – quickly realized.[11]

Although Villela does not appear in the list of IPB's founding members (she is not even a lawyer), she is in the photograph that IPB itself chose to illustrate its beginning moment.[12] This choice makes sense. A large–law firm lawyer recalls it was Villela, even before Vieira, who first introduced the idea of pro bono to some lawyers in São Paulo (Interview 1). As the UN had made 2001 the International Year of Volunteers, Villela organized meetings with business representatives to discuss their CSR practices and initiatives they could do together. The business community was Villela's main target, but she also invited some lawyers and other professionals.

At one of these meetings, this large–law firm lawyer reports, Villela asked him and his peers: "What could [they] do to exercise social responsibility as the other business-leaders [were] doing?" When they failed to respond, Villela suggested that free – pro bono – legal work for companies structuring CSR projects might be a way forward. "That was the first time we had actually heard of pro bono," he stated (Interview 1).[13]

2 Traditional Legal Elites, Professional *Noblesse*, and the Local Roots of Pro Bono

Another important force behind IPB was São Paulo "grand jurists" – lawyers whose successful careers combine experience in government, positions in academia, a great deal of family capital, and commitment with liberal values in politics and the profession.

Examples include Dalmo Dallari, José Carlos Dias, and Belisario dos Santos Jr., leading providers of free legal services to political prisoners in Brazil in the 1960s and 1970s, working closely with progressive sectors of the Catholic Church. Dallari, now a retired professor from the University of São Paulo Law School, also helped social movements lawyers in the 1980s in cases involving

[11] Milu Villela combined family and social capital and a leading position in a globalizing business sector (finance), all of which may have made her a leader in the corporate move toward CSR in Brazil. In 2002, a popular magazine in Brazil characterized her and two of her family members as "the controlling shareholders . . . of 33% of the shares of the Itau Bank, which was founded by her grandfather." The publication also reported that she "embraced social causes like a religion" and that she "impressed governments and businesspeople with her success in this area [and] represented the elite that makes a difference" (Vitoria 2002).

[12] In one of the public events observed in this research, Vieira considered Villela to be IPB's godmother.

[13] In the wake of this and other meetings, Villela created the NGO Faça Parte, which seeks to provide companies and professionals with opportunities for volunteer work.

indigenous rights and served as São Paulo's chief legal officer from 1990 to 1992. Dias became justice minister under Cardoso (from 1999 to 2000), and Santos Jr. was the state secretary for justice affairs in São Paulo from 1999 to 2000.

Other examples include Miguel Reale Jr., who appears in the picture shown here, and Marcio Thomaz Bastos Reale Jr., a professor at the University of São Paulo Law School, served as São Paulo state secretary in 1983 and 1995 and as Cardoso's justice minister in 2002. Bastos, president of the São Paulo state bar from 1983 to 1985, drafted the legal memorandum that gave the basis for the impeachment of president Collor de Mello in 1992, and served as justice minister during Lula da Silva's first term (from 2003 to 2006).

These lawyers could seldom be part of a story of pro bono's global diffusion. They were not based at big corporate law firms (some, like Dallari, were not even active practitioners) and the scope of their work was fundamentally local. However, their involvement with IPB had a crucial impact on pro bono development in São Paulo. They infused pro bono with the symbols of an old tradition of professional noblesse that values the involvement of private lawyers in public affairs and that they saw as inspirational to their own careers. In their written pieces and public speeches, these lawyers constantly associated pro bono with examples of other "grand jurists," including Ruy Barbosa, Sobral Pinto, and Luiz Gama.[14] Hence, instead of sounding like an import by young lawyers brainwashed by US law schools and global corporate clients, pro bono became an expression of a deep-rooted local tradition.

As this helped pro bono gain legitimacy, bar leaders grew in sympathy toward it. For instance, Carlos Miguel Aidar, then president of the São Paulo state bar shown in the picture here, became himself a founding member of IPB.

[14] Barbosa was a writer, lawyer, and politician who played a lead role in the first republic (from 1881 to 1930) and later used "the courts, newspapers, and his position as a senator to promote the rights of dissidents, including those of his opponents." He also "represented rural workers and women in their struggle for equal salary and labor conditions" and "contributed to the expansion of the use of habeas corpus as a remedy against any kind of discrimination and the arbitrary use of power" (Vieira 2008, 226). Pinto was a lawyer who protected political dissidents and union leaders against Getulio Vargas's authoritarian regime, which occurred 1930 and 1945. Although Pinto was a fierce Catholic, he defended communist leader Luiz Carlos Prestes (Vieira 2008, 227). Gama, who lived from 1830 to 1882, was a former slave who received informal legal training and, after being fired from his job for political activism, "started to place advertisements in several newspapers announcing his activities as a pro bono solicitor in cases linked with the liberation of slaves" (Vieira 2008, 224–225). His death "brought thousands . . . to the streets and generated several laudatory editorials and obituaries in major newspapers. Slavery was finally abolished six years later" (224–225).

3 Law Firm Rationale: Institutional Incentives for Engagement with Pro Bono

Law firms also began to realize advantages of engaging with pro bono. One was that they could create value out of an already established practice among their staff, if informally. For example, a large–law firm lawyer notes that "it was common to do free legal work for friends and relatives of (his) colleagues and employees in cases involving family law, consumer law, and small claims" (Interview 2). Another such lawyer recalls being "still an intern when [she] took on her first cases pro bono." It was something she and her colleagues did "during lunch time," normally on behalf of "firm janitors dealing with family law issues like child custody and child support" (Interview 3).

With pro bono, all of this could be converted into firm capital and reputation, at a time when prospective clients – especially multinationals and foreign investors – wanted to know how much pro bono firms were doing.

INTERVIEWEE 6: It is a matter of reputation, especially in the eyes of foreign clients. They have increased expectations that law firms will do (pro bono).

INTERVIEWER: Has this ever appeared in your conversations with them?

INTERVIEWEE 6: Yes, they ask, "Do you do pro bono?" Clients have this expectation. "What is your work in terms of social responsibility?" It is like any other service provider they recruit: "Our providers must meet these criteria, in terms of service quality but also of governance practices," and that is where community service is considered. So, there is this positive aspect (of doing pro bono). (Interview 6)

Indeed, clients began to use this information to distinguish between the law firms they would consider hiring. A general counsel stated that:

> [A medium-sized law firm], for example, started doing pro bono because we suggested it, but we are moving towards making it a real requirement and hiring services only from law firms that do pro bono.[15]

Law firms also perceived an advantage in staff satisfaction. When asked about what they found good about pro bono, many interviewees made statements like:

[15] Pro bono has not been the only such factor, but Interviewee 3 states that "it became a sort of tiebreaker, if they wanted to work with five firms and had to decide among many with similar conditions, this is something they began to consider." This is consistency with the tenets of the modern CSR model, as described, for example, in Kramer and Porter (2011) and Porter and Kramer (2006).

> Those who do pro bono have incredible satisfaction. We hear the most incredible things from them. They feel they are using their skills to effectively help a nonprofit that helps other people. In a business law firm like this we do grand projects but we can't see they helping actual people as we can in pro bono. (Interview 4)

> There is a personal aspect of it, which is that I like doing it. I think it is a way to contribute to something good with what we know. I can't donate to a nonprofit. I'd love to, but I can't. So what can I give? I can give my capabilities. So it's personally satisfactory to feel I can use what I have to help somebody. (Interview 5)

Indeed, pro bono managers and coordinators in law firms report having no difficulty in recruiting lawyers for this type of work – at least when it comes to meeting the existing demand. As a large–law firm lawyer put it,

> There is willingness to help, especially among new generations. For example, IPB promotes Mutirao Pro Bono, a day when a group of lawyers goes somewhere in the city and gives free legal counsel. There is a line, you hear a problem, and you give advice. Being the pro bono person in the firm, I sent an e-mail to our lawyers asking whether they would like to participate. A bunch of people replied. So I called IPB and said I had a list of lawyers. They said, "We can't get them all, we only have two slots, one for welfare benefits and one for labor law. Sorry, too many people showed up." So folks have much willingness to help. (Interview 3)

Lawyers' satisfaction also comes from other factors, like the chance to do different kinds of work and to be exposed to different experiences and realities. For example, as a large–law firm lawyer put it,

> You have to be creative, as the solutions you use for regular corporations don't fit to nonprofits. You can't come to a nonprofit and say it must do its balance sheet using all these accounting norms; they don't have expertise and won't hire an accountant for that. What they would pay for this accountant's services is what they need to assist a kid. They won't let a kid unassisted to pay for an accountant. You must find ways to work with what they have; there is no other way around it. (Interview 5)

Yet, pro bono could produce even further benefits. Interviewee 1, a large–law firm lawyer, recalls that pro bono was once crucial to retain clients grappling with CSR obligations:

> The client would approach you to negotiate a package of legal services and explain he helped maintain this charity foundation or project, which also

> needed services in taxes or other corporate affairs. You would say that was something you could do. And he would reply, "Great, but obviously this is something you are not going to charge me for, right? It is something you can take pro bono." You would agree with that, for there were many other firms he could go to, which would agree with these terms and, therefore, which he could hire instead of us. (Interview 1)[16]

4 An Original Alliance Takes Shape

While pro bono may have seemed initially foreign to the Brazilian legal profession and its growing corporate hemisphere, different interests and perspectives converged to create a context favorable for its promotion. A new legal elite made of lawyers with US legal training and socialization sought to promote pro bono in a broader struggle for the rule of law. The business sector saw pro bono as a good way to meet its needs for legal services in CSR projects. Elite corporate law firms saw good reasons to commit to pro bono, like retaining clientele, enhancing image in a globalizing market, and bringing satisfaction to their staff. "Grand jurists" saw pro bono as an expression of what they understood to be essential attributes of lawyers and gave IPB their endorsement; so did bar leaders. Accordingly, pro bono could grow as a pastiche of CSR, entrepreneurship of new professional elites, and the public spirit of traditional liberal lawyers. IPB's inauguration both galvanized this alliance and built on it to take the first steps toward successful pro bono adoption in Brazil – that is, until pro bono began to face resistance from other forces in the legal field.

B *Pro Bono Meets Resistance*

Convergence among legal elites, the business community, corporate law firms, and bar leaders was yet insufficient to free pro bono from conflict and resistance. Resistance emerged from several sources, including those pushing for publicly funded legal aid, corporate law firms that wanted to stop others from using pro bono to enhance their competitive image, and individual lawyers fearing competition for low-end clients. Bar leaders sought to mediate these tensions through regulation, which placed considerable restrictions on pro bono. Meanwhile, IPB officials and corporate law firms sympathetic to

[16] Pro bono policies, which we will discuss later, are the resources some firms have relied on to deal with these kinds of requests.

pro bono took advantage of the limited room left available to advance their objectives; they never fully accepted the constraints that had been imposed on them. Nevertheless, their willingness to challenge the bar would vary over time, with some corporate law firms backing off.

1 Local Market Disputes and Regulatory Struggles: Drivers of Resistance

Activists for publicly supported access to justice were the first to show skepticism toward pro bono. At the time the IPB was being inaugurated, the São Paulo state government was actively resisting the implementation of a public defender's office (PDO), which the 1988 Federal Constitution ruled should be the core of a state-based system to provide free legal services to the poor in civil and criminal cases. Hundreds of groups and social movements were then standing for the PDO. To these folks, the sudden emphasis of the legal profession on pro bono sounded like a threat, as it could discourage government investments in PDOs and inform a privatistic, market-based approach for access to justice policies (de Sa e Silva 2013; Moura et al. 2013).

A much stronger resistance, however, came from a force hitherto sympathetic to pro bono: the bar (Fuchs 2004; Vieira 2008). The reason lied in disputes for market jurisdiction at both the and the low ends of the bar, in which pro bono was perceived to be associated with unfair competition. At the high end, these disputes had resulted in a formal complaint being filed against one of the first corporate law firms to show engagement with pro bono. At the low end, solo and small-firm lawyers paid by the state to provide legal services to the poor saw pro bono as a threat and urged the bar leadership to curb it.[17]

Hence, a few months after IPB's inauguration, the context for pro bono at the São Paulo state bar had changed dramatically. Bar officials began to argue that pro bono created room for client cooptation and thus needed to

[17] Many private lawyers in Brazil are unable to provide more complex services and must compete against one another for the demands of middle- to low-income citizens. Accordingly, they frequently seek market protection against free legal services by state and civil society organizations and resist forms of alternative dispute resolution, which could make their services unnecessary. Because these lawyers are in great number, bar leaders tend to be responsive to their needs. Hence, Almeida (2006) observes that even though until the mid-1980s the bar – especially in São Paulo – was closely associated with liberal values and transformative politics, after that it became increasingly oriented toward protecting the market for private practitioners. For example, recent legal reforms in family law allowed divorce claims in which there are no property-or child custody–related issues involved to be processed administratively and at the request of the interested parties. The bar lobbied for the inclusion of a provision that would require attorneys to "supervise" this procedure, which the Brazilian Congress ultimately welcomed (República Federativa do 2007).

be restricted.[18] Robison Baroni, then president of the São Paulo Bar Ethics Court, stated to the press, "We are not against free-of-charge legal work, but this can be a means for advertisement of legal services, which is prohibited. It can be also a way for lawyers to insinuate themselves to clients with similar needs" (Souza 2002a). Jorge Eluf Neto, then president of the Bar Ethics Commission, corroborated these concerns: "The ethics code rules that lawyers must be committed to the larger society, [yet regulation of pro bono is necessary] to avoid that such solidary services fuel client cooptation, immoderate advertising, and unfair competition" (Souza 2002b).

As both an IPB's founding member and the president of the São Paulo state bar, Carlos M. Aidar tried to be conciliatory and appointed an ad hoc working group to draft regulation of pro bono practices. That regulation, entitled the "Pro Bono Resolution" and drafted in August of 2001, placed considerable limits on pro bono. To begin with, it ruled that pro bono should include "solely legal advice, not litigation." It also ruled that the only legitimate pro bono clients were "not-for-profits lacking resources to pay for legal services." Moreover, it ruled that lawyers should observe a "two-year quarantine before they can provide paid services to the same clients they had served pro bono." Finally, it ruled that lawyers should submit to the bar "an initial request of authorization to perform pro bono, as well as reports every six months, detailing the pro bono services they had provided."

While some law firm lawyers I interviewed were favorable to the bar's regulation, which they saw as a reliable basis for organizing their pro bono work in the absence of more specific policies within firms, they ever rejected the idea that pro bono could be a means for unfair competition and client cooptation. Even if retaining corporate clients was something these lawyers perceived as an advantage in pro bono at the high end of the bar, they argued that the market has its own means of regulating this aspect of firms' conduct. For example, Interviewee 5, a mid-sized law firm attorney noted:

> Firms that provide pro bono to nonprofits are not targeting at the corporations supporting these nonprofits. And even if they are, they should know that corporations will not hire them because they helped the nonprofits these corporations support. If they are doing pro bono to get paid work they will get frustrated, as corporations see these things in very separated terms these days. (Interview 5)

[18] This argument may hold some truth, at least in the United States. Philip R. Lochner Jr. (1975) and Carroll Seron (1996) show that solo and small-firm lawyers preferred to provide pro bono work to people who had backgrounds similar to their paying clients. But this would clearly not be the case for the mid-size and large firms that IPB wanted to reach out to in Brazil.

Interviewee 12, the head of an in-house legal department reinforced that perspective:

> Law firms will not use [pro bono] to get contracts, they will not work free of charge for [a nonprofit a bank is known to support] to get paid work from [this bank]. They are not going to work free of charge for Mr. [a businessman]'s family to get paid work from [the company this businessman heads] . . . This doesn't happen in countries like the US, where law firms are totally free to do pro bono . . . It won't happen here either. (Interview 12)

A similar understanding applies to the argument, central to the bar's regulatory initiative, that pro bono threatens the low-end market for legal services. Lawyers I interviewed argued that if they were firms were completely free to do pro bono work, this would have little to no impact on the demand of low-income clients for legal services. The needs for such services in Brazil far exceeds the capacity of law firms to supply services pro bono, they reasoned.

It was thus a matter of time for some of the forces behind pro bono to publicly challenge the terms of the Pro Bono Resolution. The absolute restrictions to pro bono work for individual clients became a major point of contention. The bar did not back off from its regulatory doctrine. In 2012, as an NGO lawyer was facing ethical charges for providing pro bono services to low-income members of his organization, the São Paulo Bar Ethics Court upheld the Pro Bono Resolution ruling that:

> The Resolution allows pro bono work to be provided solely to nonprofits lacking resources to pay for legal services. *Work for NGOs' members may be seen as charity that masks client cooptation and unfair competition, which the Lawyers' Statute and the Ethics Code prohibit.* Low-income people in need of legal services must be sent to free-of-charge services, such as those provided under the agreement between the bar and the PDO, law schools' legal aid offices . . . and the PDO itself (Precedents E–3.765/09, E 3.542/07, E–3.330/06, E–2.278/00, E–2.392/01 e E–2.954/04). Case No. E–4.0852011 – Unanimously decided on December 15, 2011. Attorney Marcia Matrone writing for the Court. (emphasis added by the author)

This decision caused outrage among IPB's constituencies. Marcos Fuchs, IPB's executive director, wrote that, "The bar should be concerned with making access to justice available for the poor rather than with maintaining its monopoly of poverty" (*Ultima Instancia* 2012). Alberto Z. Toron (2012), a respected criminal lawyer in São Paulo and IPB founder wrote to an attorney-targeted website. His letter stressed the traditional roots of pro bono in Brazil and denounced the bar's intention of protecting lawyers at the low end of the legal market:

> Not only is [the prohibition of pro bono to individuals] illegal but also it ignores the history of lawyering, a professional occupation that was meant to care about people. In the early days [of the profession] nobles practiced law in exchange not for money, but for recognition of honor. In my 30 years of legal practice I provided numerous individuals with pro bono legal defense... and have always believed I was honoring our best traditions [in doing so]. I hope I can keep doing that without being prosecuted; actually whoever works for a better and more solidary country expects to be left in peace. Borrowing from [Supreme Court] Justice Gilmar Mendes, "there are poor people for everyone." There is no need to protect the market when there is so much anguish among the families of incarcerated people [the clientele he serves pro bono]. (Toron 2012)

The conflict would escalate even further, but this would occur amid interesting changes in the coalition that supported pro bono, as I describe next.

2 International Market Disputes and New Local Compromises: Resistance Kept Up

The economic liberalization in the 1990s made Brazil an attractive place for foreign investors. Foreign law firms quickly saw this as a profitable opportunity. The bar identified this as a threat and enacted Provimento No. 91/2000, a regulation that placed severe limits to what foreign law firms could do in Brazil. Per this *provimento*, foreign law firms could only provide legal advice and would need a special, bar-issued license to operate.

The economic growth and international importance that Brazil achieved in the late-2000s, just as a huge economic crisis was happening internationally, reinforced the good feelings about the Brazilian market among foreign lawyers. As shown in Figure 7.2, the number of foreign law firms in Brazil grew significantly from 2001 to 2013 (Chapter 6).

Some of these firms found a way around the bar's *provimento* by developing associations with Brazilian law firms to provide services under both Brazilian and transnational law. Most of these joint ventures were established in São Paulo (Figure 7.3).

In 2005 one such joint venture (Lefosse–Linklaters) was subject to disciplinary action, but it reached a confidential agreement with the bar involving

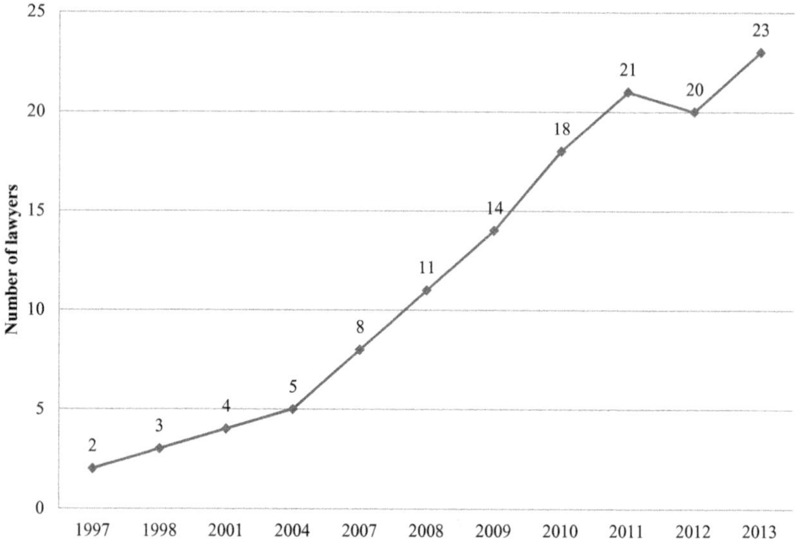

FIGURE 7.2 Foreign law firm activity in Brazil from 1997 to 2013.

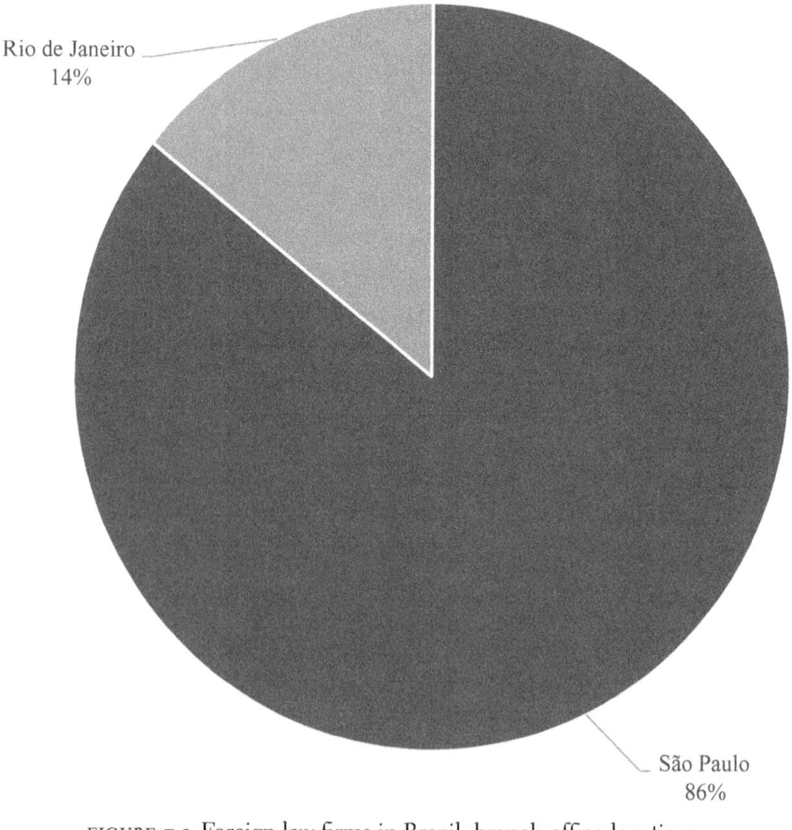

FIGURE 7.3 Foreign law firms in Brazil, branch office locations.
Source: Almeida and Nassar, Chapter 6, this volume.

operational changes to comply with the *provimento*. As other joint ventures continued to be established, CESA formally requested the São Paulo Bar's Ethics Court to determine whether this model was consistent at all with the *provimento*.

In 2011, this consultation was responded. The Court decided that, like fully foreign law firms, joint ventures risked being directed by individuals not familiar with Brazilian laws and the regulations of the Brazilian legal profession, given that they were not certified bar members. This would compromise the independence of Brazilian lawyers working in these joint ventures and expose their clients to risks.

Accordingly, the Court established several conditions for joint ventures to be consistent the *provimento*. These included complete physical separation between the local and the foreign law firms, and strict advertising restrictions, such as the prohibition of cross-references in firms' letterheads and business cards (Estadao 2011). Some firms disagreed with this ruling and took the issue all the way to the federal bar, only to see its Ethical Commission extend the basics of the São Paulo ruling to the rest of the country. In the wake of these decisions, the Lefosse–Linklaters joint venture was terminated (Vasconcellos 2013, Almeida and Nassar, Chapter 6). The bar has explicitly threatened other firms with same this fate as well (Cristo 2014).

The entry of foreign law firms into developing countries and the resulting conflicts over professional jurisdiction deserve separate treatment. Of more relevance to this chapter is the impact of these conflicts on the development of organized pro bono. Elite corporate law firms affiliated with CESA had been both a core audience and an important source of donor support for IPB's work. Because these firms faced a threat from foreign firm competition, they turned to the bar in search of protection. This led to new compromises, with an eventual split in firms' positions regarding the bar's regulations on pro bono.[19] Some firms maintained their support to IPB against the bar, but others took a step back (interviews with pro bono activists and local specialists). IPB's leadership had to search for other sources of support.

[19] Support to pro bono may have always been restricted to a few of the corporate law firms in the São Paulo market. Among a total of 533 pro bono providers working with IPB, 497 were listed as "individuals," which means they were solo or small-firm practitioners, 3 were listed as "in-house corporate legal departments," and 33 were listed as "law firms." This means there was a total of 36 providers from the corporate bar as opposed to 497 from outside of it. By contrast, CESA counts on 386 affiliates in São Paulo and 728 nationwide. IPB did not become CESA's philanthropic branch, as Interviewee 17, a local expert in the legal profession predicted.

C *Rationalizing Pro Bono*

In this meantime, law firm rationale – once important to make pro bono take off – continued to mold the reproduction of this practice. Law firms are organizations that seek the most favorable cost-benefit ratio (Rhode 2008). Initially, these concerns with results made many firms handle pro bono informally, with work being provided on a case-by-case basis. Over time, however, they favored firm investments in the opposite direction. Lawyers in charge of pro bono cases were compelled to show that "It is possible to provide these services within the available structure and that pro bono will not be a burden to the firm," as a mid-sized law firm lawyer said to me (Interview 2). As such, they had to think of pro bono more strategically and adapt it to the managerial culture of their firms. Interviewee 3, a large–law firm lawyer and pro bono coordinator explains:

> We have no policy for pro bono work; we do it case by case. It depends on the case and the partner who is bringing it. We need to check if the case is adequate to our firm culture and capability; sometimes there are cases we don't want to take or we can't take because we lack the required expertise. For example, we don't have a criminal law area in the firm, so if it is a criminal law case has we won't take it. If it involves tax law or commercial law, it's part of our everyday work, and we can donate these hours. But with criminal law, we wouldn't be willing to take responsibility for something we don't usually do. (Interview 3)

Hence, she believes that time has come for her firm to design and enact a formal policy to govern its organization and provision of pro bono:

> I do believe pro bono work should be institutionalized, because when you can do it in a better organized way, you know how many work hours you are providing and you can check how these hours are being allocated. Sometimes you feel that you are putting too many hours per year on pro bono cases and you are not, you are doing much less than you intended to. Conversely, sometimes you undertake a project that takes much more time than you originally envisioned. (Interview 2)

This vision was shared by this external observer, a pro bono activist who helped the Vance Center and *Latin Lawyer* implement the latest edition of their regional pro bono survey in Brazil. She reports that,

> When the firms had to send information about their pro bono hours for this survey, many had to find that out. And they found things they hadn't expected, like lawyers doing pro bono work for their own domestic workers

> or their family and marking those hours as pro bono for the firm. And that is because there's no universal policy in place. (Interview 2)

In addition to allowing a better quantification and better management of pro bono hours, policies also increase fairness in their distribution within the firms. Said Interviewee 3:

> Not every partner likes to do pro bono work, and the demands for the different areas of the firm vary as well. Some areas will likely never take a pro bono case; others will always be requested to do so. You may end up always sending cases to the same person. So, you need to ensure balance in the distribution of pro bono work – otherwise some areas and professionals at a firm will be disproportionally burdened.

The classic issue of whether pro bono hours are counted as billable hours appears as one such expressions of fairness, especially at large law firms.[20] As said by Interviewee 3, "If you get paid by the hours you bill, there's no other incentive to do pro bono work aside from your individual satisfaction in helping someone . . . Law firms must count pro bono work as billable hours so that lawyers will get paid and have the stimulus to work on these sorts of cases . . . This must be in their policies."

Of course, firms vary with respect to maturity in their policies. Firms with about a decade of pro bono experience demonstrated to have stronger procedures and structures of governance. As an example, Interviewee 2 says:

> We have a pro bono committee in the firm. This committee has lawyers from all areas and works as a filter – it is where we discuss whether to take the cases or not. We look at many aspects: Is the nonprofit unable to pay for legal services? Is the case worth taking? Is there any conflict of interest for the firm to work in this case? We also make an estimate of how many hours we would need to allocate to the case. If it is litigation, although we normally don't do litigation pro bono, it is more difficult; you never know how many years it will take. After looking at all these aspects, we make our decision.
>
> Other firms are just beginning to draft their policies, but already have a sophisticated idea of what these should involve, an interesting signal of organizational mimesis in the São Paulo corporate law sector. Thus, when I asked a mid-sized law firm lawyer that is just starting to do pro bono whether her work is guided by any policy, we had the following exchange:

20 For a similar discussion in the US context, *see* Dinovtizer & Garth (2009), and Sandefur (2009).

INTERVIEWEE 6: Our policy is not yet officially enacted. We want to make it simple so that lawyers can easily understand it. There's a flow chart we are working on. After we have checked who the client is, determined whether there is conflict of interest, and prepared a proposal, we open the case, record the time we spend with it, and follow its development within the firm.

INTERVIEWER: And how do you receive these prospective cases?

INTERVIEWEE 6: Via IPB and other sources, like our lawyers and their contacts in the NGO sector. But the most important thing to us are the criteria that we will use to accept or reject a pro bono client, along with issues like how we will account for the billable hours we donate – because we want to prove that we fulfill the twenty hours per year per lawyer, a moral commitment we have made by signing the Pro Bono Declaration of the Americas.

INTERVIEWER: These are the same aspects that law firms with more established pro bono practices are normally concerned with.

INTERVIEWEE 6: Yes, we know that, and we had in mind that once we started doing pro bono it should be systematically, rather than informally implemented.

This push to rationalize pro bono reestablishes the global-local relationships that have ever constituted pro bono in Brazil,[21] as some of this exchange already anticipates. Organizations and resource centers from the global North appear again as sources of best practices that can help firms in the global South meet their needs. For example, as Interviewee 7, a mid-sized law firm lawyer helping structure pro bono in her office was telling about their efforts in this area, she explained:

> We had a connection with the Vance Center, strengthened by one of our lawyers who went to study in NY and worked at a law firm with Vance lawyers. So, a Vance Center official came to visit us and we signed the PBDA. Vance has a lot of informational materials, which guided us through implementation of a pro bono program in the firm . . . These guidelines were useful. For example, today we are going to discuss our next project with our pro bono partner – a law firm partner focused solely on pro bono cases – something they recommend and we have adopted.

[21] Interviewee 13, a pro bono activist, summarizes: "We have had a very productive relationship with international organizations, which has helped us develop our ideas and practices. For example, Oscar Vieira met Daniel Grunfeld at the 2001 annual conference of the Pro Bono Institute, from Washington, D.C. I too had my first contact with pro bono at one of these events, in 2002. We work a lot with PILnet; they are very sensitive to the needs of countries, rejecting the idea that 'one size fits all.' We have organized courses with PILnet and New Perimeter and hope to set up a Latin American Forum on Pro Bono soon."

D *Sustaining and Radicalizing Pro Bono*

As resistance to pro bono grew at the bar and some law firms became hesitant in providing it with continued support, the strategies and choices of the pro bono movement had to change. Instituto Pro Bono became an advocacy center for the cause of volunteer legal work. A great deal of its energy went to mobilizing stakeholders who could help sustain pro bono against the corporate bar's agenda.

1 Old Ties Made Stronger

Bound by CSR goals, corporate clients quickly stood along with IPB. Many of these clients were already including pro bono requirements in their dealings with law firms. IPB worked to have these decisions made more explicit, systematic, and coordinated among corporate clients. The goal was to send a clear message to law firms regarding the importance of their commitment with pro bono, if not for moral reasons, at least for economic ones. Said Interviewee 13:

> I recently had lunch with an old law school friend who had just become the general counsel of [multinational] in Brazil and told her about these issues. She left the conversation saying she was going to issue a letter to the law firms she hires, showing her commitment to pro bono and stating that, in line with what happens to be her company's policy worldwide, she was no longer going to hire law firms that do not provide a minimum amount of pro bono work. (Interview 13)

Firms' concern with their public reputation – especially internationally – became another weapon for the pro bono movement to explore. The surveys conducted by *Latin Lawyer* and the Vance Center, for example, appeared to constrain firms just by asking them to report on the amount of pro bono hours they do annually.[22] Participation in conferences and gatherings, and subscription to symbolic documents such as Pro Bono Declaration for the Americas (PBDA) may not have had an immediate effect of increasing the corporate bar's commitment to pro bono in Brazil, but they open a window for further mobilization by local actors such as IPB. As Interviewee 14, another pro bono activist from my study put it,

[22] Interviewee 4 said, "We are committed to doing 3,000 hours of pro bono work annually. We report our progress to *Latin Lawyer*. We have reported done so for the past three years."

> The interest of *Latin Lawyer* in firms' performance in pro bono did shake things up here…We reached out to them and they did embrace the cause…They keep publishing about it…And as law firms are always interested in being on their pages, they have become more aware of how pro bono can be important. (Interview 14)

Yet, the more structural challenges to pro bono in Brazil led IPB to make other strategic moves. Old opponents like the PDO turned into allies, and some established relationships were strengthened, building a platform for new ventures. Projects and initiatives were diversified, while the notion of pro bono became the basis for stronger, more innovative, and more practical forms of legal activism.

2 New Alliances and New Working Definitions of Pro Bono

Whereas the bar's "Pro Bono Resolution" attempted to confine pro bono work to a single form of practice (transactional work and legal advice to underresourced NGOs), IPB gradually expanded the scope of its work and its working definition of pro bono.

Legal rights education, for example, became a new item in IPB's agenda. IPB launched *mutirões*, an initiative in which volunteer lawyers would go to public places to listen to people's stories and refer them to legal services or other agencies, if any, wherein their problems could be addressed. Similarly, IPB partnered with *Casa Saude da Mulher* (Women's health house), a project at the Federal University of São Paulo that offers medical assistance to women victims of domestic violence. Lawyers in this project would listen to victims' stories with an interest in the legal aspects they involved, and would refer them to the police or to the courts, if appropriate (Vieira 2008; Nascimento 2015).

Moreover, IPB continued to play an advocacy role for pro bono in Brazil by publicly asserting the importance of volunteer legal work for the legal profession and society in general. It is involved with initiating pro bono work at law schools as well.

Yet more intriguing, IPB undertook a more political turn: it became vocal in issues of public interest, developed ties with other organizations operating in this area of law, and began to participate in more confrontational strategies (Fuchs, 2004; Vieira, 2008).

Examples of this turn can be observed in high-level disputes related to access to justice policies and the establishment of PDOs in Brazil. In *ação direta de inconstitucionalidade* (ADI) lawsuits No. 3892 and No. 4270, a public defenders' association asked the national Supreme Court to deem unconstitutional a state policy on access to justice based entirely on ad hoc appointments of private lawyers to defend poor clients in civil and criminal cases.[23] The court favored the plaintiff, ruling that states must provide legal services to the poor primarily through PDOs. Along with NGOs like Conectas, IPB appeared as amicus curiae on behalf of the plaintiff (Conectas Direitos Humanos 2015a).

The same happened in ADI lawsuit no. 4163, which challenged an aggressive strategy by the São Paulo state bar to put private lawyers at the heart of access to justice policies (Almeida 2006). In the lack of a state PDO and as an alternative to having judges compulsorily assigning lawyers to the defense of poor clients, the bar and the São Paulo state government signed an agreement determining that (1) the bar would recruit lawyers who wanted to serve as appointed counsel in one or more state counties; (2) when an individual claimed she had no resources to pay for lawyer's fees, government officials would assign her case to a lawyer in the list; and (3) the state government would pay for the lawyer's fees (monthly) based on the specific services undertaken by the lawyer, according to the price list previously set.

When the São Paulo state PDO was established, it took control of the funds available for that agreement and sought to dictate the terms of contract of lawyers recruited through it. This caused much noise between the bar and the PDO.[24] Interpreting local legislation, the bar claimed it should be a mandatory intermediary in this kind of recruiting process.[25] The Ministerio

[23] Acao Direta de Inconstitucionalidade (ADI) is a lawsuit used to challenge legal norms on constitutional grounds directly before the Brazil Supreme Court. Only some legal subjects have standing to bring up ADI lawsuits.

[24] This infuriated the bar. With support from São Paulo state representative Campos Machado, head of the coalition of state representatives for lawyers, the bar sent a bill to the state house of representatives seeking to transfer control of the funds used to hire these lawyers from the PDO to the Secretary of Justice Affairs. With this move, the bar intended to recover its influence over the decision-making process regarding how those resources are spent. It also hoped to have more room for negotiation with state officers other than the PDO's leadership.

[25] The figures in these agreements are impressive. In the first quarter of 2011 they involved about R$160 million (or US$80 million), a monthly average of about R$22 million (or US$11 million) at the time. The agreement signed for the July 2011 to July 2012 period estimated expenditures of R$284 million (or US$142 million). And the list of lawyers providing services under this agreement for the year 2012 included no fewer than 44,609 individuals. Hence, the clear goal of the bar in this conflict was to protect – and to some extent to control – the market for legal services to the poor, like when it resisted against pro bono and against PDOs themselves.

Publico[26] intervened in favor of the PDO and took the issue all the way to the national Supreme Court. The Court favored the Ministerio Publico, breaking the bar's monopoly over the supply side of legal services in these agreements. The decision was applicable in the entire country (Conectas Direitos Humanos 2015b).

The involvement of IPB in these kinds of legal mobilization go beyond issues of access to justice. For instance, the Brazilian Constitution ensures to descendants of slaves (*quilombolas*) the right to maintain possession over lands "traditionally occupied" by those. The conservative party Democratas filed ADI lawsuit No. 3.239 to question the criteria that the federal government has used to certify such "traditional occupation." The Democratas party argued that these criteria were too permissive. The IPB took the opposite side (Fuchs 2004), thus confronting the interest of big landowners. The case is pending a court decision.

These examples show a pattern of high-level collaborative legal activism between IPB, its previous antagonist PDOs, litigation-oriented NGOs, human rights advocacy groups, and the Ministerio Publico. This has expanded IPB's support base at the bar and civil society. But it may have driven pro bono toward a much more radical route, not originally expected by many of its initial promoters.

V RESTRICTIONS REMOVED AND THE FUTURE AHEAD

On February 23, 2013, the Federal Ministerio Publico in São Paulo – one of the new allies of the pro bono movement – called a public hearing to discuss the bar's Pro Bono Resolution. Forty expert witnesses were heard, all of them critical to the restrictions placed by the Resolution. At the end of the event, the prosecutor who called the hearing indicated he had been convinced that the resolution was illegal, recommending it should be revised.

Bar leaders felt that the Federal Ministerio Publico might litigate against the resolution. And as the Brazilian Supreme Court had recently ruled against the bar in similar issues (see item D, 2 above), they feared for a backlash in their attempt to regulate pro bono as well. To avoid such a backlash, they appointed Luiz Flavio Borges D'Urso, São Paulo's elected state delegate, to write a report and point out to future directions on this issue.

[26] The Ministerio Publico is a body of independent public prosecutors operating at both the federal and state levels in Brazil, which, in addition to conventional criminal prosecution, has legal standing to bring about class action lawsuits against private parties and government organizations in defense of minorities, the environment, consumers, and the –public interest|| (Vieira 2008; Arantes 2002).

D'Urso recommended that "any regulation on pro bono that might exist in state bars" be suspended as he prepared his report (the Alagoas state bar had also produced regulation similar to the São Paulo Pro Bono Resolution). On June 17, 2013, Marcos V. Furtado Coelho, president of the federal bar, upheld this recommendation. The restrictions of the São Paulo state bar's Pro Bono Resolution were temporarily removed.

My fieldwork research in São Paulo was concluded a short while after these events. Interestingly, the suspension of the resolution did not cause much impact. Most firms continued to do pro bono work to the same extent and under the same protocols as they were doing before (others argued there was more uncertainty, which they felt to be discouraging). Some of the firms I interviewed suggested that they would accelerate their investments in rationalizing pro bono: with no clear-cut guidelines from the bar, it became even more important to have their own policies in place. The pro bono movement, in turn, was trying to take advantage of the suspension and push the legal profession, especially the corporate bar, to fully embrace its commitment to pro bono. Global players such as *Latin Lawyer* and Latham & Watkins were some of their partners in these efforts.

The chance to provide pro bono work to individuals appeared as a new factor in this conversation. Yet firms were not sure whether and how this was something they could or would like to do. Service to individuals could bring corporate lawyers and law firms closer to a vast number of people in need, as well as allow firms to contribute more intensely in cases of high impact. But the firms I researched were pondering about several organizational and institutional factors before taking such steps.

On June 14, 2015, D'Urso's report was issued and approved by the bar's governance. The hitherto controversial restrictions to pro bono, after all, had been removed. The news article on the bar's website in which the results of this process were announced is revealing of the intricacies of the process this chapter has described. The bar's president Coelho built on the "traditional" roots of pro bono to justify the new regulatory directions then adopted. He stated, "The bar drew from the good and just example of our colleague Luiz Gama, who worked pro bono to liberate slaves in the country. We hope to [continue to contribute to build] a more just and solidary society. Pro bono has been a tradition in Brazil since the XIX century, and it is one the bar wants to continue" (Ordem dos Advogados do Brasil 2015).

On October 19, 2015, the bar passed a new Ethics Code, which adopted the conclusions of D'Urso's report. A chapter on "Pro Bono Lawyering" was included in the Code, defining pro bono as free-of-charge legal services rendered to both organizations *and individuals* unable to pay for such services.

Restrictions continued to exist, but only to pro bono done for political parties or electoral candidates or "in benefit of institutions that pursue these objectives." Pro bono services should not be used "as a means of advertisement to attract clientele" either.[27]

Can or will these new circumstances affect the development pro bono? This question, as I discuss in the next section, is part of the crossroads at which pro bono in São Paulo currently is.

VI A LONG STORY SHORT: THE CROSSROADS OF PRO BONO

Based on what has been covered in this chapter, I argue that pro bono work in São Paulo is currently at a crossroads. The politics of bar regulation and international competition of law firms have hindered broad dissemination of pro bono in Brazil. Yet, because of the opposition raised by the bar and the ambivalent position of corporate law firm toward such opposition, IPB could stress the "traditional" roots of pro bono and develop closer alliances with the São Paulo state PDO, litigation-oriented NGOs like Conectas, and human rights advocacy groups.

The alliances with these organizations, all of which have a relatively radical approach to legal mobilization, has been helpful to sustain and broaden the legitimacy of pro bono against the will of the bar and the discouragement of big law firms. But the more IPB becomes part of such radical strand – or the more pro bono grows as an expression of professional noblesse – the less it may be possible to engage big law firms and the corporate clientele in this practice. Ultimately, pro bono can become the platform of more unorthodox forms of law practice that challenge the status quo. As a specialist in the Brazilian legal profession explained, "I can see IPB becoming an NGO like Conectas, relying on a small staff and network of lawyers to take few cases of high impact. This approach would already contribute to make the São Paulo legal profession more diverse and to democratize access to justice. However, it was certainly not what drove IPB founders in the early 2000s." Likewise, as a pro bono activist remarked during a more open moment when we were speculating about the future of pro bono movement,

> One of my ideas at IPB was to launch a low-income law firm with hired lawyers. It would be a nonprofit we would run like an actual business, but we would reinvest part or most of its money in the organization. This law

[27] But notice that this regulation was designed and applies to both private lawyers doing pro bono work and counsel appointed by courts or selected through financial agreements. Hence, the bar took this opportunity to make it clear it still supports the interests of such groups (Ordem dos Advogados do Brasil 2015).

> firm could then partner with bigger, for-profit law firms to have pro bono lawyers sitting in to provide some help. This would be one of the factors that would lower costs. So, there would be interns, secretaries, a permanent staff, and these pro bono lawyers. The firm would adopt a low-bono model. There would be resistance from the bar, but we would deal with it. I know people from a large corporate firm who have presented a similar project to a foundation and got support to do it. Now they are in the process of detailing the plan, and they are keeping it secret, because if it all works out they would have to leave their firms to undertake this project.[28]

The corporate bar is also at a crossroads in its engagement with pro bono. Corporate law firms and in-house legal departments must strategically situate their will to engage with pro bono among many possible approaches, as the meaning of pro bono itself has become more diversified to include alternatives from transactional work for nonprofits to legal rights education projects, from strategic litigation to legislative advocacy, and so on. Furthermore, the corporate bar must decide between more systematic and more ad hoc ways of undertaking pro bono work. For example, will they use more sophisticated managerial structures, design and implement policies, and deploy standards of measurement and evaluation, or will they merely act in response to pressures from the corporate clientele and other stakeholders?

While my research cannot provide a definitive answer to these questions, it points out to structural factors and institutional mechanisms molding the potential pathways that parties can take. Such findings, which have significance for future attempts to research and theorize about law, lawyers, and globalization, are presented next.

VII IMPLICATIONS FOR RESEARCH AND THEORY

The stories of pro bono detailed in this chapter present many implications for research and theory about law, lawyers, and globalization. A first of these implications relates to the global character of pro bono. For many of the forces shaping this practice in São Paulo, it has been important to stress what is often called its "local roots." Though this can sound powerful as a discourse, my research shows that pro bono could seldom develop in São Paulo in the absence of global forces. From the desire of global businesses for CSR policies;

[28] The IPB leadership has contended that these ideas "do not represent the core of pro bono," and compare them with "using pro bono lawyers to do mediation in cases like family law, housing, and consumer," as they have also been suggested do to (informal interviews during fieldwork). However, these ideas are revealing of the different ways in which pro bono can be and has been appropriated socially and professionally.

to cultures of professional practice in the corporate world; to circulation of people, resources, and ideas that stress the role of private lawyers in promoting the public good and building the "rule of law" internationally, there are many examples of such global inputs.

But while these examples reiterate the importance of globalization in local developments of law and the legal profession, they also show that globalization is not a univocal experience. Instead, globalization is a result of multiple processes, with participation of multiple actors, who hold multiple interests and resources, and who operate in multiple coalitions. Researchers must identify and account for these multiplicities and their impact on lawyers' professionalism. For example, an intriguing fact that my research came across is the variety of international organizations promoting pro bono in Brazil and the global South. What similarities and differences exist in their approaches? How do these approaches speak to different interests locally? How do they impact the extent to which and the meaning with which pro bono develops? These are some of the questions that this broad and more nuanced concept of globalization invites us to ask.

A second implication relates to the institutional organization of pro bono. Encounters of local and global forces shaping pro bono take place within institutional contexts, like law firms, NGOs or courts. Researchers must figure out the relationships and schemas that structure such contexts (Powell and DiMaggio 1991) and that mediate their relationship with pro bono or other comparable practices. For example, firms embraced pro bono when they felt it would meet the needs of their clientele, but some withdrew support from pro bono when they felt that doing so would help them protect their market share in a globalizing market of legal services. This led pro bono activists to mobilize corporate clients, because these were the only voices that could speak to firms in (financial) terms they understood.

Yet institutional contexts, like firms, exist within an even larger context, which Bourdieu and others have called the "legal field": a system of social positions structured in terms of power relationships (Bourdieu 1986; Dezalay and Garth 2011; Dezalay and Madsen 2012; Garth and Dezalay 2012). In the stories told above, for example, a new legal elite relied on "grand liberal lawyers" to promote pro bono – an expression of the same old tradition that these grand liberal lawyers were part of. Likewise, IPB allied itself with members of the Public Defender's Office to confront the dominant interests in the São Paulo state bar. Legal practices like pro bono grow out of conflict, cooperation, and struggles for legitimacy among participants in a given legal "field" (Dezalay and Garth 2002b; Dezalay and Garth 2011).

Finally, much of the existing thinking about law, lawyers, and globalization implies a set of economic relations bound to corporate power and hegemonic capitalist development. Both the professional power and need for legitimacy of corporate lawyers emanates from this vision of how the boundaries between state and market should be divided. Yet, as countries like Brazil, India, and China challenge the established consensus in political economy, rigorous research must be done to determine how the resulting economic arrangements may feed back into the social construction of dominant legal practices and ideologies.

This research offers a good example: as pro bono was rejected in São Paulo for arguably representing a privatistic approach to legal services for the poor,[29] which did not match the social-democratic model of the Brazilian 1988 constitution, those who supported pro bono had to look for other sources of legitimacy. They encountered these, if partly, in the "old traditions" of "grand jurists." Alternative models of political economy and development can create and destroy opportunities for legal engagement and affect the established hierarchies in the field. A challenge for future research is to identify and account for these mutually constitutive relationships, across both different domains of lawyers' professional agency and different points in time.

REFERENCES

Abel, Richard L. 2009. "State, Market, Philanthropy, and Self-Help as Legal Services Delivery Mechanisms." In *Private Lawyers and the Public Interest: The Evolving Role of pro Bono in the Legal Profession*. Edited by Robert Granfield and Lynn Mather. Oxford: Oxford University Press.

Almeida, Frederico Normanha Ribeiro de. 2006. "A advocacia e o acesso à justiça no estado de São Paulo (1980–2005)." PhD Dissertation, Political Science.

Arantes, Rogério Bastos. *Ministério Público e política no Brasil*. São Paulo: Editora Sumaré. 2002.

Bourdieu, Pierre. 1986. "Force of Law: Toward a Sociology of the Juridical Field." *Hastings Law Journal* 38 (5): 805–853.

Boutcher, Steven A. 2009. "The Institutionalization of Pro Bono in Large Law Firms: Trends and Variation across the AmLaw200." In *Private Lawyers and the Public Interest: The Evolving Role of pro Bono in the Legal Profession*. Edited by Robert Granfield and Lynn Mather. Oxford: Oxford University Press.

2010. "Rethinking Culture: Organized Pro Bono and the External Sources of Law Firm Culture." *University of St. Thomas Law Journal* 8 (2): 108–128.

[29] In the United States, the debates go in the opposite direction. As described and debated in Elefant (1991), Kilwein (1999), Minow (2002), and Abel (2009), private lawyers have been seen as partners, not rivals of publicly funded legal services.

Conectas Direitos Humanos. 2015a. "ADI 3892 E ADI 4270 – Criação Da Defensoria Pública – Conectas Direitos Humanos." www.conectas.org/pt/acoes/stf-em-foco/noticia/adi-3892-e-adi-4270-criacao-da-defensoria-publica.

2015b. "ADI 4163 – Convênio Obrigatório Da Defensoria Pública – Conectas Direitos Humanos." www.conectas.org/pt/acoes/stf-em-foco/noticia/24193-adi-4163-convenio-obrigatorio-da-defensoria-publica.

Cristo, Alessandro. 2014. "OAB-RJ Ameaça Fechar Banca Tauil & Chequer Por Associação Com Estrangeiros." *Consultor Jurídico*, July 29. www.conjur.com.br/2014-jul-29/oab-rj-ameaca-fechar-tauil-chequer-associacao-estrangeiros.

Cummings, Scott L. 2004. "The Politics of Pro Bono." *UCLA Law Review* 52 (1): 1–149.

Cummings, Scott L., and Deborah L. Rhode. 2010. "Managing Pro Bono: Doing Well by Doing Better." *Fordham Law Review* 78 (5): 2357–2442.

Cummings, Scott L., and Rebecca L. Sandefur. 2013. "Beyond the Numbers: What We Know – and Should Know – About American Pro Bono." *Harvard Law & Policy Review* 7 (1): 83–111.

Cummings, Scott L., and Louise G. Trubek. 2008. "Globalizing Public Interest Law." *UCLA Journal of International Law and Foreign Affairs* 13 (1): 1–53.

Cyrus R. Vance Center for International Justice. 2015. "Our Approach." Accessed August 2. www.vancecenter.org/vancecenter/index.php/what-we-do.

Dezalay, Yves, and Bryant G. Garth, eds. 2002a. *Global Prescriptions: The Production, Exportation, and Importation of a New Legal Orthodoxy*. Ann Arbor: University of Michigan Press.

2002b. *The Internationalization of Palace Wars: Lawyers, Economists, and the Contest to Transform Latin American States*. The Chicago Series in Law and Society. Chicago: University of Chicago Press.

2011. "Hegemonic Battles, Professional Rivalries, and the International Division of Labor in the Market for the Import and Export of State-Governing Expertise." *International Political Sociology* 5 (3): 276–293.

Dezalay, Yves, and Mikael Rask Madsen. 2012. "The Force of Law and Lawyers: Pierre Bourdieu and the Reflexive Sociology of Law." *Annual Review of Law and Social Science* 8 (1): 433–452.

Dinovitzer, Ronit, and Bryant G. Garth. 2009. "Pro Bono as an Elite Strategy in Early Lawyer Career." In *Private Lawyers and the Public Interest: The Evolving Role of Pro Bono in the Legal Profession*. Edited by Robert Granfield and Lynn Mather. Oxford: Oxford University Press.

Dong, Jin. Forthcoming. "Does the Work Environment Impact the Meaning of Pro Bono? A Sociological Analysis Using Chinese Data." In *The Chinese Legal Profession in the Age of Globalization*. Cambridge: Cambridge University Press.

Elefant, Carolyn. 1991. "Can Law Firms Do Pro Bono – A Skeptical View of Law Firms' Pro Bono Programs." *Journal of the Legal Profession* 16 (1): 95–125.

Estadão. 2011. "O Cerco Aos Escritórios Estrangeiros – Economia." March 14. http://economia.estadao.com.br/noticias/geral,o-cerco-aos-escritorios-estrangeiros-imp-,691486.

Estadao Educacao. 2011. "Coisas Que Eu Queria Saber Aos 21: Oscar Vilhena Vieira." December 11. http://educacao.estadao.com.br/noticias/geral,coisas-que-eu-queria-saber-aos-21-oscar-vilhena-vieira,810129.

Fuchs, Marcos. 2004. "Expanding Access to Justice: The Instituto Pro Bono in São Paulo." Edited by Liam Mahony. The New Tactics Project of the Center for Victims of Torture.

Galanter, Marc, and Thomas Palay. 1995. "Public Service Implications of Evolving Law Firm Size and Structure." In *The Law Firm and the Public Good*. Washington, DC: Brookings Institution Press.

Garth, Bryant, and Yves Dezalay. 2012. "Corporate Law Firms, NGOs, and Issues of Legitimacy for a Global Legal Order." *Fordham Law Review* 80 (6): 2309–2345.

Granfield, Robert. 2007a. "Institutionalizing Public Service in Law School: Results on the Impact of Mandatory Pro Bono Programs." *Buffalo Law Review* 54 (5): 1355–1412.

2007b. "The Meaning of Pro Bono: Institutional Variations in Professional Obligations among Lawyers." *Law & Society Review* 41 (1): 113–146.

Granfield, Robert, and Lynn Mather (eds.). 2009. *Private Lawyers and the Public Interest: The Evolving Role of Pro Bono in the Legal Profession*. Oxford: Oxford University Press.

Gupta, Arpita. 2017. "Pro Bono and the Corporate Legal Sector in India." In *The Indian Legal Profession in the Age of Globalization*. Edited by David B. Wilkins, Vikramaditiya S. Khanna, and David M. Trubek. Cambridge: Cambridge University Press.

Halliday, Terence C., and Pavel Osinsky. 2006. "Globalization of Law." *Annual Review of Sociology* 32 (1): 447–470.

Heinz, John P., and Edward O. Laumann. 1994. *Chicago Lawyers: The Social Structure of the Bar*. Chicago: Northwestern University Press.

International Bar Association. 2015. "IBA – About the IBA." www.ibanet.org/About_the_IBA/About_the_IBA.aspx.

Kilwein, John. 1999. "The Decline of the Legal Services Corporation: 'It's Ideological, Stupid!'" In *The Transformation of Legal Aid: Comparative and Historical Studies*. Edited by Francis Regan. Oxford: Oxford University Press.

Kramer, Michael E., and Mark R. Porter. 2011. "Creating Shared Value." *Harvard Business Review*. https://hbr.org/2011/01/the-big-idea-creating-shared-value.

Latin Lawyer. 2015. "About Latin Lawyer." http://latinlawyer.com/about/.

Latin Lawyer and Cyrus R. Vance Center for International Justice. 2012. "The Latin Lawyer and Vance Center Pro Bono Survey." New York. www.vancecenter.org/vancecenter/images/stories/vancecenter/survey.pdf.

2014. "The Latin Lawyer and Vance Center Pro Bono Survey." New York. www.vancecenter.org/vancecenter/images/stories/vancecenter/survey.pdf.

Levin, Leslie C. 2008. "Pro Bono Publico in a Parallel Universe: The Meaning of Pro Bono in Solo and Small Law Firms." *Hofstra Law Review* 37 (3): 699–733.

Lochner, Philip R., Jr. 1975. "The No Fee and Low Fee Legal Practice of Private Attorneys." *Law & Society Review* 9 (3): 431–473.

Marshall, Martin N. 1996. "Sampling for Qualitative Research." *Family Practice* 13 (6): 522–526.

Mather, Lynn M., Craig A. McEwen, and Richard J. Maiman. 2001. *Divorce Lawyers at Work: Varieties of Professionalism in Practice*. Oxford: Oxford University Press.

Minow, Martha. 2002. *Partners, Not Rivals: Privatization and the Public Good*. Boston: Beacon Press.

Moura, Tatiana Whately de, Rosier Batista Custódio, Fabio de Sa e Silva, and André Luis Machado de Castro. 2013. *Mapa Da Defensoria Pública No Brasil*. Brasília: ANADEP e Ipea.

Nascimento, Gilberto. 2015. "Advogados Do Bem." *Aprendiz*. www2.uol.com.br/aprendiz/n_colunas/g_nascimento/ge081003.htm.

Nelson, Robert L., and David M. Trubek (eds.). 1992. "Arenas of Professionalism: The Professional Ideologies of Lawyers in Context." In *Lawyers' Ideals/Lawyers' Practices: Transformations in the American Legal Profession*. Ithaca, NY: Cornell University Press.

New Perimeter. 2015. "DLA Piper New Perimeter – Mission." www.newperimeter.org/about/.

Ordem dos Advogados do Brasil. 2015. "OAB Aprova Advocacia pro Bono No Brasil." *Conselho Federal Da OAB*, June 14. www.oab.org.br/noticia/28512/oab-aprova-advocacia-pro-bono-no-brasil.

PILNET. 2015. "About Us." www.pilnet.org/public-interest-law.html.

Porter, Michael E., and Mark R. Kramer. 2006. "Strategy and Society: The Link between Competitive Advantage and Corporate Social Responsibility." www.fsg.org/downloads?file=5021&nid=1701&cmpn=70170000000J5skAAC.

Powell, Walter W., and Paul DiMaggio (eds.). 1991. *The New Institutionalism in Organizational Analysis*. Chicago: University of Chicago Press.

Pro Bono Institute. 2015. "About Us – Pro Bono Institute." www.probonoinst.org/about-us/.

Republica Federativa do Brasil. 2007. "Lei N° 11.441. Altera Dispositivos Da Lei No 5.869, de 11 de Janeiro de 1973 – Código de Processo Civil, Possibilitando a Realização de Inventário, Partilha, Separação Consensual E Divórcio Consensual Por via Administrativa."

Rhode, Deborah L. 1998. "Cultures of Commitment: Pro Bono for Lawyers and Law Students." *Fordham Law Review* 67 (5): 2415–2447.

2005. *Pro Bono in Principle and in Practice: Public Service and the Professions*. Stanford, CA: Stanford University Press.

2008. "Rethinking the Public in Lawyers' Public Service: Pro Bono, Strategic Philanthropy, and the Bottom Line." *Fordham Law Review* 77 (4): 1435–1452.

Sa e Silva, Fabio de. 2013. "Lawyers and Governance in a Globalizing World: Narratives of 'Public Interest Law' Across the Americas." http://iris.lib.neu.edu/law_pol_soc_diss/28.

de Sa e Silva, Fabio. 2015. "Lawyers, Governance, and Globalization: The Diverging Paths of 'Public Interest Law' across the Americas." *Oñati Socio-legal Series* 5 (5): 1329–1350.

Sandefur, Rebecca L. 2007. "Lawyers' Pro Bono Service and American-Style Civil Legal Assistance." *Law & Society Review* 41 (1): 79–112.

2009. "Lawyers' Pro Bono Service and Market-Reliant Legal Aid." In *Private Lawyers and the Public Interest: The Evolving Role of Pro Bono in the Legal Profession*. Edited by Robert Granfield and Lynn Mather. Oxford: Oxford University Press.

Sarat, Austin, and William L. F. Felstiner. 1995. *Divorce Lawyers and Their Clients: Power and Meaning in the Legal Process*. New York: Oxford University Press.
Seron, Carroll. 1996. *The Business of Practicing Law: The Work Lives of Solo and Small-Firm Attorneys*. Philadelphia: Temple University Press.
Shamir, Ronen. 2010. "Capitalism, Governance, and Authority: The Case of Corporate Social Responsibility." *Annual Review of Law and Social Science* 6 (1): 531–553.
2011. "Socially Responsible Private Regulation: World-Culture or World-Capitalism?" *Law & Society Review* 45 (2): 313–336.
Souza, Raquel. 2002a. "OAB Cria Polêmica Sobre Prestação de Advocacia Gratuita." *Tempo Real – Gilberto Dimenstein*, January 9. www1.folha.uol.com.br/folha/dimenstein/temporeal/gd090102.htm.
2002b. "OAB Regulamentará Advocacia pro Bono." *Tempo Real – Gilberto Dimenstein*, January 15. www1.folha.uol.com.br/folha/dimenstein/temporeal/gd150102.htm.
Toron, Alberto Zacharias. 2012. "Ética – Migalhas Dos Leitores." *Migalhas*, January 8. www.migalhas.com.br/Leitores/147706.
Trost, Jan E. 1986. "Statistically Nonrepresentative Stratified Sampling: A Sampling Technique for Qualitative Studies." *Qualitative Sociology* 9 (1): 54–57.
Trubek, David M., and Alvaro Santos. 2006. *The New Law and Economic Development: A Critical Appraisal*. New York: Cambridge University Press.
Ultima Instancia. 2012. "Instituto Critica Decisão Da OAB Que Proíbe Advogados de Prestar Atendimentos Gratuitos." January 7. http://ultimainstancia.uol.com.br/conteudo/noticias/54485/instituto+critica+decisao+da+oab%20+que+proibe+advogados+de+prestar+atendimentos+gratuitos.shtml.
Vasconcellos, Marcos. 2013. "Decisão Sobre Bancas Estrangeiras Gera Fim de Parceria." *Consultor Jurídico*, January 24. www.conjur.com.br/2013-jan-24/decisao-oab-bancas-estrangeiras-gera-fim-parceria-escritorio.
Vieira, Oscar Vilhena. 2008. "Public Interest Law: A Brazilian Perspective." *UCLA Journal of International Law and Foreign Affaiirs* 13 (1): 219–261.
Vitoria, Gisele. 2002. "Entrevista Milu Villela." *Isto E Gente*, June 3. www.terra.com.br/istoegente/148/entrevista/.
Wilkins, David B. 2004. "Doing Well by Doing Good? The Role of Public Service in the Careers of Black Corporate Lawyers." *Houston Law Review* 41 (1): 1–92.

List of Interviewees

Interviewee 1, Male, 60s, large–law firm lawyer
Interviewee 2, Male, 40s, large–law firm lawyer, pro bono coordinator
Interviewee 3, Female, 40s, large–law firm lawyer, pro bono coordinator
Interviewee 4, Female, 30s, large–law firm lawyer, pro bono coordinator
Interviewee 5, Female, 30s, mid-sized law firm lawyer
Interviewee 6, Female, 50s, mid-sized law firm lawyer, pro bono coordinator
Interviewee 7, Male, 40s, large–law firm lawyer
Interviewee 8, Female, 30s, mid-sized law firm lawyer
Interviewee 9, Male, 30s, mid-sized law firm lawyer, pro bono coordinator

Interviewee 10, Female, 30s, mid-sized law firm lawyer
Interviewee 11, Male, 40s, mid-sized company
Interviewee 12, Female, 40s, mid-sized company
Interviewee 13, Male, 40s
Interviewee 14, Female, 30s
Interviewee 15, Male, 40s
Interviewee 16, Female, 20s
Interviewee 17, Male, 30s, researcher

8

Legal Education in Brazil

The Challenges and Opportunities of a Changing Context

Luciana Gross Cunha and José Garcez Ghirardi

I INTRODUCTION

Globalization and its multiple cross-border exchanges in virtually every area of human life has led to a growing demand in the legal arena for global lawyers – legal professionals capable of proficiently thinking and practicing law from a global, rather than local, perspective (Flood and Sosa 2008). In many ways, the demand for such professionals is the result of an often uneasy interplay of differing legal systems, some based on the nation-state sovereignty and bounded by defined geographical borders and others based on the transnational rules and norms that characterize the social, political, and economic dynamics of globalization (Silver 2009). Economy and trade have already incorporated the international context as an intrinsic element into their thought processes and practices, but the same cannot be said for law, which continues to operate on the territorial-national basis that characterizes the institutions that surfaced during the rise of the modern state.

Law's predominantly local approach is struggling to meet the demands of a "poststate" world (Horsman and Marshall 1994). While law undeniably remains a vital field in a globalized world, it has come under significant pressure to change its workings, institutions, and dynamics. Moreover, such change must consider the pressure from several actors – markets, governments, groups with specific interests, nongovernmental organizations – whose interests when pulled together represent a powerful homogenizing force. To function properly, a political, social, and business environment that operates through multiple borders requires a degree of uniform in its legal structures.

This new framework requires global lawyers who understand their role and can work efficiently within a multijurisdictional framework. For this reason, the challenges in designing adequate spaces and mechanisms to educate these new global lawyers in each country, as well as the difficulties of this task, have dominated a large part of the more recent literature on legal education (Lockwood 2003).

This need for global lawyers – and for the educational institutions to form them – is particularly urgent in Brazil, whose fast economic growth is inextricably linked to its more complex involvement in the global market (and its equally complex international regulations). In fact, as has already been noted (Falcão 2010), one of the major hurdles the country must overcome on its path to sustainable development is precisely that of its lack of skilled legal professionals. Brazil needs – and lacks – lawyers who can not only understand the complexities of law in this new international scenario but also design novel ways to adjust them to meet both the country's international interests and its local peculiarities. Such professionals are key in the country's mission to establish sustainable, inclusive development.

This chapter presents an overview of the current state of legal education in Brazil. The first section presents a brief account of the main socioeconomic changes over the past two decades since they are key to understanding the new context and challenges for legal education in the country. The second discusses the way in which such changes have helped shape a new scenario for educating lawyers in Brazil, the difficulties this poses for substantial reform, and the strategies adopted by several actors in the legal profession to attempt to meet the challenge of providing the country with the global lawyers it needs.

The background assumption informing the data and ideas discussed here is that Brazil's need for a new type of lawyer, including the regional specificities, changing emphases, and educational solutions it prompted, is deeply linked to the development model the country has adopted since its return to democratic rule in the late 1980s. This link between the characteristics of the legal profession and the broader political and economic landscape, though arguably true in every country, is much more central for emerging countries due to the sharper institutional reshaping they have had to undergo to adequately respond to the needs of globalization.

In Brazil, such reshaping has translated into a profound transformation in the way the state and market operate in the economy, as well as in an intense demand for better governance and more effective accountability of both these actors. This has led to socially far-reaching, conceptually innovative legislation and practices that demanded, for their design, implementation, and adjudication, legal professionals the country obviously did not have in sufficient numbers.

This shortage of legal professionals has grown more and more evident as the country rose as a regional power and a relevant player in the global world. New policies demanded changes in the traditional legal framework, in the legal education associated with it, and in the types of lawyers it produced. Decisions by successive Brazilian administrations both to open markets and privatize major state-owned companies (mostly in the 1990s) and to have the state play a key role as a development engine (mostly since the 2000s) have demanded sophisticated legislation to create the new institutional apparatus required (Schapiro and Trubek 2012). To bring about these changes, new laws, legal education, and types of lawyers were needed.

The changes in Brazilian legal education this chapter tracks must therefore be seen as a broader chapter in the story of the country's effort to adapt its political, legal, economic, and social institutions to the inescapable, often threatening, new dynamics. The authors believe that no sensible analysis of the way the country has perceived and acted in response to the need for the formation of new legal professionals can be decoupled from this deeper understanding of its broader sociopolitical context or from the varying development models it has embraced over time. Regarding the educational dimension specifically, analyses of legal education must consider that a key promise of all the postmilitary rule administrations has been to enhance access to universities, mainly to the vast majority of the population who had been historically denied this access. They also need to factor in that this new policy for universities was linked to the promise of providing the new, ascending groups with a professional expertise that would allow them to thrive in a booming and increasingly competitive market.

Unsurprisingly, given the country's pent-up demand for university education, the market for legal education has become one of the largest – if not the largest – in the world and it is mainly carried out by private, for-profit institutions created in the wake of the market-opening policies of the 1990s and boosted by the cash-transfer and tax-break policies of the 2000s. Catering to an enormous public, which was hungry for social ascension via university degree and had the financial backing of the government to pursue it, private law schools created an educational program for the masses, with low fees, low teacher wages, little or no concern for academic research, and uncertain overall educational quality. They also adopted the traditional lecture as their default methodology (which allows for very low costs as a single teacher can easily teach more than 100 students at a time), the traditional manuals as their teaching material (which they can sell in great number to students), and the traditional curricula as their course content (the traditional syllabus that most elite law schools follow is part of what the emerging social groups believe will guarantee their acceptance in the market).

These new law schools are not primarily concerned with forming new legal professionals, let alone corporate or global lawyers. They are aware that a sizable portion of students are looking for a university degree rather than specifically a law degree because people who have attended university have a greater chance of finding a job in a country still plagued by precarious education. Most of their alumni have dismal bar exam results, but this does not prevent these law courses from continuing to be attractive for those who want certification rather than professional training. They are certainly not the place to look when one wants to understand the response of Brazilian education to the need of global lawyers.

In fact, a number of different institutions adopting different strategies have responded. Mainly in São Paulo and Rio de Janeiro, new law schools have been created with new curricula, materials, and methodology provided by prestigious educational institutions sensitive to the new role of law in the country's development. Law offices have started offering in-house courses, and there has been a boom in enrollment for LLMs and continuing education both in the country and abroad (mainly in the United States).

II CONTEXTUAL BACKGROUND

The restoration of democracy and the ensuing economic stability set the stage for Brazil to become one of the main emerging powers in the beginning of the twenty-first century. Returning to a democratic lifestyle reopened the channels for the public to participate in public life, for authorities to resume inspection of academic programs, and for operation of mechanisms to ensure accountability of government agents. The need to render accounts to society and to compete for votes in general elections, which characterizes working democracies, allowed the functioning and design of institutions to improve across the board and deeply affected public governance (Ghirardi 2014).

In the economic field, the Real Plan (1994) came to grips with Brazil's disastrous hyperinflation. The currency's recovery, together with adjustments to taxes and exchange rates, among other efforts, allowed successive governments to recuperate the capacity to invest and the country to become more attractive to direct foreign investments (FDIs). These benefits were boosted by an international economic scenario favorable to Brazil. Indeed, between 2002 and 2012, Brazil went from being the thirteenth main economy in the world to the seventh.

The presence of Brazilian companies abroad and foreign companies in Brazil, an important element for such economic advance, increased in intensity and complexity. Throughout this period, arrangements based on mixed capital (foreign/national; public/ private) grew and became more sophisticated, as did business strategies bringing both Brazilians and foreigners together. The qualitative shift in the economic approach was made possible only due to changes in the ways law in Brazil was conceived of and implemented.

The redesigning of state governance methods throughout the 1990s is one of the most significant changes made within the legal field. Redefining the state's role by means of privatization in several areas as well as creating regulatory agencies and new legal models (such as the legal concept of consumers) required the innovative transformation of legal institutions and mechanisms (see Chapter 10).

Similarly, governmental entities have created a growing demand for legal professionals who have the instruments needed to make a broad range of new socioeconomic policies work. The lack of skilled professionals to do so, and the limits that such a shortage instills on implementing policies and supervising markets, soon becomes glaringly evident.

In addition to the transformation of the state, the private sector also underwent changes to become and remain competitive in the new globalized world. Creating new markets and governance rules based on international standards was just one of the many innovations that has helped redefine the dynamics of the Brazilian market over the past two decades.

Insofar as law offices were concerned, market changes became perceptible by the mid-1990s. The market for legal services became more competitive as a new type of law office started to become hegemonic. Professionally managed law offices, with career plans and employee-lawyers not on retainers, started to overshadow the family-owned, family-managed law offices that had traditionally controlled the market (Nelken and Feest 2001; Cunha et al. 2011).[1]

The increasing number of mergers and acquisitions involving Brazilian and foreign companies, coupled with the soaring presence of Brazilian firms in foreign markets, as well as other changes, worked together to shape a novel and rather complex scenario that required some local adjustments to a global reality. Here also the country suffered from a dismal number of legal professionals capable of skillfully taking on the multiple challenges stemming from this new business framework.

III CHALLENGES AND OPPORTUNITIES FOR EDUCATING GLOBAL LAWYERS IN BRAZIL

All the changes resulting from this new context only heightened the problem of preparing legal professionals to meet the challenges of corporate-led

[1] For a detailed discussion of the corporate law firms and general (in-house) counsel, see Chapters 2, 3, and 4 of this volume.

globalization and handle its multiple local implications. Space for such education in Brazil has changed as various actors attempted to design ways to meet the new demands. Different responses to what must be done to adequately train legal professionals have generated tensions between new models and traditional institutions. The current story of Brazil's legal education today is largely the story of such tensions.

Accordingly, any debate on legal education in Brazil is obliged to take into consideration the importance that traditional colleges have as formal educational spaces. As the main locus for legal education, they play a key role in the landscape of legal education in the country. Their focus on traditional curricula, their low regard for methodology, and their exclusive focus on preparing students for success in the Brazilian Bar Association (OAB) exam, rather than on developing professional abilities, have often led them to oppose changes in the way law is taught in the country. They are the canvas on which a colorful clash is taking place to develop other spaces and other logics for legal education.

Law courses in Brazil are five-year undergraduate courses. The curricula are regulated by the Ministry of Education, which by means of the Education Guidelines Act (no. 9,394/96) defined the prerequisites for private and public schools across Brazil, regardless of the region. Students in the fifth year of a law course or those with a bachelor of law degree from a Brazilian school (or the equivalent thereof) recognized by the Ministry of Education may sit the Brazilian Bar exam, which is mandatory for those who want to work as an attorney. According to some critics, this approach, in which the law schools see themselves primarily as issuers of the certificate required to sit the bar exam, has put training for the exercise of the profession in second place. More and more, critics show that most colleges prioritize training students for the exam rather than educating them for legal work.

This exam (which, one must recall, is also a requisite for most other high-level government positions, such as a judge or a prosecutor) is held nationwide three times a year and has two phases. The first phase is eliminatory and focuses on professional knowledge of law in all areas. The second tests professional skills in a specific area of law, which the candidate selects upon registration. Those areas include administrative, civil, constitutional, corporate, criminal, labor, and tax law.

The exam's format, which requires memorizing legislation (first phase) and producing legal documents (second phase), demands very little in terms of skills that are essential to global lawyers such as context analysis and legal creativity. As approval is key to surviving in an especially competitive educational market (in 2012, there were 1,149 law courses in the country), institutions are understandably reluctant to incorporate changes that do not rely on the bar exam as a basis to organize curricula and methodologies.[2]

According to a census conducted by the Ministry of Education, some 87 percent of the courses are offered by private schools and 65 percent in cities in the interior of the country. The Southeast Region presents the largest number of courses (43 percent), more than double the number in the South and Northeast regions, which are tied for second place with 20 percent of the courses each. The overwhelming number of courses offered by the private sector highlights the importance of the business aspect in Brazil's current legal education.

This is also evident in the relative concentration of the courses. The Central West Region, which covers the federal capital and a high per capita income, has the highest number of law courses per million inhabitants (8.53), even though it is least populated region offering 11 percent of the law courses in the country. The Northeast Region, with a low income per capita, has the lowest number of courses per million inhabitants (4.15) even though it is the second most populated region and offers 20 percent of the law courses.

The National Institute for Educational Studies and Research "Anísio Teixeira," a special research agency linked to the Ministry of Education–INEP that is responsible for overseeing undergraduate courses in Brazil, shows that between 2009 and 2012 the yearly average number of law graduates in the country was 93,000. Since 2009, when the bar exam became uniform throughout the country, the national approval rate varies from 14 percent to 16 percent. Despite such a dismal percentage of successful candidates, the Order of Attorneys of Brazil (OAB) counts today 833,000 members.

The gap between law graduates and registered lawyers suggests that in spite – or because – of the exponential rise in the number of law schools, the quality of legal education remains quite poor. Reservations about the dynamics of the bar exam notwithstanding – e.g., it is virtually oblivious to questions on business and corporate law as these are seen as areas of expertise not belonging to a basic training in law – it is certainly valuable as an index of the overall (dire) scenario of legal education in Brazil.

The high number of courses and their geographical concentration has influenced the federal government to become the centralizing figure behind regulation, often dialoging with the OAB. To help students choose between so many courses, the OAB has designed a quality certificate it awards to the courses that meet minimum standards. Of the almost 1,200 courses in the

[2] Eight hundred eighty different law schools have offered such courses (http://emec.mec.gov.br/).

country, only 84 (around 7 percent of the total) were deemed worthy of receiving the OAB Recomenda certificate. The body representing lawyers clearly distrusts most of the law schools.

Apart from the bar exam approval rate, law schools are also assessed by three other rankings that monitor the quality of university courses in general: the above-mentioned INEP, the São Paulo–based newspaper *Folha de São Paulo*, and the *Guia do Estudante*, a prestigious annual magazine devoted to offering candidates in-depth information about the major universities in the country.

The INEP's assessment of law schools is structured around three major axes: (1) student performance, (2) infrastructure (e.g., facilities, resources), and (3) faculty academic profile (e.g., degree held, teaching/research load). Student performance is measured by their average score on the National Exam for the Assessment of Student Performance (ENADE) weighted with data gathered when students enter the course and their expected performance. The ENADE is a triennial exam mandatory for senior students on the year of their graduation.

The Folha de São Paulo ranking (the Ranking Universitário da Folha, or RUF) is based on the assessment of (1) market perception of the course (based on the performance of the institution with a survey carried by the newspaper with 1,970 HR professionals responsible for hiring lawyers); (2) the quality of legal education offered (which is measured by weighing ENADE grades, MA and/or PhD programs offered by the institution, faculty career plans, and faculty serving as consultants to the Ministry of Education); (3) the faculty educational background and degrees; and (4) a Datafolha survey on the quality of courses with Ministry of Education consultants.[3] The Guia do Estudante ranking of undergraduate courses takes into consideration criteria such as faculty educational background and degrees, number of academic articles published, and course facilities.[4] Taken together, these rankings function as the benchmark for students to decide which law school to apply for and for employers to assess the quality of the academic background of candidates. The growing importance of these rankings notwithstanding, family ties and attendance at prestigious traditional law schools (regardless of the teaching actually being offered) still function as a decisive element in the competition for jobs in the legal services market.

Efforts to change this situation often translate into attempts by the federal government to design and enforce mandatory (supposedly) quality-enhancing

3 The Ranking Universitário da Folha (RUF) has been published since 2012. It ranks undergraduate courses and law schools all over the country (http://ruf.folha.uol.com.br).

4 *Guia do Estudante* (http://guiadoestudante.abril.com.br/blogs/melhores-faculdades/entenda-como-e-feita-a-avaliacao-do-guia-do-estudante-2/).

strategies. The minimum required curriculum in law courses is thus directly regulated by the National Education Council, an organ of the Ministry of Education. The most recent regulations were published in 2004. Although they refrain from defining the minutia of curricula or listing the subjects that should be covered in law courses, they offer strong guidelines concerning minimum content requirements and the skills that should be developed within these courses. Governmental efforts to regulate law schools have not, unfortunately, translated into high-quality education. On the contrary, traditional legal education practices in Brazil have been so devastatingly ineffective that many now consider them to be a hurdle in furnishing the country with the professionals the new global scenario requires.

The vast majority of law schools in Brazil still rely on outdated methodological practices and curricular designs. The preferred teaching method at most Brazilian law schools is still the century-old lecturing style with its glossing of statutes and critique of judicial decisions (Falcão et al. 2012). Curricula, unsurprisingly, bespeak the same logic of replicating the design that has prevailed for the past decades: most courses are still structured around the minute analysis of virtually every article of the most important laws (e.g., civil, criminal, commercial, and procedural codes), as well as the debate on doctrinal and judicial discrepancies when interpreting them – often with little theoretical and practical significance.

Combining traditional practices and outdated curricula has translated into an appalling number of poorly prepared undergraduates, as made evident by the remarkably low pass rate in the bar exam (which oscillates between 10 percent and 25 percent). It has also caused the acute shortage of legal professionals who display the skills that are elemental to facing the everyday needs of a socially complex country and a heavily international economy.[5] It has become almost a truism to say that legal education in Brazil has a choice between changing profoundly and becoming irrelevant for everything but the certification required to sit the bar exam.

In response to this challenge posed by the inertia and inefficiency of traditional legal education, some meaningful efforts have been made to initiate this change. New undergraduate, graduate, and continuous education courses have appeared over the past decade, and some of the top traditional law schools have taken preliminary steps to update the way they teach law.[6]

5 Unsurprisingly, the arrival of lawyers and law firms and/or partnerships with firms from abroad has experienced a surge in the recent years, causing the Bar to pay closer attention to their activities; see Chapter 6.

6 FGV DIREITO's pioneering experience both in São Paulo and Rio de Janeiro are cases in point, as is the creation of IBMEC and the new curriculum at USP de Ribeirão Preto.

The university Fundaçao Getulio Vargas (FGV) has championed radical transformation. The campuses the university has opened in São Paulo and Rio de Janeiro represent a radical breakaway from the traditional organization of law schools. Adopting student-centered, case-based methodology, rather than lecturing and glossing, they have become a benchmark in discussions on the future of legal education in the country. The impressive social prestige of the Foundation (which is responsible, among other things, for producing a number of key economic indicators for the country, including inflation and unemployment indexes) and its deep understanding of national and international markets (foreign companies investing in Brazil consider it a key reference) has helped amplify its impact on legal education much beyond what might be expected from its (intentionally) limited number of students.

The very positive response FGV has received from the market and the remarkable success of its alumni are an index of the urgent need for new, global lawyers in Brazil. FGV's alumni census shows that more 90 percent of FGV graduates get hired even before finishing university. Indicative of the broad skills offered by the new curriculum and the efficiency of its multidisciplinary approach is the fact that students are sought for by corporations as well as law firms. About half the alumni of FGV Direito SP work for law firms – 95 percent of which are the most prestigious law firms in São Paulo: Pinheiro Neto, Demarest Almeida, Machado Meyer, and Mattos Filho. Another 30 percent render legal services to major corporations, especially in the banking and financial sectors.

This has led other institutions to experiment with new formats. The prestigious Universidade de São Paulo, apart from implementing changes at its headquarters in São Paulo, has opened a course in the city of Ribeirão Preto that departs significantly from the more traditional design of its mother institution. UFMG, in the state of Minas Gerais, is currently discussing the possibilities of instilling a deep change to its curriculum. At the heart of all these efforts to break away from traditional forms of legal education and to foster a renewal in legal teaching, thinking, and practice – and in their remarkable success with markets and students alike – there is a radical transformation of the curricula and the assumptions on law that informs them.

Common to these successful proposals to change legal education is the drive to overcome the traditional rendering of law as a self-contained system, impervious to the realities of everyday life. The Latin adage Quod non est in actis non est in mundo ("What is not in the lawsuit documents does not exist") has been much abused in traditional legal education to justify the still prevalent view that we must first understand every tiny detail in the statutes, laws, and decisions before we can go out into the world and act as a legal professional. Traditional legal education thus works to present law as an insulated social institution, untouched by the uncertainties and perplexities of everyday realities.

Changes to curricula in Brazil have been marked by the complete reversal of this perspective. They espouse the belief that law cannot be understood in isolation, i.e., that the law in the books is incomprehensible – even in its most abstract renderings – without reference to the law in practice.

This change in the way law is perceived has led to radical curricular transformation. As a direct result of this, there has been a surge in transdisciplinary subjects (the "law and" subjects – e.g., law and economy; crime and society; law and the arts; law and development), which aim at driving students to think about law in its relation to other areas of knowledge and from the perspective of its concrete impact on society. Extensive, exhaustive presentation of statutes has supposedly lost ground in these new curricula to the discussion of concrete situations and a critical assessment of the role law could – and should – play in them.

Methodologically, this has translated into new teaching methods (e.g., problem-based learning; role-playing; case method) that ask students to think about law as it works in and affects real situations, about the choices that legal designs and solutions imply, and about their relative effectiveness and ethical implications.

Of growing importance within these methodological shifts is the growing role that moot courts and international competitions have been playing in the menu of extracurricular activities of top law schools. In 2000, the country hosted a round of the Philip C. Jessup International Law Moot Court Competition. In 2001 and 2002 competitions took place at the Universidade Federal de Santa Catarina, but it is only in 2003 that a team of Brazilian students reached the final round. Brazilian students have also took part in the Willem Vis International Commercial Arbitration Moot. In 2013, the event brought together a total of 290 law schools from around the world, 14 of them from Brazil (5 public and 9 private, including students from São Paulo, Minas Gerais, Rio Grande do Sul, and Paraná e Rio de Janeiro).

Law offices have responded favorably to this innovation and have often sponsored teams of students. The international experience provided by such competitions, coupled with the integration of skills they require, are seen as quite valuable by employers – though, of course, not enough by themselves to guarantee the solid legal training they expect from their lawyers.

Perhaps even more telling of the urgency to create new layers than the attempts to change law schools is the phenomenon of the exponential multiplication of continuing legal education programs (CLE, known as lato sensu graduate certificate courses). Outside the reach of the Ministry of Education's strict regulations (at least for the time being; attempts have been made to bring them into the fold), such courses attract large crowds of undergraduates who are clearly aware of the inadequacies in their legal knowledge, despite certificates and bar memberships.

CLE courses have become a prime locus for the formation of corporate lawyers in Brazil. Unlike law schools, which remain for the most part faithful to their traditional syllabi, the curricula of the CLE courses clearly display concern with the impact of globalization on the practice of law in the country. From the 1990s onward, when for-profit educational institutes were authorized to offer such courses, the number of CLE offerings has expanded dramatically. Lack of official regulation makes it hard to have precise numbers, but some estimates indicate that they are probably five times more numerous than regular law schools. They typically offer a wide choice of courses, quite often related to business and corporate matters, and attract many recent graduates who are eager to learn more about areas that, though critical for the advancement of their careers, were not part of their regular law school classes.

These courses usually offer classes on topics that hold immediate relevance in the practice of law in Brazil's new socioeconomic setting rather than dwelling on the traditional subjects taught in most universities. IT, environmental, and intellectual property law are common subjects, as are classes on mediation, law and economics, and financial law. Teachers are quite often professionals with hands-on knowledge in the relevant market who often lack academic degrees. Owing to the new menu of subjects (usually presented in very traditional lecturing-for-professionals style) and the large number of students taking such courses, CLE has become one of the new frontiers in the debate on legal education in Brazil.

The CLE courses cater to those lawyers aspiring to greater professional possibilities in the global-oriented, rapidly expanding corporate law and international law markets in Brazil. According to various national and international surveys, in 2013 there were approximately 8,000 law offices devoted primarily or exclusively to these areas. This has created a demand for legal professionals who can effectively work in an international, highly competitive environment and are learned in many areas, including economics and management.

Thus, in the country's financial center – mainly São Paulo but also, to a lesser degree, in other cities such as Rio de Janeiro, Belo Horizonte, and Porto Alegre – there has been a rise in the offering of interdisciplinary CLE courses (the "law and" subjects: law and accounting; law and economics, law and banking, etc., all absent in almost all regular law school curricula). It is thus possible to suggest that the most relevant impact of globalization in legal education in Brazil is to be observed outside the law schools. The task of forming the global lawyers the country needs is being carried on elsewhere. CLE courses are, by far, the most visible locus for this training but certainly not the only one.

Much smaller in size but much more revealing in design is the phenomenon of in-house training, which has become trendy among the top law firms in the country. Disappointed by the legal training that most law schools offer and aware of the limits of the topics offered and methods used by CLE institutions, which more often than not do not include lawyer skill-building, some of the most prestigious law firms in Brazil have started programs to train their own personnel.

These corporate courses have become much more common in the large law firms in São Paulo and Rio de Janeiro, and it is believed there are around 300 such in-house programs throughout the country. They aim not only to explain the office routine and policies to new employees but also to improve what law offices see as the defective legal training of their personnel. Although initially focusing only on their internal public, such "in-house universities" have been approached by corporations that want to have them train their own employees. Like the CLE programs, these courses are also outside the scope of official regulation (Castro and Eboli 2013).

The case of Pinheiro Neto Advogados, arguably the top law firm in the country, illustrates both the movement and the reasons for its rising importance. In 2012, the firm started an in-house program that aimed to improve the skills of hundreds of its lawyers. According to the firm's website, if all the activities of all the participants in the course are factored in, they total an impressive 18,000 hours per year in training. Other major law firms are developing similar programs.

Such in-house training strategies must be understood alongside the new requirements for hiring staff, as the training programs' efficacy depends heavily on new lawyers possessing a set of nonlegal skills. Data gathered by the GLEE interviews with partners of major law firms in São Paulo and Rio de Janeiro show that proficiency in English (written and oral) is a sine qua non condition for prospective candidates, as well as advanced knowledge of the most used computer programs and internet research tools (see Chapter 2).

Displaying such mandatory sets of skills, though essential for one to get a job at a major law firm in Brazil, is certainly not enough for one to keep a job. To become a permanent member of the legal staff, junior lawyers must possess a certificate from an internationally renowned institution and, even more importantly, be able to prove some professional experience in law firms abroad.

An international certificate is also a requirement for hiring lawyers to corporate legal departments of the largest national and multinational companies in Brazil. In fact, over the past two decades, corporate legal departments have become an increasingly attractive option for young lawyers with a degree, such as an LLM, from a foreign institution.[7]

As for the professional experience abroad, the highly competitive market for legal services in Brazil, coupled with the global nature of the services rendered, demands that it be translated in more than a firsthand knowledge of the functioning of a foreign legal system. Lawyers must also display a sophisticated understanding of the economic, cultural, and political dimensions of the countries in which their clients are conducting business. This need for broad, in-depth expertise of a foreign country has led some of the law firms studied by the GLEE project to create teams that specialize in a specific region or country. A good example of this trend is Felsberg e Associados, which in 2001 created a China Desk to work exclusively on Brazil–China commercial deals (see Chapter 9).

Another locus for the formation of young lawyers that emerged within the context of globalization is the Training Program for Young Attorneys in the Brazilian Mission in Geneva. Better known as the Geneva Program, it was created in 2003 to train new lawyers by offering them an internship at the Brazilian Mission at the World Trade Organization (WTO). This program, a partnership between the Ministry of Foreign Affairs; the Brazilian Institute of Studies on Competition, Consumer Affairs, and International Trade (IBRAC); and the Center for Studies of Law Firms (CESA), aims at training lawyers to work according WTO parameters for arbitration, negotiation, and multilateral commerce rules (Shafer et al. 2012).

These new loci for training, their goals and strategies, unmistakably reveal the impact globalization has had on legal education in the country. Not unlike other areas in the market in Brazil, the context for legal education has been shaped by two complementary trends: on the one hand, the fast-paced multiplication of low-budget law schools, catering mostly to a new host of consumers and focused mainly on the bar exam and local practice, and on the other hand, the equally speedy emergence of a few niche high-quality institutions, catering mostly to elite students and focused primarily on developing the skills necessary for successful lawyering in a global context. The

7 See Chapters 3 and 4 of this volume for a complete discussion of the educational credentials of in-house lawyers in Brazil, including their educational credentials.

Brazilian scenario in this area suggests a profound, complex, multilayered interplay between corporate-led globalization, national models for development, and national-global models for legal education.

The model of development adopted by recent administrations has attempted to put together, with mixed results, strategic state intervention, a market-friendly environment (with at least lip service being paid to fiscal responsibility, control of inflation, and reduction of government debt), and social inclusion (mainly via cash-transfer programs) (Schapiro and Trubek 2012). The upshot of this broad policy for legal education has been a dual movement: niche institutions and programs have been created to train the global lawyers indispensable for the strengthening of Brazil as an emerging power, and due to a large extent to direct and indirect federal financing, hundreds of low-budget, questionable-quality law schools have been created, catering to a public with very little prospect of being engaged in lawyering in general and especially lawyering in a global context.

Both phenomena, as suggested, arguably spring from the same decisions on broader development policies at work in Brazil today. Recognizing this connection only adds to the importance of understanding the loci and dynamics of the formation of global lawyers in Brazil and the role they have been playing in the context of corporate-led globalization, which is the question at the core of the GLEE project.

The challenge is to find strategies and develop institutions capable of forming new lawyers who possess a set of skills indispensable for efficiently responding to the complex demands brought about by globalization. Brazilian lawyers need to be able to handle the complexity of global corporate issues by adopting an interdisciplinary approach to law. They must also understand the multilayered reality of corporate dynamics and couple their legal expertise with a solid knowledge of accounting, management, and corporate governance techniques. They must be able to grasp the specific nature of their contribution to the designing and achieving of the core corporate goals. This chapter claims that the majority of legal education institutions in Brazil have so far proved utterly incapable of meeting such challenges.

IV THE FORMATION OF GLOBAL LAWYERS

As pointed out earlier, the social, political, and economic transformations that deeply reshaped Brazil since the return to democratic rule in the late 1980s have translated into an urge for a radically new legal professional. The need has become acutely evident, mainly in the corporate sector, for professionals capable of proficiently responding to a new globalized, intensely competitive marketplace that requires both solid knowledge of the new legal technology, an interdisciplinary perspective, and sensitivity to the new dynamics of the actual function of law. The questions posed by this scenario and adopted as a starting point for this chapter are as follows:

- Have these new professionals been formed in Brazil?
- If so, what is their profile and where have they been formed?

According to the data gathered by the Globalization, Lawyers and Emerging Economies (GLEE) research project, such lawyers have been and keep on being formed. Legal professionals working in the corporate area are formed by the law offices themselves, who recruit promising candidates from regular law schools, sometimes even sophomores, to train and educate them directly. For these offices, which work and compete for clients on a global scale, such in-house formation programs for young talented interns, which offer a prestigious educational locus outside the traditional law schools, can function also as a marketing strategy in the fierce competition for legal services.

Interviews with law firm partners verify the hypothesis that almost all Brazilian law schools fail to produce professionals and rely on law offices to complement the education of their students via mandatory internship programs. They also confirm the strong resistance Brazilian legal education institutions show overall toward changes in traditional curricula, materials, and methodology. The traditional model serves the needs and social expectations of both the new mass-oriented, low-cost law schools and the old, family-structured law offices, which have done well using the older approach to recruitment.

Saying that law schools do not produce professionals is far from saying that they are irrelevant to one's professional prospects. GLEE research data have shown that the universities students attend are a key factor in job recruitment and that the human resources professionals responsible for hiring new lawyers are aware of the new and innovative law schools and the set of skills they are furnishing their alumni with (e.g., foreign languages, deeper knowledge of economics and accounting, mediation and arbitration techniques). When one is applying for a job, the law school's reputation still carries great weight.

Once hired, however, the chance of young lawyers moving up in their career depends on their continuing their education and updating their knowledge and skills, mainly in prestigious foreign institutions (notably in the United States); on their ability to attract and keep clients; on their displaying an interdisciplinary approach to law, which allows them to better understand broad corporate interests and hurdles; and on their being knowledgeable of accounting, management, and corporate governance techniques. The mere list of these abilities, indispensable for any successful corporate lawyer in Brazil, is enough to bring forth the stark gap between the country's needs in legal education and the reality of its current educational scenario.

REFERENCES

Análise. 2013. *Análise executivos jurídicos e financeiros*. São Paulo: Análise.

Castro, Claudio, and Marisa Eboli. 2013. "Universidade Corporativa: gênese e questões críticas rumo à maturidade." *RAE Impresso* 53 (2): 408–414.

Cunha, Luciana., Maria da Gloria Bonelli, Fabiana Luci de Oliveira, and Natalia Barboza da Silveira. 2011. "Sociedade de advogados e tendências profissionais." *Escola de Direito de São Paulo da Fundação Getulio Vargas, Revista DIREITO GV* 3 (6): 111–138.

Falcão, Jaoquim. 2010. *Classe Dirigente e Ensino Jurídico – Uma Releitura de San Tiago Dantas*. Rio de Janeiro: FGV Direito Rio, Cadernos FGV Direito Rio.

Falcão, Joaquim, Gabriel Lacerda, and Tania Rangel. 2012. *Aventura e Legado no Ensino Jurídico*. Rio de Janeiro: FGV Direito Rio.

Flood, John. 2011. "Legal Education in the Global Context: Challenges from Globalization, Technology and Changes in Government Regulation" (research paper no. 11–16, University of Westminster School of Law, London).

Flood, John, and Fabian Sosa. 2008. "Lawyers, Law Firms and the Stabilization of Transnational Business." *Northwestern Journal of International Law and Business* 28 (3): 489–525.

Ghirardi, Jose. 2014. "O Mercado da advocacia em um mundo em transformação," in print.

Horsman, Matthew, and Andrew Marshall. 1994. *After the Nation-State: Citizens, Tribalism and the New World Disorder*. New York: HarperCollins.

Lockwood, Fred. 2003. "Learning and Teaching in a Changing World." *Journal of Online Journal of Open, Flexible, and Distance Learning* 7 (1): 30–39.

Nelken, David, and Johannes Feest. 2001. *Adapting Legal Cultures*. Oxford: Hart.

Schapiro, Mario, and David Trubek. 2012. "Redescobrindo o Direito e desenvolvimento: experimentalismo, pragmatismo democrático e diálogo horizontal." In *Direito e Desenvolvimento: Um Diálogo Entre os BRICS*. Edited by M. G. Schapiro and D. T. Trubek. São Paulo: Saraiva.

Shafer, Greg, Michelle Ratton, Sanchez Badin, and Barbara Rosenberg. 2012. "The Transnational Meets the National: The Construction of Trade Policy Networks in Brazil." In *Lawyers and the Construction of Transnational Justice*. Edited by Y. Dezalay and B. Garth. New York: Routledge.

Silver, C. 2009. "Educating Lawyers for the Global Economy: National Challenges" (Georgetown Public Law research paper no. 1519387).

9

Transforming Legal Capacity in Brazil

International Trade Law and the Myth of a Booming Practice

Rubens Glezer, Vitor M. Dias, Adriane Sanctis de Brito, and Rafael A. F. Zanatta

I INTRODUCTION

The establishment of the World Trade Organization (WTO) created a demand for lawyers who could understand the WTO's rules and defend Brazil's interests in the organization's dispute resolution system. Lawyers were needed to use WTO law to support Brazilian exporters seeking access to foreign markets and to protect domestic policies and market players against complaints in the WTO. To meet this need, in 2003 the Brazilian Ministry of Foreign Affairs (or "MRE" in Portuguese), alongside organizations from the private sector, created a program in Geneva to train Brazilian lawyers in WTO law and practice (Shaffer et al. 2008). This project created a cadre of lawyers familiar with international trade law and WTO legal procedure. The reason was also political. As the one Brazilian ambassador claimed, the program aimed to "train professionals able to understand and master the rules of international trade" and to reduce Brazil's "dependence on foreign experts" (Seixas Corrêa 2005, 4).[1]

The legal scholarship has already produced excellent studies about the Brazilian governmental effort to "build legal capacity" in the field of international trade law, as provided by Shaffer et al. (2008) and Santos (2012).[2] In

[1] While the Geneva Project and related efforts focused primarily on creating the technical capacity to handle WTO claims, Brazil's effort went further. As Santos has pointed out, Brazil managed not only to build technical capacity; it also created "developmental" trade capacity, that is the ability to relate trade measures and WTO law to the country's developmental policy and be able to protect core developmental policies in WTO litigation (Santos 2012). This meant that if Brazilian trade lawyers were to effectively fight for national interests, they had to understate domestic economic policy as well as trade law itself.

[2] Such studies are representative of a line of social and legal investigation dedicated to understanding the development of legal capacity concerning foreign trade in developing countries.

this chapter, we build on this literature to investigate how international trade lawyers in Brazil have adapted to the changing nature of demand for trade law and related expertise over the past ten years.[3] Our investigation tried to answer two questions regarding the Brazilian legal profession: (1) How did international trade lawyers react to the decline of WTO cases involving Brazil and the decline of the multilateral system as a whole? (2) Were they able to use their knowledge and networks inside the community of international trade lawyers for new forms of professional activity and, if so, how?

We claim that the initial capacity-building efforts created an oversupply of trade law experts in Brazil. With the decline of WTO litigation work, these lawyers needed to find other areas to use their professional skills. The survival of these highly specialized lawyers has required boldness and a shrewd approach to remodeling their own legal capacity to meet market demands. In sum, this practice has gravitated to trade remedies (*defesa comercial*) antidumping disputes that have been brought under Brazilian law.[4] Demands made by Brazilian and foreign clients interested in applying antidumping measures, along with the creativeness of the professionals in this area, burgeoned new organizational models for legal practice in international trade law in Brazil. As we show in this chapter, Brazilian lawyers in this field have increasingly participated in global consulting networks, created "foreign desks" in large law firms, worked at firms specialized in government relations, and lobbied government agencies.

This study attempts to provide several contributions on globalization and the legal profession to the literature. First, we assess how important professional networks are to lawyers working in foreign trade, strengthening the idea that attorneys play an active role in building an elite field (Dezalay and Garth

They analyze how the legal profession influences litigation and how it affects WTO rules, favoring or blocking developmental policies (Shaffer et al. 2014). In an investigation conducted in India, the authors chose to work with the following definition of legal capacity: "the ability to use law to engage proactively in the development and the defense of international and domestic policy." This definition, as well as the one discussed here, encompasses the ability of lawyers to work directly at the WTO, and it applies to the foreign trade rules that influence public policies on a domestic level.

3 In this sense, our approach is similar to Dezalay and Garth (2010), Papa and Wilkins (2011), and Galanter and Robinson (2013).

4 Trade remedies (or trade remedy measures) are of three natures: (1) antidumping, applied when "the product is sold to export at a value below the normal value that it was sold in the internal market of the exporting country"; (2) countervailing, applied when "the product was subsidized by the exporting country"; and (3) safeguards, applied when "the product has been imported in increased quantities in a short period of time" (Kramer 2015, 35). All the measures require the demonstration of injury and causality between the action of the exporter and the injury of the domestic industry.

2002; Flood 2007). Second, we show that when disputes brought to the WTO declined and new industrial policies increased protection for Brazil's domestic industry, legal capacity that had been developed for WTO litigation (Shaffer et al. 2008; Santos 2012) was adapted and deployed in trade remedy litigation and foreign trade consulting. WTO-trained lawyers became active in the Brazilian trade remedy system and set themselves up as consultants offering economic and business services as well as legal analysis. Lastly, we identify new ways by which these firms are working, going beyond the traditional American law firm format[5] to embrace consulting networks and consulting firms specialized in government relations.

Aiming to analyze this transformation, we have observed Brazilian attorneys at work and their different practice sets. We used ethnographic methods and carried out twenty-one interviews between 2012 and 2013 with professionals in international trade law in the country.[6] We interviewed lawyers from

5 For a precise description of the classic US model, see Galanter and Palay (1994), Flood (2007), and Dezalay and Garth (2010).

6 The fact that we have used interviews conducted with foreign trade attorneys in Brazil for a broader interpretation of the redefinition of legal capacity in a changing political and economic scenario could lead the reader to question two issues. The first is that our conclusions come from the premise that perceptions put forth by these agents are reliable, due to their place in the current market. This premise is not a product of naïveté, but of the limitations in the research. Obviously, there is bias in the interviewees' words. However, we diversified our sample to understand the perspective of attorneys who work with different clients, whether they are Brazilian or foreigners. Also, we avoided any generalization that appeared in isolated comments or impressions. The ideas offered in this article are the result of a holistic analysis of primary data, based upon theoretical references. The second issue that could be directed at our work is that by focusing on how these attorneys are impacted by the opening of the economy and globalization, and by relying on their perceptions, it would not be possible to gauge how these attorneys have influenced and shaped such effects. In this case, the method adopted here has attempted to collect responses from the interviewees as to what they and their law firms have been doing in response to market changes. We are aware, however, of the limitations of our methods and possible interference from our data. Still, it is important to bear in mind that we are not interested in understanding perfectly how these attorneys influence changes in international trade law in Brazil. First, we want to provide a general overview of recent transformations in this area and how elite foreign trade attorneys have changed their legal capacity to work with new services, using new organizational models to meet clients' demands. Both issues open the door to further research. Namely, it would consist of gathering and systematizing data to question the narrative provided by the interviewees regarding how the market is structured (its supply, demand, and framework). In addition, it would consist of identifying the alumni from the most important law schools, especially the Geneva Program, analyzing the influence these agents have on the market. However, such research would require an initial exploration of elite law school courses on international trade law. Our study is, therefore, a first necessary toward that direction. These points have been raised with extreme clarity, precision, and respect by Iagê Zendron Miola and Emerson Ribeiro Fabiani. Another possible research agenda from this investigation was suggested by Professor Fabiano Engelmann, which would focus on the perception of controlling agents, such as the Brazilian Bar Association and how it relates to the legitimacy of this new "institutional environment."

seven of the eleven law firms in Brazil listed in trade law by Chambers and Partners (C&P).[7] We also used *snowball sampling* to expand our sample.[8] Specifically, we conducted semistructured interviews, which consisted of previously defined questions in a script focusing on the interviewees' professional background as well as their perception on the changes in foreign trade legal practice in Brazil over the past two decades.[9]

This chapter includes this introduction and three sections. First, in Section II, we analyze the general perception about the decline of WTO litigation and its impact in the work of international trade lawyers in Brazil. In Section III, we discuss the change in the international trade law market in Brazil and the rise of trade remedies as the center of legal practice. Following that, in Section IV, we discuss how attorneys used their training in international trade law to diversify legal services and assess new organizational models for legal practice in foreign trade that have arisen in the post-2008 scenario.

II THE MYTH OF A BOOMING FIELD: IDLE CAPACITY

Nowadays Brazil is a strong player in the multilateral system of trade. In the 1990s, this was not the case. Since the early 2000s, there has been a strong effort by the Brazilian government, together with the businesses elites, to master the rules of international trade and to train young lawyers to negotiate and litigate following WTO rules. Many scholars claim that Brazilian lawyers took advantage of this scenario to build strong connections with diplomats in Geneva (Thorstensen 2009), obtain legal training in foreign law schools (especially universities in the United States), and generate legal capacity in the field of international trade law, carving out spaces for developmental

7 It is worth emphasizing that our sample of interviewees represents approximately 65 percent of Brazil's law firms listed by Chambers and Partners in the area of foreign trade/WTO. Chambers and Partners organizes their ranking in bands. These bands are Senior Statesmen, Bands That Go from Band 1 to Band 4, Up and Coming, and Associates to Watch. With the exception of the Senior Statesmen and Associates to Watch bands, we interviewed professionals listed in all other bands. Visit Chamber and Partners current list: www.chambersandpartners.com/41/455/editorial/9/1#RankedFirms_Tab.

8 Regarding the use of the *snowballing* method in legal research, in particular, in a relatively restricted market as international trade law in Brazil, please refer to the study conducted by Krishnan and Purohit (2014, 4) on law firms and attorneys that work with commercial disputes at the Dubai International Financial Centre (DIFC) Courts and in the Dubai International Arbitration Centre.

9 The interviews were conducted mostly in person and over the telephone when required. As Marc Galanter and Nick Robinson did in their recent study on elite legal practitioners in India, we chose to keep interviewees anonymous in this article (Galanter and Robinson 2013). We believe that individual identification is not required to understand how legal capacity is redefined in this small professional niche.

policies inside the framework of the rules of the multilateral system (Shaffer et al. 2008; Santos 2012; Badin and Ratton 2013).

In the mid-2000s, the field of international trade law (ITL) grew in Brazil, with more than 100 lawyers trained in the "Geneva Program."[10] This was the period in which ITL became an autonomous field of practice inside big law firms. However, this growing sector of legal practice reached a limit years ago. The Brazilian lawyers in this field agree that "the positions have been taken"[11] – in other words, there are no huge expectations for future expansion in the professional field, which has already been restricted to an elite group of Brazilian attorneys.[12] While initially many thought there would be an increasing volume of WTO work, by 2005 it had become clear this was not going to happen. One interviewee noted:

> It is a small market, with few professionals. Everybody knows everybody. I have spoken to a few colleagues: if you are in, you're in; if you aren't, you aren't. Now, this is how it is going to be. These are the professionals, and that is it. The WTO lost the glamour it had when I was in law school. It was different in 2005. Nowadays, it is like: "What is this thing with the WTO? It never changes? Aren't we going to close any deals?" People are moving to new areas: the Bribery Act, the FPCA [Foreign Corrupt Practices Act], anticorruption. This is the cooler segment in the international area. There are many fads in law.

An analysis of WTO data reinforces the opinion offered by the attorneys interviewed. Table 9.1 shows the total number of cases filed at the Dispute

10 The most important training ground for Brazil's elite trade lawyers was the Geneva Program, officially labeled as the Training Program for Young Attorneys in the Brazilian Mission in Geneva, designed by Vera Thorstensen (a senior economist). The Geneva Program began in 2003 and has trained more than one hundred Brazilian attorneys who learned how WTO litigation worked "from within." The program stems from the cooperation between the MRE and two private organizations, the Brazilian Institute for Studies on Competition, Consumer Affairs, and International Trade (IBRAC) and the Center for Studies on Law Firms (CESA).

11 The Chambers and Partners list of foreign trade attorneys in Brazil shows the market is small. In total, only twenty-six attorneys are listed as reference professionals in the country.

12 The concept of "elite lawyering" in Brazil has been discussed in the works by Fabiano Engelmann: "Attorneys with higher international involvement comprise a relatively small number if compared to the thousands of law firms in Brazil. Situated mostly in São Paulo, the large partnerships expanded with the privatization of publicly owned companies in the 1990s, which is made evident in the increasing number of associates and the quantity of firms founded during this period. Considering the biographical profiles of the most renowned partners published in the year books, one can see the presence of international capital retained in the form of education abroad and licenses to practice law internationally, as well as the presence of organizations and associations that emphasize their ties with the financial-corporate market and expertise related to the technical aspects of financial and business operations" (Engelmann 2012, 499).

TABLE 9.1 *Breakdown of Brazil's trade remedy system*

CAMEX	Decides to apply antidumping laws and can determine retroactive charging; extends antidumping laws when there is circumvention; ratifies price commitments
SECEX	Decides to initiate, extend, or end investigations
DECOM	Conducts the whole investigation; aids Brazilian companies in investigations abroad
GTIP	May recommend that the CAMEX suspends and changes antidumping laws due to public interest
RFB	Collects payment derived from antidumping enforcement fines

Source: Brazilian National Confederation of Industry (CNI 2013, 19).

Settlement Body (DSB) involving Brazil since 1995, both as complainant and respondent.[13] It shows that there was a peak in demand by the beginning of the 2000s, the period in which Brazilian lawyers started training in the Geneva Program.

Bearing that in mind, there is a clear perception that the groups of Brazilian attorneys who deal with international trade, in particular the multilateral system, have been consolidated and will roughly stall at the same size. Given this context, the respondents stress the idea that "everybody knows everybody."[14] The small Brazilian network is connected to a small international network of attorneys.[15] According to a lawyer working at a large firm, such network connections are crucial in obtaining clients and mutual favors, that is, reciprocity among such professionals.

Most of the respondents did not expect major expansion of legal practice in international trade. There has been no substantial change in the number of WTO cases in which Brazil is either a complainant or a respondent, even though there is some oscillation in the number of cases in which the country features as the third party (World Trade Organization 2015). While the Luiz

[13] The following cases were analyzed, according to the order in which they were filed at the WTO: 1995 (DS4, DS22), 1996 (DS30, DS46, DS51, DS52), 1997 (DS65, DS69, DS70, DS71, DS81, DS112), 1998 (DS116, DS154), 1999 (DS183), 2000 (DS190, DS197, DS199, DS208, DS209, DS216, DS217, DS217, DS219), 2001 (DS222, DS224, DS229, DS239, DS241), 2002 (DS250, DS259, DS241), 2005 (DS332), 2006 (DS355), 2007 (DS365), 2008 (DS382), 2010 (DS409), 2012 (DS439) 2013 (DS472). All cases are available at www.wto.org/english/tratop_e/dispu_e/dispu_status_e.htm.

[14] The international network format will be addressed in the sections below.

[15] The practice of international trade law is also a restricted niche in other countries, such as India (Shaffer et al. 2014, 10). Besides the Brazilian and Indian markets, it is possible that the American market relies on a relatively small number of law firms that Chambers and Partners recommends. Out of 212 law firms listed by the C&P in the United States, only 48 are listed in international trade when we filtered the search using the criteria "area of law."

Inácio Lula da Silva (2003–2010) and Dilma Rousseff (2011 to present day) administrations have encouraged antidumping to protect domestic firms, even this activity may have leveled off. By the time the interviews were made, one lawyer noted that

> [the years] 2012 and 2013 were high points. With a higher exchange rate, [the domestic] industry is already protected, and the number of investigations tended to decrease in 2014. It does not stop, but it is a cyclical area. Foreign clients participate when the investigation is initially filed. If there is an investigation filed, they will participate if the market is important. They are reactive.[16]

At the same time, there has been little progress in negotiating commercial agreements between Mercosur and the European Union (Thorstensen et al. 2013). The debate on exchange rates as trade violations seems to be stalled.[17] In a pragmatic view – focused on "doing what can be done" and avoiding atrophy of the WTO – the administration of WTO, President Roberto Azevêdo, has focused on trade facilitation.[18] According to Brazil's foreign trade attorneys,

[16] As it has been reported worldwide, the situation of the exchange rate in Brazil has substantially changed, in particular, since the beginning of Rousseff's second term. Whether this new context will lead to an increase in the number of antidumping investigations is a question yet to be addressed by further research. However, Brazil has experienced some economic instability since the end of Lula da Silva's tenure as president; nonetheless Brazil and major companies within the country have maintained their antidumping strategies. For that reason, and based upon the interviewee's opinion that this is a "cyclical area," it is expected that the current status quo persists, unless either the exchange rate changes in an unfavorable manner against Brazilian exporters or import patterns become different vis-à-vis exports. In the end, it is too soon to have a precise answer, but it is possible to infer from the opinion of some lawyers interviewed for this project that historically the number of antidumping investigations is more deeply related to policy strategies than economic conjuncture.

[17] Thorstensen notes, "For countries with overvalued exchange rates, depending on the level of such appreciation, their bound and applied tariffs can be nullified and become negative, implying that the country is granting a stimulus to imports and waiving the tariff protection negotiated within the WTO. For countries with undervalued exchange rates, depending on the level of such depreciation, their bound and applied tariffs can be increased in greater proportions than the exchange rate" (Thorstensen et al. 2013, 105–106).

[18] "What we did, in Bali, was to unblock multilateral negotiations, which had been completely paralyzed for almost twenty years. Access to markets is not limited to a specific topic. It is not just agriculture, industrial goods, or services, but the three areas at the same time. It is very difficult to negotiate progress individually, in only one of these areas. A developed country willing to make compromises in the agricultural area will want more access to its products and services in other markets. We already knew it would be impossible to reach a deal for the three areas" (interview with Roberto Azevêdo in a *Istoé Dinheiro*, January 1, 2014, www.istoedinheiro.com.br/noticias/entrevistas/20140110/comando-organizacao-mundial-comercio-omc-desde-setembro-2013-embaixador-brasileiro-roberto-azevedo-passou-por-seu-primeiro-teste-impedir-morte-entidade-sediada-genebra/139525.shtml).

there will be neither a considerable expansion in the area nor a return to a practice focusing on the WTO. To be sure, one lawyer noted:

> The WTO has lost most of its power due to successive economic crises, which have made countries more individualistically minded, establishing an "every country for itself" situation. Why should a client go to the WTO to claim that someone, like the United States, is breaking a rule, in an extremely expensive case, if they can simply refuse to export to this country? Until every door is closed, exports can always be transferred someplace else. Except for situations in which changing countries is more difficult, as is the case of subsidies, antidumping at the WTO is not interesting due to the current economic situation.

There is, however, a minority who see potential for market changes. For one lawyer working at a large firm in São Paulo, the work performed by Brazilian attorneys is still quite limited to topics such as trade remedies. For him, there are still matters that are not being discussed in Brazil and that are important to other foreign trade attorneys abroad:

> I believe it is a relatively small group for the size of Brazil's legal market. They are people who know one another and meet in seminars and events. The area has grown, no doubt. Fifteen years ago, it was a much smaller group of attorneys. It has expanded. Today, it is virtually an area unto itself, but it is still quite concentrated. Many attorneys now handle only antidumping. I do not mean that antidumping is not foreign trade; this is unquestionable. It is what the client asks for and what is on your desk. But international trade has a much broader spectrum, which we do not realize. For instance, there is an extremely important debate on controlling exports in American and European law firms. At the International Bar Association, this is a very important issue. Attorneys are concerned with prohibition, controls, and restrictions on exports that many countries impose. We do not see this discussion here.

In sum, most of our interviewees did not see a need for further capacity building in this area. The chances to work on WTO litigation cases are very limited. Since the Geneva Program was created in 2003, Brazil has featured as the complainant at the WTO in only four cases and as the respondent in only three. Brazil has been the third party in a larger number, fifty-nine since 2003 (World Trade Organization 2015). Yet, generally speaking, they think the work is limited and could easily be handled by the existing group of specialists.

Given that situation, the international trade bar has had to reinvent itself. Professionals have migrated to other areas, offered new services, and developed new ways to attract businesses and communicate with foreign clients.

The legal capacity initially created to help the government and a limited number of Brazilian economic groups at the WTO has been used to expand legal services for clients either affected by imports or engaged in exports. Two major areas with potential for growth have been litigating antidumping cases under Brazilian law as well as consultancy on governmental relations, which comprehends specialists in international taxation and specific foreign jurisdictions. In the next two sections, we will explore in detail how the Brazilian lawyers managed to adapt themselves to a new political and economic scenario and how they actively created new fields of professional activity that were previously occupied by economists and "technicians" without legal training.

III REINVENTING INTERNATIONAL TRADE LAW

In this section, we will address several recent transformations in the field of international trade in Brazil. Broadly speaking, Brazil's economic policies have influenced the change in the structure of Brazil's commercial relations. Consequently, attorneys in the country have adapted to new needs and restructured their firms as well as strategized new models to attract clients, as it will be outlined below.

In Brazil, political and economic transformations have altered international trade legal practice in the country. First, we will discuss the growing importance of trade remedies and the impact of this policy on legal services. Afterward, we will explain some characteristics concerning how Brazilian law firms working with foreign trade are organized; how they have adapted to a period in which the WTO has lost predominance; and how competition and protectionist policies in Brazil and around the world have become more important. Finally, we will analyze how some professionals aimed at the nuances of international trade as it relates to governmental affairs.

A *Industrial Policies and Trade Remedies*

The pioneering generation of attorneys trained in Geneva and Washington has headed the development of several areas in international trade practice since the beginning of the 2000s.[19] According to interviewees, the areas that expanded more were trade remedies,[20] international contracts, and international taxation.

[19] For a full description of how this triple alliance (diplomacy, business associations, big law firms) was formed for strategic reasons, see Shaffer et al. (2008) and Thorstensen (2009).

[20] Brazil is considered one of the developing countries that most uses antidumping investigations, being behind only India. For instance, between 1995 and 2010, India was responsible for 1,394 antidumping investigations, followed by Brazil with 364 and China with 357 (Castelan 2012, 32). Yet the data show that the percentage of negative outcomes from dumping is higher

Namely, these areas stem from a context in which WTO cases involving Brazil have declined. Accordingly, attorneys may handle international contracts and the respective disputes that arise from contractual disagreement. This means that firms are usually hired to advise on negotiating and writing contracts and, in cases in which differences arise, to assist in disputes that will need to be decided, whether in arbitration or in courts.[21] Furthermore, given the complexity of taxes on imports and exports, some firms have created an international taxation practice area. Even though some professionals in this area come from tax law, they emphasize that there are specificities in tax involving international trade that require qualified trade professionals to handle them. This may include negotiating with the Brazilian Inland Revenue Service (Receita Federal do Brasil, or RFB), of the Ministry of Finance, which handles payments related to antidumping cases, as well as dealing with customs officials about customs clearance, all areas that present substantial difficulties. One professional reported that, while other authorities with jurisdiction over international trade law, e.g., the Department of Trade Remedies (DECOM),[22] encourage more interaction with the private sector, the RFB and the structure of the Ministry of Finance itself are more restricted.

Therefore, attorneys and law firms are hired to handle bureaucratic aspects of imports and exports, as well as to negotiate tax matters and the respective procedures that may involve fines or rebating tax(es) paid in excess. Finally, most of our respondents reported that many attorneys who were trained to help resolve disputes at the WTO currently work with trade remedies antidumping.[23] Attorneys interviewed on the proceedings involving antidumping investigations, in general, assessed them as positive. Even though there is a bureaucratic structure involving different secretariats and other governmental bodies, professionals have shown optimism regarding the possibility to dialogue with several organizations. Although this is a positive sign of the Brazilian government, rendering high-quality and efficient services depends on the negotiating skills of these attorneys, which shall not be disregarded when we look at the official structure that exists in Brazil.

in Brazil, because 16 percent of investigations ended with a negative result (33). According to more recent data, the situation is similar: in 2012, sixteen cases had a negative outcome, while this number rose to forty-three in 2013 (www.gazetadopovo.com.br/economia/conteudo.phtml?id=1460104).

21 Although this area may be important to the changes in the legal profession, its complexity has left it beyond the scope of our research.

22 The Department of Trade Remedies (DECOM) is part of the Ministry of Development, Industry, and Foreign Trade in Brazil.

23 The term *antidumping* is often used as a euphemism in relation to trade remedies, namely because the interviewees have informed us that antidumping has been the most required service derived from trade remedies.

Brazil's trade remedy system comprises the following entities: the Ministry of Development, Industry, and Foreign Trade (MDIC) is responsible for directly organizing Brazil's international trade system. It is responsible for the Chamber of Foreign Trade (CAMEX) and the Secretary of Foreign Trade (SECEX). The latter is responsible for the DECOM, an administrative authority responsible for handling antidumping investigations. Although these are the main players in Brazil's structure, after an investigation has been carried out and the decision regarding fines has been made, the Technical Group for Assessing Public Interest (GTIP) – connected to the CAMEX – can rule over antidumping matters in the case of an important public interest. Lastly, the RFB applies and collects fines applied in the aforementioned cases. Table 9.1 outlines the activities performed by the authorities listed in this paragraph:

Bearing that in mind, trade remedies have emerged as a major new source of employment, and certainly profits, for Brazil's trade lawyers. The decreasing number of WTO cases, along with the manner in which the antidumping investigation system is organized in Brazil, makes it possible for lawyers skilled in antidumping to find new trade clients. Accordingly, one respondent noted:

> The noblest practice in international trade would be to take part in [WTO] panels... but Brazil went from being a complainant and now participates often as a third party. However, considering the country's current situation, I do not see Brazil opening a panel. This is a complex area in which there exist few qualified firms. What has grown significantly is antidumping investigation.

Indeed, some scholars have noted the growing importance of antidumping as being a result of new industrial policies instituted under Lula da Silva but that continued and expanded under Rousseff. With the rise of Brazil's New Developmental State, more emphasis has been placed on supporting domestic industry (Trubek 2013). Under the Production Development Program (2008)[24] and the Greater Brazil Plan (2011),[25] the government has sought to facilitate exports and expand antidumping remedies. Through Executive Act no. 541/2011 (later converted into Act no. 12,545/2011), the federal government expanded the resources made available to the Export Financing Fund (FFEX) and created 120 positions for foreign trade analysts. In 2013 the Rousseff administration, under pressure from the São Paulo Federation of Industries

24 The program aims at promoting long-term competitiveness for the country's economy, in particular, because of its efforts to make the cooperation between the government and the private sector work. See www.pdp.gov.br/paginas/objetivo.aspx?path=Objetivos.

25 See www.brasilmaior.mdic.gov.br/conteudo/128.

to strengthen trade remedies,[26] issued new regulations of administrative procedures in antidumping actions.[27] This created legal formalities and hence more opportunities for lawyers.[28] In fact, one lawyer noted:

> Currently, Brazil applies the highest number of antidumping measures in the world. This happened during the Dilma administration due to the Greater Brazil Plan, one of the pillars behind *defesa comercial* [trade remedies]. Besides industrial policy, this plan aims at desperately protecting our industry so that it does not suffer from freer trade, and that is where antidumping comes into play. With that, over the past two years, Brazil became the world leader in applying antidumping measures. The number of measures we [as a country] filed is scary. There is no political barrier to filing a case to investigate antidumping. With the current protectionist policy, our work tends to grow.[29]

This view is also confirmed by the literature. Cynthia Kramer claims that "several countries are accusing Brazil of being protectionist" because the country "has started more investigations and applied more antidumping measures in the past two years" (Kramer 2015, 41). However, as she notes, "as long as the antidumping proceedings follow the procedure and rules established by the WTO Anti-dumping Agreement, nothing could be argued against Brazil" (41).

Interestingly, this phenomenon has also had geographical effects and spurred trade services throughout Brazil. São Paulo and Rio de Janeiro – economic centers where you can traditionally find the largest corporate law

26 Considering Brazil's deindustrialization, caused partly by the increasing imports of Chinese goods, Brazilian businesspeople asked the federal government not only to "shorten deadlines in the investigation of unfair importations, but to be more strict regarding the inspection of suspicious products and extend the reach of surcharges or rights to goods that have proven unfairly damaging to domestic goods." See Leo (2011).

27 Decree no. 8,058/2013 creates the formal procedures to determine the existence of dumping through a formal system of petitioning, educating, and administrative decision making with fixed deadlines.

28 Prior to this time, antidumping was largely handled by technocrats as it was considered an administrative proceeding for which lawyers were not required. One respondent notes: "This has been another clear movement. Large law firms were able to take advantage, in a good sense, of a new niche. Rendering services in *defesa comercial* [trade remedies] was in the hands of consultants, who often were former DECOM technicians. They are people who retired and started consulting." In Brazil, administrative legal proceedings do not require attorneys.

29 Between 2011 and 2013, the government received proposals and suggestions to change the regulatory framework for trade remedies. This resulted in the publication of Decree no. 8,058 of July 19, 2013, which, among other aspects that are related to policies, was drawn up in the Plano Brasil Maior. For an understanding of Plano Brasil Maior, besides antidumping investigations, it is interesting to note the context in which the plan was embedded while it was part of Brazil's industrial policy agenda. For this, see Almeida (2009, 50–54).

firms in the country – are no longer the only places to practice international trade law in Brazil. Brasília, the country's capital where the ministries and the center of federal public bureaucracy are located, became an appropriate place to practice trade law as well. As we will explain in the next sections, the importance of antidumping measures and the legal procedures in the DECOM generated a strong demand for a new type of work, more connected with governmental relations and lobbying in the capital of Brazil.

B *Organizing Trade Law Practice and the Inverted Pyramid Phenomenon*

The changing nature of trade law practice has led to a variety of organizational responses in the firms. The first deals with the flow of trade law cases and the problem it creates for staffing. At least until recently, it was hard to predict the annual volume of trade remedy cases. In fact, the government does not release longitudinal data on trade remedies used in Brazil, even though Brazil has been a major player in using such tools, according to the existing literature. With that said, one observer noted that unlike customs law and other areas, international trade work itself is episodic and disputes can drag on with long periods in which there is nothing for the attorneys to do, which makes workload hard to predict.

> In the old law, we were talking about one year or one year and a half of work [on a trade remedy case], with seasonal peaks. In certain months, you might not bill one minute to that client. But in the customs area, it is the opposite. There are ad hoc consultations, whether they are smaller or larger, with more or less recurring clients, but it demands the attorney's time. So, if we work only with trade remedies, at certain times, attorneys will have to work many nights, and during others they will have nothing to do. We are under the impression that, with the new law, this seasonality will become more predictable. The forecast is that investigation lasts ten months. As a rule, [work with trade remedies] is very seasonal, so it is good to have a large volume of consultations, customs matters, contracts, etc.

While the new laws passed by the Brazilian government may change this situation as the volume of actions increases, firms have needed to find ways to keep attorneys at work during trade law downtime. Largely for this reason, in most of the law firms examined, the team working with trade remedies also handles competition law cases. The explanations offered by interviewees stress two factors: (1) competition law professionals have taken advantage of their expertise and started working in an area with growing influence on general trade regulations, not restricted to international trade only, and (2) clients' demands prompted synergies in complex international trade law disputes within law firms, which forced professionals to simultaneously deal with competition problems and trade remedies altogether.

In other organizational models, trade remedies cases are handled by the same team that deals with taxation. Specifically, one or a few tax attorneys, usually the most experienced, are deployed exclusively to international trade. These attorneys are in direct contact with the client in key matters, and they define the general strategy for handling cases, while other team members, who deal with a variety of trade remedy and other issues, work on everyday tax legal proceedings.

Despite the focus on competition or tax law, we noticed some specific team formats within the organization of law firms. Even though the number of lawyers per team may vary according to the size of each firm – which are different, for example, between full-service offices or boutiques[30] – it is not so common to see the pyramid model that is common to the legal profession, in which the lesser the qualification and experience, the larger the number of professionals.[31] In fact, many teams, according to the interviewees, had the same number of interns, junior attorneys, and senior attorneys. In sum, some interviewees indicated that the international trade law market is marked by a phenomenon known as the "inverted pyramid": some teams have more experienced attorneys than newcomers.

The inverted pyramid is coherent with the narrative that "the positions are taken" in the field of international trade law in Brazil. However, considering the scope and method of this research, there is still no way to tell how permanent and widespread this trend is. We gathered this perception from small and large firms alike, but it would be a mistake to conclude that all the main international trade law firms are affected by the inverted pyramid feature. However, it is certainly a new facet of the Brazilian market that is deeply connected to the cyclical rhythm of international trade law demands.[32]

30 "'Boutique' has come to refer to highly specialized small firms residing in the corporate 'hemisphere.' These firms cultivate their comparative advantages in selected specialties and suppress any push to general coverage in order to maintain their attractiveness for referral work from big firms" (Galanter and Palay 1994, 916).

31 According to Marc Galanter and Thomas Palay in a classic study on the "tournament of lawyers," firms working with business law in the United States are structured as follows: they have a large group of salary-based junior attorneys, selected from the best law schools in the United States; they impersonalize relations with clients (the relationship is with the office), promoting hierarchy and separating "full-time" and "senior" attorneys; and they promote competition within the "up or out" logic (attorney makes partner or moves to a smaller firm) (Galanter and Palay 1994, 77–120).

32 Categorizing attorneys as junior, senior, and partner appeared in several interviews, even if there was not a specific criterion to define how each firm handles this classification. Yet it was possible to note that higher education – e.g., graduate degrees abroad – and time of service are the main criteria mentioned by the interviewees to classify attorneys working with

C *Trade Lawyers onto Government Relations*

Finally, another development has been the rise of consultancy firms specializing in international trade and the ascension of lawyers within them. The growing role of public policy in the trade area, including efforts to both stimulate exports and protect domestic industry from imports, has created a demand for information about these policies as well as for lobbying efforts to influence them.[33] Within this context, over the past few years in Brazil, new consultancies specializing in government relations and lobbying have appeared. These groups develop relations with the key decision makers who determine how export policies are structured and import protections enforced. This business, largely based in Brasilia, has attracted trade lawyers as well.[34]

In the next section, we will explain how the rise of consultancy firms in international trade law is part of a bigger transformation in the field in Brazil, spurred by the move from WTO litigation to trade remedies and the return of protectionism in a context of global economic crisis. This transition has also produced effects in the way that these lawyers work and collaborate globally. Some lawyers have created international desks inside big law firms, while others have developed new organizational models to work in this field via consultancy networks and firms specialized in governmental relations. These changes are evidence of how these professionals are actively creating new fields for highly valued legal work.

international trade law. For instance, a female professional reported that all attorneys participating in the Geneva Program are currently in leading positions, i.e., as seniors or partners in their firms. For a comparative view of the internal organization of law firms, refer to a study conducted by Gabbay, Sica, and Ramos in this volume (Chapter 2), who gathered the followed information: "We have an assessment of what weight varies depending on whether you are a junior or senior attorney. Obviously for seniors, what matters the most? Relations with the client. For a junior, what matters the most? If they are learning, if they are evolving. So, even a sophisticated assessment, which varies according to seniority, can generate importance. According to this importance, you may be promoted annually until you make partner."

33 Such movement had already been identified by Richard Baldwin and Simon Evenett after the financial crisis of 2008: "Trade is experiencing a sudden, severe and globally synchronized collapse. Protectionist forces have already emerged and will strengthen as the recession gets worse. But this is not 1930s-style protection. Governments' crisis-fighting measures have spawned new, murkier forms of protection which discriminate against foreign firms, workers and investors – often in subtle ways. The use of WTO legal protection, such as antidumping measures, is also up sharply" (Baldwin and Evenett 2009, 1).

34 A good example is Welber Barral, a former professor of international trade law and secretary of foreign trade under the Lula Administration. Barral now runs a foreign trade consultancy in Brasilia.

IV REINVENTING SERVICES AND WAYS TO ATTRACT CLIENTS: DESKS, NETWORKS, AND GOVERNMENT RELATIONS

The literature on the sociology of professions has emphasized the existing tensions in implementing a "single model" law firm, which was promoted by the international law firms in the United Kingdom and the United States with a presence in several European and Latin American countries (Morgan 2009; Muzio and Faulconbridge 2013). However, it is problematic to assume that the globalization of the legal profession has led to mastering a single method to attract clients and work in the international trade area.[35] In fact, there is still some heterogeneity in organizational models in legal practice across countries, with different ways to work with and aim at clients. According to the interviews, this seems to be true regarding international trade law in Brazil and the diversity in the structures of Brazilian international trade firms.

Indeed, in Brazil, it is common to separate full-service from boutique firms (Ghirardi 2014, 74). The former work with all the main areas of law and render services to clients of different sizes, with a large team of attorneys in different hierarchical positions that eventually work together in big projects.[36] The latter offer services focused on specific areas of the law and rely on a small team of attorneys, which often includes legal academics.[37] Yet interviewees were skeptical about the possibility to create new boutique firms focusing on international trade today for the following reasons: the unpredictable demand, the specificity of the work, and the challenges of having specialized attorneys working solely in international trade. Therefore, in Brazil, over the past two

[35] Recently Galanter and Henderson (2008) explained that the concept of large law firms and the promotion-to-partnership tournament might be revised, considering the transformations taking place in the organizational models in corporate business in the United States.

[36] According to the *Análise* 500 ranking in 2012, the main full-service offices in São Paulo are Pinheiro Neto Advogados; Machado, Meyer, Sendacz e Opice; Mattos Filho, Veiga Filho, Marrey Jr. e Quiroga Advogados; Demarest e Almeida Advogados; Siqueira Castro Advogados; Dannemann Siemsen Advogados; TozziniFreire Advogados; Veirano Advogados; Barbosa, Müssnich Aragão Advogados; Souza, Cescon, Barrieu & Flesch; Trench, Rossi e Watanabe Advogados.

[37] Also according to the *Análise* 500 ranking in 2012, the boutique law firms are Advocacia Mariz de Oliveira; David Rechulski Advogados; Gusmão & Labrunie; and Kasznar Leonardos Propriedade Intelectual. Concerning this classification, the paper "Corporate Law Firms: The Brazilian Market" places these denominations into relative terms. The common meaning of a full-service firm is one with broader practices in several areas of law, while a boutique firm is more specialized in one or a few areas. However, due to the respect that these terms have acquired over the past years, some firms call themselves boutiques for more prestige, to escape the fame of little personalization that the so-called full-service firms have (see Chapter 2).

decades, there has been a trend for the larger full-service firms to handle international trade.[38]

Despite the limited size of the international trade area in large firms in Brazil, it was possible to see some other important transformations over the past ten years (2004–2014) that are related to the impact globalization has had on this segment of the legal profession. The first is the rise of specific units ("desks") to work with foreign clients. The second is the appearance of "network firms" focused on consulting for international trade, relying on professional relations constructed globally. The third is the growing importance given to government relations and the growth of consultancies focusing on antidumping and other trade remedies.

A *The Rise of International Desks at Large-Scale Law Firms*

The first important transformation seen in the organization of firms working with international trade was specialized relations with foreign clients. Some large and medium-sized firms implemented desks to attend to clients from specific countries, an approach established in the 2000s that seems to be expanding. In 2001, for instance, Felsberg e Associados created a China Desk for "matters related to business between Brazil and China."[39] In 2005, Trench, Rossi e Watanabe announced the inclusion of a desk to "tend to clients in business with companies from Brazil and the Popular Republic of China."[40] In 2011, Machado, Meyer, Sendacz e Opice also announced their China Desk "in response to the intense demand for consulting services and advisory generated by business involving China."[41]

38 Work with international trade, however, is found in different types of firms: boutiques and large full-service firms. In India, there are more boutique firms working in areas involving international trade (Shaffer et al. 2014, 10–11).

39 Later, in 2005, Felsberg e Associados hired an attorney in China. In 2008 they began operating an outpost office in Shanghai, which allows them to offer Brazilian clients not only "the infrastructure required to make deals in China, but also direct contact with local clients and partners, as well as allowing for constant update on the legal and business environment in China and Asia." See www.felsberg.com.br/desks/china-desk/.

40 The "China Desk" at Trench, Rossi e Watanabe was taken on by Daniel Cheng Chen, who graduated from Universidade Presbiteriana Mackenzie and worked at Baker & McKenzie International in Shanghai and Hong Kong.

41 In the case of Machado, Meyer, Sencacz e Opice, the China Desk is led by a Chinese attorney who graduated from the University of São Paulo Law School. According to the information provided by the firm, "an important differential for the China Desk at Machado Meyer is the support provided the attorney Tang Wei, consultant for matters related to China. Tang was born in the capital city, Beijing, and has lived in Brazil since 1988. Here, he learned to speak Portuguese and attended law school at Largo São Francisco, São Paulo University. Today, besides being the head of the China Desk, Tang is the general-secretary at

Basically, the desk model consists of (1) allocating within the firm professionals with experience in other countries' legal systems and (2) allowing and facilitating communication with foreign clients in their local languages. It is a modality of work that is easily identifiable in large law firms in other countries, such as the United Kingdom[42] and Turkey.[43] Among the law firms analyzed in our research, most of them in São Paulo, it was possible to identify the predominance of "national desks," focused on working with clients from certain countries, instead of "regional desks."[44] There are examples of Korean desks as well as the Chinese desks mentioned above, similar to those in US, Italian, and European law firms that focus on the Chinese market (Bocconcelli and Pagano 2013, 7). To better understand how desks in Brazilian offices work, we refer to the description by an attorney working at a desk in a full-service firm in São Paulo:

> We used to work with approximately 90 percent Korean companies. We provide attorneys with the theoretical and practical background in national law. The most significant challenge for firms with desks is to have attorneys who are not merely translators. By offering qualified attorneys in technical aspects, the firm started to attract larger cases from the Asian market. In parallel, I took part in creating the Korean Desk at the firm and then other desk areas were created from the perception that it was necessary to show the client that there are people here who understand their culture. The attorney who does not have the flexibility to meet communication standards imposed by the client has no way of surviving in this market. Understanding the best format to communicate with the clients is key to standing out [in the international trade law market].

the Brazil–China Chamber of Economic Development (CBCDE) and offers consultancy to most of the Chinese companies operating in Brazil." See www.machadomeyer.com.br/noticias/para-atender-demanda-crescente-nos-negocios-com-a-china–machado-meyer-advogados-lanca-seu-china-desk.

[42] David Wilkins and Mihaela Papa, in a study on the impact of globalization in India, noted that most international firms work actively in cross-border transactions related to India. The most important firms in the United Kingdom have an Indian Desk with dozens of attorneys. These professionals are hired from the best Indian schools, and their work consists of dealing with Indian clients and handling commercial transactions related to India (Papa and Wilkins 2011, 185–187).

[43] Kiliç & Partners, a law firm based in Turkey, also has "special desks" to provide services focused on specific regions and legal systems. The firm's model revolves around "regional desks" (African Desk, American Desk, Asian Desk, CIS Desk, EU Desk, Middle East Desk) and does not have "national desks," as identified in Brazil. See www.kilicandpartners.com/international.php.

[44] An exception is the Tozzini Freire Advogados firm, which, besides having desks for China, Japan, and South Korea, also offers "regional desks" for German-speaking and Latin American countries. See www.tozzinifreire.com.br/areas-de-atuacao/.

The desk model enhances services in international trade law, initially not due to a simple matter of an expertise in international trade law but rather to a receptive structure for foreign clients, strengthened by the presence of a fellow countryman attorney for the foreign client (e.g., this situation can be visualized when one sees a Chinese attorney providing services to Chinese clients in a Brazilian firm). This work model has already been adopted by several large law firms worldwide, impelled by the need to search for new strategies to strengthen ties with clients from different origins but involved in commercial relations on a global scale. For the globalizing Brazilian profession, this organizational framework can be adjusted to work with law firms in international trade (Papa and Wilkins 2011).

B *Building "Networks" and the Rise of New Consultancies*

The second important change this research sheds light on is the development of collaborative work between international trade law firms in Brazil and elsewhere. These joint efforts have been improved by the rise of network consultancies that adopt a flexible work model based on projects.

Legal representation in cases involving Brazil at the WTO tended to be done through the association between Brazilian firms and specialized offices from abroad (Shaffer et al. 2008, 430–435). As Brazilian firms expanded their expertise in this area, they maintained relationships with major firms in the United States and Europe. At the same time, because of the increasing number of Brazilian attorneys, including trade lawyers, who received their LLMs at American universities (Engelmann 2010, 18–20) and stayed on for internships at US firms, ties with US firms also strengthened. The prosperous relationship between the small elite group of trade lawyers in Brazil and those elsewhere confirmed that Brazil was aligned with global trends (Shaffer et al. 2008).

Namely, international networks for Brazilian law firms became more available, playing a key role in international exchanges.[45] Many of the demands for work in international trade law come from such networks,[46] with no formal ties at horizontal or vertical levels. Brazilian law firms are often hired by foreign offices to clarify specific points or to work together on cases involving Brazilian matters. This has favored the creation of informal partnerships and facilitated the expansion of the network among international trade offices.

45 Namely, when the firm works for the client investing abroad, it does so in partnership with local firms.

46 We have adopted the concept of "network" from David Wilkins and Mihaela Papa, which, in general terms, means any collection of actors pursuing a continuous relationships for exchange but does not have any legitimate organizational authority to solve or arbitrate conflicts that may emerge in this relationship, constituting a horizontal social acentric organization (Wilkins and Papa 2013, 1165).

According to one interviewee working with tax law, informal partnerships with foreign firms are crucial to obtaining foreign clients, sometimes even splitting fees:

> When it comes to customs, much of the work comes from other firms. There are always specific questions from their clients or studies on how [organizations] in several countries work. In [antidumping], when an investigation is filed, we let our contacts know. They often have clients whom they refer us to, and we handle the case directly with the company. They get part of the fees because they will have to do something.

One of the reasons behind the coordination of such networks is the active search for clients through referrals, considering the limited size of the market in this area. Recurrent demands are usually related to international trade practice, which requires the attorney to work in the structuring phase of commercial operations with the client. In the end, trade remedies matter for everyday trade lawyering, whereas international litigation at the WTO occurs episodically and unpredictably:

> You do not have WTO cases every day. Neither here nor in the United States. You do not have law firms dedicated exclusively to the WTO. You have stages. Even in trade remedies, you do not get a recurring demand. Recurring demand is operational aspects of foreign trade. So, the main issue is actually that we [the lawyers] need to generate demand all the time.

These three factors – a random flow of work, high specialization, and cooperation to strengthen international trade law – have helped form a coherent network of professionals in this legal field. As our interviewees attest, international trade law in Brazil is a small field but is relatively well connected to attorneys from other parts of the world. One attorney, for instance, said that all Chinese companies her company served have become clients due to referrals and contacts from Chinese attorneys. Such referrals are crucial to creating "social capital"[47] to stabilize expectations and "build trust"[48] among agents from different locations (Chinese companies and Brazilian attorneys):

47 We use the expression "social capital" in the definition given by French sociologist Pierre Bourdieu, who became influential in the sociology of law (Bourdieu 1987; Dezalay and Garth 2002). The concept of "social capital" puts emphasis on conflicts, on the role of power, and on the social relations that increase an actor's ability to further their interest.

48 The process of building trust, according to one of the attorneys interviewed, is multifaceted: "It is difficult to answer how relationships of trust are built among these professionals. The relationships are very much word of mouth. It is case by case. 'You did well, you showed you master the subject.' 'You either won or lost, but it was not your fault; you could have foreseen the defeat.' I have some contacts from Georgetown, but only one still works in the area. The rest of them jumped on a plane, went to visit the consultancies, shook hands, asked for referrals from other consultants – this type of approach."

> All of our work, our client referrals, comes from attorneys. We have referred our clients to foreign attorneys and receive clients from attorneys abroad. All my Chinese clients were referred to me by Chinese attorneys in the international trade area with whom I deal, namely because the international trade market is small, not only in Brazil. It is small everywhere. Everybody knows who is who all over the world. There are very few here, very few in China. There are very few in the United States, very few in Brussels. So, everybody knows everybody. Attorneys specialized in international trade in China know who I am. They refer me to their Chinese clients. Attorneys specialized in international trade in the United States know who I am and refer me to their clients from there. And so on. There is a very well established network of contacts. Most have graduate degrees from the same places. There are people who have a graduate education, but there are also those who work in the area and know each other from conferences and law school.

Over the past few years, the importance given to building professional networks has been noticed by some Brazilian attorneys, who decided to experiment with new ways of working, using foreign models for consulting firms.[49] The clearest example is Uno Trade Strategy Advisors. Founded in 2006, Uno is based on connections between international trade attorneys from different countries (Brazil, Argentina, India, and the United States, among others).[50] It is a flexible work model in which consultants with different abilities are called in to assist companies, associations, and governments for specific cases. According to one of the interviewees, Uno is based on relationships between professionals from different parts of the world. It is a model for network-based and multidisciplinary consultancy:

> Some professionals are independent; some are partners. We have a firm here in Washington and a consultancy in Argentina. This is who we are. Now, in other parts of the world, it always [works through] partnerships and other professionals like us. What is interesting in international trade is that the legislation is the WTO, so all of our background is the WTO. All of our legal framework is there, even if each country has internalized the rules its own way. So, with my knowledge of the WTO and dumping and subsidies, I can work without much difficulty in the United States, in South Africa, in

49 See, e.g., the World Trade Advisors: http://worldtradeadvisors.com/.

50 "UNO offers a full range of consulting services related to international trade strategy: trade remedies, market access, tariff and non-tariff barriers, customs, trade creation and enhancement, capacity building, negotiations for preferential arrangements, among others. UNO is a network of multidisciplinary advisors with different professional backgrounds and nationalities, whose experience and diversity uniquely position UNO to analyze complex issues creatively and accurately, and assist governments, business associations and companies develop and implement tools for maximizing the results of their international operations."

> Europe, in Argentina, or in South Korea. What happens? Usually, there are attorneys who defend exporters who sell to Brazil, petitioners here, or there are attorneys defending our exporters in other parts of the world. So, there is this confluence of works. I may be here working in Brazil on an investigation that Argentina started against Brazil, and the basis is going to be more or less the same. What do I need to know? A lot of accounting, a lot of figures. Preparing the company to present an answer, it is good for me to have a local partner to remind me of specific deadlines there, which are different, and a contact with the authorities. Thus, we work a lot with global partnerships. We have reliable consultants in Indonesia, Thailand, South Africa, India, et cetera.

Such a consultancy model sets itself apart from traditional law firms in at least three aspects. First, consultants are not formally connected to the office, and the work is referred to as "ad hoc."[51] Second, professionals who engage in these different consulting projects work in different parts of the world and communicate electronically. Third, there is the flexibility to discontinue or suspend the professional relationship with the consulting firm at any moment, considering that these professionals work with specific projects. Therefore, such a model is different from the traditional Brazilian law firms, which mostly have stable working relationships with their attorneys (see Chapter 2).

Besides the characteristics described above, it is possible to see that the model for consulting firms specializing in international trade helps create professional networks on a global scale (Dezalay and Garth 2010), considering that the flexibility in hiring consultants from different countries allows new professionals to be referred by members already connected to the network. In other words, the existence of a network model for professional organizations generates the potential to expand existing connections among and between these professionals.

C *The Legal Profession into Government Relations*

The third important change in Brazil's legal practice in international trade is the appearance of consultancies and law firms focused on government relations (or public affairs). This phenomenon is connected with at least three factors: the fragmentation of the multilateral trade system and the strengthening of industrial and commercial defense policies; the economic destabilization

[51] According to Galanter and Palay (1994), one of the main characteristics of the organizational model at a large law firm is salary-based work and the hierarchical relationship among professionals.

resulting from the 2008 financial crisis; and, in Brazil, the modernization of trade remedies as a pillar in the Greater Brazil Plan of the Rousseff administration (Ramaswamy 2014; Kramer 2015).

Working with government relations has always existed at law firms. However, it was decentralized with no organized practice group. Conversely, this is currently coordinated, and the area is increasingly seen as important to Brazilian law, with the potential to expand to a larger number of firms seeking to solve their clients' demands. While in the United States this kind of activity is regulated, in Brazil there is still some resistance to regulating the relationship between public and private organizations, as talking about "lobbying" has a very negative connotation. Interviewees offer the idea that cooperation between the public and the private sector is something that still needs to be developed in the country. According to one interviewee:

> Government relations are directly related to trade. [T]rade . . . effectively has this contact with the government. That is where it was developed, and it is from this point on that the [law] firm also nurtures the new area for us [lawyers], which is . . . an unusual area. There are few firms where you are going to find it. My office already did it in a decentralized manner, that is, many areas have, albeit with their own attributions, a relationship with the government, but not in a coordinated, centralized way, using the Brasília teams, and that is what we started to do. And, clearly, it is an activity for the future. American firms have had government relations for much longer. It is a regulated activity in the United States, and in Brazil it is not. But we believe that at some point lobbying will be regulated, and I believe firms have to pay attention to this. This will take up some room. As for quality services, our legal knowledge is crucial in the relationship with the government due to matters of compliance, even in formulating proposals for public policies. So I think this is the side Brazil has yet to develop, right? Today very few proposals that are being discussed by our congress, or that are put forward by the executive branch – which is the driving factor behind legislation here in Brazil – come from the private sector. Thus, law firms will acquire this capacity, and I am totally against this theory that "oh, the private sector cannot . . . " You have to be hands-on. Of course, the government has to play its part in understanding whether it is something that will benefit a company or if it is beneficial from the public interest point of view. This is something else. The private sector should be the main motivator for reform and legislation proposals, but it is not.

Among some interviewees, whose firms have developed a specific area for government relations, there is the notion that public affairs will grow and that Brazil will adopt the American model to regulate lobbying.

> This is an area [government relations] I believe will tend to grow. Brazil needs to lose a little of that old feeling that it had: fear of lobbying. A law firm offers the client a guarantee that all this [government relations] will be done as ethically and as correctly as possible. Another important part that is also taking place is negotiations with governments, at different levels – municipal, state – regarding tax incentives and benefits. You are going to set up a factory somewhere – and we have been doing this a lot – a greenfield project, something new . . . we negotiate, and there was a time when there was an entire floor of our office dedicated to negotiating with several different cities, with several governments, with corporate people, who set up camp here [for] weeks, negotiating with everybody. And discussions [being held] like this: what is the package of benefits each state and municipal legislation allows, and what is each government willing to offer in order to receive a new factory with all the benefits it will bring?

Trade remedies work invariably involves government relations, according to many interviewees. In fact, there is no uniformity in their discourses regarding precise services provided, but a common aspect lawyers pay attention to is to offer a service that encompasses negotiation skills to handle the many faces of the Brazilian government, i.e., federal, state, and municipal. Negotiating, for instance, tax subsidies to implement factories, as well as more complex import and export operations that require negotiations with a federal level entity, is increasingly becoming part of these lawyers' agenda. There are also those who negotiate trade remedies tools, proposing services that require a safe conversation with government agencies. Even though professionals prepare and build up expectations to develop this market, according to some interviewees, not every agency regulating international trade is willing to maintain a conversation with the private sector and their respective representatives. The opinion of one attorney working with international trade since before Brazil opened up commercially highlights how Brazil still needs to develop intraorganizational communication mechanisms:

> Inside this area [government relations], when the government – the Ministry of Industry and Trade, the SECEX – has to make a decision . . . regarding international trade, it has to look to inside and outside. There has to be a certain balance. So, what we tell our clients who are here [in Brazil], who manufacture, who are settled, is that you [the client] cannot be anonymous. The Secretary of Foreign Trade cannot ignore you. You need to go there, . . . [and] when it does something there [inside the Secretariat's normative attributions] that will affect us here [the private sector], it needs to listen to people. This usually happens within the scope of the Ministry of Industry and Trade, and there are always those public hearings. It is important for the company to

> have a relationship, in the positive sense of being there [in the arena of communication with the government] constantly, informing the government of what it is doing, what it is investing in, where it is going to. Within the framework of the Ministry of Industry and Trade, this dialogue is very easy. But in the framework of the Ministry of Finance, it is a lot more distant. There is virtually no [contact with customs authorities]. That is, there is the customs control, the government [exists], but for you to go there and ask to speak to the [customs] authority that is working on the clearance and explaining, "Look, this is wrong because of this, this, and that," forget it. It is the "middleman" who goes there and has extremely limited access. If there is constant turnover of agents . . . regarding the decision makers, the [administrative] processes are ruled upon in other regions . . . , so there will be no contact, there is no influence. Which, on the one hand, of course, is noble in the sense of avoiding any problems with corruption, . . . but also you cannot overdo this thing [the justification to restrict communication]; on the other hand, you cannot speak with the person because presumably . . . you want to corrupt them.

There are evidences that, besides the focus on government relations offered by large law firms, consultancies specialized in trade remedies and public relations have appeared in Brazil. They offer consulting services in foreign trade focusing on accompanying investigations, adjusting to meet special customs regimes, obtaining appraisals and import licenses, just to name a few.[52] In this consulting work, obtaining clients is similar to how large law firms and network consultancies operate. In sum, the networks are crucial to forming truthful relationships with foreign clients.

Despite the different ways to work and organize international trade practice in Brazil, the narrative offered by Brazilian attorneys shows that they are strongly connected to foreign professionals and work constantly to find foreign clients, generating demand for legal services and expanding contact networks in the area. Creating desks and network consultancies corroborates

[52] Guidance offered by law firms for trade remedies and public relations is, in a certain way, related to Brazil's industrial policy and the close relationship between the executive branch and leaders from the industrial sector. As noted by Muruga Ramaswamy, given the exponential growth of China, "Brazil has reviewed its antidumping legislation and broadened the scope" (Ramaswamy 2014, 94). Behind this "modernization" there is "growing domestic pressure and an industrial lobby to rejuvenate the manufacturing sector," forcing the Brazilian government to "appeal to litigation measures such as antidumping." The reaction the Brazilian government had was to "announce its intention to use this remedy to mitigate concerns held by the domestic market" (95). Law firms have followed this trend, actively participating in lobbying through institutions, such as the IBRAC, and started offering specific services to Brazilian and foreign clients, focused on consulting for foreign trade and commercial trade.

the interpretation that globalization and the increase in cross-border transactions have modified part of the Brazilian legal profession, making it more connected to and dependent on international contacts and services. Conversely, the return of industrial policies in a postcrisis moment and pressures from applying antidumping measures to protect domestic industry have impacted the focus of work for some clients and the strategy to attract clients, whether it is Brazilian companies interested in antidumping measures or foreign companies that feel harmed by barriers blocking exports to the Brazilian market. In the end, while it is true that external factors have impacted the Brazilian legal profession, it is also noteworthy how ably and savvy Brazilian trade attorneys have been in protecting their field by expanding their connections abroad and with representatives from the government.

As shown in this chapter, international trade law in Brazil is a small legal field in which law firms compete with new "network consultancies" and consultancies specialized in governmental relations.

V CONCLUSION

The globalization of the legal profession in Brazil, particularly in the field of international trade law, comprises "multiple carefully negotiated and highly complex processes at the intersection of the local and global realms of legal activity" (Papa and Wilkins 2011, 27). The changing pattern of litigation at the WTO, the decline of the multilateral system for trade, and the rise of protectionism in a scenario of global crisis have affected how Brazilian lawyers organize themselves and how they envision their activity in this field. In fact, while this work was being written, a panel on international taxation involving Brazil – the respondent in this case – was composed at the WTO on March 26, 2015, which shows that the "WTO market" is indeed changing, but not extinct. Purposely, this case was omitted from Figure 9.1 in order to reinforce the idea of adaptation that international trade lawyers face. Currently, Brazil has able legal professionals to handle this type of dispute, and this is good news. However, such fluctuations in this legal market can make one wonder whether Brazil has trained more professionals than it needed.

Our research allows us to draw some conclusions on the nature of these changes in this field. First and foremost, the fear that Brazil could not develop legal capacity was substituted by the anxiety created by the perception that there is no room for more international trade lawyers, which is consistent with lawyers' accounts of organizational structure, innovation in the workplace, as well as the different models for rendering services that each firm offers. The low demand for litigation and dispute solution services at the WTO, an

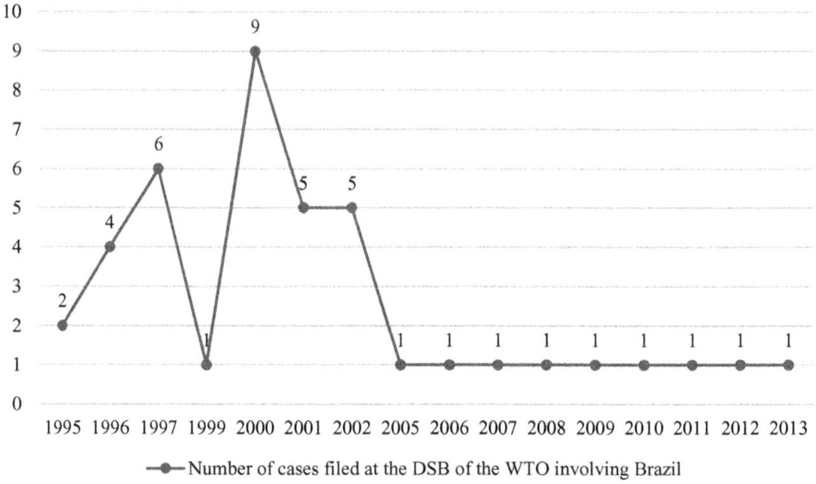

FIGURE 9.1 Brazil's participation at the DSB of the WTO (1995–2013).
Source: Prepared by the authors from WTO data.

important issue that was not covered in the previous work of Shaffer et al. (2008) and Santos (2012), had several impacts on the market recruitment to the field. Regarding law firms' structure, the services slowed down to the point where an inverted pyramid organizational model (where the cohort of skilled senior attorneys is significantly larger than the number of newcomers) has increasing relevance. In addition, although taxation and international taxation have been important areas to Brazilian law firms, the boundaries between international trade and international taxation have become "blurred," to use Sida Liu's words when he writes that globalization makes "the distinction between professional jurisdictions ambiguous" (Liu 2013, 676). To be sure, the interviewees acknowledged the necessity of having specialized teams to work on international taxation matters that arise from international trade disputes; in fact, these teams usually deal with cases brought to either the WTO or the DECOM in Brazil.

Bearing that in mind, to face the issues related to demand, attorneys started offering their services in correlated areas, such as tax law and, especially, trade remedies. They also created international desks inside big law firms and developed new organizational models, such as "network consultancies" and "government relations consultancies." These innovations should be understood as a response to a changing pattern in the field of international trade law in Brazil, namely that lawyers are working much less with WTO cases. Trade remedies, such as antidumping measures, constitute the major demand for legal work in this field – an administrative procedure that involves domestic industries injured by imports and exporters from foreign countries. This fostered a double movement inside the legal profession of trade law: a closer attention toward international clients (via desks and networks of lawyers) and governmental relations.

Finally, the interviews indicated that Brazilian lawyers have been successful not only in building legal capacity for international trade law but also in adapting it to prosper in an unstable context, changing the services they offer and seeking Brazilian and foreign clients as well as strategic partners in different ways. Instead of relying passively on demand, law firms had to prepare new types of services and reach out for clients offering an array of options. These lawyers demonstrated skills not only in the law but also in business strategy, organizational methods, and marketing. Although none were prepared for these challenges by their legal education, they developed the appropriate aptitudes and relevant contacts through a variety of strategies, which allowed them to adapt to a changing market and overcome its vicissitudes.

REFERENCES

Almeida, Mansueto. 2009. "Política Industrial e Crescimento. Instituto de Pesquisa Econômica Aplicada." *Radar: tecnologia, produção e comércio exterior. Diretoria de Estudos e Políticas Setoriais, de Inovação, Regulação e Infraestrutura*, no. 1.

Badin, Sanchez, and Michelle Ratton. 2013. "Developmental Responses to the International Trade Legal Game: Cases of Intellectual Property and Export Credit Law Reforms in Brazil." In *Law and the New Developmental State: The Brazilian Experience in Latin American Context*. Edited by David Trubek. Cambridge: Cambridge University Press.

Baldwin, Richard, and Simon Evenett. 2009. *The Collapse of Global Trade, Murky Protectionism, and the Crisis: Recommendations for the G20*. Geneva: Center for Economy Policy Research.

Bocconcelli, Roberta, and Alessandro Pagano. 2013. "Foreign Law Firms in China: The Role of Relationships and Networks" (*Accademia Italiana di Economia Aziendale* (AIDEA) Conference). www.aidea2013.it/docs/253_aidea2013_management-organization.pdf.

Bourdieu, Pierre. 1987. "The Force of Law: Toward a Sociology of the Juridical Field." *Hastings Law Journal* 38: 805–853.

Castelan, Daniel R. 2012. "O Uso de Medidas Antidumping no Brasil, na Índia e na China: características de regulação e de participação no setor privado." *IPEA – Texto para discussão*, n. 1756, Brasília. http://repositorio.ipea.gov.br/bitstream/11058/1107/1/TD_1756.pdf.

CNI. 2013. *Cartilha Antidumping*. Brasília: Confederação Nacional da Indústria. www.fiepr.org.br/cinpr/uploadAddress/Cartilha_Antidumping%5B61102%5D.pdf.

Dezalay, Yves, and Bryant Garth. 2002. *The Internationalization of Palace Wars: Lawyers, Economists and the Contest to Transform Latin American States*. Chicago: University of Chicago Press.

2010. "Marketing and Selling Transnational 'Judges' and Global 'Experts': Building the Credibility of (Quasi) Judicial Regulation." *Socio-Economic Review* 8 (1): 113–130.

Engelmann, Fabiano. 2010. "Direito e espaço econômico: a difusão do movimento Law & Economics no Brasil." *Anais do 7o Encontro da Associação Brasileira de Ciência Política*.

2012. "Globalization and State Power: International Circulation of Elites and Hierarchies in the Brazilian Legal Field." *Dados* 55 (2): 487–516.

Farhat, Saïd. 2007. *Lobby: o que é e como se faz*. São Paulo: ABERJE Editorial.

Flood, John. 2007. "Lawyers as Sanctifiers: The Role of Elite Law Firms in International Business Transactions." *Indiana Journal of Global Legal Studies* 14 (1): 35–66.

Galanter, Marc, and William Henderson. 2008. "The Elastic Tournament: A Second Transformation of the Big Law Firm." *Stanford Law Review* 60: 1867–1930.

Galanter, Marc, and Thomas Palay. 1994a. "The Many Futures of the Big Law Firms." *South Carolina Law Review* 45 (5): 905–930.

1994b. *Tournament of Lawyers: The Transformation of the Big Law Firm*. Chicago: University of Chicago Press.

Galanter, Marc, and Nick Robinson. 2013. "India's Grand Advocates: A Legal Elite Flourishing in the Era of Globalization." *International Journal of the Legal Profession* 20 (3): 1–25.

Ghirardi, José G. 2014. "O Mercado da advocacia em um mundo em transformação." *Cadernos FGV Direito Rio, A Formação da Advocacia Contemporânea* 10: 69–78.

Hapner, Paulo Afonso. 2002. *O Estado Organizacional nos Grandes Escritórios de Advocacia no Brasil: dois estudos de casa, Escola Brasileira de Administração Pública e de Empresas*. São Paulo: Fundação Getulio Vargas. http://bibliotecadigital.fgv.br/dspace/bitstream/handle/10438/3761/PauloAfonso.pdf?sequence=1&isAllowed=y.

Kramer, Cynthia. 2015. "Brazilian Trade Remedies Practice against China." In *Settlements of Trade Disputes between China and Latin American Countries*. Edited by Dan Wei. Berlin: Springer.

Krishnan, Jayanth K., and Priya Purohit. 2014. "A Common Law Court in an Uncommon Environment: The DIFC Judiciary and Global Commercial Dispute Resolution." *American Review of International Arbitration* 25: 497–534.

Leo, Sergio. 2011. "The Government Begins Modernizing Anti-dumping Rules." *Jornal Valor Econômico*, October 10. www.valor.com.br/brasil/1044186/governo-comeca-modernizar-regras-antidumping.

Liu, Sida. 2013. "The Legal Profession as a Social Process: A Theory on Lawyers and Globalization." *Law and Social Inquiry* 38 (3): 670–693.

Morgan, Glenn. 2009. "Globalization, Multinationals and Institutional Diversity." *Economy and Society* 38 (4): 580–605.

Muzio, Daniel, and James Faulconbridge. 2013. "The Global Professional Service Firm: 'One Firm' Models versus (Italian) Distant Institutionalized Practices." *Organization Studies* 34 (7): 897–925.

Papa, Mihaela, and David B. Wilkins. 2011. "Globalization, Lawyers and India: Toward a Theoretical Synthesis of Globalization Studies and the Sociology of the Legal Profession." *International Journal of the Legal Profession* 18 (3): 175–209.

Ramaswamy, Muruga. 2014. "Sino-Brazilian Trade and Antidumping Concerns." In *The Rise of the BRICS in the Global Economy: Changing Paradigms?* Edited by Vai Io Lo and Mary Hiscock. Cheltenham, UK: Edward Elgar.

Santos, Alvaro. 2012. "Carving Out Policy Autonomy for Developing Countries in the World Trade Organization: The Experience of Brazil and Mexico." *Virginia Journal of International Law* 52: 551–995.

Seixas Corrêa, Luiz F. 2005. "Apresentação." In *Vera Thorstensen & Marcos Jank. O Brasil e os Grandes Temas do Comércio Internacional*. São Paolo: Lex Editora.

Shaffer, Gregory, James J. Nedumpara, and Aseema Sinha. 2014. "Indian Trade Lawyers and the Building of State Trade-Related Legal Capacity" (research paper no. 2014–14, HLS Program on the Legal Profession, Cambridge, MA), http://ssrn.com/abstract=2401015 or http://dx.doi.org/10.2139/ssrn.2401015.

Shaffer, Gregory, Michelle Ratton Sanchez, and Barbara Rosenberg. 2008. "Trials of Winning at the WTO: What Lies behind Brazil's Success?" *Cornell International Law Journal* 41 (3): 383–501.

Thorstensen, Vera. 2009. "O Programa de Formaçao da Missão do Brasil em Genebra." In *O Brasil e o Contencioso da OMC*. Edited by M. L. Pádua Lima and B. Rosemberg. São Palao: Saraiva.

Thorstensen, Vera, Daniel Ramos, and Carolina Muller. 2013. "The 'Missing Link' between the WTO and the IMF." *Journal of International Economic Law* 16 (2): 353–381.

Trubek, David. 2013. "From Humanitarian Assistance to Professional Education: Fifty Years of the Wisconsin Law School's Engagement with the Global South." http://hosted.law.wisc.edu/wordpress/wilj/files/2013/01/Trubek.pdf.

Wilkins, David B., and Mihaela Papa. 2013. "The Rise of the Corporate Legal Elite in the BRICs: Implications for Global Governance." *Boston College Law Review* 54 (3): 1149–1184.

World Trade Organization. 2015. www.wto.org/.

10

Lawyering in New Developmentalism

Legal Professionals and the Construction of the Telecom Sector in Emerging Brazil (1980s–2010s)

Fabio de Sa e Silva and David M. Trubek

I INTRODUCTION

This book tells the story of a segment of the Brazilian legal profession – corporate lawyers – whose complexity and importance has increased as the country has experienced greater economic development and integration with the global economy. In most of the preceding chapters, we see how Brazil's changing economic structure has had an *independent* effect on the social organization of lawyering, driving changes or posing new challenges to practices and institutions that form the Brazilian corporate law sector. This chapter takes a different approach. Taking into account that the economy requires a legal basis in order to operate – and that the construction of that legal basis is heavily mediated by lawyers – it seeks to explore the role of legal professionals in constructing the new economic forms and processes that have been crucial to Brazil's pursuit of emerging economy status. It provides a thick description of the development process within which the new corporate legal elite in Brazil has grown, while examining the way this new legal elite has helped shape that very process. Instead of seeing the social organization of the law and lawyering as mere results of changes in the economy, we see them as forces that also help constitute these changes.

The chapter draws on a case study of lawyering in the telecom sector in Brazil, a sector whose trajectory in political economy resembles that of the country as a whole. After decades of state monopoly, established in the context of "old development" policies, telecom was the first sector to be privatized during the privatization drive launched in Fernando Henrique Cardoso's first presidential term (1994–1998).[1] Yet two decades later, it has become one of

[1] As we shall explain later, "old developmentalism" refers to state-led industrial development and economic growth, which prevailed in countries like Brazil in the early twentieth century, normally in authoritarian regimes.

the main provinces for civil society activism and renewed state intervention as issues like citizens' privacy and universal access to broadband Internet have become salient.[2] In the 1990s state policy favored a regime in which private companies were free to compete, subject only to limited regulation by an independent agency. In recent years, however, an additional dimension has been added as the governments of Luiz Inácio Lula da Silva and Dilma Rousseff have intervened more actively to align this sector with their industrial and social policies. How has this process taken place? What changes and continuities has it entailed? What legal challenges has it presented, and how have different actors dealt with them? What can all of this suggest about the political economy of lawyering in emerging economies like Brazil?

The chapter is divided into six sections, including this introduction. Section II situates our inquiry amid broader theoretical debates about lawyers and capitalist development in the Global South. Section III details the research design. Section IV addresses the history of the telecom sector in Brazil and the main shifts in state policy and political economy from the 1950s to the 2010s. Section V describes lawyers' engagement in four stages of that history, beginning with the fall of state monopoly, in the 1980s. Section VI discusses these findings and presents final considerations, with emphasis on the current moment.

II LAWYERS AND CAPITALIST DEVELOPMENT IN THE PERIPHERY: A REVIEW OF THE LITERATURE AND ITS PERSISTENT BLIND SPOTS

We begin by placing our inquiry into the intriguing yet little understood domain of lawyers and capitalist development in recent years. We construe this domain with support from two scholarly traditions: law, lawyers, and globalization (LLG) and law and development (L&D).[3]

[2] After the Snowden controversy, a coalition between the Brazilian government and activist groups led to the approval of groundbreaking legislation on Internet governance, Marco Civil da Internet. Known as an "Internet bill of rights," Marco Civil seeks to protect freedom of expression and privacy, as well as to promote "net neutrality," ensuring that providers will not set lower speeds for different contents or services. Beyond these demands, other groups have mobilized for the "right to broadband Internet access" under the Banda Larga é um Direito Seu (Broadband Internet Access Is Your Right) campaign.

[3] Both of these traditions stem from the law and society movement from which they draw their main premises. As such, LLG and L&D scholars (1) examine the way lawyers help fill in the gap between *law in books* and *law in action* in their interaction with ordinary people and the inner workings of institutions; (2) reject that lawyers play simply an instrumental role in these social processes, such as enunciating the objective contents of statutes and legal doctrines that should govern social relationships; and (3) understand that lawyers are deeply embedded

What we will call LLG is a body of thought pioneered by Yves Dezalay and Bryant Garth (Dezalay and Garth, 2002a, 2002b, 2011). This approach is primarily concerned with the social processes in which lawlike institutions of governance gain prominence and lawyers' professional power gets reproduced at a global scale. In particular, LLG focuses on the construction of US hegemony post–Cold War, whose twin pillars of "free markets" and "political liberalism" have in corporate law firms and NGOs the outposts of a "non-imperial empire" (Dezalay and Garth 2010; Trubek and Santos 2006; Halliday et al. 2012). This "grand transformation" began in the 1980s, with the fall of the Berlin Wall, took off in the 1990s, with the Washington consensus and the advent of neoliberal administrations, and led to massive changes in law and legal professions around the world. LLG draws on studies of recent transformations in Europe and the United States, but the focus is on "emerging economies."[4] To understand this process and how it affected and was affected by lawyers in emerging economies, LLG builds on notions like the logic of capitalist accumulation in open economies, diffusion, core-periphery relations, and the sociology of the legal profession (see Chapter 1 of this volume).

Early accounts of the role of lawyers in the grand transformation treated it as a simple one-way imposition of models from the center to the periphery, which would "modernize" the legal profession and replace a traditional elite – in the case of Brazil, "jurists" who combined family capital with part-time positions in prestigious law schools and ties with the state – with a new legal elite – lawyers with foreign education and stronger ties with global capital and philanthropy. LLG took a different approach, presenting lawyers in both the North and South as active participants in processes of diffusion. In these processes, lawyers in the South engage in collaborative initiatives that help disseminate global norm-based systems and lawlike structures of governance. But their collaboration is limited to the extent that it enhances their position in their particular "palace wars," i.e., their local struggles in the field of state power. The result is hybrid structures and what Dezalay and Garth have called "half-successful, half-failed transplants" (Dezalay and Garth 2002, 247). Examples are law school reforms in the South that empower a new intellectual elite, which, nonetheless, not only does not uphold the liberal values that reformers were expecting to see upheld but also builds on its new status to reproduce oligarchic practices in the local legal field.

in these relationships and their corresponding arrangements of power, which affect and are affected by the way they mobilize their expert knowledge and distinct professional status.

4 For a discussion of transformations in Europe, see Trubek et al. (1994).

While the LLG literature obviously contributes a lot to a critical understanding of the role of lawyers in the recent economic development in countries like Brazil, it focused on a moment in which US hegemony and its pillars were relatively uncontested. Hence, it may have limitations at a time when Brazil and other emerging economies chart new terrain, in which reinvigorated state activism and concerns with industrial development and social equality challenge the discourses and practices of development that reigned since the 1980s.

This is where the L&D literature becomes useful. Working at the intersection of economics, law, and institutional practices, L&D scholars have identified three historical moments in late capitalist development: the developmental state, the neoliberal market, and a "third moment," which they have devoted themselves to exploring in further detail (Trubek and Santos 2006; Trubek et al. 2014a; Trubek et al. 2014b).

The original "developmental state," whose existence generally correlated with authoritarian regimes, emphasized state-led industrialization and economic growth via protection of domestic industries and direct state participation in economic production via state-owned enterprises (SOEs). In this context, legal developments were supposed to organize state intervention and enhance bureaucratic capacity. The "neoliberal market," which was built in the wake of the Washington consensus, emphasized private transactions and property rights. Now, legal developments were supposed to constrain state intervention and enable the working of private businesses. The "third moment" builds on the critique of both the developmental state and the neoliberal market periods. It emphasizes concerns with social equality and democracy, absent in the "developmental state," as well as new forms of state-market collaboration, absent in neoliberalism. Thus, in this "third moment," legal developments are expected to enable public participation in state planning and decision making, as well as to articulate new ("experimental") forms of economic production across the state-market divide (Trubek and Santos 2006; Trubek et al. 2014a; Trubek et al. 2014b). Yet, whereas the L&D literature moves toward postneoliberal theories and practices of economic development, it fails to incorporate an analysis of how these theories and practices impact – and are impacted by – legal professionals (Deakin et al. 2015). Up to this point, all that it has tried to do is to establish a general relationship between "the law" and the policy repertoire of this "third moment."

This chapter explores the gaps in these literatures (Table 10.1). In particular, we wish to apply the approach of LLG to the scenario explored through L&D. We understand that this may produce descriptions and explanations for new forms of professional engagement, which can feed back into both of those

TABLE 10.1 *Traditions of inquiry on lawyers and capitalist development*

Tradition	Claims	Gaps
LLG	• Lawyers are active participants in recent economic transitions. • This takes place not through foreign imposition of norms and practices but rather through North–South collaborations to sustain institutional transplants relevant to hegemonic projects. • Lawyers engage in these processes because and to the extent that they enhance their position in their particular "palace wars."	• Focuses on the construction of neoliberal hegemony
L&D	• Examines different moments in the theories and practices of development • Discusses the role of law in these moments • Distinguishes among three different moments: old developmentalism, neoliberalism, and a "third moment"	• Does not include the legal profession in its analysis

theoretical traditions by making either their accounts more comprehensive or the questions they ask more accurate. The next section details the empirical strategy employed.

III RESEARCH DESIGN: A CASE STUDY ON TELECOM IN BRAZIL

To explore these gaps, we conducted an exploratory case study of the transformation of the telecom sector in Brazil. In addition to extensive reviews of the literature and collection of secondary data, our research included fieldwork activities in Brazil in 2014 and 2015. We conducted in-depth interviews with lawyers and nonlawyers who deal with telecom in a variety of settings, including the corporate bar, government agencies, nongovernmental organizations (NGOs), and academia. The purpose was to obtain a multiperspectival, thick description of (1) the developments of the telecom sector, especially in the period since state-owned telecom services were privatized in the 1990s and (2) the way corporate lawyers have participated in this process (Oberman 2013; Nielsen 2014).

We chose telecoms to explore the interrelation of LLG and L&D because we had access to the sector and thought it would offer a microcosm of changes

TABLE 10.2 *Sample for in-depth interviews*

Government sector		Legal profession		Civil society	Specialists	
Executive (GOV)	Regulatory (REG)	Firm lawyers (LAW)	In-house (IHC)	NGOs (NGO)	(SPE)	Total
4	5	7	3	2	4	
N = 9		N = 10		N = 2	N = 4	N = 25

going on in many sectors in Brazil. As telecom was the first sector to be privatized in the 1990s and encompasses services that are relevant to several aspects of modern life, it has experienced the changes and continuities in the Brazilian political economy and development models in great intensity.

Fieldwork was structured in three steps. First, after reviewing the literature, we selected key individuals for preliminary conversations. Second, we developed, tested, and updated our interview protocol with some of these individuals. This protocol had two kinds of questions. On the one hand, we wanted interviewees to narrate their experience with telecom and the changes they had seen in it over time. On the other hand, we wanted interviewees to place legal professionals, their practices, and ideologies within that overarching narrative.[5] Finally, we conducted successive rounds of data collection with additional informants. While we have selected these informants through techniques like snowball and the literature review itself, we made sure that crucial variables were observed, such as years of experience in the sector and workplace setting.

In total, our research involved twenty-five interviews, divided according to Table 10.2, which also includes the coding scheme used to refer to interviewees throughout our text (firm lawyers will be referred to as LAW-1, LAW-2, etc.). These conversations generally took about two hours each, and when they were not audiotaped, the researchers took extensive notes. Analysis followed the basic standards of case studies, with qualitative coding of the transcripts and triangulation across interviews and other sources of secondary data. The subsequent sections present the main findings.

[5] By ideology we do not mean a false consciousness of reality, as in traditional Marxist thinking. Rather, we refer to processes of meaning creation that permeate concrete struggles for power (Ewick and Silbey 1998; Silbey 2005). As such, we see that ideologies as forces that constitute the legal profession and its role in society (Nelson and Trubek 1992). For some the meanings that lawyers give to their own work eventually "become part of the material and discursive systems that limit and constrain future meaning making," as it is clear, for example, in Bourdieu's notion of *habitus* (Silbey 2005, 333–334).

IV THE POLITICAL ECONOMY OF THE TELECOM SECTOR IN BRAZIL: THREE STYLIZED MOMENTS (1950S–2010S)

For the purpose of this section, *political economy* means an area of inquiry and practice that deals with the relationship between (1) decisions about the allocation of scarce resources and the production of wealth at the state-nation level, and (2) the social, political, cultural, institutional, and eventually legal forces that enable and/or constrain these decisions (Weingast and Wittman 2008; Mosco 2009; Ramos 2010).

Consistently with this approach, this section places the construction of the telecom sector in Brazil in the long history of the country's struggle to grow as a modern, industrial economy. Drawing from the available literature, as well as from interviews, we highlight three moments in that trajectory: the rise and fall of state-owned telecoms (Section IVA); global restructuring, neoliberalism, and privatization (Section IVB); and the rise of a new developmental state (Section IVC).

A *The Rise and Fall of State-Owned Telecoms (Late 1930s–Late 1980s)*

Brazil experienced a rather late process of industrialization. Starting after the 1929 crash, the country took a route later known as *import substitution industrialization.* This included both trade protection for domestic industries and stronger state activism in the economy (Bolaño 2003; Furtado 2007; Tavares 2011). Import tariffs were raised, local currency devalued, and excesses in commodity production purchased by the state, thus sustaining demand and creating capital that could be used for industrial investments by domestic capital owners. Also, the state itself became an economic agent, whether by getting directly involved in basic industry, such as in steel and oil via the SOEs Volta Redonda and Petrobras, or by funding investment projects in heavy infrastructure via the national investment bank BNDES.

During this period, telecom services were rather fragmented. Multiple levels of government were entitled by law to grant permission for telecom companies to operate. More than 900 different companies handled telecom services in the country, with poor integration and no overarching regulation or even minimum coordination in aspects such as tariffs, coverage, and interconnectivity among different networks (Almeida 1998; Bolaño 2003; Aranha 2005; Pieranti 2011; Braz 2014).[6]

[6] Because tariffs were under the control of subnational governments, sometimes companies would be forced to keep them low, which frequently led to financial deficits. Lack of coordination or regulation on coverage and interconnectivity caused some parts of the countries to experience complete shutdowns now and then.

By the 1950s Brazil had become a full-scale industrial economy, with capacity to produce both consumption and capital goods. It became clear that the structural insufficiencies in telecom would be a barrier for further development. Accordingly, João Goulart, who became president in 1961, took measures to restructure this sector. In 1962 he passed an innovative Code of Telecommunications.[7] The code gave the federal government the authority over interstate and international services, as well as over "trunks" that would create nationwide service integration. It also gave the federal government power to plan and coordinate development of the sector via a steering committee called CONTEL, as well as to put together an SOE to operate in the sector and pursue new policy goals (Almeida 1998; Bolaño 2003; Aranha 2005; Pieranti 2011; Braz 2014).

Amid promises of furthering structural economic reforms, namely in agrarian ownership, and escalation of Cold War fears against communism in Latin America, Goulart's term was suddenly interrupted by the civil-military coup of 1964.[8] While the authoritarian regime that followed initially embraced an orthodox economic agenda, after 1967 it shifted toward development policies similar to import substitution. The result was the "Brazilian miracle," a time period when the country grew considerably and made progress in new industrial sectors.[9]

Telecom evolved accordingly. While there were debates in the cabinet as to whether the state should get involved in the sector, nationalist forces

[7] Months before Goulart was elected, then president Jânio Quadros had suspended the activities of *Radio Jornal do Brasil* – which was technically possible to do on the basis of existing law – in response to critiques broadcasted against his government. Hence, private companies handling radio-TV services saw the code as an opportunity to obtain protection from governments. In the meantime, military studies on issues relevant to national security had been critical about the fragmented structure of Brazilian telecom and thus supported the code's centralizing philosophy. Goulart vetoed some provisions of the code, trying to increase government power over the sector. Yet his vetoes were struck down by Congress given the power of radio-TV companies' lobbying, a fact of which the Brazilian political elite of the 1990s will seem to be mindful when it goes about restructuring the system again (Pieranti 2011, 27–34).

[8] Following contemporary discussions about this period, namely in the transitional justice community, we prefer to use the term *civil-military*, rather than just *military*. This is to emphasize the prominent role that civil forces played in the coup and in the subsequent phases of the government, which the term *military* tends to conceal.

[9] Yet this came along with aggravated inequality and lack of democracy and respect for civil rights. Then-minister Antônio Delfim Netto became famous for stating that Brazil would "let the cake grow first so that when it is big enough, everybody can have his own piece," which obviously never really happened. Also, recent initiatives such as the Truth Commission have documented the systematic use of torture and violence against individuals and groups who were supposed to be dissenters of the regime, about which there has been little accountability so far.

concerned with economic development and security prevailed.[10] In 1965, President Castelo Branco (1964–1967) established Embratel, an SOE that would create interstate integration and handle international telecom services. In 1967 the federal government established the Ministry of Communications (MINICOM) and centralized authority over all telecom services. In 1972 it established Telebras, a holding SOE that began a drive to merge all the small companies operating in the sector into state-level SOEs that Telebras controlled. This created a single, integrated network under public ownership. Finally, in 1975 the government established the Centro de Pesquisa e Desenvolvimento Tecnologico (Center for Technological Research and Development, or CPqD), a public R&D unit that would lead projects in areas relevant to telecom (Almeida 1994; Pereira Filho 2002; Bolaño 2003; Aranha 2005; Pieranti 2011; Braz 2014).

This state-owned telecom sector did remarkably well. From 1975 to 1985, landline phones went from 2 million to 12.4 million, while teledensity went from 1.9 to 8.1 landline phones/100,000 habitants. CPqD became one of the top five R&D units in telecom in the entire world (Almeida 1994; Bolaño 2003; Aranha 2005; Pieranti 2011; Braz 2014). But demand was growing at an even faster pace, and by the late 1970s, when Brazil faced severe financial strain, prospects for the sector became extremely negative.

By the late 1980s, when Brazil was beginning its transition to democracy, the telecom sector was falling apart.[11] Services were scarce and outdated, and the Telebras system was highly underfunded.[12] The breakdown in state monopoly and possible participation of private companies in the sector had become part of the conversation, and every government would try to find a way to increase private participation. In the mid-1990s, one would succeed.

[10] According to Oliveira, "When Castelo Branco's term (1964–1967) began, an executive decree had been issued creating Embratel, but within the government there were two visions for telecom: some wanted to create Embratel, as the code ruled; others thought Embratel shouldn't be created and a private company, perhaps foreign, should be called to do this job. What did Castelo do? He said: 'I'm going to suspend this.' I can't figure out who gave him this idea. But a year after that (and amid struggles in the cabinet), Castelo made up his mind. He said: 'This is over. We are going to do what is in the law. We are going to create Embratel.' When he said that, [Jose Claudio] Beltrão [Frederico] (a navy officer and CONTEL's president at the time, who favored the private company solution) wrote a letter of resignation saying he didn't agree with that" (Oliveira 2005, 78–79).

[11] An anecdote from 1994 illustrates these difficulties as they persisted: When the Brazilian team was playing the World Cup semifinals against Holland, hundreds of people were photographed standing in line in front of the Pacaembu Stadium in São Paulo. All that sacrifice was to apply for a landline phone, for which they would pay US$1,200 in two years, hoping that by the end of that period, they would be able to get it (Pieranti 2011, 215).

[12] This was partly because of the public nature of Telebras, which allowed some of its returns to be directed to fund other government activities at a time when the external debt crisis was squeezing state expenditures of all kinds.

B *Global Restructuring, Neoliberalism, and Telecom Privatization in Peripheral Brazil (1980s–1990s)*

In the late 1980s Brazil had a lot on its plate other than the problems in telecom. It had to deal with high levels of public debt, a low rate of growth, and high levels of inequality. But there was international pressure to open the telecom market. With telecom becoming more strategic for both economic and political reasons, core countries, especially the United Kingdom and the United States, made major changes in their telecom sectors to expand coverage, modernize infrastructure, and reinforce leadership in R&D (Bolaño 2003).[13]

These changes led to oligopolies, in which national champions (private or SOEs) normally played a key role. As these companies faced saturation of their local markets and needed to obtain greater returns on their investment, they began to look for opportunities overseas. This move was supported by home governments, which began demanding global liberalization in telecom services. There was growing diplomatic activity in international organizations like the United Nation's International Telecommunication Union (ITU).[14] In the early 1980s, ITU's predominant philosophy had emphasized national sovereignty over telecom networks and was critical of privatization. In 1988 the United States and the United Kingdom lobbied aggressively for a more open stance by this organization regarding global competition and private participation in the sector, and by 1991 ITU had begun to support the view that developing countries should restructure their telecom sectors along those lines.[15] Meanwhile, telecom services in Brazil kept deteriorating, and

[13] With chains of industrial production and circulation of financial capital fragmented and spread, fast worldwide technological changes made telecom a crucial component to reduce costs and increase efficiency. When it became crystal clear, as White House policy advisor Zbigniew Brzezinski stated in 1974, that "world domination would no longer take place through armies, but rather through networks" (Bolaño 2003, 5), core countries felt pushed to restructure telecom to keep and expand their relative economic power. And telecom became part of yet another structural transformation in modern societies: the constitution of a new public sphere. Similarly to what TV represented in the welfare state, new technologies in telecom provided the means through which public opinion was to be formed, strategic decisions in politics and business were to be made, and a growing variety of products and services was to be globally advertised and commercialized (Bolaño 2003).

[14] On the role of the World Bank in promoting the same agenda, see Ismail (2006).

[15] Braz (2014, 134) explains that at this time another United Nations agency, UNESCO, had published the so-called McBride Report, which "acknowledged unequal access to information and communication, reinforced the importance of communications for national sovereignty and development, criticized the concentration in the media, and urged nations to regulate and implement policies for the communications sector." Disagreeing with the report, the United States, the United Kingdom, and Japan left UNESCO, while increasing their diplomatic investments in the ITU.

solutions to improve Telebras's finances, like cross-subsidy between local and long-distance calls, were proving to be dysfunctional for the company and the larger economy (Almeida 1994; Bolaño 2003; Aranha 2005; Pieranti 2011; Braz 2014).

There had been earlier attempts to hand telecom services to the private sector, but these were either dropped from the government agenda or successfully blocked by Telebras workers and nationalist activists (Dalmazo 2002).[16] However, in 1994, Cardoso was elected president with an explicit promise of opening up telecom to the private sector. Cardoso appointed his close friend, Sergio Motta, thus far a relatively unknown figure, as his minister of communications. Motta – nicknamed "Tractor" for his ability to get things done, "running over" his opponents if necessary – took on that challenge.[17]

Motta was facing a more favorable context than his predecessors.[18] Cardoso had a solid basis in Congress, Telebras lacked public support, and even its workers and traditional allies felt they would no longer be able to block government initiatives to liberalize the sector. In fact, some of them had already agreed that participation of private capital was the only hope for the sector. Internationally, the so-called Washington consensus was in full swing, and organizations like the IMF and the World Bank were requesting indebted developing countries to go through structural adjustments to have access to their credit programs. In plain words, this meant reducing government expenditures and public deficits, privatizing existing SOEs, and making local economies more open for global capital (Almeida 1994; Dalmazo 2002; Bolaño 2003; Aranha 2005; Pieranti 2011; Braz 2014).[19]

[16] In 1987, in what became known as the Victorigate, MINICOM announced that Brazil would open up its market for satellite communications. Yet this would be particularly beneficial to the Victori Communications S/A multinational, which had the Brazilian media group Organizações Globo as one of its primary investors. This caused strong reaction from Embratel workers and administrators, and the minister had to take back his word. Similar tensions and critical events took place in 1988, before and during the constitutional assembly; 1991, with attempts to hand B band cellular phone services in to private companies; and 1993, during a constitutional reform assembly.

[17] For more about Motta and his days at the office, see Prata et al. (1999).

[18] Then again, Motta and Cardoso were careful enough not to signal that they were considering privatizing the Telebras system until that decision was finally made. Dalmazzo shows that during his presidential campaign, Cardoso had said he was only going to make state monopoly "more flexible." Braz shows that in eight months Motta made three different public statements about his plans for the sector, none of which reflected what ultimately happened.

[19] From this perspective, the Washington Consensus actually implied a form of "technocratic" expertise, in which a science-like approach to economic development predicted that attraction of foreign capital in developing countries would cause them to flourish. This causal narrative provided legitimacy for institutional reforms focused on removing barriers for global capital in the 1990s (Gupta 2015).

After securing a constitutional amendment that broke the state monopoly over telecom services, Motta and his staff began to discuss alternatives for the sector. While several options were available that would maintain some role for Telebras in the sector, Motta and his staff took a different approach.[20] Braz reports that in 1995 MINICOM signed a multi-million-dollar agreement with ITU to obtain technical assistance to restructure the sector.[21] Through this agreement, ITU would hire consulting firms and legal professionals who would provide decision makers with policy solutions and legislative drafts.

Braz demonstrates that the consulting firms hired had been central producers of theories and solutions aligned with the Washington consensus. Hence, he argues, the very presence of ITU and these firms in the restructuring process in Brazil was a sign of the script decision makers were to follow: Telebras would be sold off; the government would collect a considerable amount of capital with this sale, thus reducing the fiscal deficit;[22] and a new structure of

[20] Maculan and Legey (1996) analyzed parallel experiences internationally and encountered a vast spectrum of possibilities for regulation and governance of the sector after privatization. In debates specific to the Brazilian context, Telebras workers were embracing the Brazil telecom project, in which Telebras would be reorganized and subject to regulated competition against other entrants in the market while remaining a public company. Others agreed with the transferring of Telebras ownership to the private sector, but claimed that the Brazilian state should hold golden shares, which it could use to promote national and strategic interests within the resulting company (Dalmazo 2002; Braz 2014).

[21] This agreement was first signed in 1996, with a budget of $US5.1 million, then was renewed in 1997 with an updated budget of $US16.6 million (Braz 2014, 154, 159).

[22] Analysts find that maximizing returns in the sale auctions of the Telebras system was an essential concern of the government. Consequences were twofold: several obstacles to investment were removed, while other developmental objectives were deemphasized. For example, when the restructuring process began, the government artificially distinguished between radio-TV and other telecom services, while channeling all of its efforts to restructure the latter. This avoided political disputes (and the consequent delay) that would emerge if this whole package were subject to review, as what happened in the legislative process related to the 1962 Code. In addition, prior to selling Telebras, Cardoso created the Programa de Recuperação e Ampliação do Sistema de Telecomuniçãcoes e do Sistema Postal (Program for Recuperation and Expansion of the Telecom and Postal Systems, or PASTE), which heightened investments in telecom. This lowered future costs of telecom's infrastructure, making the sector more attractive for prospective investors (Almeida 1998). Also, the state actively participated in the privatization process by funding private consortiums put together to purchase fragments of the Telebras system. This financing was provided by the Brazilian Development Bank at below-market interest rates, which again increased the perspective of high returns and made private investment in Brazil more attractive (Braz 2014). Finally, Telebras was reorganized into twelve smaller companies, each one with jurisdiction over a region and with permit to explore a certain kind of service. In this division, the highly populated and industrialized state of São Paulo was treated as a region in itself. São Paulo could have been placed in a region with less developed states or cities, which would be sure to be served by a vigorous provider. Yet this would likely reduce the market value of São Paulo, something that Motta and his team, briefed by consulting firms, would not agree to.

telecom regulation and governance, much more friendly to foreign capital, would be erected,[23] thus driving a larger process of change in the Brazilian state.

With this inspiration, the restructuring of the Brazilian telecom sector evolved at a fast pace. In less than three years, Motta and Cardoso proposed and passed (1) a constitutional amendment breaking the state monopoly over telecom services in 1995, (2) a minimum law enabling participation of private companies in B band cellular phone services in 1996, and, finally, (3) a comprehensive reform in the sector via the Lei Geral de Telecomunicações (General Communications Act, or LGT), in 1997. This reform had two main components: (1) establishing new, more market-friendly legal regimes to govern telecom services and (2) creating an independent agency to regulate the sector.[24]

In April 1998, Motta died, but his widow was invited to participate in the celebration of the sale of Telebras.[25] Not long after, the promises and perils of telecom in postprivatization Brazil would become visible. State-market boundaries had been dramatically redefined, and private companies were now fully responsible for handling these services. The demand was being met more easily; and other services and technologies – namely cellular phones in prepaid plans – were spreading rapidly.[26] Yet, tariffs actually increased, and – as

[23] In 1996 and 1997, Motta led a series of "road shows" about Brazil's telecoms. These were "gatherings with international businessmen carefully selected" in which Motta would "give presentations on the economic reforms undertaken in the country over the last five years . . . and talk about the context and the recent changes in telecom services in the country." They took place in Tokyo, New York City, London, Frankfurt, Paris, and Lisbon. President Cardoso himself joined Motta in Tokyo and Paris (Braz 2014, 153).

[24] For details about these components, see Sections IVB and IVD.1.

[25] She was photographed along with President Cardoso and the new minister of communications Luiz Carlos Mendonça de Barros, holding the symbolic hammer used in the bid auction in which the Telebras system was handed in to private capital. Later on, Barros and other officials, such as BNDES president André Lara Resende and President Cardoso himself, were caught on taped conversations discussing measures to put together the Telemar consortium. Telemar had purchased segments of the Telebras system with jurisdiction over the North-Northeast regions of Brazil, according to the regional divisions through which the system was reorganized. In these conversations, Cardoso authorized Barros to speak on his own behalf to Telemar representatives, with promises of BNDES funding for the acquisition of the regional company. Except for Cardoso, all the other individuals involved resigned from their positions in government.

[26] But see Cavalcante (2011, 8–9): "Some argue that telecom services have been democratized, as there is virtually universal access to cellular phone services in the country. However, this is not a simple equation . . . since it does not mean that people communicate effectively through these cellular phones for communication, which in fact can be more accurately compared to 'portable pay phones.' The main indicator of this is the great discrepancy between postpaid and prepaid plans in the country. In 2009, out of the 175 million users of cell phone services, 143.6

telecom had essentially become a market good – access to these services was contingent on ability to pay.[27] Also, the sector was being denationalized: the preference for attracting global capital in the privatization process led to domination of the sector by foreign multinationals. Finally, the new telecom structure in Brazil seemed to reinforce the technological gap between the country and central economies. With growing reliance on foreign multinationals and diminished state-owned infrastructure to conduct bold R&D initiatives, Brazil could likely lag behind developed countries, with short- and long-term implications for its development trajectory. In Bolaño's words:

> Here lies a paradox, for although users, consumers have had access to the products of revolutionary changes in telecom, Brazil seems to have lost its capacity to learn and internalize technological progress, which it had in the context of the old Telebras system and its connections with CPqD and local universities, which even made Brazil become an exporter of technology in telecom. What we have these days, on the contrary, is an accelerated growth of imports in components, equipment, and final products, which increase the trade deficit in the sector. (Bolaño 2003, 3)

In 2002, as this model matured and contradictions became more apparent,[28] metalworker and Workers' Party leader Luiz Inácio Lula da Silva was elected president. Internationally, the winds of the Washington consensus had weakened amid economic stagnation and high rates of unemployment in peripheral economies. It was a fertile time for new philosophies and practices in development. Would Brazil face the challenges of this new moment? Would that have any impact on the telecom sector? If so, what kind of impact would that be?

million had prepaid plans (i.e., 82.55 percent). This is a form of reversed subsidy, for those who can pay less have greater expenses with phone services, while the 'good consumers' – people with higher income and big businesses – have plans with free-of-charge devices and low tariffs."

27 As we explain later, landline phone services providers must meet obligations of universalizing these services. However, this has been understood as expanding the number of landlines, installing and maintaining pay phones, and meeting standards of accessibility for people with disabilities. There have been no initial requirements, for example, that cheaper services be provided to low-income families, which in fact was seen as inconsistent with a model of regulated competition. (For a critique of this policy choice, see Coutinho 2005.)

28 This claim went beyond the political left. Rhodes reports that in 1998, Delfim Netto, the right-wing intellectual and former minister noted earlier, commented, "Brazilian consumers didn't realize the high prices they were paying, and concessionaries were not meeting their obligations. As long as this went on . . . , Brazil would continue to be a prisoner of the 'neocolonialist worshippers of the free-market God' and would not become a 'global player'" (Rhodes 2006, 162).

C *Telecom and the New Developmental State in Then-Emerging Brazil (2003–2010)*

The trajectory of telecoms[29] under Lula follows a pattern that can be seen in other areas like economic policy (Barbosa and Souza 2010; Teixeira and Pinto 2012; Trubek et al. 2014a; Trubek et al. 2014b) and social policy (Campello and Neri 2013; Coutinho 2014; Rego and Pinzani 2014). Tension between transformative expectations and structural constraints led to a more or less painful, more or less successful process of learning.

In fact, Lula's first years in office caused much political malaise and institutional tension in telecom. Along with Miro Teixeira (Rede-RJ), the minister initially appointed to MINICOM, Lula inherited a market-based system (Bolaño and Massae 2000; Mattos and Coutinho 2005). Private companies were the sole providers of telecom services; an independent regulatory agency, ANATEL, oversaw and adjudicated issues related to these services; and the laws governing the sector and informing the agency's activity stressed minimum constraints to competition. Hence, the federal executive had very limited capacity to redefine the objectives and means for development of the sector.

Lula and Teixeira were critical about this institutional structure and challenged it when they could. In reference to ANATEL, Lula once said that Cardoso had "subcontracted the business of governing."[30] In 2003 there was fierce debate about rates for landline phone services contracts (Mattos 2003). ANATEL had authorized rate increases, but consumer protection groups and federal policymakers deemed them too high. They argued that these rates had become distorted and would contribute to inflation.[31] Facing these

[29] From now on in this chapter, we will refer to telecom in the narrower sense of the LGT, i.e., as structurally separated from radio-TV and the multimedia complex. This is because radio-TV and multimedia have raised other discussions, proposals, and tensions within Lula's and Dilma's (left-wing) governments in aspects like economic and political concentration of media ownership, content-rating systems, and public interest obligations by media vehicles. While these are all fascinating issues – and the always artificial distinction between telecom and radio-TV is blurry at a time of fast technological convergence – they unfortunately extrapolate the objectives of this article.

[30] "Lula Criticizes Agencies and Says He Will Make Changes," *Folha de São Paulo*, February 2, 2003, A1, Edição São Paulo ("'Brazil was subcontracted. Agencies rule the country,' said Lula at a lunch with congressional leaders. The president complained that he learns about increases in tariffs through the newspapers: 'Decisions that affect the people are not made by the government,'" A4).

[31] Teixeira proposed that "the adjustment would be according to a consumer price index (IPCA) instead of a general price index (IGP-DI). The consumer price index indicated inflation of 17 percent, while the general price index was indicating a rate of 32 percent. The proposal, however, encountered fierce resistance even inside the government because some believed

challenges, ANATEL stuck with the rates previously agreed upon with the companies. Teixeira gave a speech declaring that he could not do much about it but that ANATEL was wrong and consumers should go to court to get the rates reviewed. The *Ministerio Público*, the Brazilian prosecutorial agency whose mandate includes protecting the "public interest," built on the minister's suggestion and filed a lawsuit. Federal courts gave a preliminary injunction, which prevented ANATEL from applying higher rates.

ANATEL defended its position before these courts and was eventually successful. Yet this episode left extreme mistrust between ANATEL and the federal executive. Lula sent to Congress a draft bill seeking to reduce the power of regulatory agencies vis-à-vis the federal executive. While this draft bill never went to floor deliberation, in June 2003 Lula signed executive decree no. 4.733, through which he began to reestablish government control of the telecom sector by defining "social inclusion" and "industrial development" as key objectives for telecom policies and by requiring the agency to implement cost-based methods to assess tariffs in landline phone services. In January 2004, the president of ANATEL resigned and left the agency, even though he was entitled by the law to keep a position on the board of directors until November 2005.

Although Lula appointed another president to ANATEL, he was still not able to fully overcome the existing institutional constraints and change the course of the sector. Initial signals of change appeared in 2006, when a renovated board of directors at the agency began to ask for "counterpart obligations" when examining requests filed by the companies in areas other than landline phones. These obligations, which were presented by the agency as a "precondition" to grant the requests, generally related to objectives of social inclusion, such as making coverage or technologies available to poor communities. Companies did not like this new regulatory rationale, but ANATEL continued to use it anyway. IHC-3 describes these changes in the following terms:

> In the past, we would file requests before ANATEL, and they would look at whether or not our requests were in accord with the law. Then they began to introduce counterpart obligations. For example, we wanted to provide satellite TV services. We filed the related request for authorization. They said:

that it would imply breaching statutory provisions and concession contracts. The president then presented a new proposal limiting the 2003 increases to 17 percent and rolling over the remaining percentage to the next three years... ANATEL, however, did not accept the government's proposal" (Prado 2008, 455–456). Aranha adds: "In an appeal to the Supreme Court... companies even declared that they would give up the difference between the indexes if the court revoked the preliminary injunction" (Aranha 2008, 17).

"We approve it if you accept a counterpart obligation in the benefit of society, which involves installing satellite TV antennas in schools, poor communities, etc." We thought: "No way we can do this. If we accept, they will place these preconditions in all our requests. We have a right to obtain these authorizations." But we did.

In 2007 another series of events led to further changes (Peixoto 2010; Pena et al. 2012; Aranha 2015). It all began with Lula reaching out to one of his closest advisors with a request for ideas to connect public schools to the Internet. According to this former government official (GOV-2):

> Lula thought it was unacceptable that we were entering the twenty-first century and our kids going to public schools were growing digitally illiterate. He had discussed that with his ministers of communications and education, but he thought this was not going to go much further without coordination from the presidency. It is always difficult to do things that involve two authorities; there is always too much conflict, too much disagreement, too much dispute for leadership. I didn't even work with anything related to that, but he asked me to take the lead on it and I committed myself to doing so.[32]

To understand what comes next and how it furthers changes in telecom regulation and governance, we must have in mind that the concession contracts the companies had signed with the government imposed certain obligations as a condition of the authorization to operate landline services. One of these obligations was to work toward universal citizen access, which was defined in periodic universalization plans issued by the government after public discussions led by ANATEL. Initially, these plans called on the companies to install pay phones throughout the country. Later Lula expanded this obligation to include multiservice stations that added fax and dial-up Internet.[33]

[32] Political reasons may also have contributed to strengthen this concern with expanding Internet access. For example, GOV-4 argues that, although there had been crucial tensions in the field of communications policy during the first Lula administration, "the majority of the government had not understood how strategic communications are. And I understand that this began to change after [the corruption scandal referred to as] *Mensalão*. At that point, the government realized that there was a mainstream media discourse, against the government and highly disseminated, and that there were not alternative voices around. This was more or less at the end of Lula's first term. Then he gets reelected and brings [journalist and left-wing activist in the 1960s] Franklin Martins to his cabinet… and Martins transforms communications into a public problem."

[33] GOV-2 commented: "We began to understand how the telecom sector worked and realized that there were periodic reviews of obligations with universalizing landline telecom services, which companies should meet as part of their concession contracts. In 2003 we had a first review of this plan, and MINICOM began a conversation about introducing obligations related to installation and maintenance of multiservice telecom stations. These should offer

By 2008, it was clear that multiservice stations were both expensive and obsolete. The companies approached ANATEL and offered to replace them with "backhaul," an infrastructure for Internet connection.[34] ANATEL appreciated this proposal, as it would make broadband Internet available to 3,439 municipalities by December 2010 (Duarte and Silva 2009). But Lula's advisor and his aides saw these conversations as an opportunity to get more. They approached ANATEL and the companies and demanded that the exchange also involve an obligation to provide free broadband Internet services to 56,865 public schools by that same deadline. Companies initially resisted this solution, dubbed the Banda Larga nas Escolas (Broadband Internet in Schools) project, but ultimately agreed to it.[35]

Other than yielding such innovative policy solutions, the making of Banda Larga nas Escolas helped mobilize several groups with transformative ideas about telecom within Lula's administration. As it emerges from our exchange with that same former advisor (GOV-2):

INTERVIEWER: So if I understood it correctly, it was the president's call for making broadband Internet access available to public schools that challenged people at ANATEL and MINICOM to engage in discussions about expanding Internet access in the country.

INTERVIEWEE: I wouldn't say that ANATEL and MINICOM were not engaged in these discussions, but the visions they had were much more moderate than ours, I mean, than the visions we had at the presidential office.

INTERVIEWER: I guess what I'm trying to understand is how such a narrowly constructed demand, i.e., getting Internet to schools, triggered a much broader process, in which the government began to understand the Internet and the expansion of Internet-related infrastructure as something strategic.

INTERVIEWEE: Well, it did not "pop" like this either. It came through the president's demand, but it also resonated with our people in telecom, those who

not just access to pay phones but also to services like fax, dial-up (dial-up!) Internet, etc. In 2006 we had a second review of the plan and included these stations."

34 "*Backhaul* is the telecommunications industry term that refers to connections between a core system and a subsidiary node. An example of backhaul is the link between a network – which could be the Internet or an internetwork that can connect to the Internet – and the cell tower base stations that route traffic from wireless to wired systems" (Moore 2013, 19). "Visualizing the entire hierarchical network as a human skeleton, the core network would represent the spine, the backhaul links would be the limbs, the edge networks would be the hands and feet, and the individual links within those edge networks would be the fingers and toes" (http://itlaw.wikia.com/wiki/Backhaul).

35 Civil society organizations were also skeptical about these solutions, anticipating issues that would come up later. Since the resistance of both companies and civil society organizations refer to technical-legal issues, we will get back to their specific terms later in this chapter.

conceived the multiservice stations back in 2006 ... unionists, researchers, former Telebras and Embratel workers. This process allowed us to gather all these people ... and build on their expertise and their lifelong activism.

In 2009, Lula built on this momentum to strengthen the authority of the executive branch vis-à-vis both the independent regulator and the companies increased. In that year, he signed executive decree no. 6.948, establishing the presidential Comitê Gestor do Programa de Inclusão Digital (Managing Committee for Digital Inclusion), or CGPID. This reinforced the ability of his advisors to influence developments in the telecom sector. In 2009–2010, ANATEL and MINICOM began to draft a new universalization plan for landline phone services. Influenced by the ideas nurtured at the CGPID, they decided to further what they had begun with Banda Larga nas Escolas. Now they wanted to have companies install and run backhaul in all Brazilian municipalities. Moreover, they wanted this expanded Internet infrastructure to have greater capacity than that required in 2008 and be available to be used by governmental organizations for public businesses.[36]

Companies reacted aggressively against this proposal, raising legal and economic arguments and even filing lawsuits to deter it. To move beyond this deadlock, the government began to work on a more comprehensive policy, once again under the CGPID's leadership. This was called Plano Nacional de Banda Larga (National Plan for Broadband Internet), or PNBL. In 2010, after extensive backstage meetings and public debates, Lula signed executive decree no. 7.175/2010, which made the PNBL official.

In its core, the PNBL reflected a new compromise between the state and the market: the plan relied on private companies, which signed terms committing to provide cheaper broadband Internet services to Brazilians.[37] But it also signaled a reinvigoration of state activism. Most remarkably, the government reestablished Telebras, which was assigned with two tasks.[38] First, it should ensure technological infrastructure for federal policies and administration, which included building and maintaining a separate network

[36] The underlying intention was to radically modernize the public sector. For example, health care units would be able to exchange patients' records online or the criminal justice system would be able to create a national database.

[37] Companies agreed to provide broadband Internet services at 1 mbps speed, a monthly fee of R$35 (about US$12), and at least 15 percent of services provision taking place through DSL cables rather than mobile devices.

[38] This required a complicated operation by the government. The SOE Eletrobras had a 16,000 km network of optical fiber cables, which was part of the infrastructure it used to transmit and distribute energy. Eletrobras contracted Eletronet to operate these cables. Eletronet had gone bankrupt, and litigation pended over its debits. The government intervened in the bankruptcy court case to regain access to Eletrobras's cables. In the context of the PNBL, Telebras should take control of this network and use it to meet the tasks it had been assigned with.

for the federal public sector. Second, it should "regulate the market" by providing broadband Internet services to private parties *at the wholesale level*, with the chance to operate at the retail level "in places where there is no adequate offer of such services" by private companies.

In addition, the federal government urged state governments to give tax breaks to telecom services, which should bring the prices of broadband Internet services down to R$29.90 (about US$10.00) a month. It also announced investments of R$14 billion (approximately US$5 billion) in infrastructure and industrial development related to broadband Internet for the 2011–2015 period.[39] Finally, the PNBL brought civil society into the discussions. As part of the plan, the government launched the Forum Brasil Conectado (Connected Brazil Forum), with participation of NGOs and activist groups along with business representatives and government officials. The forum was to be a permanent advisory panel for PNBL managers charged with implementing the PNBL. And in 2010 Brazil had its first Conferência Nacional de Comunicações (National Conference on Communications), or CONFECOM, a participatory process in which a range of different constituents gathered to discuss the challenges and alternatives for communications in Brazil, including broadband Internet.

Amid these events, Dilma Rousseff was elected for her first term in the presidency. Even before she took office, her appointed minister of communications, Paulo Bernardo, met with CEOs from telecom companies. Bernardo agreed to discuss and perhaps review the backhaul obligations, which led the companies to withdraw the lawsuits they had filed to challenge these obligations. Indeed, in 2011 the new government decided to make the PNBL its core instrument to expand broadband Internet and in doing that relaxed backhaul obligations. In 2014, Rousseff was reelected with the promise to transform the PNBL into an even larger program, which she dubbed Banda Larga para Todos (Broadband Internet for All). It was not clear what this new program would entail. But as the PNBL had produced limited results, she might need to look for alternative policy solutions.[40] These might include new backhaul

39 In 2011 this budget was adjusted for RS$12.7 billion (about US$4 billion). It should include: (1) construction of infrastructure to create a national network for broadband Internet provision – R$7.142 billion; (2) communications satellite – R$716 million; (3) support for projects related to content and applications – R$270 million; (4) digital cities project – R$1.2 billion; (5) support for public digital TV channels – R$652 million; and (6) development of an operating system for a national, public digital TV – R$2.8 billion (Brasil 2012).

40 By the end of 2014, when Rousseff was running for reelection, there was much dismay about the PNBL. In December, the Brazilian Senate released a report stating that two-thirds of Brazilian households still lacked access to broadband Internet. Only 2.6 million individuals, or 1 percent of all cable Internet users, in the country had signed up for the PNBL's cheap plan, half of whom were in the state of São Paulo. Telebras had reached only 612 cities out

obligations, which would trigger conflicts along the state-market-society continuum yet again.[41]

While it is tempting to discuss the merits and the degree of success of these policies, we are more interested in the changes they represent in theories and practices of development over time in Brazil. From this perspective, we see them as a move toward what L&D literature calls the "new developmental state" (Trubek et al. 2014b). While policies like Banda Larga nas Escolas and the PNBL represent active state efforts to structure the sector to meet developmental goals, this is to be achieved not by renationalization but in partnership with private entities. While this new state intervention continues to seek economic growth and industrialization, it also shows a concern with equity, social justice, and even political liberties.[42] And while the state now intervenes more, it is concerned with building legitimacy for its intervention.[43]

For us, the key questions are: how have corporate lawyers participated in this process? What kind of mediation have they provided? Which of their skills have been more decisive? We address these questions in the next section.

V CORPORATE LAWYERS IN THE CONSTRUCTION OF THE MODERN TELECOM SECTOR IN BRAZIL: FOUR STAGES OF ENGAGEMENT

This section reports four stages in which corporate lawyers participated in the construction of the modern telecom sector in Brazil, with an emphasis on the last three decades (late 1980s–late 2010s).

of the 4,278 it was committed to reaching when it was reestablished. The CGPID, arguably the coordinating mechanism for PNBL implementation, had had its last meeting in 2010. The forum had been deactivated.

41 For example, in December 2014, ANATEL began to review the universalization plan for landline phones and signaled that it wanted to reinstate backhaul obligations for companies. According to documents made public, ANATEL's plan was to have companies install and run fiber-optic backhaul in 2,888 municipalities that do not have such infrastructure yet. Companies were obviously against this.

42 As an example (rhetorical, at least), the statute that ensured the R$12.7 billion resources for the PNBL treated this as an investment in "communications for development, inclusion, and democracy" (Brasil 2012).

43 Although for some left-wing intellectuals none of this was a reason to see a radical turn in Brazil's telecom policy. For example, Cavalcante (2012, 156–157) argues: "The PNBL and the revival of Telebras . . . reactivate the state's purchase power, which has brought local industry back to life like a phoenix [and] recognizes that the market alone is not capable to provide public utilities with quality and universal coverage. But . . . the predominant vision in the government is that markets can handle public utilities and the 'competition' regime is applicable to all areas of public utilities, even if an SOE is in place. [Hence] the return of development does not necessarily mean that the basic interests of popular classes will be met." Of course, there are critics to this increased state intervention as well, such Sousa et al. (2013).

The first two stages focus on the transition between state monopoly and a regulated market (late 1980s–1997). They reveal two ways in which corporate lawyers contributed to that process. Initially, they sought to provide legal legitimacy and the necessary legal tools for ongoing attempts to open up the sector. They engaged in creative interpretation of existing laws and produced drafts of administrative norms that could enable private participation in the telecom sector. Yet none of these efforts were sufficient to produce an atmosphere favorable to private investment.

When the government made a more decisive move to open up the sector and seek foreign investment, corporate lawyers had a chance to prosper. In a first "transitional moment," when the government allowed the private sector to offer B band cellular phone services, they intervened to ensure that the demands of foreign investors would be met. As the process moved forward and the government was convinced that it needed to make major changes in Brazilian law to make the sector more attractive to such investors, it turned to corporate lawyers to identify specialized professionals who could get the job done. These experts helped create a competitive market system governed by a US-style regulatory agency.

The third stage focuses on the initial operation of the sector as a regulated market under a new legal structure (1998–2007). This time, corporate lawyers ensured that the previous legal reforms were administered the way they were intended. Initially, the new legal forms were in conflict with an enduring technocratic ethos among ANATEL directors, who had been socialized in the context of the state-owned Telebras system. By undertaking opaque and idiosyncratic regulatory practices, which translated into demands that companies saw as exceeding legitimate regulatory concerns, these old-style technocrats tried to pour the old wine of developmentalism into the new bottle of the regulatory state. Corporate lawyers curbed the powers of these technocrats by imposing legal constraints on regulatory discretion through the use of courts and administrative proceedings. By the end of this period, with regulation operating under stricter legal constraints and ANATEL placing more value on the law and legal reasoning, corporate lawyers had acquired considerable professional power, which they could use to exercise more substantive influence on the workings of the agency and drive the sector toward the original aspiration of a regulated market in which private companies enjoyed significant freedom.

The fourth stage focuses on the changing scene in the sector after the emergence of new state activism in the late 2000s. Now, concerns for social inclusion, industrial development, and democracy led to new demands on the companies, producing conflicts along the state-market-society continuum. At the core of these conflicts are different visions about where the lines dividing the continuum should be drawn, with the companies preferring not to take on the new obligations while facing both a stronger state bureaucracy and a more active civil society. Corporate lawyers mediating these conflicts present two accounts for their professional engagement, which we describe in more detail at the end of this chapter: *resistance* and *negotiated engagement*. At this point, both approaches coexist in the telecom corporate bar. It is unclear which will prevail. But if negotiated engagement were to flourish, it would mean a fundamental shift in the political economy of corporate lawyering and require modifications to the account provided by LLG.

A *From "Muddling Through" to the Need for a New Legal Infrastructure: Corporate Lawyers and the Opening of the Brazilian Telecom Market (Late 1980s–1995)*

When telecom services in Brazil were under state monopoly, most things in the sector took place within a single complex informed by a state-driven rationale. When monopoly began to wither, the sector became open to a new array of interests and perspectives. Tensions emerged, new and old, between policy and business, public and private, national and foreign.

Within Telebras, these and other tensions used to be managed through a technically informed culture of legality. Whereas companies in the Telebras system were subject to a number of laws and regulations, they had relatively broad discretion to organize their internal proceedings. These technical decisions were translated with little or no mediation into normative commands, the well-known Telebras norms or patterns. These norms or patterns ended up governing a myriad of operations in the sector and were treated as if they were formal legal obligations.

This overlap between technical solutions and normative commands – or perhaps subordination of a legal order to a technical order – gave engineers much power in the everyday life of the sector. Hence, as LAW-4 recalled from conversations between Telebras and foreign multinationals, which he was one of the few lawyers to witness, top Telebras officials paid little if any heed to strictly legal issues and cared only for technical matters. He exemplified with:

> This project . . . , which used satellites operating in low Earth orbit. Embratel didn't show any interest for this project, but the president of Telebras liked it and wanted to discuss it. We had a meeting – he was an air force commander – and I said that from my perspective there was a *legal* issue to be dealt with, for I wasn't sure these satellites could connect with the SOEs that

were part of the Telebras system. Technically I knew that they could, but legally I wasn't sure, for calls in this project worked like international phone calls – you had to dial an international number to have your call completed. So I had doubts whether Telebras companies could make this kind of call or whether they were exclusive to Embratel. He said: "Let's find it out now," then turned to his assistant and said, "Call the engineers." I said, "Listen, commander, I know that technically it is possible to make the calls. This should not be the problem. My question is strictly legal. Wouldn't it be better to call the lawyers?" And he replied, "Do you want a response or not?" (laughs long and loud). So this is to say that in the normative aspect of the system, what really existed were the Telebras norms, which had been written by engineers.

For a small group of early career lawyers with elite degrees from São Paulo, Rio de Janeiro, and Brasília, who had decided to venture in the then nascent field of telecom corporate law, the erosion of the Telebras system presented both opportunities and challenges. While there was an obvious need for mediation between the interests and expectations of incoming foreign investors and local legal rules and practices, these rules and practices were neither produced nor organized in a coherent and autonomous fashion. Amid the resulting uncertainty, lawyers had to muddle through both existing normative systems and established social hierarchies: not only did they have to sort out what "laws" could be applicable to specific transactions and operations, but they also had to build legitimacy for their reasoning against arguments coming from engineers on the one hand and foreign businessmen on the other.

LAW-3 shows an extraordinary consciousness of this context and the challenges it entailed. After she had provided numerous examples of her experience in the sector, we had the following exchange:

INTERVIEWER: So let me try to understand. In these first days you were mostly mediating between the existing legal rules in Brazil and the expectations of foreign investors who were arriving in the country?

INTERVIEWEE: If you look at my files, my e-mails were almost legal memoranda in English, Portuguese, French, etc. They asked about everything; they wanted to learn about everything. And I worked in this gap between a *lex mercatoria* and a *lex juridical*, i.e., between international business practices and local rules, including Telebras norms.

She went on to provide an instructive example:

We started to draft consumer contracts. Consumer protection institutions began to challenge our practices, and we had to respond. Then there was this British executive who came to me and said: "In case of unpaid bills, I want to

> have services to consumers interrupted immediately"; and I said, "You can't. This is not like Britain. There are consumer protection laws and the Telebras norms that we need to observe"; these norms hadn't been cancelled yet. But the British had urgency; he wanted the company to shut down services the next day, provided that consumers had not paid the bill on its due date. And I was showing him the norms and the legislation, but he wouldn't accept my advice. So I had clerked for a judge, and I went to talk to her. I said, "Your honor, if you had to decide a case like this, what would you consider 'immediate cancellation?'" And she said, "Well, I'd say 48 hours; you can't disconnect someone faster than that." Then I got back to the British officer and said: "Listen; here is what a judge said . . . "

Obviously, simple iterations of such ad hoc proceedings would not provide a legal basis that private investors would feel comfortable with. With the opening of the market progressing at a fast pace, a more autonomous and comprehensive legal order to govern the sector would be necessary, if not inevitable.

B *From Interpreting Existing Laws to Legitimizing New Legal Drafters: Corporate Lawyers and the Construction of a New Legal Regime for Telecom (1995–1997)*

Getting involved in efforts of lawmaking was not something foreign for the growing telecom corporate bar. In the mid-1980s, when government officials were looking for ways to hand some telecom services to the private sector, corporate lawyers sought to contribute by engaging in creative interpretation of the existing legal infrastructure, the 1962 Code. LAW-4 refers to one of the events in such history as the "hyphen battle":

> Cellular phone services were considered "restricted public utilities" under the 1962 Code. Lawyers began to argue that this could be read as either *restricted-public utility* or *restricted public-utility*, and this created much debate. Those against privatization argued that it should be read as *restricted public-utility*: as such, it would refer to *public utilities* available to *restricted groups of people*, but as *public utilities*, these should be necessarily provided through Telebras. In contrast, those who favored privatization argued it should be read as *restricted-public utility*: as such, it would refer to *utilities* available to a *restricted public*, which, nonetheless, were not necessarily *public* and, therefore, did not need to be provided through Telebras.

Although the "hyphen battle" had made it clear that substantial disagreements existed as to whether it was possible to open the market for cellular phones under the 1962 Code, subsequent government officials kept trying to do it. Corporate lawyers sought to help again. This time, they focused on producing suggestions for administrative norms that could operationalize opening. LAW-4 mentions that, at the time:

> There was no such a thing as a public consultation, but they asked for suggestions. So we took part of that process, along with [cites local and multinational companies] and others . . . ; and we had lots of meetings. It was through these experiences that I established myself in this sector; I was part of a small group of corporate lawyers whose primary mission was to *draft* suggestive norms to govern the opening process. We would read materials, get together, have discussions, and attempt to produce these suggestions for the government.

Nevertheless, uncertainties typical of transitional moments prevailed. LAW-4 recalls that, in the wake of all these meetings and drafting work, "the government ended up enacting . . . three different norms to open cellular phone services to the private sector"; yet none of them was able to attract companies: "Without the amendment breaking state monopoly, no one felt safe to invest."

The passing of that amendment in 1995 and the minimum law in 1996 provided the safety that private investors demanded. And it also provided corporate lawyers with an opportunity to engage in the changes affecting the sector. Indeed, not all the terms of these transitional regulations met the demands of foreign investors, and corporate lawyers were called to perform critical interventions. LAW-4 details:

> Somewhere in this transitional moment there was a rule requiring that more than 50 percent of the shares in the investing companies ought to be in the hands of Brazilians. So all foreign businessmen and [we] their lawyers went to the ministry, and we had a meeting with the minister, and we all said: "Listen, do you think that we are going to invest billions of dollars and will not be able to control the companies in which we are going to invest, even if that is a shared control with a local partner?" At the end, the minister interpreted the law in a way that Brazilians were either legal residents in Brazil or companies incorporated according to Brazilian laws. It was not explicit, but we all implied that companies could have all of their shares in the hands of foreigners, as long as they were "incorporated according to Brazilian laws." And this later informed the rules adopted for Telebras's privatization.

Then again, these were just the beginnings of a much broader restructuring process, which involved the splitting and selling of the Telebras system and the move from state monopoly toward a market-based regime.

Now legal professionals would be hired to work full-time with the authorities in charge of this process. These professionals had a complex task to deal with. As the restructuring operations were initiated, the government became convinced that it needed to undertake major institutional reforms to make the sector more attractive to the foreign investors it was seeking. Not all kinds of reforms were sufficient to meet the expectations of these investors – McKinsey consultants hired in the context of the ITU-MINICOM agreement maintained that the government's chance to succeed in its plan was contingent upon Brazil's ability to emulate foreign models of regulation and governance. As LAW-2 explains:

> There were many doubts about the extension of the reform, and things were not bright and clear, but there was a lot of international pressure. The fact that legal counsel was hired through ITU was meaningful. Everywhere in the world ITU was "supporting" telecom reforms, as they used to say, which means they were putting pressure for telecom reforms. And ITU had a certain menu of ideas, which I assume had been discussed with the government, as there was consensus among MINICOM officials about aspects such as the need for a regulatory agency, for independent regulation, for competition, things that were very much in line with reforms taking place internationally.

Needless to say, the reforms advocated by McKinsey consultants conflicted with Brazilian legal and political repertoires. Beyond another instance of *law-making*, they looked more like a call for *state reconstruction*. Given the existing nature of Brazilian administrative law, robust legal assistance would be necessary for the government to find a way to create such radically new forms.

As government officials needed to identify legal professionals who could get this job done, corporate lawyers who had built reputations for their "deep knowledge" in telecom legislation were called to advise would-be drafters of the new legal regime. In fact, when LAW-2 described his recruitment for that job, we had this informative exchange:

INTERVIEWEE: [The government] hired McKinsey as the consulting firm for economic issues and three individual lawyers. These people [we] had nothing to do with telecom; they were referred by the minister of communications' personal attorney, who also had nothing to do with telecom or even public law.

INTERVIEWER: Can you tell me more about this attorney?

INTERVIEWEE: His name was [omitted] He is known for later becoming the president of the bar. But I didn't know him in person at the time, and he didn't know any of us either. In fact the minister talked to [omitted], a telecom lawyer in São Paulo. Foreign companies were preparing to enter the telecom market in Brazil, and she was working for them. She had deep knowledge of telecom laws and was the correspondent for [Minister's attorney, omitted] in São Paulo. And the minister asked: "Who would be good lawyers to do public-law-related work, etc.?" and she referred the three of us. So this is how I got there.

Much beyond "good lawyers to do public-law-related work, etc.," the selected professionals bore a distinctive set of political, social, and cultural capitals. They had considerable practical experience working in both the public and the private sectors. They were well-established administrative law professors at a leading São Paulo law school, the Pontifical Catholic University of São Paulo (PUC/SP) Law School.

As the restructuring process evolved, that combination of capital and expertise would prove to be of great importance. After much back and forth with McKinsey consultants and government officials, these lawyers decided on what would be seen as a "revolution" in Brazilian public law. The LGT draft they produced included substantial innovations, given the existing forms and structures governing public entities in the country.

One of the primary and most interesting aspects of this "revolution" was the construction of ANATEL as an independent regulatory agency. Independent agencies were not part of the Brazilian public law repertoire, while alternative solutions such as a steering committee within MINICOM had been successful before. Yet consulting firms estimated that the independent agency solution would be more attractive to foreign investors, which should lead to higher returns in the privatization auctions.[44]

To meet the standards set by consulting firms, LAW-2 and others initially proposed a completely new institutional form, the Ofício Brasil de Telecomunicações (Brasil 1997; Prata et al. 1999; Braz 2014). The Ofício would be a completely independent agency, with power even to collect resources for its own maintenance so that no relationship with governmental organizations would exist. But amid fears that this form would be seen as unconstitutional, LAW-2 and others had to work out something different. This involved tweaking an existing legal form, the *autarquia*.[45] Hence, the LGT draft conceived ANATEL as a *special autarquia* linked to MINICOM. As such, ANATEL would have administrative independence, no hierarchical subordination to any other entity, fixed terms and stability in the office for its directors, and financial autonomy (LGT, articles 8 and 9). In addition, ANATEL was given

[44] It did not take much for critics of privatization to realize and denounce that this built on US models of economic regulation and governance, such as the Federal Communications Commission (Ramos 2003, 2004).

[45] *Autarquias* are a legal form in Brazilian administrative law, which refers to public entities with relative self-governing capacity. *Autarquias* were introduced by the civil-military regime in 1967 as a more flexible form for public entities. For example, for quite some time *autarquias* were able to hire personnel using regular private-sector employment contracts. In 1992 all forms of public entities became subject to the same labor regime, and much of the flexibility of *autarquias* was reduced.

power to produce and enforce norms governing corporate conduct in the sector (LGT, articles 19).

These innovations produced immediate and "violent" reaction within and beyond the legal field (LAW-2). The legal status of *special autarquia* and the norm-making power assigned to ANATEL were extensively criticized by more traditional jurists like Celso A. Bandeira de Mello, from the Pontifical Catholic University School of Law, and Maria Sylvia Z. Di Pietro, from the University of São Paulo Law School. Di Pietro (2010) argued that *autarquias* could not serve the purposes they were being given by the LGT, for, in Brazilian administrative law, they were ultimately prohibited from creating norms. Mello (2009, 157) shared this vision and added that by granting ANATEL the status of a *special autarquia*, reformers sought "to give a new flavor to an old concept, while also building on the putative prestige of a US-related terminology."[46] He predicted and feared that

> these "agencies" are likely to trespass their power. Based on the label they were given, they will believe – and so will all the naive – that they are invested with the same power as US "agencies," which would be totally inconsistent with Brazilian law. (158)

As the changes brought about by the LGT were able to survive these and other tests,[47] the corporate bar would come out of this restructuring process considerably more empowered. The reform introduced new ideas into the sector, which, in many ways, were more attuned to interests and expectations of corporate clientele. LAW-2 shows the vision about the future of the sector that was held among drafters of this new legal regime. Explaining the solutions they produced, he stated:

> We thought a lot about concession contracts, and we feared that there would be huge losses for the federal government in the expiration of contracts . . . as there had been, for example, in electricity and railroads. This was something we were extremely concerned about, even more than business consultants. This made us come up with a model . . . that would allow the

46 In similar ways but outside of the legal academy (Ramos 2003, 2004; Braz 2014).

47 Opposition parties, labor unions, and individuals filed more than a hundred lawsuits attacking the privatization process and the LGT. Most of these lawsuits were dismissed and, while some of them resulted in temporary constraints to the process and minor modifications in the law, no one really impeded state monopoly from falling and a regulated market from emerging in Brazilian's telecoms. Interestingly, one lawsuit was personally filed by Bandeira de Mello and other dissenting administrative and constitutional law scholars. This demonstrates how that changing context affected the legal field and academy: it triggered conflicts for power and influence among different generations and habitus of scholars, which began to clash with one another over the capacity to say what the law is all about.

> development of the sector to take place with minimum regulation and regulatory obligations.[48] Over time this would become more and more general, although there would be some unprofitable investments, like to serve certain regions or kinds of users, that the state would be able to meet via concession contracts. It would be able to terminate with large-scope concession contracts and focus the use of concession contracts on specific situations.

In addition, the reform created a unique, specialized body of law whose mastery would become an asset in many modern law firms, general counsels' offices, and beyond. LAW-2 himself would not escape this fate: in 1998, when Telebras was privatized, he finished his contract with MINICOM and ITU and "went to work for the private companies, obviously."

C *Legalizing Regulation: Corporate Lawyers Making Legal Claims to Uphold Market-Friendly Institutions* (1998–2007)

The passing of the constitutional amendment and the LGT formally made the telecom sector more market-friendly. But institutional memories of the Telebras era continued to affect theories and practices of governance within the new regulatory agency ANATEL.

The first board of ANATEL directors was recruited from among the same engineers who used to draft and implement the Telebras norms. Like many other respondents, REG-5 recalls that "the first composition of ANATEL's board of directors was exclusively of engineers . . . as the agency was originally staffed with former Telebras workers and the commanders of the Telebras system were normally engineers."

This continuous professional dominance led to survival of old characteristics in the new structures. One of them was the relative disregard for a lawlike reasoning. For instance, LAW-2 recalls that one of his tasks after privatization was to help ANATEL draft its first regulatory package. He reports that this allowed him to do "fascinating things," among which he emphasizes:

> For example, the first bylaw of the agency had a code of administrative procedure within it. At that time there were no laws governing administrative procedures. And the interesting thing was that at the first meeting of the board of directors, I brought with me a draft of these bylaws. And I said: "The

48 This will make more sense to the reader when we introduce the discussion about the two legal regimes that the LGT created: one (public) with heavier regulatory burden, initially limited to landline phone services, and the other (private) with much more flexibility, although, as we will see, later on the government would begin to blur the distinction between these two regimes.

> first institutional challenge this agency will need to meet is to have its bylaw. And according to the law, bylaws need to go through public consultation before being enacted. Here is a first draft that we prepared; you will need to read it carefully." They looked at me, all engineers, and replied: "We will have to read this all? This is impossible." And I said: "Well, this is about how the agency is going to work; you need to read it, raise questions, make suggestions . . . " We then had this deadlock, and they ended up submitting the draft to public consultation without having read it.

Obviously, the passing of that bylaw was not enough to make ANATEL directors more aware and considerate of law and legal reasoning in their everyday work. ANATEL directors routinely disdained legal opinions and memoranda – even when produced internally to the agency – while also asserting their expert knowledge and technical rationale as the primary basis of legitimacy for regulatory practices.[49] LAW-4 recalls that in this period:

> From a lawyer's perspective, it was hard to understand . . . that ANATEL directors would say to ANATEL lawyers that their memoranda were wrong. Now imagine having your legal memorandum being rejected by five engineers. They were all in good faith – I'm not suggesting they were doing anything wrong – but we had what we called the "rubber ball" memorandum, a memorandum that would bounce back from the board of directors because it was written in terms that did not match their reasoning and therefore ought to be redrafted. I had a case in which, probably by mistake of ANATEL staff, I retrieved a case docket and there were two legal memoranda with the same number, same date, same signatory; the only difference was that one was for [something] and the other was against [it].[50]

This ethos had a clear and obvious impact on the interests and expectations of private companies: norm making and norm implementation by ANATEL was more opaque and idiosyncratic than they could have anticipated, and this made their relationship with the agency more conflictual than they would have preferred.

49 IHC-3 adds: "They were averse to legal arguments. If we sent them memoranda that were too legalistic, they would say: 'What the hell is this? Get this out of here.' It seems folkloric, but when we argued that ANATEL lacked jurisdiction over a matter, they took that as an offense. They rejected lawyers. Many times I heard from my bosses: 'We are not taking you to ANATEL with us today, otherwise we will have trouble.'"

50 LAW-6 adds that "ANATEL even tried to formalize these practices, which is incredible. The fact that they handled the cases secretly so that reports and opinions could be changed to conform to final decision, they tried to formalize this. They put on public consultation a draft proposal for new bylaws that had this exact provision."

Oversight and sanctioning activities by ANATEL in regulatory commands relating to universal access and quality of services led to an escalation of these conflicts. The agency took a rather ironfisted approach, which included periodic assessments of compliance: ANATEL began to launch a flood of administrative procedures (PADOs) to assess compliance.[51] Suggesting that this was designed to scare companies, LAW-1 noted that heavy fines were levied and some companies "went bankrupt." REG-1 added:

> This was a time of many PADOs, initially with very low fines, but that became tougher, especially in issues of quality, universalization, and oversight obstruction. The person doing oversight would ask for information, which would not be sent on time to the agency, and we would give the company a R$10–20 (approximately US$3.5–7 now) million fine. There was a landmark case in which the inspector went to inspect a telecom facility and the company's representative, who was having food nearby, said, "Sorry, I don't have the keys. There is a quick maintenance taking place today, and I don't have the keys. You have to come back tomorrow." So the inspector went there the next day, got in, and things were all right. But he filed a complaint for oversight obstruction, and we gave the company a fine of R$20 (approximately US$7) million. This is how we began to lose track of things.

Once again, this context provided corporate lawyers with both challenges and opportunities. Whereas lawyers are known for their ability to challenge power on the basis of norm-based systems, making legal claims in telecom was not easy. The regulatory culture established at ANATEL had made the administrative domain averse to legal arguments and lawlike reasoning. LAW-1 details how ANATEL proceeded in cases like the ones we just addressed:

> Companies would receive by mail what ANATEL understood was necessary for their defense. Generally, this would not include the technical reports, let alone the legal memoranda produced within the agency. Later, companies began to raise legal issues in their defenses, like lack of due process and motivation. These were frequent issues in their defenses. But the board of directors liked to issue concise decisions, no more than three pages long, which obviously limited the room for complex legal issues to be dealt with.

Going to court against this regulatory culture and its products was risky in many ways. First of all, corporate lawyers wanted to keep the courts out of the regulatory business. The theory of regulatory agencies, which was actively and

[51] PADO is an acronym that refers to an administrative proceeding within ANATEL in which the agency assesses the accomplishment (or lack thereof) of regulatory obligations and imposes sanctions, if need be.

widely disseminated in the wake of privatization, held that courts should limit their review of regulatory measures to formal aspects like limitation of discretion and due process. Corporate lawyers were not so sure that the Brazilian bench would embrace that theory in full and leave the substance of regulation to regulators.

Second, corporate lawyers were doubtful that courts would be able to handle and even understand the complex issues that telecom regulation involved. LAW-5 recalls:

> We thought that courts might not be equipped to deal with regulatory issues and understand regulation. Judges had grown in a preprivatization context; they had trouble understanding how things worked. We felt that whenever we needed to take anything to court, we had to explain the very basics. So our attitude was much more reactive.

Third, the corporate lawyers and ANATEL were facing common antagonists in the courts: the *Ministerio Público* and NGOs were beginning to file lawsuits to address regulations acceptable to the companies but which they saw as threats to the "public interest" and the interests of consumer groups. LAW-5 continues his account:

> We would not fight against ANATEL; sometimes we would line up with ANATEL in lawsuits filed by the *Ministerio Público.* One example is in prepaid cellular phone credits: ANATEL established a ninety-day limit for use of these credits, after which they would expire and users had to refill their phones. The *Ministerio Público* said this was outrageous, but this is actually what allowed prepaid phones to exist and become widely available. And we had to explain to the court the economic reasoning behind prepaid phones...and at that time we worked closely with ANATEL to explain to courts and prosecutors these services' regulations, which were being interpreted simply through consumer laws, with no understanding of the economic reasoning behind them.

Finally, going to court could produce consequences directly adverse to the corporate clientele. The plain reason is that technocratic ANATEL would not hesitate in retaliating against companies that chose litigation. LAW-1 explains:

> In the first ten years these disagreements were dealt with mostly at an administrative level for...I don't know how to put this, but the fact is that ANATEL would retaliate, so if you went to court, ANATEL would not give you the annual tariff increase, you know what I mean? So companies had a fear of going to court against ANATEL, for they would not remain unpunished: if they filed a lawsuit discussing interconnection, the agency would impose

> obligations or it would not give the company something it needed in another area that had nothing to do with interconnection.

Yet corporate lawyers were not willing to play a peripheral role in this story. As dealing with administrators was hopeless and going to court on behalf of their clients was too risky, some of them ended up filing lawsuits on their own behalf. They would claim that, as "citizens," they had been denied due process rights within the agency.[52] Little by little, this creative insurgence would help generate a body of judicial decisions setting standards for administrative proceedings in ANATEL and other regulatory agencies.

There came a point, as fines imposed by ANATEL reached seven figures, that oversight and sanctioning activities became a real burden for companies. Their fear of submitting their claims to court was overcome by a rational assessment of the short-term benefits they could gain if they did so, in view of the huge fines they faced. LAW-1 explains:

> Companies began to see that, in some cases, there was a real chance they could avoid a multimillion-dollar fine by arguing that some due process rights had not been respected. This was risky pursuing, but the potential benefits could outweigh the risks, depending on how one saw it. And they began to be more tolerant with the risks and more considerate with the benefits.[53]

[52] In our research, we came across some of these cases. One involves a lawyer who requested documents to prepare the defense of his clients before ANATEL. As his request was denied, he filed an injunction against the agency, on the basis of article 5, XXXIV, of the federal constitution, which states: "It is ensured to everyone the right to petition and to obtain certificates before public bodies in order to defend her own rights and clarify situations of personal interest." The court issued the injunction, which was confirmed by the Court of Appeals (AMS no. 17512 DF 2005.34.00.017512–0, Writing for the Court: Federal Appeals Judge Daniel Paes Ribeiro, division six. Decided on January 18, 2008, decision published on March 3, 2008, e-DJF1, 289. TRF1).

[53] The fact that Lula took office and tried to gain some control over ANATEL reinforced the technocratic ethos at the agency. As ANATEL staffers saw changes in the presidency and the board of directors as political – and therefore as a threat to the technical reasoning they valued so much – they looked for ways to keep control over the normative power of the agency. Corporate lawyers and their clients initially nourished this midlevel bureaucratic power. They mistrusted the new leadership arriving at ANATEL and the way Lula was handling the sector and saw midlevel superintendents as more reliable and predictable actors with whom to have a meaningful conversation about their businesses. Yet with time this proved to be wrong. ANATEL superintendents had the same technocratic background as the preceding agency's directors and could be even less accountable than directors. As superintendents were not meant to be norm makers, they ended up using ad hoc, fragmented events to rule, like when issuing an authorization or examining a request. LAW-1 refers to this as a time when "regulation began to be issued through letters": ANATEL began to introduce new regulatory commands or even impose penalties through simple communications from superintendents to companies.

At the same time, changes occurred in government legal services, which helped unsettle the relationship among technocracy, law, and lawyers. These (1) made it mandatory for legal counsel internal to regulatory agencies to be recruited from among career government lawyers and (2) required general counsel at these agencies to report to the *advogado-geral da união*, who is the chief lawyer for the executive branch, instead of agency presidents.

This gave lawyers acting internally to ANATEL considerable leverage and independence vis-à-vis the board of directors. As a consequence, ten years after ANATEL was established, its lawyers began to issue legal memoranda that called for much higher procedural standards for regulatory practices at the agency. And although the board was not required to meet the vast majority of these standards, which were written as mere legal recommendations, rejecting them would help corporate lawyers make even more robust cases in court against the reigning practices within the agency.

The result was a substantial shift in the sector. As regulatory activities within ANATEL had to be more considerate of internal legal procedures and eventually of court decisions, the old technocratic ethos at the agency had to make room for more lawlike institutional practices and professional expertise. For instance, REG-1 reports:

> Given the number of PADOs, we began to hire lawyers and more lawyers, and the agency began looking more like a mini-court. This was even reflected in the agency bylaws: if you compare our first bylaws to what we have now, you will see that we now have much more regulation over legal proceedings, much more procedural rules. These all bind the way the board of directors operate, with much of a law look or judicial look. The board decisions were named *acts*; now they are named *opinions of the board*. So let's face it: this is becoming a court. It's hell.

SPE-2 adds:

> The presence of lawyers in the ANATEL board of directors increased significantly; in the beginning they were all engineers and occasionally some economists. Now I'd say there was a shift – there are more lawyers than economists and engineers in the board. And there are changes in the administrative proceedings. Last month . . . ANATEL allowed parties in their proceedings to make oral arguments. Who's that for? It's obviously for legal professionals: they are pressuring for greater participation in decision-making processes within the agency. In fact, the new facet of the agency as an administrative court is something that benefits legal professionals.

Of course, all of this had a significant effect on the telecom corporate bar. From actors with limited means and significance maneuvering between ANATEL engineers and corporate managers, corporate lawyers became necessary resources for companies trying to navigate through a regulatory web that was itself becoming more and more legalized.

Having achieved such a privileged position, corporate lawyers could expect to complete the transformational process initiated with the LGT. Facing continuous legal questions and legal claims, ANATEL would have to meet a much higher legal burden to exercise its regulatory power. These increasing legal constraints could drive telecom regulation back toward its intended track after Telebras's privatization: a market-friendly regime, with minimum, rationally conceived, and impersonal state intervention into private affairs. Except that a new impulse of state activism was on its way.

D *Amid Resistance, Negotiated Engagement, and New Institutional Constraints: Corporate Lawyers and the Emergence of a NDS in Telecom (2007–2014)*

After a decade of opening up and rapid change in the telecom sector in Brazil, corporate lawyers had attained a distinctive status in telecom regulation and governance, which they could mobilize to mold the sector in accord with principles cherished by their clientele. But this state of affairs changed in the late 2000s, when the government began to introduce new requirements. The most important of these were requirements that the companies make broadband Internet widely available. This created tensions between the government and the companies and led corporate lawyers working for the latter to explore new professional skills and roles.

1 NDS in Telecom and the Challenges to Law and Lawyers

The legal issues created by the emergence of a new developmental state in telecom and the challenges the corporate lawyers had to deal with stem from the structure of the basic law (LGT). The law divided telecom services into two regimes: public and private. Public telecom services were those deemed to be essential, affect a wide range of interests, and require continuous provision. Private services were any telecom services not meeting those tests.

The system was designed to separate services thought to be an essential state responsibility and require close regulatory scrutiny from those that could be left largely to market forces. The regulatory process varied: for services deemed public, providers must be selected through public bids and are regulated by a detailed concession contract; for those deemed private, a simple authorization is all that is required. The prices of public services are controlled, and there are obligations for universal access; there is no mention of such requirements for services deemed to be private. Infrastructure created for public regime services reverts to the government at the end of the concession; this is not required for private services.[54]

When the telecom sector was privatized in the 1990s, the only services that were included in the public regime were landline phone services. All other services, including cellular phones, came under the much looser private regime. Landlines were subject to a strict regulatory regime, including the requirement to fulfill plans to promote universal citizen access to telecom; other services were free of such requirements.

This system was challenged by both Banda Larga nas Escolas and its successor Plano Nacional de Banda Larga (PNBL). These policies depart from the logic of the basic law in two ways. At a more general level, they embody a new philosophy of governance. Strict rules and limited state regulation on businesses, while never completely implemented in the sector, gave way to open-ended bargaining across the state-market divide as government seeks to engage private parties in attempts to meet developmental goals in industrialization, social welfare, and democratic participation. Hence, when we pushed LAW–6 to articulate a vision of the current moment of telecom policy, he said:

> It is a time of "let me help you deal with this problem you are facing, as long as you make an investment here or there." This is what telecom regulation has become. The government is looking for what to put on the table to put pressure on companies so that they will do this or that, as it wants, like to invest in broadband Internet. It is a time where the president's chief of staff is drafting regulation and in which we engage in political negotiations about the core issues of interest to companies in the sector.[55]

But at a more specific and contentious level, these policies challenged the reigning "spirit" of the LGT. In fact, in Banda Larga nas Escolas, companies

[54] This helps explain why companies resisted new backhaul obligations in their concession contracts, although they had initially embraced this solution. GOV-2 notices that "companies no longer want to invest in backhaul, as they know that this will revert back to the government at the end of the concession contracts; this is not interesting for them."

[55] This is consistent with Taylor's characterization of contemporary Brazilian capitalism, which stresses that the line between autonomous regulatory agencies and executive agencies "has become less clear" (Taylor 2015, 18) and "the system of regulatory bodies has reduced but not significantly eliminated government influence" in the economy (Taylor 2015, 19–20).

providing landline services in the public regime had an obligation to make these services universal, as mandated by the concession contracts they had signed with ANATEL. Installing and running backhaul became a means to do that. But the same case could not be made for the obligation they were assuming to provide Internet access to schools, which was not really related to landline services and therefore could not be formalized in the context of those concession contracts.[56] As a way around this, this obligation was included in addendums to authorizations that the same companies had been granted to provide *other services* under the private regime, like cellular phone services. But obligations of this kind were not supposed to exist in the private regime. LAW-7 shows his discomfort with this solution. He says:

> The biggest surprise we had in this negotiation [over backhaul] was Internet to schools. Because for me exchanging multistations for backhaul was a mathematic operation – what the former was worth against what the latter was worth. But then they said: "We want something more, since we are exchanging things anyway." And Internet to schools appears as this "something more." And then came this addendum to authorizations for companies to provide services under the private regime, establishing obligations that were not in exchange for anything, stating that companies are voluntarily assuming an obligation to deliver broadband Internet to schools. This is something that creates a lot of uncertainty.

The PNBL appears more beneficial to companies, but it follows the same pattern as Banda Larga nas Escolas. Instead of installing and running backhaul infrastructure, companies were selling Internet plans at cheaper prices to Brazilians. Prices and other conditions for these sales were established in Terms of Commitment, which those companies "voluntarily" signed with MINICOM. But such terms of commitment did no less than create formal legal obligations for services in the private regime. So in both cases the bright line between the public and private regimes was breached, with regulatory requirements being introduced in areas thought to be strictly governed by market mechanisms. Even government officials, like GOV-1, acknowledge this, when they say, for example:

[56] But notice that consumer protection NGOs also questioned whether backhaul could relate to landline phone services at all. ANATEL and companies had prepared extensive reports treating backhaul as infrastructure that works "in support to landlines." NGOs understood that broadband Internet should be subject to new contractual relationships and feared about whether backhaul resulting from Banda Larga nas Escolas would revert back to the government.

> Telecom companies have been operating under these contracts since 1998, but they do not cover broadband Internet: this is offered under the private regime. Now we no longer want to invest so much in landline phone services, but we can't abandon these companies, which will be here until 2025. So we have created some weird or unorthodox tools, to say the least, to make things move forward without having to deal with problems related to the concession contracts. In 2008 we had Banda Larga nas Escolas. In 2011, as part of the PNBL, we had these Terms of Commitment, as we wanted companies to diffuse broadband Internet access but could not put that into their universalization plans. These Terms of Commitment work as if companies had come to us and said: "Hey, we want to offer broadband Internet access nationwide," to which we replied: "Great, so let's sign a document stating what your obligations will be." And we came up with this, which ANATEL oversees and imposes fines if obligations are not met, etc. So this is a time when there is great room for legal creativity.[57]

Needless to say, corporate lawyers and their clientele are critical of this approach. For example, when we asked IHC-2 about the main legal challenges he faces these days as an in-house lawyer in the sector, he said:

> We notice that ANATEL is imposing additional obligations over our provision of some services. In addition to what the agency is doing in concession contracts... we began to see that in spectrum auctions related to cellular phone and multimedia services, ANATEL is including some obligations that mark a clear attempt to undertake public policies through private service providers, i.e., to undertake public policies in the context of service authorizations.

He concluded:

> It is one thing to do it in the context of concession contracts, where you sort of expect to see greater state presence and there are legal obligations to universalization... but I'm talking about authorizations... and we see ANATEL imposing some obligations to universalization that I believe are much closer to or make much more sense in the context of concession contracts.

While all companies and their lawyers face these new conditions, the corporate bar's reaction to this approach has not been uniform. Two competing

[57] Similarly, GOV-3 considers that "Banda Larga nas Escolas is a weird thing. It was really a remarkable policy initiative that, nonetheless, took place through weird pathways. We tried to put it as a clause in the concession contracts; we tried to draft a new concession contract; all these alternatives had legal problems. We ended up drafting an addendum to these companies' authorizations to provide multimedia services, which, nonetheless, ought to include obligations of revertibility" (GOV-3).

accounts of professional identity have circulated: *resistance* and *negotiated engagement*.

2 Resistance and Negotiated Engagement: Variation in the Meaning of Corporate Law Practice in the Rise of a NDS in Brazil's Telecom

As a NDS-like approach in telecom has emerged in Brazil, new forms of professional engagement have been experienced and the meaning of corporate law practice has become diversified. There are two accounts. The first we call *resistance*. It really includes denial of state authority to drive the sector (as compared to the market), a belief that policy solutions like Banda Larga nas Escolas or the PNBL are illegitimate in view of the law and a concomitant willingness to resist them.

One way resistance has manifested itself is through legal scholarship. Corporate lawyers have written articles and opinions denouncing the recent moves by the state as being inconsistent with the existing legal infrastructure governing the sector, or "the law." These argumentative constructs have helped sustain the aspiration of a market-based regime for telecom services and reclaim the original intents of the LGT against the will of NDS supporters.

An example is with Marques Neto (2010). In a leading peer-reviewed journal in telecom law, he argues that policies like the PNBL show "disregard for . . . mechanisms" that exist in the LGT, while "seeking alternatives aside from or against the LGT" (Marques Neto 2010) For the author, this "may ultimately lead to an increase in the offer of broadband Internet to Brazilians. This is possible, but will result in the dismantling of a successful model and a throwback in the institutional robustness of the sector" (Marques Neto 2010).[58]

Resistance also appears in legal mobilization, in which corporate lawyers build on the capital and expertise they have acquired after years of struggles to legalize regulation to resist new policy solutions. Banda Larga nas Escolas provides an example: through a single-shot lawsuit, lawyers challenged the universalization plan in which the government wanted to include more aggressive backhaul obligations. This froze the process and ensured temporary protection to the interests of their clientele. As Aranha et al. explain these events:

58 This is a signal that resistance builds on some of the academic capital corporate lawyers have accumulated, which they can build on to advance positions relevant to their clientele. In fact, Marques Neto is a corporate lawyer and a law professor at the University of São Paulo law school.

> The reaction to these new [backhaul] obligations took place via formalistic legal claims, when Telefónica argued that the 24-month minimum period for companies to learn about their obligations under the universalization plan ought to be observed, which meant that the plan should have been approved by December, 31, 2008, in order for it to be effective on January 1, 2011. By establishing more time for public consultation, court orders prevented the program from coming to force. On December 13, 2010, . . . the federal government formally proposed that companies gave up their lawsuits in exchange for further discussion and commitment to reach consensus. On December 15, 2010 SindiTelebrasil filed a petition withdrawing the lawsuits (after which the government enacted the PNBL).[59]

Resistance coexists and potentially conflicts with negotiated engagement.This involves accepting state authority to drive the sector, a belief that the solutions it has produced are contestable but legitimate, and a mind open enough to examine how clients can take the most benefit from this new context. In some ways, it is like corporate lawyers were back to the time when strict legal reasoning was at best ancillary to regulatory debates; the difference being that old-style technocracy has been replaced by new developmental "experimentalism." Thus LAW-4 describes his more recent experience in dealing with those new regulatory demands in the terms that follow:

> In many cases it continues to be that practical advocacy; so when a public consultation is released (now there are public consultations before norms and other kinds of administrative actions are enacted), and sometimes there are public hearings, we take the chance to make our comments and engage in public discussions about the issue. And . . . we sometimes set meetings with ANATEL directors or superintendents to try to understand what they are trying to accomplish and see what we can do about it. Now there is much less fear to bring about lawsuits against ANATEL, but I think that these debates and meetings are the most efficient ways we can do our job.

Likewise, when IHC-3 was addressing the most recent developments in telecom regulation and governance, she said:

[59] But notice that this injunction was granted for violation of *procedural* rights. Corporate lawyers still have much skepticism about whether judges can effectively decide the substance of telecom policies or address the regulatory practices of the agency. LAW-6 stated: "We bring very neat cases to the courts, we present forceful legal opinions, but we get no response. It seems that our cases only get decided when they become of statistical relevance to courts, like in mass litigation. We go to court because there is nothing else we can do once we are imposed a R$50 million fine, but these cases have no regulatory impact; judges don't say: 'ANATEL, watch yourself.' We are just discussing numbers."

> Banda Larga nas Escolas and the PNBL involved extensive negotiations . . . with endless meetings with the ministry, the president's chief of staff; we had to really move to Brasilia for a few weeks. And we have been learning how to deal with this world of negotiation. For example, there is a provision in the LGT that says that concession contracts must be ensured economic equilibrium. We have studies showing that by 2018 concession contracts will have become unprofitable. Along with the need for clarification about revertibility, this is the most pressing issue for companies nowadays. But we know that notwithstanding the existence of that legal provision, if we approach the government to discuss these issues, they will say: "We are willing to do what it takes, but you need to give me something in exchange, namely broadband." Now, the government is promoting discussions about how to improve telecom laws and regulations, and this is what we are going to put on the table.[60]

As lawyers "learn how to deal with . . . negotiation," they also face the need to develop and deploy a different set of professional skills. Beyond handling transactional services and litigation cases, they are increasingly required to give their input to ongoing conversations between companies and the government. This means assessing risks of suggested operations vis-à-vis the existing laws but also imagining institutional arrangements that could better reconcile the interests of both companies and the government, thus acting again like "drafters" of a new, hybrid legal regime. Hence, as LAW-6 was describing his current work, he said:

> Sometimes we are called to say what can be possibly done; whether this or that component could be included [in the deals] and in what terms. To the extent that the government opens the doors for some discussions, we are called to work on these more concrete issues: if we need to present new solutions for the issue of revertibility, for example, what could we present?

The persistence and prosperity of "practical advocacy" and the further engagement of corporate lawyers in institutional imagination are contingent upon many factors and moves. Resistance could be benefited by future court decisions curtailing telecom "experiments," changes in government orientation, or both. Lawsuits have become a limited but viable alternative to resist government demands, and there is growing political opposition

[60] These discussions began on October 20, 2015, with an online public consultation about "revisions of the model for telecom services provision in Brazil." The consultation was introduced with considerations and questions by MINICOM, of which we emphasize: "Given the new aspiration of Brazilian society for broadband Internet, instead of landline phone services, it is necessary to redesign public policies to allow different segments of society to have access to these services" (www.participa.br/revisaodomodelo/eixo-1).

to some aspects of new state activism, which can reverberate in the telecom sector. At the same time, other forces may buttress the NDS approach. These include a stronger and more professional state bureaucracy more able to resist corporate pressures,[61] a better-mobilized and more effective NGO sector[62] pushing for universal broadband Internet coverage and public participation in telecom regulation and governance,[63] and state-based institutions of bureaucratic oversight, like the Ministerio Público[64] and the Court

61 This stronger state bureaucracy results from Lula's decision to hire career civil servants to ANATEL instead of using ordinary labor contracts, as Cardoso did. With a greater degree of job security and sophisticated education, including, in many cases, advanced legal training from elite law schools in Brazil and overseas, these new civil servants developed working methods and bureaucratic networks that favor more robust legal analyses and strategic planning for legal confrontation against telecom companies, if need be. For example, when REG-5 was asked to describe his involvement with recent telecom policies, he said: "The ministry makes a political decision and we begin to think about it in legal terms, both at the ministry and at the agency. And we focus on providing ideas about how that could be effectively pursued, as well as sustained, in the courts, because companies will obviously take it to court if they don't like it. So we construct sustainable legal solutions in the sense that they will be coherent both with other norms internal to the administration and with the language of the courts. Companies go to court against us very often, and I'll not say that we win 100 percent of the time, but we manage to prevail in courts to a great extent of the cases. Industrial policy is something we have done [in 3G and 4G spectrum auctions]; we have established obligations of domestic content and national technologies. This is something that companies regularly questioned, but that we sustained in the courts."

62 This development of civil society organizations as homologous to corporate capital has been documented in several occasions. For instance, Santos and Rodriguez-Garavito demonstrated that in the wake of neoliberal reforms in the 1990s, marginalized groups and communities in the Global South turned to the law and courts in search of protection (Santos and Rodriguez-Garavito 2005). Curiously, obsession in market-oriented reforms with the implementation of a "rule of law" system in peripheral countries gave their citizens tools to resist those same market reforms. Likewise, as Dezalay and Garth analyze the global diffusion of legal norms and institutions in the context of neoliberalism and US hegemony, they refer to *merchants* and *missionaries*, meaning that the process speaks to the need for free-market economies *and* political accountability, both of which contribute to strengthen the "rule of law" project (Dezalay and Garth 2002a, 2002b, 2011, 2012; Cummings and Trubek 2008). Existing literature suggests that telecom privatization in Brazil provided an impetus for legal mobilization via consumer protection NGOs, which has also led campaigns and collaborated with institutions like the Ministerio Público in causes for the right to broadband Internet (Rhodes 2006; Veronese 2011). These NGOs are small in number but have been able to place significant constraints on government officials and companies. For example, a lawsuit filed by one of them reinforced revertibility of backhaul in the context of Banda Larga nas Escolas, as detailed by NGO-1 and NGO-2.

63 For more on the promises and failures of public participation in telecom policy, see Leal (2001), Mattos (2006), and Aranha (2008).

64 LAW-6 states: "Sometimes negotiation also bumps into other sources of resistance, like the *Ministerio Público*, consumer protection NGOs. So if the solutions we are producing lack consistency, even if we make a deal with the government, this is going to be invalidated." For examples of requests that the *Ministerio Público* has made to ANATEL, in its capacity of the

of Accounts.[65] What is certain is that these changes in the Brazilian state and the correspondent emergence of a new form of lawyer and modes of lawyering in corporate practice challenge existing accounts of lawyers and capitalist development in the periphery. We turn to these issues in our final considerations.

VI FINAL CONSIDERATIONS

This chapter pursued a different objective than most of the other chapters in this volume. Instead of examining how changes in the economy impact corporate lawyering in countries like Brazil, we tried to understand how corporate lawyers in Brazil have participated in making the economic changes taking place around them. We used the study of lawyers and telecommunications in Brazil as a way into this complex terrain.

The study revealed three stages in the coevolution of the telecom regime and the lawyers engaged in it. These are summarized in Table 10.3.

Taken together, the elements in this figure indicate the acquisition of new professional power, which, nonetheless, faces a challenge. As corporate lawyers were able to help build, sustain, and enforce a norm-based system that favored corporate power at a global scale, they themselves increased in power and importance. Yet as this norm-based system is being challenged by the "experimental" practices of a NDS, such professional power faces a challenge as well. As LAW-3 defines it: "Lawyers did what they could have done in the sector: they made it have its norms and operate in accord with these norms. Now the challenges are at a more strategic level."

Faced with this context, the methods and meanings of corporate law practice have become diversified. Resistance has appeared in the use of expert opinion and mobilization of expert knowledge to curtail state action deemed illegitimate. But this has coexisted with negotiated engagement, which entails acceptance of NDS, the ability to operate in a more flexible legal regime that

"guardian of the 'public interest.'" See Melo et al. (2005). For analyses of lawsuits filed by both NGOs and the Ministerio Público, see Faraco et al. (2014).

65 The Court of Accounts oversees public expenditures, but in this accountability role it has become increasingly influential in the design of telecom policies. For example, in his critique to the regulatory practices by ANATEL, LAW-6 stated that the agency "now faces some problems that it created for itself. For example, they are now negotiating a consent decree with companies in order to resolve disputes about previously imposed fines. And they are under a lot of pressure, as the Court of Accounts will say they are being reckless if it understands that they were too soft in these negotiations. I know someone who is working on this who said, 'It is my career that is at stake. If I do not justify these decisions very well, I will be held responsible.'" For examples about the role of the Court of Accounts in telecom, see Brasil (2006, 2008).

TABLE 10.3 *The role of corporate lawyers in three periods in the history of Brazil's telecoms industry*

Period	Characteristics	Stories
The fall of state monopoly (late 1980s–1997)	• State monopoly begins to lose sustainability. • The government wants to open the sector but finds difficulties in doing so.	• Corporate lawyers try to help the efforts to open the sector by engaging in creative interpretation of existing laws and drafting administrative norms that could enable private participation in the sector.
Global restructuring, neoliberalism, and privatization (1998–2007)	• Mainstream forces at the domestic and international levels converge around the ideas that the sector should be handed in to the private sector, with the sale of Telebras. • The government is advised that to attract foreign investors, as it was seeking, it should undertake major institutional changes in the sector along models of "regulated competition" currently being diffused internationally.	• As the opening process begins, corporate lawyers perform critical interventions to ensure it will meet the demands of foreign investors. • As the opening process moves forward, corporate lawyers help identify professionals who could assist the government in promoting the institutional reforms necessary to attract foreign investors. • Corporate lawyers legalize regulation to constrain an enduring technocratic ethos in the system, harmful to the interests of their clientele.
NDS (2008–now)	• The government tries to regain capacity to drive the sector. • Reinvigorated state activism, driven by concerns like industrial development and social equality, engenders new ("experimental") policy solutions. • These solutions challenge the existing practices of governance and the reigning "spirit" of the law.	• Corporate lawyers resist by producing market-friendly legal ideologies and mobilizing the law, while also establishing negotiated engagement with the government's needs. • At the same time, corporate lawyers face new institutional constraints, with greater legal capacity within the state and greater relevance for mechanisms of social and public accountability. • This context places challenges on corporate law practices and professional ideologies, which can change in ways not envisioned by existing accounts.

requires continual negotiation, and the use of "practical advocacy" to influence its "experiments" so that they can better meet the needs of the corporate clientele.[66]

These findings have implications at multiple levels. For this book and the general field of studies on lawyers and capitalist development, they bring new information about the construction and subversion of hierarchies in the legal profession in view of the fast economic change and integration to the global economy Brazil has experienced. Rather than a full replacement of elites, the stories we have shown look more like a light and mirrors game. The emerging telecom corporate bar relied on – and empowered – traditional "jurists" when major legal reforms were needed to allow privatization. These reforms expanded the role of corporate law practice in telecom, eventually dragging some of those "jurists" into the world of corporate law practice: LAW–1 is the best example. Yet members of the modern corporate bar in telecom took pathways that are indeed consistent with those of traditional "jurists." They have invested in academic careers and became part-time professors at prestigious law schools, such as the University of São Paulo's: Marques Neto, cited supra, is but one example. But this symbiosis can be further affected by Brazil's turn to a NDS and the emergence of "practical advocacy" and institutional imagination. Should these all gain traction, lawyers with new skills and habitus, formed by a mixture of policy, business, and legal reasoning combined with negotiating skills, could displace more traditional "rule of law" and doctrinally oriented practitioners. Similarly, lawyers with closer ties to the state could prove to be more effective than those more wedded to global capital. It would be instructive to follow the formation of these new identities.

For L&D debates, our findings are revealing of how a mutually reinforcing dynamic was created between corporate law practice and the field of state power, which could potentially help sustain Brazil's trajectory toward a NDS, were NDS policies to survive. While the "neoliberal moment" valued the "regulatory state" and civil society – both seen as tools to constrain state action – the "third moment" or NDS in Brazil built on the established regulatory machinery and civil society participation to increasingly impose obligations over companies and pursue its new developmental goals.[67] And as some corporate lawyers have retooled to get the best possible deals for their clientele in what now looked like an open-ended process of negotiation, they

66 For similar developments in the field of antitrust law, see Miola (2015).

67 This is also consistent with Taylor's observations about the formation of this "third moment," in which: "It is ironic but perhaps unsurprising that the regulatory framework established to facilitate the privatization of a variety of firms in a number of sectors has been repurposed over time to serve as an instrument of government control over the economy" (Taylor 2015, 20).

have found ways to protect private interest, but also provided legitimacy to that NDS. Were this dynamic to keep going, there could be a new kind of "spill over" between private capital and a reconfigured field of state power in Brazil, with mediation of a new generation of lawyers – included those in corporate practice.

Finally, for LLG debates our findings are of no less significance. As we have shown, telecom corporate law and lawyering in Brazil does emerge as a byproduct of US hegemony and its tenet of "free markets." But amid changes in the field of state power leading to an NDS in Brazil, corporate law and lawyering have gotten retooled in ways that may be consistent with – and potentially feed back into – the construction of a counterhegemonic project. LLG accounts will take great benefit from investigations on how such counterhegemonic projects, which thus far have been primarily dealt with by contemporary L&D research, could affect the relative role of law in governance and the construction of lawyers' professional power in the Global South.

Some could argue that, while something new has happened in Brazil, it is hard to say how deep these changes go or how sustainable they may be. In fact, the NDS approach has shown some limits, and there are calls for a return to more market-oriented policies. Brazil is at a liminal moment, and the conflict in telecom policy and lawyering is caught up in a much larger national debate about state, market, and law. But contestation of hegemonic powers and the search for alternative developing models are recurring events in world history, as we can see with Brazil, the BRICS more generally, and even some African countries nowadays. For those venturing in these processes, whether as researchers or as their architects, the lessons we learned from Brazil are sure to be useful.

REFERENCES

Almeida, M. W. 1994. "Reestruturação, internacionalização e mudanças institucionais das telecomunicações: lições das experiências internacionais para o caso brasileiro" (PhD dissertation, Universidade Estadual de Campinas, Campinas).

1998. "Investimento e privatização das telecomunicações no Brasil: dois vetores da mesma estratégia." Campinas: Universidade Estadual de Campinas.

Aranha, M. I. 2005. "Políticas públicas comparadas de telecomunicações (Brasil–EUA)" (PhD dissertation, Universidade de Brasília, Brasilia).

2008. "Democracia participativa e a agência reguladora de telecomunicações brasileira." In *Anais do I Seminário Internacional de Regulação de Serviços Públicos*. Santa Cruz do Sul: EDUNISC.

2015. *Direito das telecomunicações: Historico normativo e conceitos fundamentais*. 3rd ed. Charleston, SC: Privately published.

Barbosa, N., and J. A. Souza. 2010. "A inflexão do governo Lula: política econômica, crescimento e distribuição de renda." In *Brasil entre o Passado e o Futuro*. Edited by E. Sader and M. A. Garcia. São Paulo: Fundação Perseu Abramo e Boitempo Editorial.

Bolaño, C. R. 2003. *Políticas de Comunicação e Economia Política das telecomunicações no Brasil: convergência, regionalização e reforma*. 2nd ed. Aracaju: Universidade Federal de Sergipe.

Bolaño, C. R., and F. Massae. 2000. "A situação das telecomunicações no Brasil ao final do processo de privatização." *Revista Brasileira de Ciências da Comunicação* 23 (1): 43–55.

Brasil, R. F. 1997. "Diretrizes gerais para a abertura do mercado de telecomunicações." Volume 4: Documentos de Suporte: Sundfeld Advogados. Ministério das Comunicações.

2006. Acórdão TCU 2109. Auditoria de natureza operacional." Avaliação da atuação da ANATEL no acompanhamento da qualidade da prestação dos serviços de telefonia. Determinações e recomendações. Monitoramento. Tribunal de Contas da União.

2008. TC023.332/2008–7. Avaliação da atuaçnao da ANATEL no acompanhamento da qulidade da prestação dos serviços de telefonia. Baixo grau de implementação de recomendações do acórdão 2109/2006-P. Reduzido grau de cumprimento das determinações. Fixação de prazo para providências. Reiterações. Novo monitoramento. Ciência aos órgãos interessados. Monitoramento. Tribunal de Contas da União.

2012. Lei n 12.593. Institui o Plano Plurianual da União para o período de 2012 a 2015., January 18, 2012. www.planalto.gov.br/ccivil_03/_ato2011–2014/2012/Lei/L12593.html.

Braz, R. 2014. *Reestruturação capitalista, firmas multinacionais de consultoria e telecomunicações: a privatização do Sistema Telebrás no lógica da mundialização do capital* (Doutorado em Comunicação e Sociedade, Universidade de Brasília, Brasília).

Campello, T., and M. C. Neri (eds.). 2013. *Programa Bolsa Família: uma década de inclusão e cidadania*. Brasília: Ipea.

Cavalcante, S. 2011. "As telecomunicações após uma década da privatização: a face oculta do 'sucesso.'" *Eptic online: revista electronica internacional de economia política da informaçao, da comunicaçao e da cultura* 13 (1): 166–183.

2012. "Estado, capital estrangeiro e burguesia interna no setor de telecomunicações nos governos FHC e Lula." In *Política e classes sociais no Brasil dos anos 2000*. Edited by A. Boito Jr. and A. Galvão. São Paulo: Alameda.

Coutinho, D. R. 2005. "Entre eficiência e equidade: a universalização das telecomunicações em países em desenvolvimento." *Revista Direito GV* 1 (2): 137–160.

2014. "Decentralization and Coordination in Social Law and Policy: The Bolsa Família Program." In *Law and the New Developmental State: The Brazilian Experience in Latin American Context*. Edited by D. M. Trubek, D. R. Coutinho, and M. G. Shapiro. Cambridge: Cambridge University Press.

Cummings, S. L., and L. G. Trubek. 2008. "Globalizing Public Interest Law." *UCLA Journal of International Law and Foreign Affairs* 13 (1): 1–53.

Dalmazo, R. A. 2002. *As mediações cruciais das mudanças político-institucionais nas telecomunicações do Brasil*. Porto Alegre: Secretaria da Coordenação e Planejamento, Fundação de Economia e Estatística Siegfried Emanuel Heuser.

Deakin, S., D. Gindis, G. M. Hodgson, H. Kainan, and K. Pistor. 2015. "Legal Institutionalism: Capitalism and the Constitutive Role of Law" (research paper no. 26/2015, University of Cambridge Faculty of Law). http://ssrn.com/abstract=2601035.

Dezalay, Y., and B. G. Garth (eds.). 2002a. *Global Prescriptions: The Production, Exportation, and Importation of a New Legal Orthodoxy*. Ann Arbor: University of Michigan Press.

2002b. *The Internationalization of Palace Wars: Lawyers, Economists, and the Contest to Transform Latin American States*. Chicago: University of Chicago Press.

2010. *Asian Legal Revivals: Lawyers in the Shadow of Empire*. Chicago: University of Chicago Press.

2011. "Hegemonic Battles, Professional Rivalries, and the International Division of Labor in the Market for the Import and Export of State-Governing Expertise." *International Political Sociology* 5 (3): 276–293.

Di Pietro, M. S. 2010. *Direito Administrativo*. 24th ed. São Paulo: Atlas.

Duarte, D. A., and L. D. Silva. 2009. "Informe Setorial: Backhaul ameaçado, consumidor atento." *Revista de Direito, Estado e telecomunicações* 1 (1): 219–232.

Ewick, P., and S. S. Silbey. 1998. *The Common Place of Law: Stories from Everyday Life*. Chicago: University of Chicago Press.

Faraco, A. D., C. M. Pereira Neto, and D. R. Coutinho. 2014. "A judicialização de políticas regulatórias de telecomunicações no Brasil." *RDA: Revista de direito administrativo: Rio de Janeiro* 265: 25–44.

Furtado, C. 2007. *Formação econômica do Brasil*. 34th ed. São Paulo: Companhia das Letras.

Garth, B., and Y. Dezalay. 2012. "Corporate Law Firms, NGOs, and Issues of Legitimacy for a Global Legal Order." *Fordham Law Review* 80 (6): 2309–2345.

Gomide, A. A. 2011. "A Política das Reformas Institucionais no Brasil: a reestruturação do setor de transportes" (PhD dissertation in public administration, Escola de Administração de Empresas de São Paulo [Fundacao Getulio Vargas], São Paulo).

Gupta, P. 2015. "From Statesmen to Technocrats to Financiers: Agents of Development in the Third World" (paper presented at the Institute for Global Law and Policy Conference, Harvard Law School, Cambridge, MA).

Halliday, T., Karpik, L., and Feeley, M. (eds.). 2012. *Fates of Political Liberalism in the British Post-Colony: The Politics of the Legal Complex*. Cambridge: Cambridge University Press.

Ismail, S. 2006. "Analyzing the World Bank's Blueprint for Promoting 'Information and Communications.'" *Federal Communications Law Journal* 59 (1): 237–250.

Leal, S. 2001. "Os mecanismos de controle-público/social presentes no regulamento do setor de telecomunicações no Brasil: a Lei Geral de telecomunicações e o Regimento Interno da Agência Nacional de telecomunicações" (master's thesis in communications, University of Brasilia, Brasilia).

Maculan, A. M., and L. R. Legey. 1996. "As experiências internacionais de regulação para as telecomunicações e a reestruturação dos serviços no Brasil." *Revista de Economia Política* 16 (4): 67–86.

Marques Neto, F. A. 2010. "Entre a legalidade e o 'puxadinho': a universalização da banda larga no Brasil." *Revista de Direito de Informática e telecomunicações* 5(9): 53–61.

Mattos, C. 2003. "Telecomunicações reajuste e contrato." *Conjuntura Econômica – IBRE/FGV* 57 (11): 60–63.

Mattos, C., and P. Coutinho. 2005. "The Brazilian Model of Telecommunications Reform." *Telecommunications Policy* 29 (5–6): 449–466.

Mattos, P. 2006. *O novo Estado regulador no Brasil: eficiência e legitimidade*. São Paulo: Editora Singular: FAPESP.

Mello, C. A. 2009. *Curso de Direito Administrativo*. 29th ed. São Paulo: Malheiros.

Melo, M., F. Gaetani, and C. Pereira. 2005. "State Capacity and Institutional Change: A Case Study of Telecom Regulation in Brazil" (paper presented at the X CLAD International Congress on State Reform and Public Administration, Santiago, Chile).

Miola, I. 2015. "The Politics of Competition Regulation in Latin America: Roots and Roles of Antitrust Laws in Argentina, Brazil, Chile and Mexico" (paper presented at the Institute for Global Law and Policy Conference, Harvard Law School, Cambridge, MA).

Moore, L. K. 2013. "Spectrum Policy: Provisions in the 2012 Spectrum Act." Congressional Research Services. http://fas.org/sgp/crs/misc/R43256.pdf.

Mosco, V. 2009. *The Political Economy of Communication*. 2nd ed. Los Angeles: Sage.

Nelson, R. L., and D. M. Trubek. 1992. "Arenas of Professionalism: The Professional Ideologies of Lawyers in Context." In *Lawyers' Ideals/Lawyers' Practices: Transformations in the American Legal Profession*. Edited by R. L. Nelson and D. M. Trubek. Ithaca, NY: Cornell University Press.

Nielsen, L. B. 2014. "Thinking Law: Thinking Law in Motion." *Brazilian Journal of Empirical Legal Studies* 1 (2): 12–24.

Oberman, M. 2013. "Two Truths and a Lie: Stories at the Juncture of Teen Sex and the Law." *Law and Social Inquiry* 38 (2): 364–402.

Oliveira, E. Q. 2005. *Depoimento*. Rio de Janeiro: CPDOC/Embresa Brasileira de Correios e Telégrafos.

Peixoto, E. L. 2010. "Programa Nacional de Banda Larga: Análise sobre a Formação da Agenda da Universalização da Banda Larga no Brasil" (master's thesis in public administration, Universidade de Brasilia, Brasilia).

Pena, A. G., H. Abdalla Jr., and J. L. Pereira Filho. 2012. "A banda larga e o cenário brasileiro das telecomunicações." *Revista de Direito, Estado e telecomunicações* 4 (1): 237–302.

Pereira Filho, J. E. 2002. "A Embratel: da era da intervenção ao tempo da competição." *Revista de Sociologia e Política, Curitiba* 18: 33–47.

Pieranti, O. P. 2011. *O Estado e as comunicações no Brasil: construção e reconstrução da administração pública*. Brasília: Abras/Lecotec.

Prado, M. M. 2008. "The Challenges and Risks of Creating Independent Regulatory Agencies: A Cautionary Tale from Brazil." *Vanderbilt Journal of Transnational Law* 41 (2): 435–503.

Prata, J., N. Beirão, and T. Tomioka. 1999. *Sergio Motta: o trator em ação*. 1st ed. São Paulo: Geração Editorial.

Ramos, M. C. 2003. "Tão ruim quanto uma má idéia é uma boa idéia mal copiada." *Revista Teletime* 55: 36–38.

2004. "Agências Reguladoras: a reconciliação com a política." *Revista de Economía Política de las Tecnologías de la Información y Comunicación* 7 (5): 17–39.

2010. "Crítica a um Plano Nacional de Banda Larga: uma perspectiva da economia política das políticas públicas." In *Anais da IV Conferência ACORN-REDECOM*. Brasilia.

Rego, W. D., and A. Pinzani. 2014. *Vozes do Bolsa Família: autonomia, dinheiro e cidadania*. 2nd ed. São Paulo: Editora UNESP.

Rhodes, S. 2006. *Social Movements and Free-Market Capitalism in Latin America: Telecommunications Privatization and the Rise of Consumer Protest*. Albany: State University of New York Press.

Santos, B. S., and C. R. Garavito (eds.). 2005. *Law and Globalization from Below: Towards a Cosmopolitan Legality*. Cambridge: Cambridge University Press.

Silbey, S. S. 2005. "After Legal Consciousness." *Annual Review of Law and Social Science* 1 (1): 323–368.

Sousa, R. A., N. A. Souza, and L. C. Kubota. 2013. "Desenvolvimentos Institucionais Recentes no Setor de Telecomunicações no Brasil." *Texto para Discussão*, no. 1874. Brasilia: Instituto de Pesquisa Economica Aplicada (IPEA).

Tavares, M. C. 2011. "O Processo de substituição de importações como modelo de desenvolvimento na América Latina: o caso do Brasil." In *Desenvolvimento e igualdade: [homenagem aos 80 anos de Maria da Conceição Tavares]*. Special ed. Edited by V. P. Correa and M. Simioni. Rio de Janeiro: Instituto de Pesquisa Economica Aplicada (IPEA).

Tavares, M. da C., and J. L. Fiori. 1993. *Desajuste Global e Modernização Conservadora*. São Paulo: Paz e Terra.

Taylor, M. 2015. "The Unchanging Core of Brazilian State Capitalism, 1985–2015" (research paper no. 2015–8, School of International Service). http://ssrn.com/abstract=2674332.

Teixeira, R. A., and E. C. Pinto. 2012. "A economia política dos governos FHC, Lula e Dilma: dominância financeira, bloco no poder e desenvolvimento econômico." *Economia e Sociedade* 21: 909–941.

Trubek, D. M., H. Alviar Garcia, D. R. Coutinho, and A. Santos. 2014a. *Law and the New Developmental State: The Brazilian Experience in Latin American Context*. New York: Cambridge University Press.

Trubek, D. M., D. R. Coutinho, and M. G. Shapiro. 2014b. "New State Activism in Brazil and the Challenge for Law." In *Law and the New Developmental State: The Brazilian Experience in Latin American Context*. New York: Cambridge University Press.

Trubek, D. M., Y. Dezalay, R. Buchanan, and J. Davis. 1994. "Global Restructuring and the Law: Studies of the Internationalization of Legal Fields and the Creation of Transnational Arenas." *Case Western Reserve Law Review* 44 (2): 407–498.

Trubek, D. M., and M. Galanter. 1974. "Scholars in Self-Estrangement: Some Reflections on the Crisis in Law and Development Studies in the United States." *Wisconsin Law Review* 1974 (4): 1062–1103.

Trubek, D. M., and A. Santos. 2006. *The New Law and Economic Development: A Critical Appraisal*. New York: Cambridge University Press.

Veronese, A. 2011. "A judicialização das políticas públicas de telecomunicações e as demandas dos consumidores: o impacto da ação judicial" (PhD dissertation in Sociology, Universidade Estadual do Rio de Janeiro, Rio de Janeiro).
Weingast, B. R., and D. Wittman. 2008. *The Oxford Handbook of Political Economy*. Oxford: Oxford University Press.

Index